SORTING OUT THE NEW SOUTH CITY

RACE, CLASS, AND URBAN DEVELOPMENT IN CHARLOTTE, 1875–1975

THOMAS W. HANCHETT

© 1998 The University of North Carolina Press

All rights reserved

Designed by April Leidig-Higgins

Set in Electra by Keystone Typesetting, Inc.

Manufactured in the United States of America

The paper in this book meets the guidelines for
permanence and durability of the Committee on
Production Guidelines for Book Longevity of the
Council on Library Resources.

Library of Congress Cataloging-in-Publication Data

Hanchett, Thomas W. Sorting out the New South city :
race, class, and urban development in Charlotte,
1875–1975 / by Thomas W. Hanchett.
p. cm. Includes bibliographical references and index.
ISBN 0-8078-2376-7 (alk. paper)
ISBN 0-8078-4677-5 (pbk. : alk. paper)
1. Charlotte (N.C.)—History. I. Title.
F264.C4H28   1998   97-40785
975.6'76—dc21   CIP

02 01 00 99 98   5 4 3 2 1

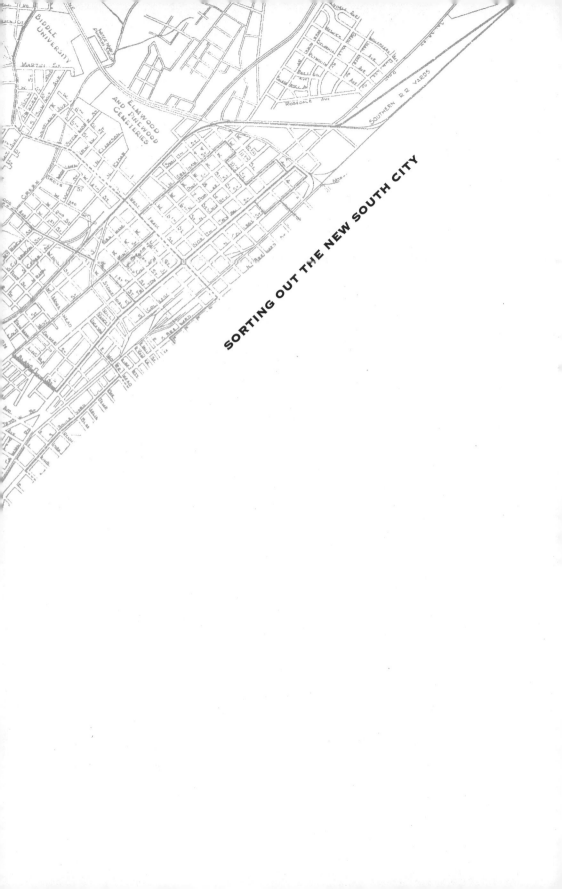

SORTING OUT THE NEW SOUTH CITY

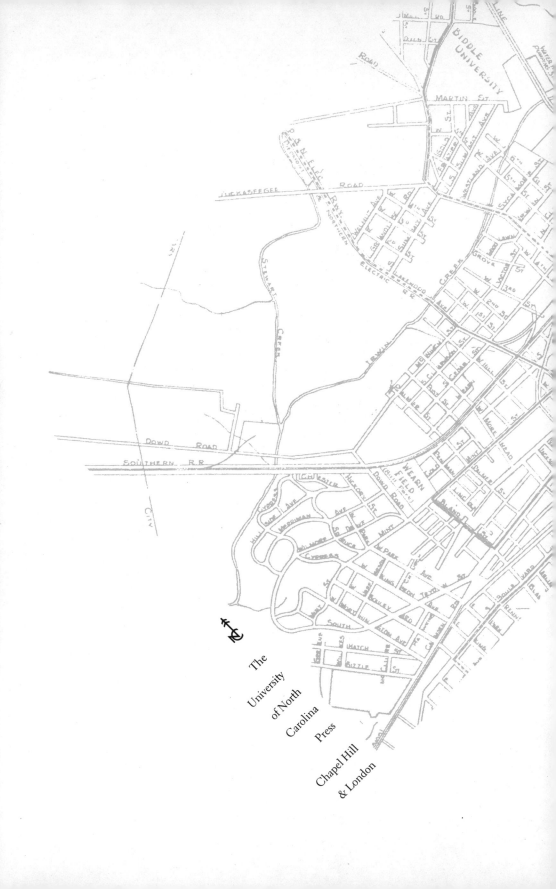

The University of North Carolina Press

Chapel Hill & London

FOR THE SAWYERS AND THE HANCHETTS,

ESPECIALLY LYDIA

CONTENTS

ACKNOWLEDGMENTS

As I have explored the story of Charlotte's development, I have incurred many debts.

An Andrew D. Mellon Postdoctoral Fellowship in Southern Studies with Dan Carter at Emory University facilitated production of the final manuscript. Awards from the St. George Tucker Society and the Urban History Association provided crucial momentum. Walter and Catherine Hanchett gave support at every stage, and Al and Ann Sawyer's generosity spurred the project to completion. At UNC Press Stephanie Wenzel, Ron Maner, David Van Hook, and especially editor David Perry provided patient assistance as the manuscript became a book.

At the University of North Carolina at Chapel Hill, thanks to faculty members William Barney, Peter Coclanis, Jacquelyn Dowd Hall, John Shelton

Reed, George Brown Tindall, Peter Walker, Joel Williamson, and especially James Leloudis and Roger Lotchin. Thanks also to the community of graduate students at Hamilton Hall, including Pamela Grundy, Lu Ann Jones, Scott Philyaw, Joel Sipress, and Lisa Tolbert.

Other historians interested in the built environment offered advice and encouragement. Stuart Blumin, David Goldfield, Christopher Silver, and Michael and Mary Tomlan read early essays. Richard Dozier shared enthusiasm and insight concerning African American neighborhoods. A comment from Mac Whatley helped me find the work's central thread. Mary Boyer, David Carlton, and James Cobb critiqued the entire manuscript in its penultimate draft, as did writing mentor extraordinaire Jon Houghton. And Catherine Bishir's untiring interest kept the project on track.

Excellent libraries and librarians made research a pleasure, especially UNC's Southern Historical Collection and North Carolina Collection, Cornell's Art and Architecture Library and Department of Manuscripts and Archives, and the University of North Carolina at Charlotte's special collections department. Charlotte is fortunate to have one of the nation's outstanding local history repositories, the Robinson-Spangler Carolina Room of the Public Library of Charlotte and Mecklenburg County. Its extremely able staff under direction of Mary Louise Phillips, Bob Anthony, Pat Ryckman, and Chris Bates did much to make this book possible.

For special help with illustrations I am grateful to Mary Boyer, Tom Bradbury, Sheila Bumgarner, the *Charlotte Observer*, Alice Cotten, the Curt Teich Postcard Archives and John Hinde Curteich, Inc., the Cornell University Department of Manuscripts and Archives, Pete Felkner at the Museum of the New South, Pamela Grundy, and Peter Wong.

My interest in Charlotte grew out of an inventory of neighborhood architecture that I carried out for the Charlotte Mecklenburg Historic Landmarks Commission from 1981 through 1985. Copies of the report may be consulted at the commission offices or at the Carolina Room of the public library. The vision for that report came from commission director Dan Morrill, who has done more than any other individual to rediscover Charlotte's New South history. He and Paul Escott, Janette Greenwood, William Huffman, and Mary Kratt made the commission an exciting scholarly environment in those years.

Community history would disappear without the ongoing efforts of committed community members. Jack Claiborne, Lew Powell, and others at the *Charlotte Observer* and the old *Charlotte News* showed special interest in the role the past plays in shaping the present. Thanks to the UNCC Urban

Institute, Hezekiah Alexander Homesite, Myers Park Foundation, Dilworth Community Association, Frances Gay and Arthur Dye and the rest of the Plaza-Midwood Neighborhood Association, Rev. DeGranval Burke and the Afro-American Cultural Center, and neighborhood groups in Washington Heights, Cherry, Elizabeth, and Fourth Ward. Thanks also to friends along the way, including Jean Ormston, Kathy Kerr, Dianne Ames McLaughlin, David and Raynell Schmieding, Stephen Jackson, Barbara Nail, Jo Mims, and Mary Lou Bennett.

I owe my greatest debt to Carol Sawyer. Her love and companionship have made the journey a joy.

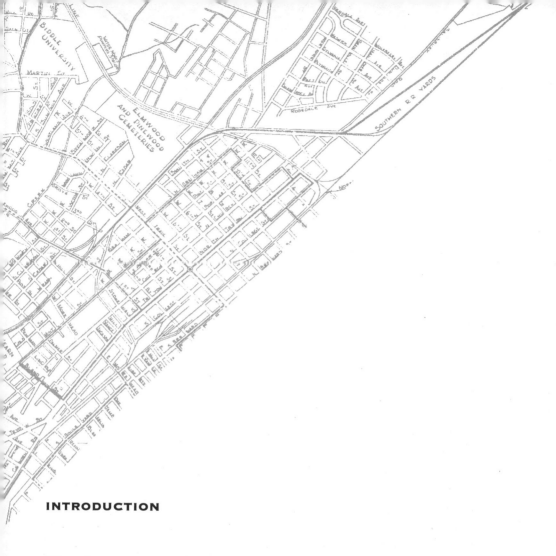

INTRODUCTION

What shapes a city? What forces mold its neighborhoods, give rise to its industries and offices, give form to its shops and skyscrapers? What determines where the streets will run, where the wealthy will build their mansions, where the poor will have their humble homes? And why do these forces seem to shift over time, transforming one area, destroying another, holding yet another unchanged?[1]

This book explores those questions for a hundred-year period in the history of Charlotte, North Carolina. Today Charlotte takes great pride in newness. Glistening towers signal its position as the nation's third-busiest banking center, young professional basketball and football teams sell out just-built arenas, and ten-lane expressways sweep past office parks and a busy hub airport.[2] Charlotteans are quick to tell you that theirs is the biggest and fastest-growing

TABLE 1. Charlotte Population, 1850–1990

Year	Population	Increase over Last Census	% Increase over Last Census
1850	1,065		
1860	2,265	1,200	112.7
1870	4,473	2,208	97.5
1880	7,094	2,261	58.6
1890	11,557	4,463	62.9
1900	18,091	6,534	56.5
1910	34,014	15,923	88.0
1920	46,338	12,324	36.3
1930	82,675	36,337	78.4
1940	100,899	18,224	22.0
1950	134,042	33,143	32.8
1960	201,564	67,522	50.4
1970	241,178	39,614	19.7
1980	310,799	69,621	28.9
1990	389,000	78,201	25.1

Sources: U.S. Bureau of the Census, *Sixteenth Census*, "Population," 1:772; Blythe and Brockmann, *Hornets' Nest*, p. 449.

Note: City population was enumerated separately for city and county for the first time in 1850.

city in both North and South Carolina, with a metropolitan population well over a million people, second only to Atlanta as the urban heartbeat of the Southeast. But Charlotte is not merely a city of the present moment.[3] It came of age in the "New South" decades of the late nineteenth and the twentieth centuries. During the 1870s–1920s Charlotte transformed itself from a rural courthouse village into the trading and financial hub for America's premier textile manufacturing region. Charlotte's oldest and best-loved neighborhoods today date from this era of transformation. From the 1920s to the 1970s the city experienced changes on an even larger scale, as the population surged from 50,000 to 250,000 and the contemporary network of highways, shopping centers, and sprawling suburbs sprang into place.

In the process, Charlotte witnessed dramatic shifts in form. The city became not merely bigger but fundamentally different in the ways people organized space. In an industrializing city, where should people work, and where should they dwell? Where should the millhand live and the mill owner reside? What was the proper mix of stores, factories, and houses? What—very important in this Southern city—was the proper arrangement of black people and white people? Who should make such decisions? Throughout the century from the mid-1870s to the mid-1970s, Charlotteans continually redefined their notions of "a good place to live." By exploring that process of redefinition we not only open a window on the past but also may better understand the unspoken assumptions that shape our cities today.

PATTERNS IN TIME: SECTORS, PATCHWORK, AND SALT-AND-PEPPER

Looking at land use in Charlotte today, it is easy to visualize the city as a pie cut in wedge-shaped slices, or "sectors," to use the terminology of urban geographers.[4] On Charlotte's southeast side, miles of oak-shaded byways define fashionable districts such as Myers Park, Eastover, and Foxcroft, which are more than 95 percent white. Opposite, on the northwest side, extends a wedge of predominantly black neighborhoods, including older Biddleville and Washington Heights and newer University Park. Less-well-to-do predominantly white wedges extend northeast and southwest, including North Charlotte mill cottages, Central Avenue apartment complexes, or compact ranch houses off South Boulevard. Lines are by no means hard and fast, but in Charlotte, as in many cities in America today, where you live tells a lot about who you are.

Such divisions turn out to be far from timeless, however. A look back at land use in Charlotte indicates that sharply defined sectors appeared surprisingly recently. As late as the 1920s the city's leading black neighborhood existed not northwest but southeast of downtown, close by the town's most elite white districts. The northwest side of the city, meanwhile, included desirable middle-income white areas. Neighborhoods were clearly defined, but separation was much less than it would later become. All around the city, black areas could be found adjoining white areas, and prosperous neighborhoods lay next to poor ones. Where Charlotte in the late twentieth century looked like a pie sliced into sectors, the pattern of the 1920s more resembled a multicolored patchwork quilt.

Turn the clock back another fifty years, and Charlotte land use gets even more surprising. In the 1870s there was very little pattern at all to residential location. Business owners and hired hands, manual laborers and white-collared clerks, and black people and white people all lived side by side. Certain vague tendencies could be discerned. The two major thoroughfares, Trade Street and Tryon Street, did hold a number of the city's larger houses. There were a few more African Americans in Second Ward and Third Ward to the south-

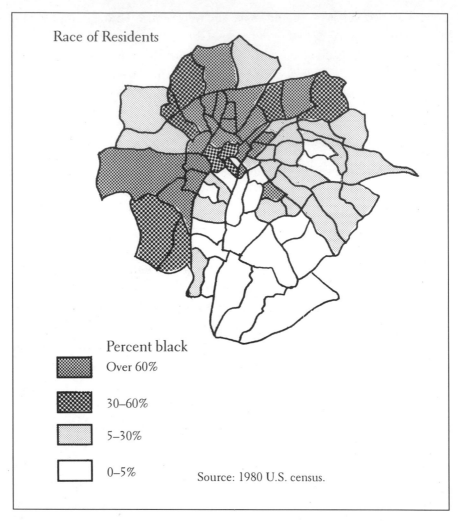

Race of Residents

Percent black

Over 60%

30–60%

5–30%

0–5%   Source: 1980 U.S. census.

FIG. 1. CHARLOTTE LAND USE, CA. 1975

Sectors. In 1975 Charlotte land uses were arranged in roughly pie-shaped sectors. Residences of wealthy whites extended to the southeast. Houses of African Americans congre-

east and southwest and a few more business owners in Fourth Ward to the northwest, perhaps. The edge of town had more smaller houses and not as many big ones. But there were no sharply delineated neighborhoods, and no direction was clearly more desirable than another. On any block the finest house might adjoin the most modest cottage. If the city of 1925 resembled a patchwork quilt, land use in 1875 looked like a scattering of salt and pepper.

Other Southern centers seem to have experienced similar changes in land use from salt-and-pepper to patchwork to sectors. Charleston, South Carolina,

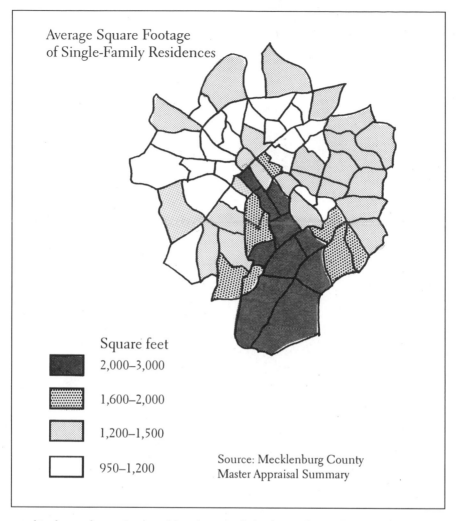

Average Square Footage
of Single-Family Residences

Square feet

2,000–3,000

1,600–2,000

1,200–1,500

950–1,200

Source: Mecklenburg County
Master Appraisal Summary

gated in the northwest. Less-wealthy whites tended to live to the northeast and southwest. This sectoral pattern has been identified by American geographers in numerous twentieth century American cities. (Maps based on Clay and Stuart, *Charlotte*)

today is noticeably segregated by color and income, but a recent study in historical geography found that rich and poor and black and white lived and worked side by side as late as the 1880s.[5] Nashville, Tennessee, in 1880 "was also mixed in a way unknown to the modern segmented city that was to dominate the twentieth century. Commercial and residential land use intermingled casually, and many merchants, professionals and artisans lived with their families in loft apartments above their shops and offices," writes an urban historian. By contrast, "in the modern city that emerged between 1880 and

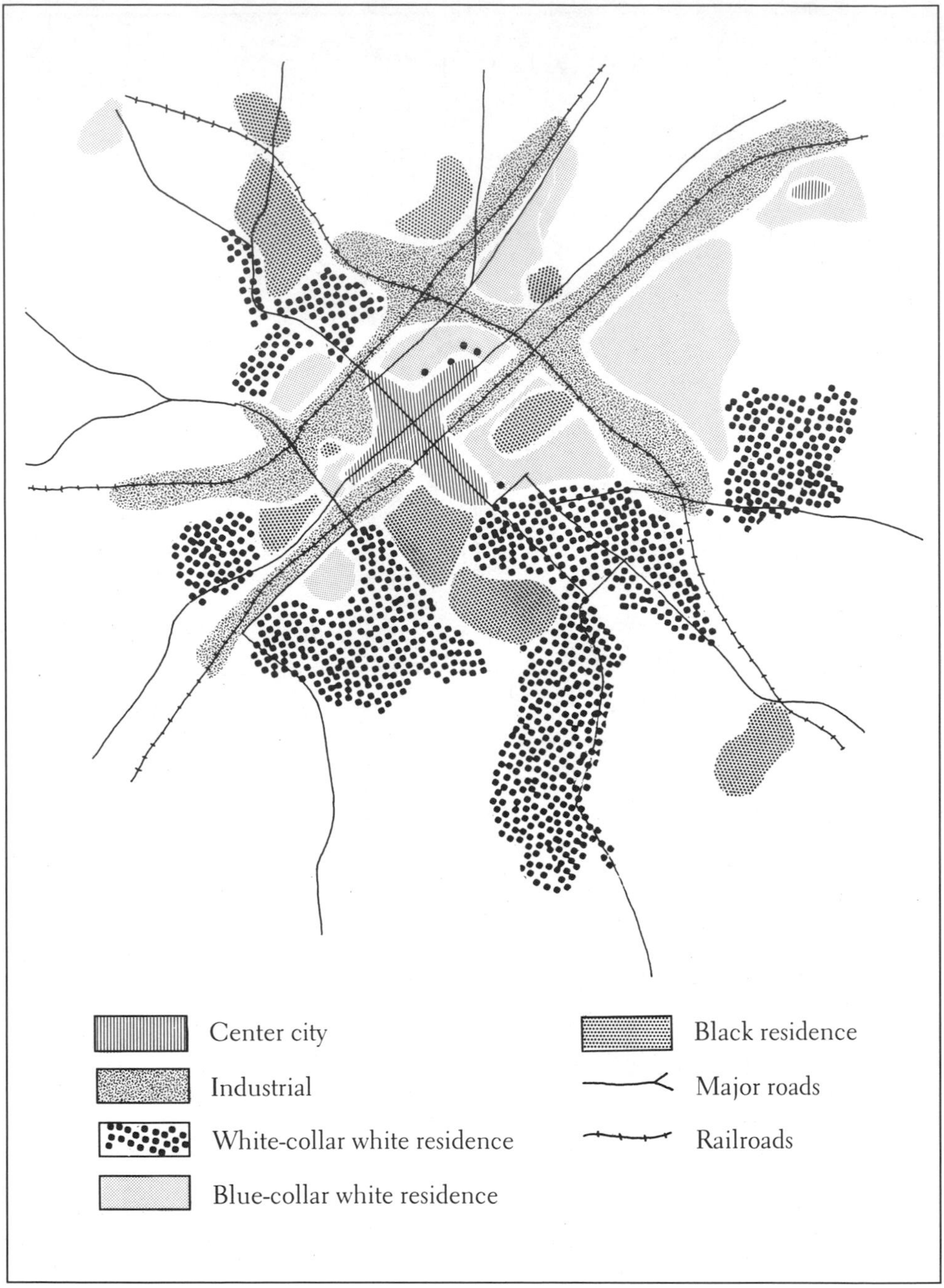
Center city
Industrial
White-collar white residence
Blue-collar white residence
Black residence
Major roads
Railroads

FIG. 2. CHARLOTTE LAND USE, CA. 1925: SCHEMATIC DIAGRAM

Patchwork. In 1925 southeast Charlotte was not yet the clear favorite of the city's well-to-do whites. Desirable white-collar white suburbs also existed on the south (Dilworth), west (Wesley Heights), and northeast (Club Acres) sides of town. Black neighborhoods likewise were scattered throughout the city, notably including Brooklyn southeast of downtown. Rather than forming sectors, neighborhoods more resembled a patchwork quilt.

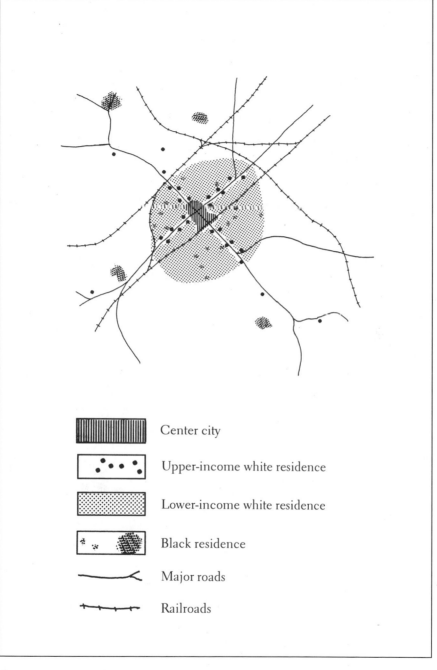

Center city

Upper-income white residence

Lower-income white residence

Black residence

Major roads

Railroads

FIG. 3. CHARLOTTE LAND USE, CA. 1875: SCHEMATIC DIAGRAM

Salt-and-Pepper. The 1870s saw even less separation of land uses in Charlotte. Well-to-do residents lived the length of Trade and Tryon Streets in each direction. African Americans settled most thickly in the southeast and southwest but made up at least one-third of the population in every ward. Throughout the city, on almost any block one could find the residences of upper-income whites, lower-income whites, and blacks mixed like salt and pepper.

1915 the lines that separated the wealthy, the poor . . . and blacks were [increasingly well] defined."[6] Looking past the 1910s, a planning history of Memphis and Richmond documents the later stage of the transformation. Both cities possessed "a patchwork pattern of neighborhoods" in the second quarter of the twentieth century, quite similar to Charlotte's patchwork quilt. Subsequently, "the demarcations between individual neighborhoods gave way to broader divisions in each city along race and class lines." By the 1970s, wealthy "white neighborhoods coalesced into a residential wedge extending eastward" in Memphis, while Richmond developed a similar zone stretching westward.[7]

In the Southern city, in short, neither segregation by income nor segregation by race has been as constant as we might imagine. Instead, the arrangement of the urban landscape changed markedly during the past century or so. From a place where people of all types lived intermingled throughout the town, the Southern city "sorted out"—first into a patchwork of well-defined neighborhoods, then into groups of neighborhoods arranged in sectors demarcated by color and class. What propelled this far-reaching transformation?

FORCES OF URBAN CHANGE

When most people today think about factors shaping land use, government agencies probably spring first to mind: city planners, highway engineers, zoning boards, and building inspectors. In Charlotte, though, these bodies appeared late in the game. The city had no planning department, no traffic engineer, and no zoning laws until well into the 1940s. Even building codes remained rudimentary and largely unenforced through most of our period. Government did play some role in matters such as annexation and street extension, as we shall see. But the impetus for new land use arrangements came from outside City Hall.

Three generations of scholars have posited models aimed at understanding land use in the city. The earliest efforts came from sociologists and economists who looked exclusively at conditions as they saw them in the 1920s and 1930s. Robert Park and Ernest Burgess proposed a "concentric ring" model, analogous to rings in a tree trunk.[8] They noted that downtown occupied the city's center, surrounded by a ring of factories and workers' housing, surrounded by a ring of middle-income neighborhoods, surrounded at last by wealthy suburban commuters. To this ring model, Homer Hoyt added a "sector theory," in which he noted that once land use got started in a spot, it tended to extend outward in that direction as the city grew, forming a wedge or sector.[9]

While the ring/sector model did a fairly good job describing the city as it appeared in the early twentieth century, the model turned out not to hold when the next generation of investigators began to look back in time. The suburbs, they found, had not always been the most desirable part of the city. In fact, in the era when most urbanites walked where they were going, the rich seemed to have congregated near the city center. Led by geographer Gideon Sjoberg, scholars proposed a new version of the concentric ring model.[10] In the "walking city" era, rich neighborhoods had occupied the inner ring and poor neighborhoods had been relegated to the periphery. Transportation innovations in the mid-nineteenth century—the horse-drawn streetcar and later the electric trolley—had simply turned the pattern of neighborhood location inside out.

Recently a third generation of studies has challenged this mechanistic "walking city/streetcar city" model. Urban historians Stuart Blumin, Robert Fishman, and Henry Binford; social historians Paul Johnson, Elizabeth Blackmar, and Sean Wilentz; and urban geographers Michael Conzen and Paul Knox, among others, have shown that early American cities did not consist of neighborhoods at all, at least not in the sense of homogeneous residential groupings of people of particular income levels.[11] Instead, land uses mixed casually in the preindustrial city. Merchants operated their countinghouses in their parlors, craftsmen lived above their workshops, and apprentices and journeymen resided with their masters or dwelled close by. Enterprises were small, seldom employing more than a handful of people. In fact, a single building often held all aspects of production—selling in the front room and making in the back room downstairs, with living quarters for the master's family upstairs and lodging for apprentices in the attic. The rise of the new industrial economy during the early nineteenth century changed all this.[12] As the industrial revolution took hold in the Northeastern United States, craft shops grew into factories with dozens and then hundreds of employees. When an enterprise expanded, manufacturing shifted to larger and less expensive space elsewhere, and the old craft shop with its high-traffic Main Street location became solely a salesroom. The master could no longer lodge his growing number of employees in his own home or find space to feed them around his own table, as he had once done with apprentices and journeymen. Working-class residential districts now formed in out-of-the-way places off the main streets. As retail activities took over the old shop, the master's family itself moved away to a house of their own. White-collar residential areas sprang up, set apart both from the solidifying "downtown" and from the districts of in-

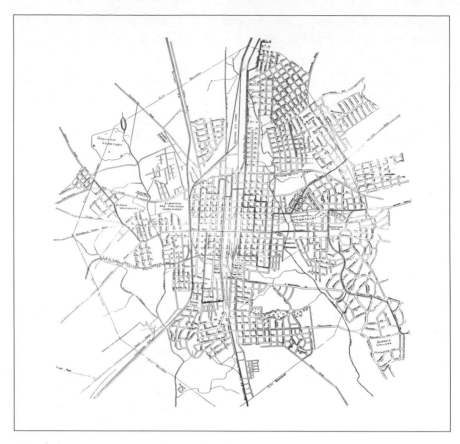

FIG. 4. THE CITY OF CHARLOTTE, 1925
This Chamber of Commerce map shows Charlotte's boundaries and the extent of its developed streets in 1925. New suburbs and mill villages swirl around the pre-1885 square-blocked grid. A keen eye can pick out streetcar lines as well. (Courtesy of the Robinson-Spangler Carolina Room, Public Library of Charlotte and Mecklenburg County)

expensive workers' housing. Well before streetcars appeared, these industrializing cities were clearly sorting out into distinct neighborhoods. Economic change, not just transportation change, propelled the reorganization of the urban landscape.

SORTING OUT THE NEW SOUTH CITY

This new model—a sorting-out driven by wider economic transformations—provides a starting point for understanding the changing landscape of Charlotte and other cities in the South. Charlotte's shift from intermingled land

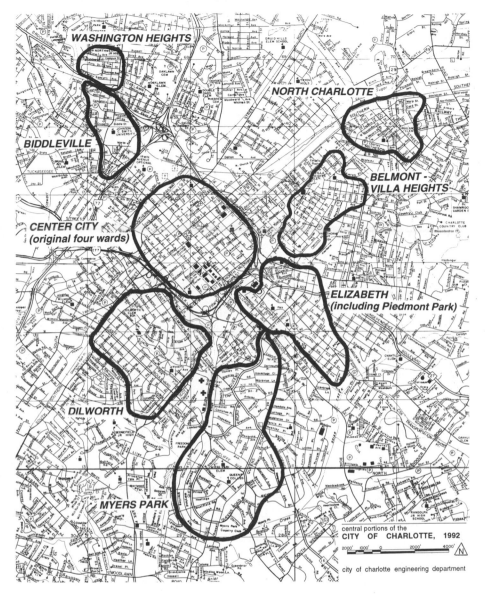

FIG. 5. NEIGHBORHOODS DISCUSSED IN DETAIL IN THIS STUDY

use to distinct neighborhoods happened two generations after the shift occurred in the North. It came hard on the heels of the post–Civil War wave of industrialization that transformed the economy of this long-agricultural region, creating a New South of factories and cities.[13] As in the North, Charlotte's initial sorting-out reflected deep changes in society brought on by the rise of new, large-scale economic enterprises.

But Southern urbanization by no means merely mirrored what had happened half a century earlier in the North. The South brought its own heritage to the process.[14] Dixie's particular agricultural economy, its traditions of leadership, and especially its historic division into black and white racial groups conspired to create a unique story. The differences could be seen in myriad issues during the 1880s–1920s, from now-forgotten debates over suburban annexation to the politics of disfranchisement.

Even into the era of interstate highways, we shall see, Charlotte's patterns of growth remained in important ways "Southern." Since the 1930s, federal aid to cities for road building, slum clearance, and sundry other projects has played an ever-expanding role in American urban development. In the South the legacy of disfranchisement resulted in tight control of local government by well-to-do whites, who put the federal dollars to work further sorting out the Southern city. Such was the case in Charlotte, which grew so divided by the early 1970s that the U.S. Supreme Court, in the landmark decision *Swann v. Mecklenburg County*, made the locality the nationwide test case for court-ordered school busing intended to reverse the effects of segregation.

The pages that follow trace Charlotte's century-long transformation from salt-and-pepper to patchwork to sectors. Chapters 1–3 begin by examining the momentous shift from an economy resting on farm trade to one based on factory production and explore what that meant to society and politics in Charlotte in the 1870s–1890s. Chapters 4–7 then focus closely on the process of neighborhood formation during the crucial years of the 1890s–1920s, when separate districts for blue-collar whites, African Americans, and white-collar whites, plus a bustling downtown, first appeared. Finally, Chapters 8 and 9 look at local government's role in urban development and gauge the impact of federal programs in magnifying the trend toward separation from the 1930s through the 1960s.

Before the Civil War . . . the better classes were very particular with
whom they associated; . . . the leveling principle was not tolerated;
but where worth was found it was always recognized.

—planter's son J. B. Alexander

PRIOR TO ITS New South industrial awakening, Charlotte functioned quietly for more than a century as an agricultural trading village, the courthouse town for Mecklenburg County. The difficult geography of the Carolina "backcountry" meant that Mecklenburg possessed few of the sprawling plantations of Old South lore. Nonetheless, the county's larger landowners securely controlled economic and political life, and they expected deference from the rest of society. The hamlet the planters built at the county's center reflected this society both in its process of city planning and in its arrangement of dwellings and shops. In the 1850s the construction of railroads would set Charlotte apart from surrounding backcountry towns and put it on the road to prosperity. This commercial growth, however, would do little initially to disrupt either traditional social patterns or urban forms.

TRADING HAMLET, 1750S–1850S

Charlotte's first white settlers arrived in 1753, choosing a hilltop site where two Native American trading paths crossed.[1] The Catawba River flowed a few miles away but the newcomers paid it little mind. Charlotte lay in the Carolina piedmont region, the band of rolling hills betwixt the Appalachian mountains to the west and the flat coastal plain along the Atlantic to the east. In the piedmont, frequent waterfalls and rocky rapids made rivers mostly unusable for transportation. Instead, the settlers followed the example of the Catawba Indians before them and did their trading overland via the old native trail southward to the port of Charleston (still in use as Interstate 77) or the Great Trading Path that ran northwest into Virginia (Interstate 85 today).[2] To better attract the commerce of surrounding farmers, the settlers pushed for designation as the county seat. They named their village in honor of England's Queen Charlotte, promised to call the county after her birthplace of Mecklenburg-Strelitz, Germany, and for good measure designated their main thoroughfare Tryon Street to flatter the colonial governor. Governor William Tryon granted the community its wish, signing Charlotte's official city charter as a courthouse town in 1768.[3]

By the time of the American Revolution, Mecklenburg County already was growing and processing enough corn and wheat to make it a military objective in the southern campaign of British general Lord Cornwallis. "The mills in its neighborhood were supposed of significant consequence," wrote a British officer, "to render it for the present an eligible position, and in the future a necessary post when the army advanced."[4] Cornwallis captured Charlotte and made it his base of operations but found little welcome from the local populace.[5] As early as 1775 Mecklenburgers had defiantly published a document called the Mecklenburg Resolves, which declared all royal commissions "null and void" and urged citizens to elect military officers "independent of Great Britain." They had even—local tradition holds—signed a Mecklenburg Declaration of Independence a year before the United States officially broke with Britain.[6] "The counties of Mecklenburg and Roban [neighboring Rowan] were more hostile to England than any in America," a British veteran of the southern campaign later remembered.[7] With British troops suffering harassment at Charlotte and defeat at the nearby Battle of Kings Mountain, Lord Cornwallis retreated, muttering that Mecklenburg was a "hornets' nest of insurrection."[8] Charlotte citizens proudly adopted "the Hornets' Nest" as their village's nickname.

In the generation following the Revolution, corn and wheat production continued to drive the economy, along with two new products of the land, cotton and gold. The gold strike came in 1799 when a farm boy playing in a creek twenty-five miles east lugged home a glittering seventeen-pound nugget.[9] Charlotte, the closest well-established town, now became the trade center for America's first gold-producing region. The city experienced no wild gold rush, but it did draw miners from as far as Europe, who sank shafts literally under Charlotte streets as well as across the surrounding countryside. To handle the wealth, a branch of the North Carolina State Bank opened in 1834, the town's first such institution.[10] In 1837 an imposing U.S. Branch Mint went up at the corner of Mint and Trade Streets, coining $1.6 million in gold pieces within a decade.[11] The mining bubble burst in 1849, however. Much richer discoveries in California eclipsed the Carolina deposits, and miners streamed westward in that now-legendary rush. Charlotte settled back into its agricultural ways.

The arrival of cotton farming meant more to Mecklenburg's long-term growth than did the discovery of gold. In 1793 American inventor Eli Whitney created the cotton gin, which allowed cotton to be farmed economically for the first time across much of the South. The new crop made its most dramatic impact in the coastal plain, where good river transportation enabled farmers to create huge plantations producing the fleecy staple. But cotton also found its way into the backcountry, taking hold particularly in the productive soils of Mecklenburg and a handful of adjoining counties in the Carolina piedmont. As early as 1802 Mecklenburg County led the entire state of North Carolina in number of cotton gins.[12] The enumerator for the 1810 U.S. census confirmed the county's impressively high output: "103 cotton gins . . . 3512 bags of cotton . . . Each bag about 250 wt. . . . and all sent to market principally Charleston, South Carolina."[13]

The offhand phrase, "all sent to market principally Charleston," made cotton selling sound simple. In fact it was anything but easy for Mecklenburg residents to get their crop to market, and that reality decisively shaped the nature of farming in the county. Farmers had to pile their cotton in wagons, then haul it southward along rutted dirt paths eighty miles or more to the nearest river port. At the fall line towns of Columbia, Camden, or Cheraw in South Carolina, they transferred the cotton to boats for the journey to Charleston. "All know what it costs to take a load of cotton to the nearest market," complained the *Charlotte Journal* in 1845. "It generally takes from 6 to 8 days—this at $3 per day would be at lowest calculation $18 to get a load of cotton to market, which at the present price of the article makes a great inroad into the amount received."[14]

The arduous journey to market meant that the backcountry had a structure of opportunity much different from that of the coastal plantation belt.[15] For lowcountry agriculturalists, a simple formula of "more land, more slaves, more cotton" seemed the surefire strategy to wealth. Historians consider twenty slaves and a hundred acres of cultivated land the minimum for a "plantation," but many planters in the coastal Carolinas amassed far more. It was not unusual to find lowcountry plantations with more than 200 slaves and thousands of acres of cotton fields, controlled from white-columned mansions or elegant Charleston townhouses.[16] In the backcountry, things were less simple. Because of the "great inroad" that difficult transportation made on profits, backcountry farmers could not rely on a single cash crop. Instead of concentrating on cotton, they found they had to raise a mix of crops, calculating what might bring a profit if cotton prices should drop too low to cover transportation costs. The same census taker who noted all the cotton flowing out of Mecklenburg County in 1810 also remarked on the high wheat and corn production. The county had twenty-one grist mills, plus a whopping sixty-two stills, corn liquor being the most efficient form in which to transport the yellow grain to the docks at Charleston.[17] By the 1850s Mecklenburg stood near the top of North Carolina agriculture in nearly every crop except tobacco.[18] Among the state's seventy-five counties, Mecklenburg placed third in cotton output, fourth in butter, eleventh in corn, and twelfth in wheat production—despite ranking only twentieth in population. At the same time Mecklenburg stood far ahead of coastal plantation counties in dollars invested in farm machinery, a testament to the way that the lack of an easy cash crop pushed backcountry individuals to innovate.

This structure of opportunity shaped Mecklenburg's society as well. In contrast to lowcountry counties, only a single farmer here on the eve of the Civil War possessed as many as fifty slaves.[19] Those few men who owned twenty slaves and thus qualified as planters usually also kept a store in town, practiced law or medicine, or pursued other nonfarm endeavors as a hedge against agricultural uncertainty. While big planters were relatively scarce in Mecklenburg, the county's fertile soil helped make smaller slaveholders unusually numerous. More than 800 households owned between one and twenty laborers, putting Mecklenburg near the top of North Carolina counties in this category. This situation boded well for town development. In the lowcountry, big plantation owners traded directly with brokers in Charleston or Wilmington and often simply ignored local towns. Mecklenburg's smaller slaveholders, by contrast, could seldom muster the time, expertise, or economic clout to deal directly with the coast and instead traded their crops to Charlotte storekeepers.

Having few planters and many small slaveholders did not make Mecklenburg a society of equals. Rather, the social structure resembled a pyramid, narrow at the peak and broad at the base. At the pinnacle stood the planters, less than 1 percent of Mecklenburg families.[20] Just below them came the merchants and smaller farmers who owned fewer than twenty slaves. Taken together, all these slaveholders made up a distinct minority of the county, roughly a quarter of the total population. Nonslaveholding whites occupied the next level of the pyramid, around 35 percent of county residents. At the bottom of the pyramid stood African Americans, whose labor made cash-crop agriculture profitable. From just 14 percent of Mecklenburg population in 1790, the number of slaves increased steadily with the rise of cotton farming until, by the 1850s, they comprised fully 40 percent of the county's inhabitants.[21]

Social and political power rested firmly at the top of the pyramid. Mecklenburg held to traditional ideas of social organization that historians have often noted in early agricultural America.[22] The family rather than the individual constituted the basic unit of society, and all members within a family were expected to defer to its senior or most able male. This family model of deference extended to the community. The most able family heads—those who amassed sizable amounts of property—controlled community affairs. Men who owned no land held only limited voting rights (women and other "dependents" possessed no voting rights at all). Community leaders thus came almost

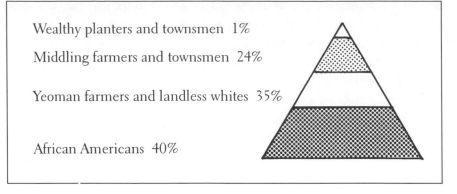

Wealthy planters and townsmen 1%

Middling farmers and townsmen 24%

Yeoman farmers and landless whites 35%

African Americans 40%

FIG. 6. MECKLENBURG'S SOCIAL PYRAMID
Before the Civil War Mecklenburg society resembled a pyramid with a small number of slaveholders at the top. Slaveowners made up only a quarter of the county's population, but that minority held considerable power over the society as a whole.

entirely from the wealthiest strata of society, and unless they proved notably rude or incompetent, they could expect to enjoy deference from their lesser fellows. As a leading historian has written of George Washington's Virginia,

> The overwhelming majority of men were agriculturalists, differing in the scale of their operations more than in the nature of them. . . . Nearly every [elected official] was a representative of agriculture; there was little else in Virginia he could represent. Under these circumstances, those who achieved most in nonpolitical life could be vested with political power without seriously endangering the interests of less successful men. It was more or less appropriate for the large planter to represent the small farmer, and the farmer accepted this leadership as natural and proper.[23]

By today's standards Mecklenburg before the Civil War was far from a democracy. Women, of course, could not cast ballots, nor could African Americans, not even the handful of free blacks.[24] Even among white men the vote was strictly limited.[25] Only men owning substantial amounts of land could participate fully in government. Well into the 1850s North Carolina law prohibited those with less than fifty acres—more than half the white population—from voting in senatorial elections. Men who wished to run for office faced much stiffer property requirements, from 100 acres for a seat in the state legislature to several hundred acres for governor. Even jurors, sitting in judgment at the humblest trial, had to be men of property. For most local offices the governor or state legislature simply appointed officials rather than going to the trouble of holding elections. Not surprisingly they tended to pick men who were landholders like themselves. This was true in Charlotte, where the legislature appointed the first city commissioners, who afterward picked their own successors, and it was true in Mecklenburg County, where most affairs rested in the hands of state-appointed justices of the peace, who typically served for life and enjoyed the informal title "squire," in open emulation of the English gentry.[26]

Men of wealth felt at ease in their position atop society before the Civil War. J. B. Alexander, scion of a leading Mecklenburg planter family, later recalled, "A half century ago the better classes were very particular with whom they associated; that is they would not allow their daughters to go riding, or attend social parties, or in any way be thrown together with people of a lower caste." This "old-time aristocracy," secure in its control of the ballot box, looked after society's interests as it saw them. Those who met the elite's approval might attain admittance to the apex of the pyramid; wrote Alexander, "Where worth was found it was always recognized." From the general populace, though, Mecklenburg's "better classes" expected obedience and deference. "Fifty years ago," Alexander remembered nostalgically, "the leveling principal was not tolerated."[27]

RAILROAD TOWN, 1850S–1870S

Despite the prosperity promised by its fertile soil, and despite the willingness of its slaveholders to experiment with crop mix and invest in new machinery, Mecklenburg County faced a frustrating barrier to growth. Geography held the county prisoner. Some cash crops could go out overland, but high transportation costs meant that most trade remained local and self-contained—nearby farmers meeting at the courthouse square to exchange surplus goods mostly with each other. By the end of the 1840s Charlotte boasted a population of 1,065.[28] It was almost exactly the same size as half a dozen other courthouse hamlets scattered over the Carolina piedmont. Salisbury, Salem, Greenwood, Abbeville, Greenville, and Spartanburg each performed similar functions for their localities, and each had about the same number of inhabitants. The Carolinas' chief cities were all ocean or river ports or political centers in the coastal plain: Wilmington, Raleigh, and Fayetteville in North Carolina and Charleston and Columbia in South Carolina. As long as rocky rivers and rutted wagon roads remained the only transportation routes into the piedmont, no backcountry town could grow much bigger than 1,000 or 2,000 souls.

The solution was obvious: build a railroad. As early as the 1830s, almost as soon as the new transportation technology had been perfected, the North Carolina legislature began discussing constructing a state-owned railway to link the fertile cotton region around Charlotte with the North Carolina coast.[29] But years passed without action. Then, in 1845, news spread that the South Carolina State Railroad was expanding. Its line from the port of Charleston would soon reach to Camden, eighty miles southeast of Charlotte. If Mecklenburg could just find a way to extend those rails, the long wagon and boat trips would be a thing of the past.

In March 1845 a committee of eighteen Mecklenburg leaders called a meeting at the Charlotte courthouse to kick off a railroad fund drive.[30] The makeup of the group reflected the nature of the backcountry elite. Though nearly all owned slaves, only one listed his occupation purely as "planter" in the census. Instead most of the eighteen gave their identities as "merchant," "lawyer," or "physician." The arguments the committee presented to prospective stock purchasers likewise illustrated the backcountry's market-oriented mindset. "In the first place," the committee said, the railroad "would enhance the value of real estate in direct ratio with its distance from the terminus."[31] This argument appealed particularly to backcountry men of property because, in comparison with lowcountry planters, they had less of their capital tied up in slaves and more invested in land.[32] And since many backcountry farmers already had town interests, they could be expected to support anything that raised town land values. Even for farmers with no town land, the committee continued, building a railroad "will afford them an easy access to market and give them an opportunity to dispose what surplus property they may have and at fair prices."[33] The promoters singled out cotton growers in particular: "Now if a Rail Road was in operation a bale of Cotton could be sent to Charleston for a mere fraction of what it would cost a planter to take it." Farmers lacking cash could contribute the labor of their slaves: "If you have not money, agree to pay in work, so that the great boon shall not be withheld from us."[34]

But such entreaties alone could not produce sufficient cash within Mecklenburg to fund such an expensive project. Committee members traveled to Charleston, hoping to find investors among the wealthy cotton traders there, but met only "cold indifference."[35] Finally in late 1847 promoters hit upon a novel solution: put the route up to bid. The railroad committee announced that it contemplated building either to Camden or to its rival, the South Carolina capital city of Columbia. The promoters opened two sets of stock

TABLE 2. Conveners of Charlotte's First Railroad Meeting, 1845

Name	Occupation	Real Estate Owned	Slaves
J. W. Osborne	lawyer	–	–
G. W. Caldwell	lawyer/mint supt.	–	1
J. B. Orr	–	–	–
J. W. Hampton	–	–	–
D. Parks	merchant	$14,000	26
W. F. Davidson	lawyer	2,400	11
W. Johnston	lawyer/merchant	8,000	11
Jos H. Wilson	lawyer	7,000	15
C. J. Fox	physician	2,000	0
W. W. Elms	merchant	34,000	36
Benjamin Morrow	planter	7,200	43
M. W. Alexander	physician	–	–
J. B. Kerr	hotel keeper	5,000	0
A. Graham	merchant	5,600	9
W. J. Alexander	–	–	–
Thomas Brem	merchant	4,500	7
R. C. Carson	merchant	6,100	3
R. H. Brawley	merchant	2,500	3

subscription books and began crisscrossing the South Carolina backcountry like traveling evangelists, holding stock-sales meetings in every hamlet and country crossroads along the two routes. Ultimately Columbia won the bidding war, and in 1849 construction commenced.[36]

On October 21, 1852, amid jubilant celebration, the first passenger train steamed into Charlotte on the new Charlotte & South Carolina Railroad. Some 20,000 people poured into the village, according to newspaper estimates, a number many times the entire county population. "Crowds came from Columbia, Chester, Winnsboro, and the surrounding country," reported one chronicler. Celebrants feasted on barbecue, sat through speeches, and listened to John A. Young's brass band from Columbia, "and at night there was a dance and a display of fireworks."[37] Indeed, the event constituted a landmark in Charlotte's economic development. The track up from Columbia was the very first railroad to tap the fertile farmlands of the North Carolina piedmont. Suddenly Charlotte possessed a distinct advantage over all those other courthouse towns that dotted the backcountry. Barely three months after the first train arrived in 1852, a farmer near Lincolnton, some thirty miles to the west, noted in his diary, "I was in Charlotte last week. You would be surprised to see its change. It has become the market for the whole country around. I went down and sold two loads of cotton and bought all my groceries for the year on as good terms as we could formerly in Columbia or Cheraw. It is a great convenience to the people and saves much time formerly spent in going to distant markets."[38]

Three additional railways opened during the next few years, making Charlotte decidedly the best trading location in the North Carolina backcountry by the eve of the Civil War. In 1854 the long-discussed North Carolina State Railroad finally reached the city.[39] Running in a great arc from Charlotte through Greensboro and Raleigh toward the ports of the North Carolina coast, it made Mecklenburg for the first time a functioning part of North Carolina, for it now became as easy to go east to the capital at Raleigh as it was to go southward to Charleston. In 1860 Mecklenburg entrepreneurs chartered a project with the grandiose moniker "The Atlantic, Tennessee and Ohio Railroad Company."[40] Intended to connect Charlotte with the Midwestern United States, it never found a way to cross the Appalachian mountains and instead served as a short feeder line bringing produce from the nearby courthouse town of Statesville, North Carolina. In 1861 the first leg of the Wilmington, Charlotte and Rutherford Railroad opened to Lincolnton, acting as a similar feeder line.[41]

The four roads—two main lines and two short lines—gave "a stimulus to the cotton trade which no other advantage could have conferred," wrote a local newspaper editor. Even farmers located fifty or sixty miles closer to the coast now often shipped their crop back up the tracks to Charlotte to be sold. "Countless numbers of bales have been brought to Charlotte from the direction of Chester and Rock Hill, in South Carolina, over the [Charlotte & South Carolina], while the North Carolina Railroad gives people all along its line, from Charlotte to Lexington, however paradoxical it might seem, a market in Charlotte for their cotton. . . . Situated at the terminus of both [main] roads," he explained, "competition between them at once enabled the cotton dealer here to pay the very highest price for the staple."[42] One bellwether of Charlotte's blossoming trade was the opening in 1853 of the Bank of Charlotte, the city's first locally owned financial institution.[43] The railroad prosperity attracted an influx of new residents, more than doubling city population during the 1850s, to 2,265 people.[44] In a single decade as a railroad town, Charlotte grew as much as it had in its entire first century.

Economic growth and the rapid rise in population did nothing to shake Charlotte's established social pyramid. Those with wealth simply added to their power, like lawyer and slaveholder William Johnston, who now also served as president of the Charlotte & South Carolina Railroad, or fellow railroad promoter W. W. Elms, a planter and merchant who after 1852 became, in J. B. Alexander's words, "the principal cotton buyer in the market. He built several elegant houses and did much to improve the town."[45] Outsiders might find a way to rise into the "better classes" if they worked hard and carefully allied themselves with existing powerholders. Robert M. Oates offered an example of these "new men." Third son of a small farmer in nearby Cleveland County, Oates was one of many country boys who came to sell cotton and found themselves caught up in the wonderful excitement of the railroad town.[46] Arriving in 1853 at age twenty-five, he first took a job as clerk in a grocery store. By 1857 he had formed a partnership with Lewis Williams, son of a prosperous old Mecklenburg family, to open a firm selling groceries to farmers and taking cotton or cash in payment. "They are clerks in produce both young men of good business habits," a credit investigator jotted approvingly that year. Williams, "probably w[orth] 5 to 6 thousand," put up most of the cash. Oates, "not w[orth] much say 1 to 2 thousand dollars," contributed the entrepreneurial drive.[47] Through such combined enterprise of new men and established families, Charlotte blossomed during the decade before the Civil War.[48]

Modern-day Southerners love to bemoan the devastation wrought by the war between the states. But for Charlotte the Civil War and the decade of Reconstruction that followed actually improved the city's competitive position in the regional economy. As soon as fighting started in 1861, Charlotte geared up to support the Southern war effort.[49] Entrepreneurs started small concerns to turn out gunpowder, chemicals, woolen goods, and canteens, and the Mecklenburg Iron Works, a mining equipment firm that was the town's only industry, switched to casting Confederate cannon. Most noteworthy and least likely for this landlocked town, the Confederate government made Charlotte the site of its main naval yard in 1862. Fearing capture of the port of Norfolk, the Rebels moved their "smith, foundry, machine shops, rigging loft, laboratory and other departments" for two years to a spot on the railroads near downtown.[50] The siting was wise; thanks to Charlotte's sheltered backcountry location the city never came under direct attack from Northern troops. Mecklenburg County furnished some 2,700 men to the Southern military, a sacrifice "strikingly illustrated in the many representatives of the 'crutch and cane' order, habiliments of mourning, and the vacant seats in the home circle," a visitor observed at the war's end in 1865. Yet as seriously as Charlotte felt the loss of her young men, he wrote, "war—ruthless war—has not fallen so heavily on this place as many places."[51]

Surviving the Civil War unscathed gave Charlotte great advantage in the first months of peace. The entire world clamored for Southern cotton after the scarcities of the war. Any community that could transport crops to market could virtually name its own price. Charlotte's excellent rail connections remained remarkably intact, except for the Statesville short line cannibalized by Confederates to repair more strategic routes elsewhere, and a small, easily repairable section of the Charlotte & South Carolina Railroad wrecked by Union troops.[52] Cotton trade resumed immediately. Wrote the editor of the *Charlotte Observer*, "In 1855 the annual sales of cotton on this market was less than three thousand bales. In 1860, on account of the railroad influence, the trade had gradually become of more importance, and had reached twelve thousand bales. . . . With the crop of 1866, business of this line was again resumed, with about the same amount in the market as in 1860—12,000 bales."[53] Bringing the same number of bales to market in 1866 as in 1860 represented an extremely lucrative achievement. During the first postwar months, short supplies and difficult transportation pushed prices on the New York Cotton Exchange up from the 1850s level of around fifteen cents. Cotton spiked briefly as high as one dollar per pound, then settled at between than thirty and forty cents a pound.[54] "Cotton brought prices that would paralyze the operators of today," one Charlottean later recalled. Even as late 1869, he noted, "some grades of cotton sold at twenty-five cents per pound."[55] Money poured into the Queen City. Suddenly Charlotte was rich.

Trade flourished. By June 1867 there had "been ten or twelve new Store Houses built," cheered a local newspaper. "From our own observation, and after consultation with others," the paper added, "we estimate the number of new Dwelling Houses at seventy-five."[56] By 1869 *Branson's North Carolina Business Directory* could list 183 merchants in Mecklenburg, putting upstart Charlotte just behind the state's long-established trade centers of Raleigh and Wilmington.[57] Five new banks opened during the postwar decade, and the city briefly supported the services of an architectural firm, a luxury almost unheard-of in the backcountry.[58] To boost trade further, city fathers purchased a municipally owned cotton press in the early 1870s. The huge machine compressed cotton bales for storage or shipment to distant markets, a service that made the city even more of a magnet for the region's farmers.[59] "The scope of country of which Charlotte is the commercial cotton center," noted the 1875 city directory, included "fourteen counties in North Carolina and at least eleven in South Carolina." Mecklenburg still had a diverse agricultural output, and Charlotte was becoming a wholesale point for a variety of consumer goods; but the directory observed, "There is no channel of commerce which has added so much to our wealth as the cotton interest."[60] By 1875 40,000 bales of the white fiber passed through town annually, making Charlotte the busiest inland cotton market in both Carolinas.[61]

Recognizing how much their good fortune depended on rail links, Charlotteans freely invested a portion of postwar profits in new lines. In 1872 the Carolina Central Railroad connected Charlotte directly with the port of Wilmington.[62] In 1874 crews relaid rail on the Statesville short line and extended its roadbed northward in the direction of Richmond and southward all the way to Atlanta, creating the Atlanta & Charlotte Air Line, a major through-route across the Southeastern United States.[63] The fresh construction came as part of a regionwide railroad-building effort that massively reoriented Southern commerce. Lowcountry ports had traditionally dominated the South's trade, but lowcountry planters lost all their slave capital with Civil War defeat and now had scant cash to invest in the new technology of railroads. Most post–Civil War Southern railroad construction thus took place in the old backcountry, where it spurred the rapid rise of inland commercial cities across the piedmont. The most explosive growth occurred at Atlanta, Georgia, a hamlet that happened to enjoy the unique advantage of sitting astride the Southeast's best rail route to the Midwest.[64] Charlotte, hemmed in by the Appalachians to the west, would never match Atlanta's reach, but it likewise staked its future on railroads. By the mid-1870s, though still smaller in population than Charleston, Columbia, Wilmington, Raleigh, or even New Bern, the Queen City boasted a greater number of rail connections than any other place in North or South Carolina. With lines converging from six directions, Charlotte stood poised to step forward as a leading trade hub.

The post–Civil War prosperity drew hundreds of newcomers. "Charlotte was a boom town in those days," one such arrival recalled.[65] Despite the loss of many men in the war, city population grew at virtually the same rate during the 1860s as it had in the preceding decade, doubling once again to 4,473 inhabitants.[66] Charlotte's old-time aristocracy accepted these newcomers on much the same terms as they had those who arrived in the 1850s. Wealthy and well-connected men such as North Carolina's Civil War governor Zebulon Vance, who came to practice law from 1866 to 1876, were immediately embraced into the leadership circle.[67] Similarly, ambitious strivers who lacked famous names but added to the city's economic vitality also received warm

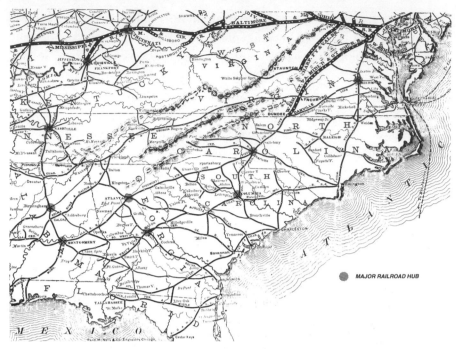

MAJOR RAILROAD HUB

FIG. 7. REGIONAL RAILROAD HUB, 1876

Railroad connections transformed Charlotte from just another backcountry town to a place of regional importance. By 1876 lines radiated in six directions from the small city, giving it the best rail connections in the Carolinas. Old ports and political centers such as Wilmington, Raleigh, and Columbia still boasted more citizens, but the future lay with Charlotte. To the west, however, lay the twisted mass of the Appalachian Mountains, blocking easy access to the Midwestern United States. Ultimately Charlotte would rank second to Atlanta as the commercial city of the Southeast, because Atlanta possessed a rail link through the Appalachians to the Midwest. (Source: adapted from a portion of "General Map of the Baltimore and Ohio Rail Road and Its Connections," 1876, courtesy of the Geography and Map Division of the Library of Congress)

welcomes. Conspicuous examples included a pair of Jewish businessmen, Samuel Wittkowsky and Jacob Rintels, who had run a hotel in Statesville before the war, then moved to thriving Charlotte in 1865 to open a dry goods store. "Doing a good business and we think safe," said a credit investigator of Wittkowsky in late 1865.[68] The pair's entrepreneurial energy quickly put them among Charlotte's top buyers of cotton and sellers of farm supplies. Even snobbish J. B. Alexander had few qualms about accepting such men into Mecklenburg society. "The Israelites," he later announced, "have proved amongst our best citizens."[69] For a man of wealth, Charlotte was a very good place to be immediately after the Civil War.

For a brief time it looked as if the postwar era might include dramatic advances for those further down the social pyramid as well. Federally administered Reconstruction beginning in 1865 promised major changes in social relations in the South.[70] Defeated Confederate officers lost their right to vote or hold office until pardoned by the U.S. government; since most men of wealth had been active in Confederate affairs, the traditional elite abruptly found itself stripped of long-held political control. At the same time, constitutional amendments ended slavery and extended full citizenship rights to African Americans. A sweeping democratization of politics compounded the affront. The government stuck down the old system of justices of the peace and insisted that ordinary citizens, not just men of property, be allowed to sit on juries. A new North Carolina constitution gave African Americans the vote and also omitted any mention of traditional property qualifications among whites. Suddenly, as never before in North Carolina history, the majority of the male population possessed political power.

The "better classes" reacted strenuously against this new democracy. Men such as J. B. Alexander, accustomed to humble deference from the "lower caste," erupted in anger. "A new code of laws [was] given to our people, with negro jurors and the baser element of whites," Alexander fumed years afterward.[71] "It was very annoying for a good citizen of the county to be subpoenaed by a former slave, acting as deputy, to appear at the bureau to answer certain complaints lodged by said freedman. It was worse to ignore the order. Here you were confronted with negroes, probably some you had never seen before."[72] To be judged by a stranger, especially a black or "baser" white man, rather than a justice of the peace you had long known and socialized with, seemed downright humiliating to the old-time aristocracy. Even worse for the "better classes" was their loss of control of politics. "Our system of voting and managing elections remained the same until the close of the Civil War. Then all was changed, the bottom rail was put on top," Alexander wrote.[73] While black assertiveness was annoying, what really galled Alexander were the poorer whites who now refused to show deference to wealth: "The negroes had never enjoyed freedom before, and if they had not been led astray by unprincipled white men, they would have listened to their best friends, their former masters," he reasoned. Instead, "the whole election machinery was in the hands of an irresponsible party, and the enemies of the best people in Mecklenburg County."[74]

Before much time passed, though, the "best people" regained their accustomed places in the South. Men of wealth won back the right to vote, and after Federal troops pulled out of Charlotte in 1872, old-line leaders moved back firmly into the seats of influence. Mecklenburg "emerged from Reconstruction politically much as it had been before the war," with "wealthy, urban, middle-aged professionals . . . in power both before and after the conflict," two recent studies of the county in this era confirm.[75] Charlotte's city government in 1876 typified the resurgence of the traditional economic elite.[76] William Johnston, president of the rail line to South Carolina, served as mayor. The city council included one black man and one white newcomer, a token of Reconstruction change. But the large majority were familiar names from the 1850s, including two former planters who were now bank presidents and three antebellum merchants—among them the enterprising storekeeper Robert M. Oates—who continued to dominate city commerce. The Charlotte economy might grow and change, it seemed, but color, wealth, and position would continue to define the social order just as they always had.

THE URBAN LANDSCAPE OF THE PREINDUSTRIAL CITY

The landscape of Charlotte expressed this confidence in tradition. Well into the 1870s, Charlotteans organized their city in ways that would have seemed familiar to a time traveler from colonial days or even from medieval Europe. "The social geography of medieval cities," say historians, "was relatively undifferentiated; apart from a few public spaces and religious buildings, most structures combined shop, workshop and private residence."[77] That custom of intermingled land use carried over into the New World. The famous statesman Benjamin Franklin, for example, built his 1770s house in the heart of Philadelphia on the same lot that held his printing shop.[78] The young apprentices who worked in the shop received lodging in his home or above the printery. Behind the house Franklin erected rental quarters that he let to journeymen (young artisans who had progressed beyond the apprentice stage but still worked for an employer rather than running their own craft shop). Such a mixture of activities—residence and business, owner and renter, and employer and employee—may seem an odd hodgepodge by today's standards, but it was no accident. Philadelphia was renowned as America's best-planned city, laid out in an orderly grid of straight avenues that marked a major improvement over the mazelike street patterns of old Europe. If Philadelphians had so desired, they could well have been as methodical about separating land uses as they were about laying out streets. But they saw no need. In a community of familylike operations such as Franklin's, there seemed no reason not to live and work in close proximity. Each master had only a handful of men, and he labored alongside them, fostering a very personal, face-to-face relationship. As apprentices and journeymen, his workers were not mere employees but, rather, junior craftsmen being trained to follow in the master's footsteps. As long as this pattern of economic enterprise held, the old medieval mingling would remain common.

In Philadelphia and elsewhere across the Northeast, however, traditional ways of organizing society and the city began to break down during the generation following Benjamin Franklin's death.[79] Around the beginning of the 1800s, enterprising masters started expanding craft shops into manufactories that exploited the new principal of division of labor. The craftsman split his work into a number of simple tasks and hired more hands. As production increased, he spent more time in the salesroom than the workroom and soon hung up his old rough blue workshirt in favor of a starched white collar. "Blue-collar" workers, meanwhile, increasingly found themselves handling repetitive, routine tasks, working as employees rather than as craftsmen-in-training. The new white-collar/blue-collar relationship eroded traditional bonds of deference. Workers, once able to air grievances directly with the master across the workbench, now organized strikes to get the attention of owners who seemed to view laborers not as family but as interchangeable parts in a machine dedicated to profit. Owners, struggling to manage bigger operations, felt a new need for employee punctuality and soberness—a sharp change from the casual customs of the craft shop where master and men often adjourned to a nearby pub for the afternoon when business was slow. A sudden enthusiasm for temperance societies, etiquette books, religious revivals, and public schools in the Northeast after 1800 can all be linked to the search for mechanisms to replace the disappearing bonds of deference.[80] The economic changes also sparked a major reorganization of the urban landscape. Intermingled work and residence gave way to a "downtown" of shops and an area elsewhere of "manufactories." Employees, too numerous to lodge in their employer's house and eat around his table, found separate dwellings of their own. By the 1820s and 1830s, historians have discovered, land use in America's industrializing cities was sorting out into clearly identifiable blue-collar and white-collar neighborhoods.[81] Such changes came much more slowly, though, to the still-preindustrial South.

Like Philadelphia, Charlotte in colonial times took pride in orderly planning. When Governor William Tryon proclaimed Charlotte the county seat of Mecklenburg in 1768, his charter specifically required a planned urban design.[82] Tryon granted the town fathers 360 acres, with the mandate that a surveyor draw "an exact plan of one hundred acres of said land" showing streets and house lots. The rest would remain as pasture to be used in common by the residents for the time being; city fathers would plat it as the village grew. Charlotte's initial surveyor laid off the town in a grid, with square blocks defined by straight streets running at right angles to one another. Trade and Tryon Streets, the two original Indian trading trails, became the main streets, and their crossroads at the heart of the grid became the courthouse square. The Charlotte plan was a bit less elegant than Philadelphia's, perhaps. No blocks were left open as parks, a hallmark of the Pennsylvania capital, and the streets were aligned with the old Indian paths rather than set rigidly to the points of the compass (to this day North Tryon Street actually heads northeast, South Tryon Street points southwest, and so on). But even in its simplicity, the Queen City's grid showed a similar spirit of community order.

As Charlotte grew throughout its first century and a quarter, it remained a planned town. The grid expanded many times from the initial 100-acre kernel. First, town officials extended the streets until they covered the entire 360 acres, roughly to Brevard Street on the east, Poplar Street on the west, Seventh Street on the north, and Third Street on the south.[83] By the time the city first registered its municipal boundaries with the state in 1815, officials had added even more blocks, eastward to Alexander, northward to Eighth, and southward to Stonewall.[84] In each expansion the new streets were planned by a decision of the community leaders rather than by any individual entrepreneur. A surveyor hired by the city fathers staked out future avenues across private farmland; as owners developed their property, they were expected to build those streets exactly as dictated. The undeviating uniformity of the grid thus became the physical representation of community control. Not until the dawn of the industrial era would that tradition be questioned.

The buildings that Charlotteans erected on top of their orderly grid likewise showed respect for long-standing habits and customs. Charlotte's first courthouse, constructed in the 1760s in the middle of the Trade and Tryon crossroads, was a two-story wooden building with a meeting room above and trading stalls for farmers below, an arrangement dating back to the market halls of medieval England.[85] The very practice of calling the crossroads the "Square," despite the fact that it was only an ordinary intersection in shape, likely also harked back to England's market squares. Well into the 1820s, age-old instruments of justice added to the Square's traditional atmosphere: a "whipping post, stocks and pillows [pillory] stood in the middle of the street . . . in full view of the judge's bench where he could see his sentence executed."[86]

Descriptions of the town in the 1820s and 1830s indicated the persistence of mixed land use throughout the community. On South Tryon Street in 1825, for instance, the home and office of "Joseph Wilson, a distinguished lawyer," adjoined an operation frequented by hunters "where all coon skins and other furs were sold."[87] Town leaders felt no need to reserve South Tryon for lawyers and other professionals, nor did they take action to separate elite residences from even such prosaic and noisome operations as trade in animal pelts. Mixed use was even more evident within individual buildings. Rich planter William Davidson operated a store in one first-floor room of his handsome house facing the Square. Nearby on the Square the banker John Irwin had a similarly elegant residence, whose ground floor "composed Mr. Irwin's store room, counting room, dining room and parlor."[88] When Leroy Springs, the wealthiest planter in the entire Carolina backcountry, erected an imposing brick mansion in town in 1830, he followed the same practice: "As was often the custom in those days the first floor of a residence was used for business purposes, and in the corner adjoining the Square Mr. Springs conducted a general store which occupied one-half the ground floor space. The north side was the family sitting room. . . . From an ornate ceiling in the sitting room hung a handsome chandelier . . . [, and] a beautiful spiral staircase extended up to the third floor."[89] What was true for fine residences also held for ruder buildings. The last "town" structure on North Tryon Street in 1825, near Sixth Street, "was a long one-story log house with a partition in the middle. One end was used as a dwelling and the other end as a hatter-shop, and belonged to a man named Thomas Capps."[90] Beyond that, farmers' dwellings straggled out along the main roads, each with agricultural acreage behind it. The farmhouses combined workplace and home functions as well, serving as both residences for the farm families and headquarters for their agricultural operations.

When the arrival of the railroads during the 1850s brought rapid growth and new land uses to Charlotte's urban landscape, residents continued to hold tightly to traditional ways of arranging their town. At the end of 1852 the population influx attracted by the just-completed rail line to South Carolina inspired Charlotte leaders to again enlarge the city. As they had since colonial times, the city commissioners hired a surveyor and directed him to "make a plan."[91] The existing grid of square blocks was extended outward to McDowell Street on the east, Morehead Street on the south, Graham Street on the west, and Twelfth Street on the north (completing the area that would comprise Charlotte's center city in the 1990s). Even the new railroad tracks carefully respected the grid, following three corridors that simply replaced planned streets. The original North Carolina State Railroad and the Charlotte & South Carolina Railroad joined to form one corridor between College and Brevard Streets just east of the Square. The Atlanta & Charlotte Air Line created a second corridor, running parallel to Graham Street west of the Square. The North Carolina Central to Wilmington and Lincolnton crossed the other two corridors at right angles, forming a third corridor parallel to Twelfth Street north of the Square.

Initially the railroads had only limited effects on land use in the city. Well into the 1870s leading citizens maintained elegant homes close to the tracks.[92] Prominent lawyer Zebulon Vance, when he moved to Charlotte after the Civil War, picked a dwelling right next to the rails on Sixth Street. Mecklenburg Iron Works chief John Wilkes owned a showplace residence on West Trade Street barely a hundred yards from the rail corridor west of the Square, and banker W. R. Myers lived on East Trade Street in an equally elegant house equally close by the rails to the east. The noise and soot of frequent steam trains was not enough to disrupt traditional residential location.

The most immediately visible change the railroads did bring was the rise of a cotton district. Warehouses, sales facilities, and the municipal cotton compress bunched along the rail corridor east of the Square, an area that Charlotteans proudly nicknamed the "Wharf" for its functional similarity to the waterfront at Charleston. Town life had once centered on the courthouse and on the handful of shops and taverns around the Square. Now the Wharf became a third center of urban activity for Charlotte. The arrival of the first cotton bale each season generated an impromptu parade. The wagon driven by the lucky farmer clattered into town, gathering men and boys in its wake as word spread of the happy event. At the Wharf, black stevedores swarmed out to meet the wagon, vying for the honor of unloading it. A sample of cotton extracted from the bale quickly passed to a cotton broker for grading, and before nightfall the town buzzed with predictions on the quality of the coming crop.

The effects of the busy cotton wharf, in turn, sparked the start of what would become a far-reaching transition in land use in Charlotte—the creation of a downtown devoted solely to business. As trade boomed following the Civil War, property near the Wharf rose sharply in desirability. Merchants scrambled to open stores as close to it as possible in order to catch the trade of visiting farmers. In the heart of Charlotte, businesses began to push out residents. By 1877 when itinerant mapmaker F. W. Beers drew the city's first detailed building map, an important innovation could be detected in land use patterns: a small but clearly defined business district. The Beers map showed

FIG. 8. COTTON WAGONS LINED UP NEAR THE WHARF
From the 1870s through the 1920s the cotton compress and warehouses of the Wharf—in
the vicinity of South College Street—constituted a hub of activity in downtown Charlotte.
(Courtesy of the *Charlotte Observer* and the Museum of the New South)

some 150 establishments crowding around the Square and extending down
East Trade Street to the cotton wharf. In some of these buildings, merchants
still held to the old custom of living upstairs over the shop, like prominent
banker Rufus McAden, who resided with his family above the new First
National Bank. But many of the two- and three-story structures were devoted
solely to commerce, and their owners walked to work each morning from
dwellings elsewhere. Charlotte's central area was beginning to become a true
downtown.

A pair of buildings on Trade Street symbolized the transition away from
mingled work and residence. In 1875 the old John Irwin house still stood on
the Square, looking much as it had in 1825. It no longer functioned as a combined residence and business, however. A drugstore took up the entire ground
floor, and the druggist went home each evening to a separate dwelling five
blocks away.[93] Architecturally the homey, gable-roofed Irwin house looked
increasingly out of place compared with the new structures springing up
during the late 1860s and 1870s. Charlotte merchants now began erecting

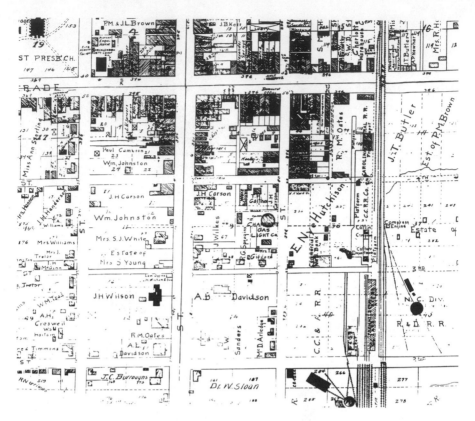

FIG. 9. COTTON WHARF AND DOWNTOWN, 1877 BEERS MAP
Completion of the railroad to Columbia (at right) made Charlotte a prosperous cotton-trading town. This portion of the 1877 Beers map shows some of the resulting changes. Along the railroad, just off South College Street between Third and Fourth Streets, stands the cotton compress and the busy cotton platform. Along Trade Street a solid row of businesses now extends westward from the tracks—the beginnings of a true downtown. (Source: Beers map of 1877, as retraced in 1911; courtesy of the City of Charlotte Engineering Department)

"business blocks," brick structures whose flat-roofed silhouettes proclaimed their purely commercial character.

The finest example of the new mode stood right alongside the Irwin house. Wittkowsky & Rintels, by the 1870s the city's largest dry goods firm, occupied a handsome new three-story brick building done up in the fashionable Italianate style, with cast-iron trim above the windows and a heavy cornice emphasizing the flat top of the facade. The boxy look contrasted sharply with the homelike pitched roof of the older, wood-frame Irwin house next door. Anyone glimpsing Wittkowsky & Rintels's building could see that it held a busi-

FIG. 10. BUSINESS BUILDINGS OLD AND NEW, INDEPENDENCE SQUARE
In this picture of Independence Square in the 1880s, two buildings neatly symbolize
Charlotte's evolving economy. In the foreground, at the corner of West Trade Street and
North Tryon Street, stands the old structure erected early in the century by merchant
John Irwin. Its homey gable roof signals the fact that it had not only been Irwin's store but
also his residence. To the left, just down West Trade Street, looms the new commercial
block put up after the Civil War by Samuel Wittkowsky. Wittkowsky and partner Jacob
Rintels operated on a new scale. With thirty employees their business no longer fit the traditional mold of a household craft shop. The boxy, flat-topped form and stylish Italianate
architecture of their building says clearly that this is no house. (Courtesy of the Robinson-
Spangler Carolina Room, Public Library of Charlotte and Mecklenburg County)

ness. Indeed, Samuel Wittkowsky resided in a handsome house on South
Tryon Street three blocks from his store, and Jacob Rintels had a mansion a
similar distance away on West Trade.

While the impetus for business block architecture came in part from competition for land near the Wharf and the Square, the firm of Wittkowsky &
Rintels also personified an even more important factor quietly at work by the
mid-1870s. In the booming postwar economy a few ambitious men reached
toward a new scale of operations. By 1876 Wittkowsky & Rintels employed
some thirty-six workers, the city's biggest workforce.[94] Fourteen of the firm's
hands were salesmen, some concentrating on local retail sales and others on
wholesaling outside the city. Eleven worked as clerks and bookkeepers, fore-
shadowing the legions of office workers who would one day inhabit downtown
Charlotte. The firm also made some of the products it sold: three women

FIG. 11. JACOB RINTELS'S MANSION, BUILT 1874
Both Wittkowsky and Rintels lived in houses that were separate from their place of business—a new pattern. Jacob Rintels's handsome residence on West Trade at Graham Street went up in 1874. The mansard-roofed tower and the slender windows with their elaborate arched tops showed Rintels's awareness of the very latest French and Italian influences in Victorian architecture. (When suburbs became fashionable in the 1910s, this house was moved—minus the tower—to suburban Myers Park, where it still stands.) (Courtesy of the Robinson-Spangler Carolina Room, Public Library of Charlotte and Mecklenburg County)

worked as dressmakers, and one as a hatmaker. Remaining employees served as laborers, moving goods and running errands. Such an operation outstripped the family model of workplace organization. Unlike Benjamin Franklin's apprentices, the many workers at Wittkowsky & Rintels could no longer be lodged with the master's family above the shop. It was entirely appropriate, then, that the firm abandon the old house form of architecture in favor of the modern business block. Though still very modest by latter-day standards, Wittkowsky & Rintels represented the start of large-scale economic enterprises in Charlotte.

Only a handful of Charlotte businesses yet operated on the scale of Wittkowsky & Rintels. In 1876 just eleven firms employed as many as a dozen workers.[95] Three were railroads (with twenty-four, thirteen, and twelve Charlotte employees, respectively). Three others were traders like Wittkowsky &

Rintels, hiring twelve or so assistants to pursue a variety of business opportunities. Another pair of outfits pursued disparate combinations of sales and manufacturing. White & Sims, who worked thirteen men, split them between a leatherworks and a grocery sales establishment, while W. R. Cochrane divided his twelve-person force between a restaurant and a cigar works. Only two concerns devoted primarily to manufacturing had as many as a dozen employees in 1876. Carolina Agricultural Works, a farm implement manufactory, engaged fifteen hands. The sash and blind company of J. Rudisill, producer of building components, had twelve employees. Large-scale economic enterprises would become a much more powerful factor in the arrangement of the urban landscape with the appearance of big textile mills during the 1880s. For now, a handful of exceptions notwithstanding, Charlotte remained a predominantly preindustrial economy. The U.S. Census of 1880 reported that Charlotte's average "manufacturing firm" had just 3.9 workers.[96]

A WALK AROUND CHARLOTTE ON THE EVE OF INDUSTRIALIZATION

Outside the nascent downtown, Charlotte retained the traditional patterns of land use typical of a preindustrial city. Somewhat miraculously—considering how small Charlotte still was in this era—two detailed data sources exist that allow us to explore those patterns close-up. Charlotte's first city directory appeared in 1875–76, containing listings giving the name, address, and occupation of nearly every household head in the community. By matching that information to the buildings drawn on the F. W. Beers map of 1877, a clear picture of local land use emerges.[97] In Charlotte, as in Benjamin Franklin's Philadelphia a century earlier, the dwellings of owners and workers, rich and poor, and even blacks and whites still coexisted in close proximity (see color fig. 1). That arrangement spoke much about the values and ideals of preindustrial society.

Our imaginary walk through the Charlotte of the 1870s begins where any newcomer might first experience the city: along the two main avenues of Tryon Street and Trade Street. Beyond the new business buildings near the Square, land use along these busy streets in 1877 quickly reverted to residential. The Beers map showed big houses, only two or three per block, set well back in spacious yards, lining Tryon and Trade in each direction. The city directory confirmed that these were the grand residences of some of Charlotte's leading citizens.

By today's standards, this pattern of imposing dwellings lining the busiest streets seems surprising on at least three counts. For one, we now expect people of wealth to guard their privacy, huddling their houses together in an exclusive neighborhood out of the way at the edge of the city. But the mansions of Tryon and Trade showed no such tendency. Second, we might expect in this walking-city era that persons of wealth would cluster as conveniently as possible near the Square. But Charlotte's fine residences lined the entire length of bustling Trade and Tryon, extending as far as the city's edge in each direction. Third, we might at least expect such dwellings to congregate on a "best side of town," forming a sector extending in one particular direction of the compass. But Charlotte's mansions appeared equally in all four directions. Walking out East Trade Street, one passed fine residences such as that of banker W. R. Myers, while in the opposite direction down West Trade Street one saw the equally elegant abode of Anna Morrison Jackson, the widow of Confederate general Stonewall Jackson. On North Tryon Street stood the grand old Phifer house (where townspeople had gallantly lodged Confederate president Jefferson Davis in the closing days of the Civil War), while South Tryon Street's estates included that of revered Rebel general D. H. Hill.

These families clearly regarded residential location on a busy street as an asset, not a liability. The roots of the practice dated back to the village's earliest days when the first settlers had built their cabins along the trading paths; some elite families of the 1870s were descendants of those original inhabitants and retained the same land. But the pattern represented more than simple persistence. Fresh arrivals to the elite such as Jacob Rintels made a point of siting their stylish post–Civil War mansions right alongside the old ones. Even as the teeming wagon traffic of the cotton boom brought more noise and more dust—not to mention more horse manure—Trade and Tryon Streets remained the most fashionable addresses in town. The reason lay in the era's attitudes toward money and power. In a traditional deferential society, Charlotte's leading men—whether natives such as W. R. Myers or newcomers such as Jacob Rintels—felt no need for modesty about their wealth. Their houses, standing proud for all to see, proclaimed their position atop the social and economic pyramid.

As we venture off Trade and Tryon on our walk, the dwellings become smaller. Environmental factors played some part in who lived where, producing a slight but noticeable social gradient as one moved toward the edge of town. One such factor was ease of access to the Square; though not a hard-and-fast rule as we have just seen, long walks tended to make the outskirts less desirable than close-in locations. Factors of topography and drainage reinforced this. In the era before sewers and storm drains, homeowners sought the highest, best-drained ground they could find. Charlotte in the 1870s had not yet outgrown its original hilltop. Tryon Street ran along the ridgeline, while Trade Street followed the highest path up one side and down the other. Away from the main streets, the land fell off gently toward Irwin Creek at the west side of town and Little Sugar Creek on the east side. In addition, "branches"— as Mecklenburgers called unnamed minor tributaries—cut into the side street districts. Fourth Ward, with the fewest branches, had larger houses than Second Ward, which was the city's worst-drained district.

While such environmental factors did make poorer people more likely to reside near the edge of town, the striking thing about Charlotte's side streets in 1877 was how little differentiation could be detected among income groups. The Beers map and city directory listed business proprietors, office employees, and manual laborers living side-side-by side on nearly every block. The proportions of the mix changed as one moved farther from the Square, but the gradient was gentle, with no sharp breaks. More store owners could be found near the Square and more laborers near the outskirts, to be sure, but in no case were residents separated into homogeneous white-collar or blue-collar neighborhoods.

Three sample blocks in First Ward, northeast of downtown, confirm this salt-and-pepper intermingling. The first lies close to the Square. Our walk starts at the spacious house of Zebulon Vance on Sixth Street at the railroad. As a former governor as well as a prosperous lawyer, Vance stood at the top of the town's elite; his choice of a residence on Sixth Street offered clear proof that not all of the city's leaders lived on Trade Street or Tryon Street. Across Sixth Street from Vance's house stands a much humbler cottage shared by two clerks, Henry Strouse and Robert Gary. Walking up Sixth to College Street, we come to the wagon-making manufactories of Robert Wearn and William McCracken. Next to them at the corner is the dwelling occupied by druggist William Wilson and wagon maker Charles Wilson. On other corners of the intersection stand the homes of widow Mrs. C. Warlick and grocery wholesaler M. C. Mayer. Turning up College Street, we pass the cottages of bookkeeper W. H. Whetmore, planing mill hand John Moore, salesman Richard Hennegan, livery stable proprietor J. W. Wadsworth, physician Robert Gibbon, and clerk James Tremain. At the College and Seventh intersection are the modest cottage of blacksmith John Lambert, the fine houses of storekeeper Ferdinand Kuester and manufactory proprietor Jonas Rudisill, and the church of the city's black Presbyterian congregation. Turning onto Seventh

Street, one passes the houses of grocer James Symons, ironworking foreman Marshall Frazier, bookseller J. K. Purefoy, and clerk Charles Rigler. Turning finally down A Street, we pass the residence shared by physicians Eli Green and Alfred Lindley, partners in a company that made medicines. In this block near the city's heart, then, many, but by no means all, residents were fairly well-to-do. The houses of prosperous professionals and businessmen such as Zebulon Vance and Jonas Rudisill comfortably coexisted with the small cottage of workman John Moore, the African American church, and the two wagon-manufacturing operations.

The second sample block lies farther away, on North Tryon Street halfway between the Square and the edge of town. Beginning on North Tryon, we walk past the fine residence of cotton and commission merchant James B. Rankin, adjoined by the much smaller house owned by carpenter John H. Connell. Next comes the Lutheran Church, then the handsome dwelling of cotton and coal merchant William H. H. Gregory, who boarded his clerk and his bookkeeper in his home. Around the corner at Ninth and North College is the residence of William I. Friday, co-owner of a general store. Turning down College Street, one passes bookkeeper Thomas Tiddy, black renter Ben Smith, and cotton and wholesale merchant T. H. McGill. Swinging onto Eighth Street, one sees the compact cottage of tailor John Stracker, which stands just behind the large Rankin residence, where we began. Again, land use here is mixed. The proportion of business owners is almost as great as it is closer to the heart of town, confirming the desirability of high-visibility locations such as North Tryon Street. Yet the block is by no means exclusive. Residences include dwellings that house boarders, the relatively humble cottage of a tailor, and a home occupied by an African American, as well as the dwellings of elite cotton and wholesale merchants.

The third sample block lies at the very edge of settlement. Starting at the corner of Ninth and Myers Streets, one sees a corner house owned and occupied by mail agent James M. Turrentine, and next to it is the residence of David White, proprietor of a downtown grocery store. Continuing down Myers Street, one strolls past the dwellings of two skilled black workmen, carpenter Anderson McKnight and mechanic Washington Owens, and then comes to the corner house owned by another skilled African American, painter Dick Pethel. Turning onto Eighth Street, one passes the residence of blacksmith Marton Vanderburg. At Eighth and E Streets carpenter Jesse Mullis owns one corner house, carpenter John Glenn owns another, and clerk Giles Miller lives in a third. Strolling up E Street to Myers Street brings us to two houses owned by members of the Eddins family, carpenter Charles W. Eddins and route agent William Eddins. Walking along Myers to the corner of Ninth takes us back to the beginning of our jaunt. Occupations in this block, too, span the range from laborer to business owner. Residents are, on the whole, less prosperous than they are in the blocks closer to downtown. Still, the houses held everyone from store proprietor White, to office workers Miller and Turrentine, to blue-collar carpenters Mullis and Glenn, to African Americans Pethel and Owen.

The appearance of boarders in our sample underscores the continuity of traditional social habits in 1870s Charlotte. Many business owners maintained the age-old practice of lodging some of their workers in their own homes or adjacent dwellings. Both merchant William Gregory and gun and lock seller Ferdinand Kuester, whom we met on our walk, listed employees living in their households. Elsewhere in First Ward, livery stable owner J. R. Davidson boarded both his stable superintendent and a driver in his family's residence. Saloonkeeper Charles Roedigger shared his house with his bartender. Grain merchant R. M. Miller, who ranked among the town's wealthiest citizens, found room for his clerk and two laborers at his elegant family home on North Tryon Street. In this city of small trading enterprises, employers had not yet given up the custom of living alongside their employees.

Our sample blocks point up another, even less expected kind of intermingling: by race. More than a decade after the Civil War, Charlotte still had no hard-edged black neighborhoods. Rather, African Americans continued to live all over the city, usually side-by-side with whites.[98] Scholars who have noticed persistence of racial intermingling in Southern cities have assumed that it was merely a case of African Americans continuing to occupy old slave quarters.[99] In slavery days, urban blacks were scattered throughout town, living in their owners' houses or in separate huts on the master's property. This pattern did seem to persist in 1876 along Trade Street and Tryon Street in Charlotte, where the city directory listed house servants, drivers, and cooks living with their employers. But elsewhere in the city, simple persistence could not explain the intermingled arrangement of the mid-1870s. Newly freed black people had poured into Charlotte after Emancipation looking for work and community with their fellows. The city's African American population zoomed from about 800 in 1860 to 1,880 by 1870, and it would hit 3,338 in 1880, comprising an all-time high of 47 percent of the city's people.[100] Such numbers could not squeeze into former slave shanties. In fact, the number of blacks by the mid-1870s exceeded the city's total population at the start of the

TABLE 3. Black and White Populations of Charlotte by Ward, 1879

	Ward 1	Ward 2	Ward 3	Ward 4	Total
White	1,393	623	881	946	3,843
Black	740	1,091	1,026	407	3,364
% Black	35	64	66	30	47

Source: 1879 Charlotte city directory. The numbers were unofficial, but the total ratio of blacks to whites exactly matched that determined a year later by the U.S. Census Bureau, a good indication that these figures were relatively reliable.

Civil War. The picture of integration seen in the 1875–76 city directory was painted on a canvas of new buildings.

The highest concentrations of African Americans appeared in Second and Third Wards, where blacks made up a narrow majority of the population. Second Ward represented an obvious locale for former slaves. Nicknamed "Logtown," its low-lying land had made it an area of inexpensive residences even before the war, and with Emancipation newly freed slaves gravitated toward its humble cabins. Location immediately adjacent to the cotton wharf added to its desirability; African Americans filled most of the jobs operating the compress and handling bales on the Wharf. Despite its obvious attractions, though, Second Ward had no more black residents than Third Ward. By the 1870s Third Ward held the city's two leading African American institutions, Clinton Chapel AME (African Methodist Episcopal) Zion Church and St. Michael's Episcopal mission school. In the shadow of those institutions, racially integrated housing remained a way of life. As late as 1889 the city directory showed three white households and ten black ones on the block with Clinton Chapel.

Similar salt-and-pepper racial mixing could be seen in First and Fourth Wards, where African Americans constituted one-third of the populace. Dick Pethel, the black homeowner we met on our First Ward stroll, was not unusual for living next to a white businessman. The 1875–76 directory showed black families residing on twenty-eight of First Ward's block fronts; only three of those block fronts were all black. Throughout the four wards, people of color fitted into the physical fabric of the city just as whites did. Like whites, most black Charlotteans lived in dwellings fronting city streets, rather than in rear alleys and courts.[101] Like working-class whites, some blacks could be found along the streets close to downtown, while more tended to reside nearer

FIG. 12. TRYON STREET, CA. 1875

On June 12, 1875, *Harper's Weekly* published this view of the heart of Charlotte, looking southward across the Square and down South Tryon Street. The string of buildings on the right neatly summed up the town's recent growth. At the extreme right is the homey, gable-roofed John Irwin house, which had once held both Irwin's home and business but now was devoted solely to commerce. Next, across West Trade Street, stands the Granite Row that was constructed at the start of the railroad boom of the 1850s. Compared with the Irwin house the Row is big and of imposing masonry construction. But its gable roof still harks back to earlier days. Past Granite Row, three post–Civil War "commercial blocks" can be seen. With their flat roofs and stylish Italianate trim they speak volumes about Charlotte's bustling economy following the war. The fledgling downtown remained small, though. Beyond the commercial blocks, the canopy of trees shades residences. (Courtesy of the Robinson-Spangler Carolina Room, Public Library of Charlotte and Mecklenburg County)

the edges of the city or in low-lying areas. Integration, not segregation, remained the rule within preindustrial Charlotte.

Just outside the city, five small "rim villages" offered an exception to that rule.[102] One rim village was called Biddleville, a group of African American dwellings initiated in the late 1860s around Biddle Institute (today Johnson C. Smith University), a college founded by the Presbyterian Church for the freed slaves. The four other rim villages included Greenville/Irwinville just northwest of Charlotte, Dulstown directly north, Blandville just south, and Myers Quarter (renamed Cherry in 1891) to the east. These communities likely dated

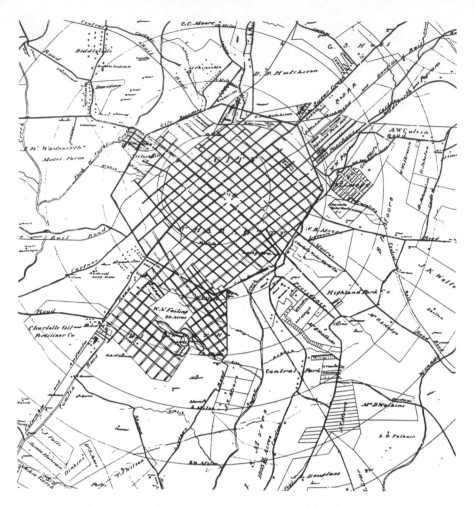

FIG. 13. A PORTION OF THE BUTLER AND SPRATT MAP, 1892

The 1892 Butler and Spratt map captured Charlotte on the verge of tremendous expansion. Southeast of town are the just-platted streets of Dilworth, and the smaller proposed grid of Belmont may be seen immediately east of the city (in both cases the mapmakers show all planned streets, through few actually had been constructed). African American rim villages are depicted as clusters of dots: Biddleville to the northwest, Greenville and Irwinville to the north, and Blandville to the southwest. South of town is the vast J. S. Myers cotton farm, future site of the posh Myers Park neighborhood.

from before the Civil War, begun either as slave quarters for nearby planta-tions (as in the case of Myers Quarter and probably Irwinville) or as clusters of free blacks and hired-out slaves, a pattern noted by historians in other ante-bellum Southern cities. The Blandville district may have started as an mining camp around the old Rudisill and St. Catherine's gold mines; its major black residential street was called Gold Street, and subsequent directories listed at least one African American as "miner, St. Catherine mine." Interestingly, Blandville—the only rim village whose inhabitants appeared in the 1875–76 city directory—had eight white households among its four dozen families, including two Italian musicians.[103]

By the late 1870s Charlotte had changed considerably from the rural courthouse town of 1850. Railroads had brought prosperity and a widening circle of trade, pushing the population from barely 1,000 to more than 6,000 people. A generation of entrepreneurial "new men" had joined with established families in the 1850s to build new business enterprises, which survived the end of slavery and flourished during the 1860s and 1870s. Handsome brick "business blocks" now defined a fledgling downtown, and a thousand houses spread out from the Square half a mile in each direction.

Yet despite the rapid growth, Charlotte remained a traditional preindustrial community in most respects. The town's enterprises were still small. Interactions between social groups remained deferential, with men of property holding tight control of political life. The urban landscape echoed that continuity. Old ways of community planning still dictated the street layout. Old habits of residential intermingling persisted. Rather than clustering in homogeneous neighborhoods, residents of all types scattered throughout the city like salt-and-pepper. Charlotte's wealthiest businessmen—who could have afforded almost any living arrangement they wished—remained at ease with the notion of residing next door to a white manual laborer or even a black workman. Charlotte was still a city of traders, with no major manufacturing industry. That would be the next step, sang the 1875–76 city directory: "When in future years . . . we shall be able to utilize the God-given privileges with which we are blessed, and convert her into a manufacturing town, as will most assuredly be done, we may justly look forward to a brighter career of prosperity than has ever dawned upon us."[104]

CHAPTER 2

HABILIMENTS OF PROGRESS

Bring the mills to the cotton!

—New South promoter D. A. Tompkins

CHARLOTTE'S success building a railroad economy put it at the forefront of a post–Civil War effort known as the New South movement.[1] Until the Civil War, many leading men of Dixie had disdained Northern-style economic enterprise. "We have no cities—we don't want them. . . . We want no manufactures: we desire no trading, no mechanical or manufacturing classes," orated one prominent Texas planter. "As long as we have our rice, our Sugar, our tobacco, and our Cotton, we can command wealth to purchase all we want."[2] Defeat wiped away that self-satisfied assurance. Southerners aggressively began to pursue Northern-style industrial and urban development. Particularly along the new inland railroad lines, factories sprang up in earnest starting in the 1880s. Counties that had once only grown cotton now built mills to spin it into thread and weave it into cloth, and promoters competed vigorously to trumpet the urban potential of each city and town. While they embraced the New South Creed of economic progress, Dixie leaders did not adopt Northern ideas wholesale. They endeavored to pick and choose those things that would enhance, not remake, their familiar society. In particular they sought to maintain the social pyramid. Such careful choices could be seen in the creation of Charlotte's early mills and millworker housing and its first streetcar district during the 1880s and early 1890s.

TRADING PARTNERSHIPS AND THE COTTON MILL CAMPAIGN

The notion of building cotton mills in the Carolina piedmont had been around long before the 1880s. As early as 1813 the state's first textile factory opened at Lincolnton, and by 1860 North Carolina had some thirty-nine operations, most located near piedmont waterfalls.[3] But the same rocky rivers that provided power sharply limited the ability to get goods to market, and the enterprises usually remained minor adjuncts to cotton plantations. Mecklenburg planter William Henry Neal operated a typical mill in the 1850s with partners Peter M. Brown and Harry B. Williams. "N is a farmer, B is a rich farmer and tanner, W a heavy merchant," reported an investigator for the R. G. Dun credit bureau. Neal "has a large farm and a large wheat mill. Does more at his mill than at his cotton factory."[4] One competitor of Neal's in the county, the Rock Island Manufacturing Company, managed to survive the Civil War but went bankrupt soon after. Not until fifteen years following the war would Charlotte businessmen amass enough capital to finance a major long-running textile enterprise.

"Col. R. M. Oates and Mr. D. W. Oates are now at the North for the purpose of purchasing the Machinery for the Cotton Factory which they will erect in Charlotte as soon as possible," announced the *Charlotte Democrat* in January 1880.[5] Since arriving with the railroad boom in 1853, Robert Oates had steadily built a small fortune buying cotton and selling supplies to farmers. The R. G. Dun credit service reported in 1879 that Colonel Oates, in partnership with his brother David, was the town's top cotton merchant: "Have been successful and are doing the leading business here."[6] The dry pronouncement constituted a notable understatement. Oates had been worth barely $1,000 in 1857 when he established his first toehold in trade through partnership with a local planter's son. Once in business, Robert Oates piled up "$8 to $10" thousand by 1873, "$20 to $25" thousand by 1875, and "$50 to $75" thousand by 1879. "He is as 'good as wheat,'" wrote the credit investigator in that year: "Probably does not owe a dollar."[7] With that kind of capital, Oates and his family could now afford to plunge into textile manufacturing in a big way.

The Charlotte Cotton Mill, as the Oateses proudly christened their enterprise, took inspiration from the latest trends in the Northeast, long the nation's premier textile-manufacturing region. The brick building located on the railroad in Fourth Ward stood one story tall—an efficient form just coming into use in New England—and was arranged in an *L* with "the roof being opened with skylights and the walls on both sides being one succession of tastefully-constructed windows."[8] Technology developed "at the North" made the Charlotte Cotton Mill almost instantly profitable. Purchasing the latest machinery, the Oateses were able quickly to create a factory of 6,240 spindles "built at a cost of $15 per spindle," a visitor reported in April 1881 as the mill achieved full operation. "Their daily running expenses are sixty dollars. . . . From these figures, with raw cotton averaging ten cents per pound, we have the neat profit of $155 per day."[9]

As Charlotte's first New South cotton mill swung into operation, a number of other textile-related enterprises appeared in the town.[10] The city's six rail lines, reaching across the piedmont, gave Charlotte easy access to most of the other cotton factories rising throughout the Carolinas and made the town a logical locus for entrepreneurs seeking trade with the mills. The Mecklenburg Iron Works, begun before the Civil War as a gold-mining machinery firm, now shifted to making and repairing cotton presses, industrial steam engines, and boilers for textile factories. A rival firm, Liddell & Co., sprang up to join it, and by the late 1880s each company regularly employed upward of seventy hands.[11] In 1883 a young merchant named Edward Dilworth Latta opened the Charlotte Trouser Company. Four years later Latta had sixty-three sewing machines in daily operation and five roving salesmen selling pants to storekeepers throughout the South and as far away as New York. Within a decade Charlotte would sport five pants factories and boast of being "the greatest trouser manufacturing city in the country."[12]

The most enterprising textile-related entrepreneur was certainly D. A. Tompkins.[13] A relative of legendary South Carolina politician John C. Calhoun, Tomkins had gone north to school after the Civil War, earning an engineering degree at highly respected Rensselaer Polytechnic Institute. In the early 1880s he chose Charlotte as a base from which to sell Westinghouse steam engines to the Southern cotton industry. Much as Robert M. Oates had done a generation earlier, Tompkins smoothed his path by joining forces with an established local family, making grain merchant R. M. Miller his partner in the D. A. Tompkins Company. The Tompkins Company designed over 100 cotton mills across the region and pioneered technology to press discarded cotton seed into vegetable oil, creating a new textile-related industry. As the machinery business became established, Tompkins busied himself in every aspect of the New South cotton mill campaign. He published how-to books for mill developers, devised investment plans to help communities start new factories, helped set up colleges at Clemson and Raleigh to train textile engineers and chemists, and bought the *Charlotte Observer* and made it a persistent voice for Southern development. Even the *Atlanta Constitution*, which considered itself the New South fountainhead, acknowledged that Tompkins "did more for the industrial south than any other man."[14]

In 1889 three more cotton mills opened in Charlotte—the Alpha, the Ada, and the Victor—confirming the city's New South zeal and further demonstrating the vitality of its economy. The D. A. Tompkins Company designed and erected all three. As with the original Oates factory, capital came almost entirely from the community itself. The Alpha Mill used a novel "installment" funding plan instead of customary sales of stock, an innovation that garnered much attention nationwide. Rather than wait for a few wealthy men to commit large chunks of cash, promoter Calvin Scott invited any Charlottean to visit his dry goods store "and pay in fifty cents per share on their stock, of which twenty-five cents is the initiation fee and twenty-five cents is the first installment of dues, and the weekly payments will be made at the same place from 4 to 8 o'clock each Saturday."[15] Fellow merchant John L. Brown organized the Ada Mill on the same type of installment plan later that same month.[16] The energy evidently spilled over to established investors. Within weeks Charlotte Cotton Mill founder Robert M. Oates and merchant

S. A. Cohen announced the formation of a new Victor Cotton Mill Company, financed conventionally.[17] "Charlotte is essentially a home-made city," boasted a local newspaper editor in 1889: "All the Cotton mills and clothing factories . . . were built mainly by Charlotte people."[18]

LOCATING THE MILLS, HOUSING THE WORKERS

The locations of Charlotte's first four cotton mills represented an interesting evolution in ideas of land use in the New South city. When Robert Oates created the city's initial mill in 1880, he chose a site right in town. The Charlotte Cotton Mill occupied a block and a half of land within Fourth Ward. The large brick factory rose just a block off posh West Trade Street, in sight of fine residences, including those of railroad owner William Johnston and socialite Mrs. Stonewall Jackson. The Board of Aldermen encouraged the location, granting the cotton mill a ten-year exemption from city taxes.[19] In a society where intermingled work and residence had always been taken for granted, this new enterprise evidently presented no threat to the social decorum of the elite avenue. The Charlotte Cotton Mill employed seventy "operatives" when it opened, nearly twice as many as any previous local firm. To house some of the workers, the Oates brothers built a short row of modest wooden rental dwellings facing Sixth Street behind the mill. "Eight tenement houses for the hands are being framed," noted the *Charlotte Observer* in 1880. "The houses will be painted and plastered, [and] will contain ample room for ordinary families."[20] The Oateses erected only eight cottages because most of their operatives would be women and children, the families of workmen employed elsewhere in town.[21] With millhands who were already part of the city's social fabric, the Charlotte Cotton Mill could be incorporated comfortably into the community.

The three mills added in 1889, however, broke that familiar pattern of locating workplaces within the urban fabric. The Alpha, Ada, and Victor each employed more hands than the first mill, hiring seventy or more adults apiece plus anywhere from one dozen to four dozen boys and girls.[22] Such a large workforce no longer could be drawn from the wives and children of already-employed Charlotteans. Now entire families fresh off the farm flocked to the city to labor in the mills. Where the Charlotte Cotton Mill had snuggled into the existing town, the three new plants were set outside the urban grid—the Alpha and the Ada beyond Twelfth Street to the north of town, and the Victor across the railroad to the west (see fig. 13). Promoters did not pick these spots to

FIG. 14. ALPHA MILL COTTAGES, CONSTRUCTED CA. 1890
Rows of humble three-room cottages on Calvine Street (off east Twelfth Street, visible from the Brookshire Freeway today) were erected as part of a village for employees of the adjacent Alpha Mill. They constitute one of Charlotte's oldest single-class neighborhoods. (Photograph by author, March 1993)

avoid city taxes; each lay within the municipal boundaries. Rather, they chose sites with an eye to erecting factory housing. Rows of company-owned cottages went up alongside each mill to hold the textile workforce.

The Alpha, Ada, and Victor mill villages represented a major innovation in Charlotte's social geography. The ancient custom of intermingled land use, a constant in Charlotte through more than a century of change and growth, no longer held here. Only blue-collar textile hands lived in these new districts, making them Charlotte's first class-segregated neighborhoods. The sense of separation was heightened in the Ada and particularly in the Victor villages by the fact that the streets of mill cottages made no attempt to extend Charlotte's long-established grid plan. Instead the lanes obeyed their own independent logic, setting the mill families even more sharply apart from the rest of the city.

Charlotte adopted the mill village concept, ironically, at a time when textile company housing was fading in the North.[23] Initially cotton mills had been located at waterfalls, often far from existing cities. Pioneering facilities such as the famous Lowell mills in Massachusetts erected company villages as a lure to attract workers to these isolated sites. That pattern of rural riverside textile villages showed up in North Carolina as well beginning in the early nineteenth century. When steam power replaced water power around mid-century, however, factories no longer needed to be located in the countryside. By the 1880s most industries in New England sought sites in town and expected that workers would buy or rent in the regular private housing market. In the newly industrializing piedmont South, however, mill men kept the village concept when they began to build cotton factories in Carolina cities.[24]

Charlotte's New South mills all ran on modern steam, but nonetheless their founders consciously chose to promote the older housing practice. Part of the reason may have been the sheer quantity of arriving workers, whose numbers perhaps strained the existing local housing supply. More significantly, the practice fit well with Charlotte's social habits. In a community where old craftwork customs of social organization still prevailed, the mill village dovetailed neatly into existing ways. Company housing encouraged millhands to feel traditional bonds of obligation to their employers, just as apprentices had felt obliged to the master with whom they lodged. Company housing also enabled employers to monitor their operatives, exactly as craftsmen had once watched over their workmen. "An important advantage," wrote D. A. Tompkins, designer of the Alpha, Ada, and Victor mill villages, "is that employees go to bed at a reasonable hour and are therefore in better condition to work in the daytime."[25]

Charlotte's 1889 mill villages thus embodied an intriguing mix of change and continuity. These separate districts of blue-collar housing represented a new phenomenon in the urban fabric, the first homogeneous single-class neighborhoods in Charlotte. At the same time the mill villages also represented powerful continuities that made them attractive to Southerners. In a society where old-fashioned deferential relations between worker and master remained very much alive, the notion of providing workers housing seemed not at all strange. The cotton mills, in fact, were not alone in this practice. In 1887 the Carolina Spoke and Handle Company, a Charlotte firm employing thirty-two hands, noted it was erecting four new tenement (that is, rental) houses next to its factory.[26] Much in the manner of customers in a clothing store, trying on items and selecting only those that complement their personal style, Charlotteans picked and chose what ideas they wished to adopt as they shaped their New South city.

That process of selection could be witnessed as well in the creation of the district of Dilworth. Launched with great ballyhoo in the early 1890s, Dilworth promised to be Charlotte's first Northern-style "streetcar suburb." Streetcar neighborhoods had appeared up North with the invention of the horse-drawn railcar during the 1830s and increased exponentially after engineers perfected electric-powered trolleys in the 1880s.[27] Speculators in suburban real estate loved the trolley, for it opened vast acreages of land to development. Indeed, real estate men usually took the lead in financing and constructing streetcar systems. They directed the lines out from downtown into the land they held in the countryside, often creating a "trolley park" at track's end to boost ridership among the general public and also to lure customers to look at suburban house lots. Charlotte's Dilworth—set at the city's edge, served by trolleys, and ornamented by a gracious park—seemed at first glance a typical example of a streetcar neighborhood. On closer examination Dilworth strayed considerably from the accepted definitions of a suburb.

Up North, streetcar suburbs were conceived as exclusive residential districts for white-collar commuters. Such neighborhoods, in other words, represented yet another variation on the idea of the sorted-out city. Land use was purely residential: homogeneous groups of mostly single-family houses surrounded by lawns and greenery. No businesses, no ugly factories with their noise and smoke, and no teeming blue-collar workers were allowed to despoil these neighborhoods. Four attributes defined the ideal, writes suburbia's leading historian, Kenneth Jackson: "non-farm residential" land use, "middle and upper status" residents, low density relative to older sections, and a daily commute to work.[28] Suburbia, agrees fellow historian Robert Fishman, is "defined by what it includes—middle-class residences—and second (perhaps more importantly) by what it excludes: all industry, most commerce except for enterprises that specifically serve a residential area, and all lower class residents."[29] Dilworth bent or broke every one of those rules. The contradictory impulses embodied in the district's design made it a fascinating mirror of social attitudes in Charlotte in the dawning years of the industrial era.

Mass transit debuted in Charlotte in 1887 with the inauguration of horse-drawn streetcar service, but promoters at first showed no inclination to push rails outward into surrounding farmland.[30] The tracks of the horsecar system simply connected the three railroad corridors with the Square, running along Trade and Tryon Streets from the train stations to the businesses and hotels at the heart of town. Charlotte's leaders certainly knew about the concept of suburbia from their frequent trading trips to the North; the up-to-the-minute architectural ornament they chose for their houses and business blocks following the Civil War showed a keen familiarity with the Northern built environment. In this city of small trading enterprises, though, there seemed no interest in the aggressive sorting-out of land uses that the suburb represented. "Charlotte Real Estate Advancing," noted 1887 headlines. "Property in the business part of the city, or within four blocks of Independence Square, is at a premium," but "suburban property remains about the same."[31] If a real estate man could find some way to change those attitudes and make it fashionable to live at the edge of town, he might reap a tidy windfall.

Edward Dilworth Latta stepped forward to seize the opportunity. A model New South entrepreneur, Latta descended from a South Carolina planter family that sent him north for his education after the Civil War.[32] After a year at Princeton, young Latta found his way to New York City, where he learned the clothing business. Traveling back south as a salesman, he discovered Charlotte's booming economy and in 1876 opened a men's haberdashery store near the Square.[33] Soon he expanded into manufacturing, creating the Charlotte Trouser Company, which by the late 1880s employed 120 seamstresses.[34] In 1890 Latta felt ready to try real estate development. Following the established practice of Charlotte entrepreneurs, he sought five partners among the city's elite: M. A. Bland, a physician and son of antebellum landowners; J. L. Chambers, manager of the Liddell Iron Works; E. K. P. Osborne, a lawyer and part-owner of the horsecar line; Eli Springs, city alderman and son of leading planter Leroy Springs; and F. B. McDowell, a prosperous merchant and longtime mayor of the city who also edited the *Charlotte Chronicle* newspaper. Together Latta and his powerful allies created the Charlotte Consolidated Construction Company, popularly known as the Four Cs.[35]

The Four Cs began amassing farmland at the city's southern edge and at the same time negotiated to purchase the horsecar system. Latta was well aware of the new electric streetcar technology from his business trips northward and from contacts in Asheville, where North Carolina's first trolley system had gone into operation in 1889. In February 1890, when the renowned inventor Thomas Alva Edison visited Charlotte to experiment with a process for refining gold ore, Latta invited him to his home. Soon after, the Four Cs purchased the old Charlotte Street Railway and announced it would spend $50,000 converting it to electricity, with track "extended in all directions." The trolley system would be "on the most improved plan, new from spike to car, entirely discarding everything in connection with the present tramway," the Four Cs stated.[36] The Edison Company got the contract and dispatched an engineer to direct a workforce of local, mostly African American laborers.[37] In July 1890 the reason for the transit improvements became clear to Charlotteans. Edward Dilworth Latta announced plans for a vast new real estate development to be created long the streetcar line. Named Dilworth, it would occupy 442 acres of fields around a wooded ravine just south of the city beyond Second Ward.

While the prospect of considerable profit certainly inspired Dilworth's formation, Latta's thinking also evinced a broad streak of New South boosterism. In a yearlong series of advertisements and editorial columns mailed to newspapers throughout Dixie, the Four Cs trumpeted its work in glowing words and flowing phrases that emphasized the New South Creed.[38] Congratulating themselves as visionaries "before whose eyes the future hangs no veil," Latta and company proclaimed that Dilworth represented "the inaugural movement in the march of improvement" that would see Charlotte "aglow with the spirit of enterprise."[39] Dilworth was not merely a real estate development but a symbolic vehicle bringing modernity for all, "a living monument . . . erected to our push and energy."[40] By creating this up-to-date district, Charlotte would throw off any last vestiges of the antiurban "Rip Van Winkle rest" that had once kept the South in the dark. Over and over the Four Cs advertisements urged readers to embrace the innovative ideas of the era: "We must go forward or retrograde—there is no resting point with progress."[41] Admonished one column, "We show what other towns are doing, with the hope that the inspiration to do likewise will pervade this community to a large extent."[42] Exhorted another, "Get out of old ruts if they are the pest houses of bad habits. Now go to work."[43] To Edward Dilworth Latta, the former clothing salesman, the process was as simple and as necessary as buying the right suit of clothes: "Don the habiliments of progress and be wiser and happier thereby."[44]

Just like suburbs in the progressive North, Dilworth would include a grand trolley park. "Please read the histories of all cities, particularly locations thereof which have been made adjacent to parks," advised a Four Cs advertisement: "Enhanced values ten-fold have followed."[45] The company set aside the ravine in the center of Dilworth as a pleasure ground named Latta Park: "The suburban attractions of the leading cities of this country and the Old World are the parks. Hyde, near London, the Central, in New York, the Prospect, near Brooklyn, the Fairmont, in Philadelphia, and the Druid Hill, in Baltimore, are notorious for their grandeur and beauty. The last named holds the leadership over the list because of its great natural harmony. . . . The park on the Four Cs property near Charlotte will lead all others of the South, save Druid Hill, at Baltimore."[46] To embellish his glade, Latta brought in two designers with impressive New South and European credentials. Gottfrid L. Norrman, a native of Sweden, ranked as the busiest architect in the booming New South capital of Atlanta. The Four Cs commissioned from him plans for an imposing pavilion at the heart of Latta Park, fitted with "four ten-pin alleys, a billiard room, ladies' reception room, ball room, and music and refreshment stands."[47] To sculpt the ravine's landscape, the promoters hired landscape architect Joseph Forsyth Johnson, a recent immigrant from the British Isles. Johnson had published a book titled *The Natural Principal of Landscape Gardening* before coming to Atlanta, where he created the grounds of the 1887 Piedmont Exposition and laid plans for Inman Park, the city's first trolley suburb.[48] For the Four Cs, Johnson created a lavish celebration of "nature in her grand attire," as Latta ebulliently put it. Johnson's Latta Park covered ninety acres (much more than it does today) around a romantic boating pond that the promoters christened Lake Forsyth in the designer's honor. Advertisements described terraced flower gardens, a lily pad pond, and fountains that would "fling their spray on an atmosphere laden with the fragrance from thousands of rare flowers and costly roses."[49] In the latest "naturalistic" style, Johnson laid out tree-shaded, curving pathways designed for picturesque effect: "At various points, broad drives diverge and wind in different directions affording space and distance for the pleasure buggies of a large city."[50]

Anticipation built toward the auction of suburban house lots that would mark the grand opening of Dilworth and Latta Park. Already in April 1891 newspapers reported that "scores of promenaders could be seen coming in from the park. On the boulevard there were probably a hundred turnouts [carriages] while at lakeside, flower gardens and groves were dotted with pedestrians."[51] On May 18 the trolley system got its first tryout. Accompanied by a "great and jolly crowd," the first pair of cars glided down "South Tryon Street, the speed increasing as it was found that the track was in good order," wrote a local reporter. "The crowds all along the line yelled and cheered."[52] Two days later, when the entire system started operation, the *Morning Star* of Wilmington, North Carolina, reported, "The streets and yards fairly swarmed with people, each hurrahing and waving as the car passed along. Bouquets were sent to adorn the cars with, and everyone was wild with joy."[53] The Four Cs skillfully whipped the enthusiasm to fever pitch. Latta paid reporters from the Atlanta *Constitution*, the Charleston *News & Courier*, the Raleigh *News & Observer*, and other regional papers to visit and write glowing columns. Adver-

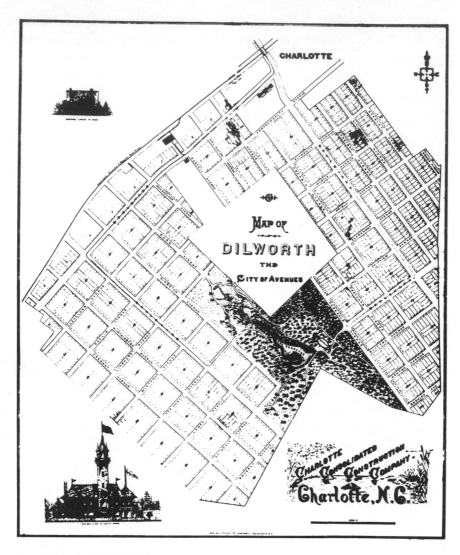

FIG. 15. ORIGINAL PROPOSAL FOR DILWORTH, 1891

The Four Cs' design for Dilworth mixed new and traditional elements. Latta Park (with a lake and naturalistic curving drives designed by Atlanta landscape architect Joseph Forsyth Johnson) formed the centerpiece—the first time Charlotte had seen land set aside purely for recreation. Three extra-wide streets made up The Boulevard (Morehead Street, South Boulevard, and East Boulevard today), a handsome promenade for carriages. Dilworth's basic street pattern, however, remained old-fashioned. Streets were still straight and blocks still rectangular, and at the east the subdivision's avenues simply extended existing city streets. (Courtesy of the Robinson-Spangler Carolina Room, Public Library of Charlotte and Mecklenburg County) tisements for the house lot sale went forth to every outlet, promising a band contest; an "inter-state baseball tournament" featuring teams from Charlotte, Columbia, and Winston; a performance of a comic opera by the celebrated Marie Greenwood traveling troupe; and "A Grand Display of Fireworks."[54]

On May 20, 1891, a throng whose size surely gladdened Latta's heart turned out for the lot auction. Since Revolutionary times local citizens had set aside May 20, the anniversary of the Mecklenburg Declaration of Independence, as a time for community celebrations. "Heretofore they have been held in honor of sentiment only," applauded the *Charlotte Chronicle*. "Today we celebrate a new era—a new business era for Charlotte."[55] Reporters counted 2,000 people in attendance as a team of professional real estate auctioneers from Tennessee worked their way up and down Dilworth's rough-graded dirt streets: "Along in front of them ran boys with red flags to mark the boundaries of the lots. Behind and all about were people in hacks and buggies, on horseback and on foot, with maps in hand eagerly bidding for the ground. There was no drag. The auctioneer's hack would stop in front of a lot. Its dimensions and location would be called out from the map. 'How much for it a front foot,' the auctioneer would call out. 'Five,' 'six,' 'seven,' 'seven-fifty,' 'eight,' 'ten,' 'thirteen,' would come in quick response. 'Sold!' "[56] Dilworth, announced a visiting reporter, "bids fair to become the resident portion of the city for Charlotte's Upper Four Hundred."[57]

After all the fireworks and festivities had ended, the auctioneers had departed, and the dust had settled, however, it turned out that the excitement was more the product of clever public relations than any indication of a genuine hunger for suburban real estate. Reporters at the auction estimated that bidders snapped up 165 of Dilworth's 1,630 lots for an impressive-sounding total of $125,000.[58] But many buyers never made payments on their bids, and barely half that number of sales were actually consummated. According to historian Dan Morrill, county deed records showed that the Four Cs transferred just seventy-eight Dilworth lots to forty-seven individual buyers in 1891.[59] Only three dozen more parcels changed hands during the next three years. Despite the national fashion, and despite Latta's best efforts to whip up a buying frenzy, white-collar Charlotteans clearly remained reluctant to embrace the concept of suburban living.

That reluctance, ironically, could be detected deeply and subtly embedded in the very design of the district itself. The layout of Dilworth betrayed an unmistakable ambivalence about the notion of suburbia as defined in more industrialized cities. In the North, suburban promoters were beginning to experiment with naturalistic street systems—curving networks of avenues that visually set a suburb apart from the adjacent city.[60] Latta Park's landscape architect Joseph Forsyth Johnson himself had devised at least one such design already in his career: the 1887 Inman Park neighborhood of Atlanta. But the Four Cs did not ask Johnson for street planning advice. Instead they laid out a variation on the old grid of straight streets and square blocks that Charlotte had known since colonial days. In the half of Dilworth closest to town (the present-day East Morehead Street area) Latta ran his streets in such a way as to extend Charlotte's existing grid, much as had been done for well over a century. The Dilworth grid used somewhat smaller blocks, but several of its avenues hooked up neatly with streets already laid out in Second Ward. In the outer half of his district, Latta tinkered with tradition a bit more but still kept the grid idea. The tract of farmland he bought happened to have an angled boundary on this side, so Latta bent his grid slightly in order to fit in the maximum number of house lots. The decision held considerable long-term import for Charlotte's urban design; for the first time in the town's history, an individual developer's convenience took precedent over unified city planning. Compared with streetcar suburbs elsewhere, however, the action seemed notable for its timidity.

Dilworth's layout of major boulevards likewise showed an unwillingness to break radically with local planning customs. In Charlotte the grand streets had been broad Trade and Tryon, busy thoroughfares at the heart of the grid. In Dilworth, big houses would also stand on special broad avenues for all to see. The Four Cs arranged Dilworth's four widest streets to form a large rectangle, making a complete circuit of the neighborhood just inside its boundaries. Grandly named The Boulevard, it would be the perfect place for residents and visitors to promenade in their carriages (today three sides of the boulevard rectangle survive as East Boulevard, South Boulevard, and Morehead Street).[61] Latta wrote a clause into his house lot deeds setting a minimum cost for houses built along The Boulevard, to ensure creation of a suitably grand streetscape.[62] Off the avenue he set no such requirements, however. Just as in Charlotte's old center city, any land use would be welcome on Dilworth side streets. That all-embracing attitude toward land use represented the most startling difference between Dilworth and Northern streetcar suburbs.

Not only could big houses and small cottages mingle in Dilworth, but both black and white families were also welcome there. Latta made no effort to create a barrier between his project and the adjoining predominantly black

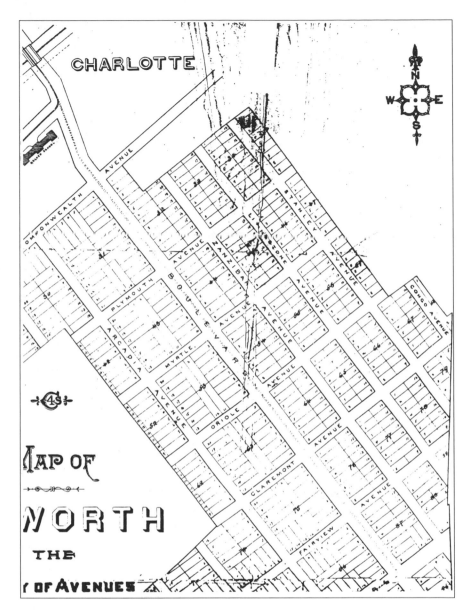

FIG. 16. DILWORTH'S PROPOSED "AFRICAN" STREETS, 1891

The original 1891 Dilworth design seemed to welcome, rather than exclude, black residents. Avenues planned east of present-day Morehead Street ("Boulevard" on this map) were designed to extend existing city streets in predominantly black Second Ward. The street names—Congo, Stanley, Livingstone, and Zanzibar—reflected that African Americans were the intended residents. The "African" streets were never built, and in 1911 the area was redesigned to cut Dilworth off from Second Ward. (Source: Dilworth promotional map, ca. 1891, Robinson-Spangler Carolina Room, Public Library of Charlotte and Mecklenburg County)

Second Ward. In fact, he thoughtfully platted small lots adjacent to Second Ward and gave the streets there African-themed names—Zanzibar, Stanley, Livingstone, and Congo—in an effort to encourage African American buyers. Like several other portions of the original plan, the "African" avenues were not developed as proposed, but Dilworth did nonetheless gain at least one cluster of black residents in its early years. Black families occupied houses in an alley off Euclid Avenue between Worthington and Tremont Streets, and the Four Cs sold land for an AME Zion church, which by 1905 stood proudly on Worthington Avenue.[63]

Even industry was welcome in Dilworth. The most basic characteristic defining the Northern streetcar neighborhood was the desire to prohibit factories and set residents well apart from the busy world of workers and smokestacks. Edward Dilworth Latta, however, included an industrial district as a major feature of his plan for Dilworth. The railroad mainline to South Carolina ran along one side of the neighborhood, and Latta made no effort to put distance between the railway and his proposed avenue of grand homes. He laid out part of The Boulevard (the portion known today as South Boulevard) close along the tracks. Directly behind The Boulevard's large house lots he set aside a strip of land for factory development. Latta erected the first structure in Dilworth there, the big brick powerhouse and car barns for the Four Cs trolley system.[64] Much as with the Oates cotton mill ten years earlier, Charlotteans evidently still felt no pressing urge to adopt the Northern fashion of separating industry from fine residential areas.

Streetcars, in short, did not automatically produce a streetcar suburb. Dilworth might possess some suburban attributes—set off from the city, served by trolleys, designed with a romantic, naturalistic park. Yet its promoters clearly thought of it more as an extension of existing urban practices than as a new type of neighborhood. The City of the Avenues was not intended as an exclusive residential district for Charlotte's Upper Four Hundred but, rather, as one Four Cs ad put it, as a sort of "neighboring town with all the modern city comforts."[65]

Indeed, as house lot sales languished in the early 1890s, the Charlotte Construction Company forged ahead boldly with development of the less-suburban components of its plan. In July 1892 the company sold land along the railroad to D. A. Tompkins, who immediately launched construction of a cotton mill intended as a showplace for his notions of textile engineering.[66] Tompkins's Atherton Mill complex soon included not only factory buildings but a store, a school and meeting hall, and an extensive mill village (remnants

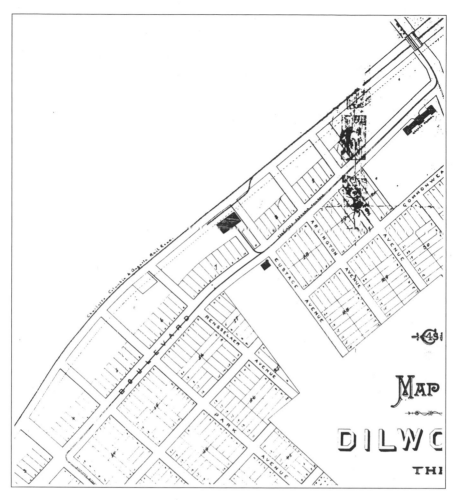

FIG. 17. DILWORTH'S RAILROAD CORRIDOR, 1891
Dilworth's design did not separate industrial and prime residential areas. The broad Boulevard was drawn running close along the railroad track that bordered the subdivision. Latta set aside a strip of land between the house lots and the railroad for factory development. The map shows the powerhouse and car barn for his trolley line as the first industrial building there. (Source: Dilworth promotional map, ca. 1891, Robinson-Spangler Carolina Room, Public Library of Charlotte and Mecklenburg County)

survive along Dilworth's Tremont and Euclid Streets today). The compact cottages, as small as two rooms, would become prototypes for plans published in Tompkins's book *Cotton Mill: Commercial Features* (1899). Meanwhile Edward Dilworth Latta himself broke ground near the trolley barn in 1893 for the new factory of his own Charlotte Trouser Company, which soon turned out 150,000 pants per year.[67] By the end of 1895 six additional factories lined

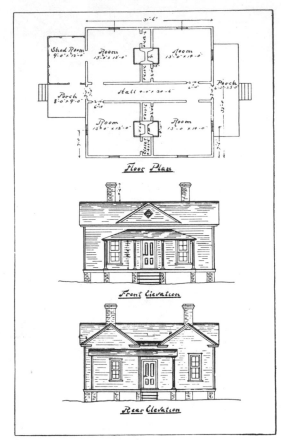

Fig. 36.   Four-Room Gable House.   Cost $400

**FIG. 18. FOUR-ROOM MILL
COTTAGE**
Houses erected in the early
1890s for D. A. Tompkins's
Atherton Mill at the edge of
Dilworth provided some of the
models for designs published
in his influential book on tex-
tile mill development. One
Atherton cottage, at 2005
Cleveland Avenue, has been
designated a Charlotte land-
mark by the Charlotte
Mecklenburg Historic Land-
marks Commission. (Source:
Tompkins, *Cotton Mill*)

the railroad, among them a spoke-and-handle manufacturer, a textile machinery firm, the Park Elevator Company, and the Mecklenburg Flouring
Mill, whose flour brands included the delightfully named Princess Charlotte,
Royal Family, and Dilworth.[68] In October 1895 the *Charlotte Observer* grandly
tagged the corridor "the Manchester of Charlotte," a reference to the celebrated industrial center of Great Britain.[69]

The Four Cs also reached out to homebuyers who did not fit the elite
profile of Charlotte's Upper Four Hundred. In March 1893 Latta announced a
tempting innovation: he would erect thirty-five houses in Dilworth to be
"purchased or rented on the building and loan plan."[70] This new financing
scheme, somewhat similar to today's long-term mortgage, constituted a considerable novelty. Homebuyers of the 1890s customarily had to put down
an initial cash payment of half the purchase price, then completely pay off

the balance in just two or three years. Instead, Latta offered to take modest monthly installments over a longer period. "He was the originator," the *Charlotte Observer* wrote later, "of the plan on an extensive scale of enabling families to own their own homes out there, accepting small payments initially for purchase of either homes he built or vacant lots in his extensive domain."[71] From 1893 on, Dilworth newspaper advertisements, trolley cars, and even the neighborhood water tower relentlessly repeated the slogan Buy a House with Your Rent Money.

Latta's assorted initiatives kept Dilworth afloat through the nationwide depression that rocked the United States in late 1893 and 1894, and gradually the neighborhood caught on with white-collar Charlotteans. In the mid-1890s two-story wood-frame houses started to dot the avenues. The first streets to attract such residents seem to have been The Boulevard, Kingston Avenue, and Park Avenue, which served as the major entrance to Latta Park. Among the earliest Dilworth houses extant today are two on Kingston Avenue. The 1895 residence of building contractor Julius Mallonee, designed by a young Charlotte architect named C. C. Hook, features an exuberant jumble of porches and sunburst gables in the Queen Anne variant of the Victorian style.[72] The 1894–95 house of Joseph Harrill, a downtown store clerk, represents a simpler version of Victorian fashion, with several wings and a broad front porch.[73] Despite his handsome new house, interestingly, Harrill soon tired of the daily commute. After two years riding the trolley out to Dilworth, he decided to move back downtown.

Harrill's ambivalence neatly symbolized the mixed feelings that Charlotteans seemed to hold toward modern fashions in urban design. On one hand, the booming economy was spawning factories of unheard-of size. Hundreds of strangers swelled the city's population to more than 18,000 people by the early 1890s. For the first time separate blue-collar residential districts were appearing in Charlotte, look-alike rows of mill cottages that stood in the shadows of the Alpha, Ada, Victor, and Atherton mills. It might seem obvious that sorting-out of residential districts represented the inevitable wave of the future here just as it had earlier in the Northern United States. Surely the New South must embrace modernity, grasp firmly the symbols of advancement, and don the habiliments of progress.

Yet at the same time Charlotteans endeavored to hold to tradition. After all, Charlotte had none of the terrible crowding, the rickety tenements, the teem-

FIG. 19. MALLONNE-JONES (TOP) AND HARRILL-PORTER HOUSES
Two of Dilworth's oldest surviving dwellings, both dating from about 1895, feature the
complicated massing favored by Victorian designers. (Photograph by author, March 1993)

ing immigrants, the angry strikes, and the political upheavals that had accompanied the industrial revolution in the North. Why give up convenient and familiar urban habits in order to commute to some white-collar suburb set apart from the city? The New South factories as yet had barely had time to affect the patterns of personal relationship that had always kept Southern business owners and workmen in close contact. Charlotte's elite anticipated little change. They talked proudly of their "all-native" workforce and boasted that such workers would never fail to show deference to employers. The *Charlotte Chronicle* caught the easy spirit of confidence perfectly in a column at the end of the 1880s: "Inequalities run all through the social fabric, irrespective of race or previous condition. Wealth and fashion, etiquette and position, erect barriers to outside intrusion and prescribe rules of intercourse." Such inequalities, such barriers and rules, embodied God's wisdom. "There always have been and always will be social distinctions," the paper assured. "All will be ordered as Providence deems best and wisest."[74]

That confident assurance would not withstand the events of the 1890s.

CHAPTER 3

INSOLENCE

You wanted to take the government out of the hands of the men who own the property and put it in the hands of those who are ignorant and own no property.—Charlotte mayor J. H. Weddington, 1897

SORTING-OUT of land uses likely would have continued gradually and haltingly in Charlotte, pushed forward by the growing size of economic enterprises but pulled back by faith in tradition, if not for a series of political upheavals that rocked the region during the 1890s. Under the banner of the new Populist Party, voters at the base of the social pyramid—small farmers, the new factory workers, African Americans—suddenly found their voice all across the South.[1] In North Carolina the Populists and their allies in the Republican Party won control of the governorship and legislature, voting out men of the elite who had long governed the state. To wealthy Southerners the Populist-Republican challenge was all the more disturbing because it came not from outside the region, as Reconstruction had, but from within. Old-line Democrats lashed back with disfranchisement—laws that barred most blacks and many poor whites from voting. While disfranchisement solved the political problem, it could not wash away the stinging reality of the challenge itself. Over the course of the decade of bitter struggle, North Carolina's elite came to see their society as sharply at odds along class lines. It became painfully clear that "lower caste" whites and blacks no longer felt deference toward "the better classes." "Prescribed rules of intercourse" and respect for "wealth and position" had only recently seemed "ordered by Providence."[2] By 1900 that traditional bedrock would lie shattered.

RURAL ROOTS OF THE POPULIST CHALLENGE

To understand the political battles of the 1890s, it helps to look back at the experiences of the three groups who joined forces behind the Populist banner. Each had their own concerns. Small farmers felt themselves losing power to the upstart railroad towns. Factory workers sought to shape the new economic system in which they labored. African Americans, who had gained freedom and the vote but not much else during Reconstruction, looked for a way to finally attain the respect and influence due them as free citizens. For all three groups, discontent with current economic leadership provided a common denominator. Individually each was a political outsider. If they could find a way to come together, they would constitute a large majority of voters in the South.

Among farmers discontent had been building for decades. Since the 1850s railroad towns such as Charlotte had taken on more and more economic power in the South. Every fall, when farmers drove their wagons to town piled high with cotton and produce, the fate of their yearlong labor lay in the hands of city merchants. As long as prices remained high, this seemed eminently reasonable. But by the 1870s the post–Civil War cotton boom had passed, and the American economy slid into a depression. Farmers found themselves scrambling to make ends meet. Many turned to new commercial fertilizers— such as the Carolina Fertilizer advertised by Charlotte merchant Robert M. Oates at $50 per ton, cash, or $55 per ton plus 7 percent interest, on credit—in order to boost yields.[3] But with cotton prices now falling, such spending could trap the unlucky, as men such as Mecklenburg's Green L. P. Fite discovered. In 1870 Fite owned a small farm on which he raised 200 bushels of corn and two bales of cotton.[4] In 1871 he went in debt $70 to Charlotte storekeepers Carson & Grier. By 1872 his debt had increased to $100, and Carson & Grier took a lien on his crop. The lien—a powerful legal tool introduced into North Carolina law in 1867—gave the merchants first right to any cash resulting from crop sale. During the next five years Fite never made enough to pay off his debt and continued to get advances each spring from Carson & Grier. In 1877 Fite gambled on a strategy that might help him produce enough to retire the loans. He mortgaged almost all of his land for the purchase of two mules. The gamble failed, and in 1878 he lost his farm. Green Fite either left the county to try farming elsewhere, became a tenant farmer on someone else's land, or took off for town to take up "public work" in a mill or manufactory. He never reappeared in Mecklenburg deed books.

New fence laws also hurt small farmers. Traditionally, as far back as pre-colonial times in England, citizens had retained the right to graze their live-stock on all undeveloped lands. Farmers built fences only around their crops; all unfenced areas remained free range for anyone's animals. This particularly helped less-wealthy families, since they could raise animals without owning vast acreages of grazing land. In the 1870s the age-old pattern abruptly reversed in the South.[5] Responding to the markets opened by the railroads, wealthy farmers planted ever-larger fields of cash crops, and they tired of spending money to fence all those acres. In 1873 leaders in the Providence, Pineville, and Steele Creek Townships near Charlotte passed a law requiring that live-stock owners fence in their own animals.[6] It was the first such law in North Carolina, the start of a trend that would sweep the entire piedmont by the late 1880s. Proponents argued that the regulations would not only protect field crops but also improve the quality of livestock, since owners would have greater control over their animals' feeding and breeding. For families who only possessed a few acres of land, not enough to satisfy a hungry herd, the fence laws represented a serious blow, however. The new system ended free-range animal raising and cut deeply into the ability of small farmers to scrape by.

The fertilizers, fence laws, and falling cotton prices transformed Charlotte's agricultural hinterland and stirred anger among rural families. Analyzing Mecklenburg census data, historian Carolyn Hoffman has shown that during the 1870s, "Large farms were getting larger and small farms smaller. The small to medium-sized farmer was literally losing his land and status. . . . By 1880, almost 43 percent of the county's farmers were tenant farmers, . . . an increase from 15 percent in 1860 and 16.8 percent in 1870."[7]

Adding insult to injury, as county families sank into poverty, the city of Charlotte grew and prospered. The proud new business blocks and the stylish houses that spilled down Trade and Tryon Streets did nothing to soothe farmers on their yearly visits. By the 1880s, Hoffman calculates, the Charlotte elite controlled 80 percent of the total real property owned by the county's wealthy families.[8] They controlled politics as well, increasingly sending city dwellers to represent Mecklenburg in the state legislature.

Signs of rural unrest multiplied during the 1870s and 1880s. White and black farmers angry at the fence law ripped down two miles of fencing in Clear Creek Township in 1875.[9] In 1879 when fertilizer companies announced a 25 percent price hike, Mecklenburg farmers called a mass meeting to threaten a boycott of town merchants, winning a partial rollback.[10] Conflicts surfaced most often at the cotton wharf. The city-appointed cotton weigher who oversaw Wharf operations became a lightning rod for disputes between farmers and merchants, resulting in an 1885 law that mandated that the county commission and the town aldermen select this key official jointly.[11] Farmers also sought ways to band together to gain economic leverage. A short-lived Farmers Mutual Aid Society formed in Mecklenburg in 1871.[12] In 1873 a local chapter of the nationwide agricultural organization known as the Grange started, and a year later eighteen branches dotted the county.[13] Grangers attempted to set up a direct trade union that would buy supplies and sell members' cotton, bypassing town merchants, but the plan proved overambitious and soon failed.

Agricultural agitation reached a new level in the late 1880s with the arrival of the national Farmer's Alliance. Led by North Carolinian Leonidas L. Polk, publisher of the *Progressive Farmer* newspaper, the Alliance took impressive initiatives to improve rural economics nationwide.[14] To stop railroads from gouging farmers, the Alliance successfully petitioned the U.S. Congress to create the Interstate Commerce Commission in 1887, America's first government regulatory agency. To cope with persistent deflation that crippled cotton prices, the Alliance proposed that the United States stop pegging money supplies to the "gold standard" and instead print enough "greenbacks" to stabilize prices (a strategy adopted only much later by Washington). In North Carolina the Alliance campaigned to cut railroad rates, and it worked successfully for creation of a state agricultural college to train better farmers, today North Carolina State University. Such action generated great excitement in rural Mecklenburg. In 1887 an Alliance chapter started under the leadership of a landowner previously active in the Grange, and less than a year later the organization boasted 2,000 members in the county.[15] When Leonidas Polk visited Mecklenburg in 1891, Alliance supporters filled the Latta Park auditorium to overflowing, hanging on his every word.[16]

BLUE-COLLAR ROOTS OF THE POPULIST CHALLENGE

Discontent bubbled as well among workers within Charlotte. As the scale of local enterprises grew during the years after the Civil War, traditional master-apprentice relations eroded. In 1871 and again in 1873 and 1877 Charlotte workingmen attempted to organize a mechanics union.[17] The term "mechanic" in this era applied to any skilled man who worked with his hands, including carpenters, cobblers, and harness makers. The Mechanics Union aimed to guard the rights of journeymen whose jobs were threatened when masters enlarged shops and experimented with production methods that used unskilled labor. Resentment occasionally boiled into walkouts. In 1874, for instance, skilled craftworkers deserted the city's two largest leatherworking manufactories in protest against plans to hire more unskilled workers.[18] A Charlotte carriage-maker summed up the discontent when he railed against the "great many men who are trying to run a business [who] have never served as apprentices. They employ men who have not served, at a small price, thus bringing the price of a mechanic on a level with an ignorant, incompetent man who ought to be shoveling dirt."[19]

In the mid-1880s a national workers' organization known as the Knights of Labor picked up adherents in Charlotte. "We learn that a lodge of the Knights of Labor was organized in this city on Monday night last," reported the *Charlotte Home Democrat* in April 1886. "As we said about the humbugging Grange when it was started in this section . . . *secret class combinations are dangerous.*"[20] The Knights especially worried Charlotte's economic elite because of the organization's success unionizing textile workers across the state. A member of the Knights from Raleigh won election to Congress, and Knights talked of striking against the cotton mills in eastern North Carolina to demand that the workday be shortened to eleven hours.

In truth, textile workers needed some way to improve their situation.[21] In addition to laboring long hours—eleven or twelve hours daily Monday through Friday, plus a half-day on Saturday—millhands faced working conditions that were often wretched. Managers kept the mills hot and damp in order to make the cotton easier to spin, and lint constantly choked the air. No laws regulated child labor. Carolina farm families had traditionally given children chores to do, and when the families moved to the mill villages, it seemed natural that eight- or ten-year-olds help their parents in the factory. Mill owners liked the arrangement, since small fingers could do useful tasks amongst the swift-moving machinery, but children in the mill missed the seasonal rhythm of the farm with its times for school and play. Parents earned so little that children virtually had to work. In 1890 skilled men in Charlotte's four cotton mills made $1.00 to $1.40 per day.[22] Unskilled men earned 65¢ to 75¢. Women and children got even less, typically 40¢ to 65¢. Until 1897 wages in Charlotte included free use of a mill cottage, but only as long as family members were employed, a situation that depended greatly on luck.[23] Mills ran according to demand for products. If the market happened to be strong for yarn but weak for woven cloth, for instance, the spinners would keep working while the weavers lost their jobs. When the world market had too much of a particular kind of fabric, mill owners simply shut off their machines until profits improved, and they turned employees out on the street with no guarantee of rehiring. "Last week night work shut down at the [Ada] mill on account of a dullness in the market," went a typically brief newspaper note. "It throws about 15 families out of work. They are now moving off."[24]

Established Charlotteans thought they saw more and more idle strangers hanging about. The continual hirings and layoffs at the mills and manufactories put a growing portion of the city's people constantly in motion, drawn from countryside to city in hope of work, moving from mill to mill and town to town in search of a better situation. Throughout the 1880s and 1890s increasingly indignant columnists decried "the unusually large number of beggars and tramps now infesting this place," the idlers "guilty of impudent, rude and vulgar conduct," and the new "class of loafers who are not at all desirable citizens."[25] In response, elite Charlotteans launched new initiatives designed to take this motley horde in hand and instill the manners, morals, and love of hard work that the "lazy, vagrant" masses seemed to sorely lack. In areas such as the control of alcohol, public education, and the provision of poor relief and other municipal services, Charlotte's "best men and women" now took up reform movements long under way in the industrialized North.

Prohibition of alcohol emerged as one of the hottest issues of Charlotte politics.[26] In the craft shop society of Benjamin Franklin's day, masters and workers had often imbibed together in the neighborhood pub. With the rise of manufactories, that sort of socialization declined. The owner was not only less able to share and supervise his workers' drinking, but the expanding investment in plant and the growing concern for productivity made inebriation less acceptable. Workmen, conversely, manfully resisted every attempt to restrict alcohol, regarding drink as a time-honored right that must not slip away in an age when so much else was changing. During the 1830s and 1840s a struggle over temperance had swept the manufacturing cities of the North. In Charlotte its time arrived in the 1880s. "Charlotte has twenty-two licensed bar rooms and twelve churches," chided the *Southern Home* newspaper as it kicked off the antisaloon campaign.[27] Alcohol stood in the way of economic progress, prohibitionists asserted. By the "dead-weight of grog-shops . . . we have been kept back," lectured a longtime resident, "our energies crippled and our advancement retarded, until Charlotte looks more like a little shriveled dwarf than a giant, as with her unsurpassed facilities and surrounding she ought to be today."[28]

Both "drys" and "wets" put the issue in a class context in their speeches. Dry proponents represented the "wealth and intelligence of Charlotte," said banker R. Y. McAden.[29] Meanwhile Manual Lord, a gardener addressing a wet rally, took pains to "impress upon his auditors the intention of the wealthy class to abolish the rule of whiskey as a first step toward encroaching upon their liberties."[30] The leader of the antiprohibition People's Ticket pointed out that closing saloons would have little effect on well-to-do drinkers who could buy liquor outside the county; the proposed law would be "the rich man's license and the poor man's prohibition."[31] Census analysis confirms that wet support came disproportionately from blue-collar men, according to a careful study by historian Janette Greenwood: "While unskilled laborers accounted for only four percent of all prohibitionists, they made up nearly a third of the antiprohibitionist ranks."[32] The drys narrowly lost at the Charlotte ballot box in 1881, tried again in 1886, and again in 1888. Each election was close. But each time a blue-collar majority succeeded in squelching prohibition.

While Charlotte's "better classes" had no luck shuttering the saloons, they did make considerable headway in education initiatives, most notably the public graded school. Education historians point out strong links between economic modernization and the rise of public education in the Northeast beginning in the 1820s and 1830s.[33] Historically, schooling had been reserved for the sons of wealthy families who could afford private academies; most children learned what they needed through apprenticeship rather than the schoolroom. Industrialization ended the apprenticeship system for blue-collar youngsters and at the same time created a growing white-collar class who felt their children merited prestigious schoolroom training. To fill these twin demands, New England reformers developed America's first extensive system of publicly funded schooling. Its hallmark was the graded school, which divided the educational experience into carefully ordered grade levels, an arrangement that had much in common with the orderly environment of the new business world. Though well known, this approach failed to catch on in the South until well after the Civil War.[34] Charlotte showed some interest in public education during Reconstruction, but by the 1870s numerous newspaper advertisements for private academies made it clear that school remained the privilege of those who could afford it. In the New South era, as manufactories expanded and cotton mills began to hum, conditions finally became right for the Northern innovation to take root. In 1882 Charlotteans moved to make public education available to city children, opening the taxpayer-funded Charlotte Graded School.[35]

For blue-collar youngsters, fresh private initiatives buttressed public education. Reformers gradually realized that many children never came to the school in town because they worked long hours in the textile mills at the edge of the city. In the 1890s, with the number of mills growing and groups such as the Knights of Labor seeking members, the need to educate such youth seemed especially urgent. "As the throngs of children go to the factories and there begin a new life, a life that has many evil temptations in the way, this work should be carried with vigor and earnestness into every quarter of the town," counseled the *Charlotte Democrat*.[36] Local churches began sponsoring Sunday Schools out in the mill districts around Charlotte. The Sunday School in nineteenth century America was much different from the familiar institution of today, which provides child care and Bible study while adults attend services. Classes, often held in the factory itself or nearby, offered the basics of modern education to working people who could only attend school on their single nonworking day.[37] Charlotte's Sunday School sessions, conducted personally by "the best men and women of the large churches," taught reading, writing, and arithmetic and—as importantly—attempted to instill the values of hard work, thrift, and obedience that factory owners thought their employees lacked. "In every direction Sunday schools have been started in the suburbs, amid the newer population settled around the factories," wrote the wife of the town's leading cotton man in 1896. "The Christian rejoices, the political economist is glad. They both trust that the discordant elements in nature and society may yet realize the harmony which the prophet predicts when a 'little child shall lead them.' "[38]

Stresses and strains brought on by "discordant elements" led to reforms in other aspects of Charlotte life as well, including poor relief and even fire protection. Well into the 1890s care for the poor remained largely informal, provided by neighbors and churches. The only public provider of assistance was the mayor, who each winter personally handed out firewood to the needy from a pile contributed by community members. With the increasing number of newcomers hired and laid off by Charlotte mills and manufactories, poor relief became too big a job for informal networks, and in 1896 citizens chartered a humane society to organize community aid.[39] The problem of "discordant elements" was also, in a very different way, behind the shift from volunteer firefighters to a paid municipal fire department in 1887. "The greatest trouble and danger of volunteer departments is that membership in them is usually avoided by those who own big shares of property and the control is left in the hands of young men who pay but little tax," explained the *Charlotte Chronicle*. "In these circumstances conflicts between city government representing property and the departments forming the protection of property are inevitable."[40]

All these changes indicated clearly that the traditional bonds uniting men of property with less wealthy members of the community were fraying in Charlotte. The old craft shop system that had once offered young men a ladder to climb from apprentice to journeyman to master no longer operated. The close-knit relationships of the small workplace were giving way to less personal interactions between the factory owner and his numerous and interchangeable employees. Workers—whether seasoned craftsmen or new millhands—felt frustrated by the seemingly arbitrary and thoughtless actions of employers who had little firsthand experience on the shop floor. Business owners felt equally frustrated. Where once their hard-won prosperity would have guaranteed them the deference of the community, now they found themselves jostled by strangers who seemed to lack respect for property, morality, and hard work. "What Charlotte needs," admonished the *Chronicle* in 1891, "is willing, persevering workers to draw her along in the onward march of progress. . . . All should work in unison and in concert; . . . grumble less and work more."[41] That grumbling would soon give way to a full-fledged challenge at the ballot box, a challenge that would call into question the very notion that government should "represent property."

AFRICAN AMERICANS AND THE POPULIST CHALLENGE

African Americans comprised the third group active in the Populist uprising of the 1890s, constituting a key component of the Republican Party that would fuse with the Populists to win control of North Carolina government. That black people could be an important factor at the polls so long after Reconstruction comes as something of a surprise to us today. The popular image of the South is of a land where African Americans lost all political voice after the brief period of Northern occupation during the late 1860s and early 1870s. In reality, historians have shown, black voters and black politicians remained an energetic political force for twenty years following Reconstruction's end.[42] They joined whites in the Republican Party—the party of the Great Emancipator, Abraham Lincoln—to form an active opposition to the old-line elite Democratic Party. In Charlotte, black Republican candidates usually won one or two of the three aldermanic seats from predominantly black Second Ward and sometimes one seat from Third Ward. From 1868 through 1894 at least one and sometimes as many as three black men always sat on Charlotte's twelve-person Board of Aldermen.[43]

For African Americas just set free from the shackles of slavery, such opportunities helped make the 1870s, 1880s, and early 1890s a time of tremendous hope. To be sure, in Charlotte as elsewhere across America, skin color constituted a powerful dividing force in society. But for a generation following the Civil War it was not at all clear that skin color would be the most important dividing force. Money, education, and heredity defined the "better classes" at least as sharply as race. When the *Charlotte Chronicle* mused about the "inequalities [that] run all through the social fabric," it pointed out that wealth and position erected barriers "more despotic, if anything, than those based on the prejudices of color."[44] If race was merely one barrier among many, African American strivers might yet break into the hierarchical social order. Charlotte's established families had always welcomed outsiders who showed economic drive and an enthusiasm for elite values. "Where worth was found," J. B. Alexander claimed, "it was always recognized."[45] Cotton mill founder Robert M. Oates provided an inspiring model, having worked hard as a clerk, allied himself with an established family, and built up his capital to climb the pyramid into Charlotte's leadership as a merchant and cotton mill owner. Edward Dilworth Latta had followed a similar route upon his arrival in the 1870s, as had D. A. Tompkins starting in the 1880s. Even members of the "Hebrew Race"—Western civilization's perennial outsiders—successfully won admittance to the ranks of Charlotte leaders, notably Samuel Wittkowsky and Jacob Rintels. It did not seem far-fetched to hard-working, forward-looking blacks that "the better classes" among the African American race, too, might duplicate that achievement.

During the prohibition fights of the 1880s, a black elite of ministers, shop owners, and skilled workers joined the white "better sort" in campaigning vigorously for temperance. In 1881 a racially integrated prohibition association under the direction of both black and white officers put forth an integrated slate of dry candidates. "Black prohibitionists shared the speakers rostrum with their white counterparts" at political rallies, writes Janette Greenwood.[46] They argued that temperance represented the route to economic uplift and, ultimately, to respect. African Americans "must prove they know how to be masters of themselves" and put aside the liquor that "brought so many of them to disgrace, kept them poor and in rags," urged a black college student from Biddle Institute.[47] "During strong political struggles," an African American schoolteacher asked pointedly, "from what walls and fronts do you most frequently or altogether hear the infamous blasphemous epithet 'd——d nigger'? Does it come from the Mecklenburg Foundry, Observer office, First National Bank, Second Presbyterian Church, or does it come from those temples of prosperity and virtue, the Retail Saloons?"[48] Prohibition sentiment ran so strong among white-collar blacks that in 1887 the city's leading black church split in two. Staunch prohibitionists, led by a prosperous building contractor, left Clinton Chapel AME Zion to found their own Grace AME Zion Church.[49] The repeated defeat of prohibition at the ballot box, however, ultimately took its toll on the black-white political alliance. The white elite wanted black prohibitionists to deliver working-class votes, but black workers turned out to be no more willing to give up drink than white workers were. Black saloonkeeper J. T. Schenck consistently won election from Second Ward no matter what black prohibitionist ran against him.[50] "The darkey, who in prohibition elections in Charlotte seems to hold the balance of power, felt his importance and was sought after by both pros and antis," sulked the *Charlotte Chronicle* following the third defeat of temperance in 1888.[51] From such grumblings, Greenwood suggests, it was but a short step for adamant white prohibitionists to ask themselves whether virtue might triumph if black voters could be removed from the equation.

Blacks became a convenient group to blame for other tensions arising in Charlotte society with the growth of mills and manufactories. African Americans comprised much of the unskilled cheap labor pool in the South, and white craftsmen who lost out to new manufacturing methods often perceived their misfortunes in racial terms. The 1874 walkouts of Charlotte leatherworkers, for instance, included complaints against the hiring of African Americans.[52] When the textile mills opened, proprietors sought to soothe labor unrest by hiring only whites for jobs inside the factories, relegating blacks to unloading cotton bales or sweeping up. A palpable rise in the number of African Americans in Charlotte exacerbated white worries. Black population growth consistently outpaced that of whites through 1880, until blacks made up more than 40 percent of the citizenry.[53] The influx sparked many of the same resentments expressed toward the wave of white millhands. Even to walk along a sidewalk when "the darkey" was "in town on Saturday night with money in his pocket," the *Charlotte Observer* complained, "a person must not take offense at a jolt, a crunch on the foot, a dig in the ribs."[54] "There are complaints from all parts of the city," wrote the *Home Democrat* ominously, "about bad conduct of idle, lazy, vagrant negroes and whites, who prowl about day and night committing depredations or guilty of impudent, rude and vulgar conduct."[55]

In contrast, Charlotte's white newspapers made scant mention of the city's impressive black achievers. Biddle Institute, the Presbyterian academy founded for freedmen after the Civil War, had now grown into a full-fledged college with black professors and, in 1891, a black president.[56] The AME Zion Church stationed its regional bishop at Charlotte and located the printing office for the entire nationwide denomination in a black-owned building in Second Ward.[57] African American newspapers, including the church's *Star of Zion* and the secular *Charlotte Messenger*, appeared regularly.[58] Black contractor W. H. Houser owned Charlotte's major brick-making plant and constructed many of the city's big new buildings.[59] Black physician and civic leader J. T. Williams would soon win appointment as consul to Sierra Leone, the top U.S. diplomat to that West African nation.[60] While such men inspired much pride in the hearts of black Charlotteans, to white residents they symbolized disquieting change. For white craftsmen coping with economic displacement or for white mill families laboring long hours in the textile plants, it did not feel good to see ex-slaves in such high places. For elite white leaders of the Democratic Party, the existence of such articulate and accomplished men in the opposing Republican organization was not comforting either.

POPULIST UPHEAVAL, ELITE RESPONSE

In 1891 newspapers across the South and the nation buzzed with news of a new third party in politics.[61] The rural activists of the Farmer's Alliance now moved boldly into the political arena, announcing formation of the People's Party, soon better known as the Populist Party. The Populist platform urged government action on behalf of agriculture, with proposals ranging from regulation of railroads, to monetary reform aimed at stopping deflation, to a system of government-run warehouses and price supports that would help stabilize wildly fluctuating crop prices. Virtually all the Populist ideas would eventually become mainstays of American government policy in some form. But in the 1890s such notions seemed highly novel, a shining hope to small farmers but radical nonsense in the eyes of entrenched economic interests.

In Mecklenburg Democratic leaders initially perceived the Populist Party as a minor concern, another skirmish in the ongoing rivalry between rural and urban interests. Agricultural landowners had bolted the Democratic Party briefly in the heyday of the Grange in 1875 and had threatened to desert again during the cotton weigher controversy of 1885, but always they had returned quickly to the Democratic fold. While such disputes might get spirited, the conflicts fell within the accustomed bounds of political discussion. The job of government, after all, was to represent property; men of property in the city and men of property in the county might naturally hold differing views, and politics offered the acceptable way to reconcile them. In any such discussions the Democratic Party, as majority party and stronghold of the propertied elite since the Civil War, naturally expected to control the debate.

It quickly became obvious, however, that Populism represented a major and fundamental threat to the status quo. The newly formed political organization picked up popular support with astonishing speed. In 1892 Populists won election to a number of county offices across North Carolina and captured several seats in the state legislature. Emboldened, the party began reaching out to voters beyond its agricultural base, making overtures particularly to the workingmen in towns. When the 1894 political season rolled around, the Populist Party announced formation of a powerful political partnership. The Populists would join hands with the established Republican Party to field a Fusion ticket across North Carolina. The move represented a racial risk; along with its many white members, the Republican organization also included the bulk of the state's African American voters. It made strong sense, though, for all political and economic outsiders to unite under a single banner. And when the ballots were counted in 1894, the strategy proved a huge success. The Populist-Republican alliance won almost two-thirds of the seats in the state legislature, ending the long tradition of Democratic control.[62]

The newcomers immediately made their presence felt. Legislators proposed fresh taxes on railroads and businesses and put a 6 percent cap on the interest that merchants and banks could charge for farm loans. They also moved to open politics to ordinary citizens. Instead of appointing local officials—the antebellum custom that had been overturned during Reconstruction had since crept back into practice—Fusionists insisted that leaders be chosen by popular election. To ensure that all could vote, the Fusionists required that party symbols be printed on ballots, a boon to the 36 percent of citizens who could not read. In the words of historians Jeffrey Crow and Robert Durden, such changes added up to a "virtual revolution in North Carolina politics."[63] In the Fusion vision of the New South, government would no longer simply represent property but instead would represent the wishes of the entire electorate.

In Charlotte the dimensions of the incipient revolution became clear as voters prepared to go to the polls in 1896. Fusion speakers and writers publicly questioned the relationship between government and moneyed interests. In a commencement address at Biddle Institute, black Charlotte businessman I. D. L. Torrence decried "the oppression of the poor by the rich" and "the weakness of the government in securing liberty to all its citizens alike."[64] Mecklenburg farmer J. A. Wilson expressed the same theme in a letter published by the North Carolina Bureau of Labor Statistics: "Owing to legislation in favor of monopolies our lands are gradually slipping from the hands of the wealth-producing classes and going into the hands of the few. I do not believe God ever intended that a few should own the earth, but that each should have a home. . . . Three fourths of our population are tenants, and are not able to buy land at present prices; they are the men who create the wealth and pay the taxes."[65] Millhands, too, were deeply disgruntled. A Democratic strategist in Raleigh spoke urgently of the need to "make a hard fight" particularly "among the factory operatives and the laboring classes," and local leaders scrambled to create a Workingmen's Democratic Club to reach out to mill folk.[66] Shortly before election day an observer calculated that while Democrats remained the biggest party in Mecklenburg with some 4,000 adherents, the combined vote of the Republicans (2,500) and Populists (1,500) exactly matched them. "The Democrats," he noted dryly, "will have some hard fighting to retain control of county matters."[67]

When the polls closed in 1896, the Democratic Party found it had lost even more ground. At the state level, Fusionists controlled a whopping 78 percent of the North Carolina legislature and for good measure elected their candidate, Daniel Russell, as governor.[68] In Mecklenburg County, Democrats lost every single countywide contest.[69] Within the city and surrounding Charlotte Township, where rural interests should have had minimal impact, Democrats did manage to eke out victories, but only by the most precarious margins. In fully seven of twelve precincts the vote had gone against Democratic candidates. A large turnout in the remaining five had barely counterbalanced the deficit. Most alarmingly, the seven offending ballot boxes included not just those in precincts with heavy black populations, which might be expected to support Republicans, but also "mill boxes" near Charlotte's textile factories.[70] Working-class Charlotteans as well as farmers and blacks were clearly deserting the Democratic Party and its traditional vision of government.

Among Charlotte's prosperous men of commerce, the 1896 election results first inspired anger. Editorials complained of a "crusade against the merchants" and decried the indignity of submitting to rule "by a portion of the white people of the state, adding their votes to those of the black people, who were always opposed to the government of the Democracy."[71] The choice of words revealed much about the elite's view of politics: traditional party leaders, not the majority of the voters, constituted the democracy. Charlotte's elite expressed fury at the "impudence," the "insolence" of having its prerogative to rule challenged.[72] "Irreverence is one of the tendencies of the age," fumed Mrs. John VanLandingham, wife of Charlotte's leading cotton broker, as she surveyed the political turnabout: "It is liberty run mad."[73] When a local Populist politician tried unsuccessfully to get the state legislature to amend Charlotte's charter to give Fusionists additional power, old-line Democratic mayor and banker J. H. Weddington erupted with an even more revealing blast. "You wanted to take the government out of the hands of the men who own the property," he steamed, "and put it in the hands of those who are ignorant and own no property."[74]

Raw anger gave way to strategies designed to regain control. In March 1897 the state Democratic captain, Samuel Ashe of Raleigh, made a widely publicized speech proposing "a constitutional amendment that no person coming

TABLE 4. 1896 Election Margins in Charlotte Township

Ward 1	
Precinct 1	140 vote Democratic majority
Precinct 2	132 vote Democratic majority
Precinct 3 ("Gingham Mill Box")	4 vote Fusion majority
Ward 2	
Precinct 1 ("one of the negro boxes")	63 vote Fusion majority
Precinct 2 (also a largely black area)	107 vote Fusion majority
Precinct 3 ("Atherton Mill box")	52 vote Fusion majority
Ward 3	
Precinct 1	106 vote Democratic majority
Precinct 2 (rural "Kidd's Store")	79 vote Fusion majority
Precinct 3 (rural "Seversville")	66 vote Fusion majority
Ward 4	
Precinct 1	265 vote Democratic majority
Precinct 2	173 vote Democratic majority
Precinct 3 (rural "Groveton")	195 vote Fusion majority

Source: *Charlotte Observer*, November 10, 1898.

Note: Characterizations in quotation marks were those made in the *Observer* article. All precincts with no characterization were predominantly white and urban. For a more detailed delineation of the precinct boundaries, consult the last page of scrapbook PC 175.19, Clarkson Collection.

of age after January 1, 1901, shall be allowed to vote unless he can read or write."[75] Similar provisions had recently been passed in Mississippi and South Carolina.[76] Ashe pitched his amendment as a public-spirited device designed purely to improve education and stamp out illiteracy. Democratic insiders did not need to be told what such a law could accomplish for their party. Most of the state's illiterate individuals were white small farmers and African Americans, precisely the "lower caste" men who rallied to the Fusion cause. The Democratic editors of the *Charlotte Observer* loudly endorsed Ashe's suggestion: "Besides proving an incentive toward education, such a law would enoble the ballot."[77] A literacy amendment to the North Carolina constitution would take time to put in place, however. Also, some Democratic strategists worried that it might do too much harm to those poor whites who continued to vote Democratic, and not enough to black Republicans. "Many of our people are waking up to the fact the young negroes of today are going to school and preparing themselves to enter into competition with their white neighbors," one observer cautioned.[78] Even as this debate went on, Democrats methodically worked a simpler, more time-honored strategy: the appeal to racial unity.

Race offered the perfect "wedge issue," something that could break up the Populist-Republican alliance by dividing blacks and poorer whites, despite their considerable economic interest in sticking together. The Democratic Party had always marketed itself as the party of the white man, but now it would push that virtue as its chief selling point. In April 1897 the men at the helm of the state party formally launched the new strategy. Under the headline "The Next Campaign Issue," the *Charlotte Observer* carried the announcement "The Ex-Governor Says That White Supremacy is the Issue."[79]

Over the next months Democrats hammered away relentlessly at the theme of black evil, white unity, and the absolute necessity of the color line. In Charlotte, party leaders breathed fresh life into the Workingmen's Democratic Club. Hastily created on the eve of the 1896 election, it now received a formal charter. Headed by party regulars—no actual workingmen among them—the club sent speaker after speaker into Charlotte mill villages to preach "white supremacy and white labor."[80] The city's Democrat-controlled newspapers pushed the same message. Stories spread rumors of scandals in eastern North Carolina, where the black majority in the population had resulted in a substantial number of African American elected officials; headlines screamed the horrors of "Negro Rule" in Wilmington and "Black Men Running Mad" in New Bern. Editorials made much of the fact that Fusion candidates appointed some of their African American supporters to state and federal jobs.[81] The papers also stepped up coverage of black crime, reporting what seemed to be every alleged rape in the South no matter where it occurred and devoting long columns to lynchings of Negro transgressors.

The next statewide election, in 1898, showed the effectiveness of the racial drumbeat. Young railroad lawyer Charles B. Aycock, stumping neighboring Cabarrus County for "the Democracy," won the crowd in a close debate against a Populist speaker by praising a local lynching.[82] In subsequent speeches, covered admiringly by the *Charlotte Observer*, Aycock applauded the noble Democrats for using the white supremacy message "to unite the white people against the negroes, an infamous race."[83] Aycock brought the message to Charlotte in person a week before the election in a "White Men's Rally at Latta Park Auditorium."[84] Demanded *Observer* editorials, "The Anglo Saxon Must Rule."[85] When officials tallied the vote that fall, Democrats happily noted the tide turning in their favor. In Charlotte Township, Democratic totals rose in every precinct, while Fusion numbers dropped. The shift was small, but it swung both of the mill boxes and one of the three rural ballot boxes into the Democratic column.[86] Statewide, similarly small but significant increases put 134 Democrats into general assembly seats, compared with 36 Fusionists.[87] Rejoiced the *Charlotte Observer*, "Fusion Downed. The State Democratic. Whites to Rule."[88]

In reality the margin remained much too close for comfort. Where it had once enjoyed unquestioned control, the Democratic Party clutched only a slim and shaky lead. Strategists now turned to producing, in the candid words of one state legislator, "a good square honest law that will always give a good Democratic majority."[89] The solution turned out to be Samuel Ashe's proposed literacy requirement, with a clever new twist. In 1898 Democrats in Louisiana facing the Populist challenge had devised a literacy amendment with a "grandfather clause."[90] In complicated legalese the clause assured that men whose ancestors had been eligible to cast ballots before 1867 would continue to be allowed to vote, whether literate or not. Since only white men had been eligible prior to that date, the grandfather clause protected whites while disfranchising blacks. To Democratic strategists the grandfather clause seemed a stroke of genius. In the atmosphere of white supremacy, few white people would likely protest a law that made a point of targeting black people. With black citizens disfranchised, the Fusion coalition would no longer muster enough votes to effectively challenge Democratic control.

North Carolina's disfranchisement amendment, though, contained a kicker. It required that illiterate whites had to register within seven years. After that date, the reading requirement applied to whites just as it did to blacks.[91] Populist and Republican leaders, struggling to save Fusion from the rising hysteria of white supremacy, urged voters to heed the fine print. Charlotte's Fusionist *Southern Workman* newspaper called desperately for "defeat of the amendment as a measure hostile to the rights and interests of white working-men."[92] The amendment, warned Republican U.S. senator from North Carolina J. C. Pritchard, "will . . . disfranchise hundreds of honest yeomen of the State, men who, because of poverty, are uneducated themselves and will not be able to educate their boys by the first day of December, 1908."[93] Such objections drowned amid the carefully orchestrated din of white supremacy.

As the vote on disfranchisement neared in 1900, Democrats pulled out all stops in a furious drive to whip up racist emotion. Party speakers went again to the cotton mills, expounding on the theme "Race Fusion is Unnatural."[94] Other Democrats donned red shirts—a conscious variation on the white robes of the Ku Klux Klan—and roamed the countryside harassing opposition voters. Newspapers harangued the "inferior race" and asserted the God-given prerogative of white men to lead Civilization. Hissed the *Charlotte News*:

Shall low-born scum and quondam slaves
Give laws to those who own the soil?
No! By our grandsire's bloody graves,
No! By our homesteads bought with toil.[95]

Though laboring diligently to set the issue in terms of black versus white, the elite's real anger leaked through. Not just former slaves but "low-born scum" were the threat. Blacks had united with the "most dangerous class of the white population," the *Observer* snarled. North Carolina's elite must wrest their state, the paper urged most memorably, from "the danger of the rule of negroes and the lower class of whites."[96]

On the eve of the 1900 election Charlotte's leading merchants and businessmen headed a gala white supremacy parade down Tryon Street. Phalanxes of red-shirted marchers, representing "the best men" from each district in the county, followed the mounted dignitaries. Applauded the *Charlotte News*, "600 Red Shirts in the Grand Horseback Parade. Tryon a Blaze of Red." The paper continued: "One float that elicited cheers all along the line was a skillfully drawn representation of the election under the [influence of the black voter], and was composed of living figures." A white man "in the act of depositing his ballot in the box" was grabbed by a "black negro" who "held him by the lappel [sic] of his coat until he could answer the challenge of another negro who pointed a pistol in his face."[97] By such elaborate visual display, "Mecklenburg's Great Rally" sought to make obvious to even the most illiterate viewer the message that the Fusion cause was dead.

On August 2, 1900, the disfranchisement amendment to the North Carolina constitution passed by a handsome margin. "The Democracy" was safe. For the next sixty years, thanks to similar laws instituted throughout the region, the Democratic Party would reign without serious challenge in a one-party South. "The business men of the State are largely responsible for the victory," wrote a *Charlotte Observer* correspondent analyzing the white supremacy campaign. The "bank men, mill men, and the business men in general—the backbone of the property interest in the State—. . . worked from start to finish and furthermore they spent large bits of money in behalf of the cause," declared the writer. "Their opinion must be respected."[98]

The battle was won, but the victors emerged deeply shaken. Ten long years of nasty fighting had been required merely to prove what should have been obvious all along, that men of property must rule. North Carolina just recently had seemed a simple agricultural state in which everyone agreed that the most successful farmers should guide politics, a deferential society "ordered as Providence deems best and wisest." Now so many interests competed for control: farmers versus merchants, factory owners versus millhands, and even blacks versus whites. Charlotte's leading citizens had encouraged much of the economic change and had profited handsomely. But they had not foreseen that the profusion of interests might bring discord and create situations in which "lesser" men would oppose those long accustomed to leading. For men of wealth whose families had constituted the old-time aristocracy, and for the successful newcomers who had worked long and hard to win admission to that elite, the Populist upheaval signaled a disturbing new reality. The traditional social pyramid could no longer simply be taken for granted. In the late 1880s Charlotte leaders had talked comfortably about society's God-given "rules of intercourse" and "barriers to intrusion." A decade later they found themselves lashing out at "liberty run mad" and struggling furiously to beat back "the danger of the rule of negroes and the lower class of whites."

Suddenly the big-city fashions in urban design that Charlotteans had casually dabbled with during the 1880s and early 1890s made sense. The "habiliments of progress"—to use Edward Dilworth Latta's phrase—now fit. In a topsy-turvy world it might well be wise to put some physical distance between one's own group and these others who could seem so strange. During the late 1890s to late 1920s, Charlotte leaders set to work to re-create their town in a modern urban image, abandoning old-fashioned salt-and-pepper intermingling in favor of a city sorted out into a patchwork quilt of separate neighborhoods for blue-collar whites, for blacks, and for the "better classes."

CHAPTER 4
CREATING BLUE-COLLAR NEIGHBORHOODS

Just at this period in the development of mill people it seems to be better to allow them to . . . form a class to themselves. . . . If this tendency to become a separate class is not resisted, and churches and schools are provided to these people, all to themselves, they . . . do better than where mill people and others are mixed promiscuously.

—Charlotte minister Rev. Gilbert T. Rowe, 1903

EVEN AS Charlotte leaders succeeded in squashing the Populist upheaval in politics, economic change continued relentlessly to pull and tug at urban society. Business enterprises were growing dramatically in number and in size; where the average manufacturing firm in Charlotte had only 3.9 employees in 1880, it reached 24.3 workers in 1900 and would hit 53.4 by 1930.[1] The arrival of more and more working-class families further stirred social conflict, including a rash of factory strikes and a heated debate over public health issues that flared around 1900. Such events exacerbated the tensions that had arisen during the 1890s and goaded the development of a new feature on Charlotte's urban landscape: sizable blue-collar residential districts. Two neighborhoods, changing Belmont and freshly planned North Charlotte, provide a glimpse of the way this new form came into being.

ECONOMIC GROWTH, 1890S–1920S

The last decade of the nineteenth century and the first decades of the twentieth saw Charlotte take its place as the leading trade center in the Carolinas, a destiny it had striven toward since construction of its first railroad in the 1850s. Financial machinations far beyond Charlotte's borders, somewhat ironically, made the local dream a reality. During the 1870s and 1880s Wall Street investors swept up a string of regional rail companies, culminating in the creation of the mighty Southern Railway by the famed financier J. P. Morgan in 1894. The Southern Railway controlled four of the six tracks that converged on Charlotte and routed its Washington-to-New Orleans mainline through the city. Lucky Charlotte now sat astride the "Main Street of the South."[2] Even more fortunately, Charlotte still retained competing rail service. In 1900 the Southern's major rival, the Seaboard Air Line Railroad, purchased the other existing tracks that entered the town.[3] Two additional options appeared in the early 1910s with construction of the Norfolk & Southern Railroad running eastward through Raleigh into Virginia and the Piedmont & Northern electric interurban line extending westward to neighboring Gastonia.[4] The multiple rail connections kept transportation prices low and helped Charlotte's economy expand. By 1930 the Queen City would surpass every town in North Carolina and even the venerable port of Charleston in South Carolina to emerge as the largest city in both states, a position that Charlotte would hold into the twenty-first century.

Cotton manufacturing boomed. Already in 1896 Mecklenburg ranked as North Carolina's third most important textile manufacturing county, boasting

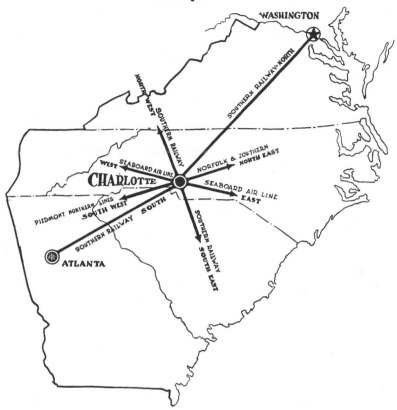

Charlotte is the Center

Transportation

Approximately one hundred passenger trains arrive in and leave Charlotte every day (Charlotte Chamber of Commerce). Four lines of independent railways operate through Charlotte, and operate lines in eight different directions—The Southern, The Seaboard, The Norfolk-Southern, and The Piedmont and Northern. Charlotte is headquarters for The Southern Railway "Lines East," and outside of Washington is the principal center of its activities. The Piedmont and Northern Railway, an interurban railway, 130 miles long, has general headquarters in Charlotte.

Charlotte should be included on every Southern list

FIG. 20. CHARLOTTE RAILROAD CONNECTIONS, 1919
(Source: *Charlotte Is the Center*)

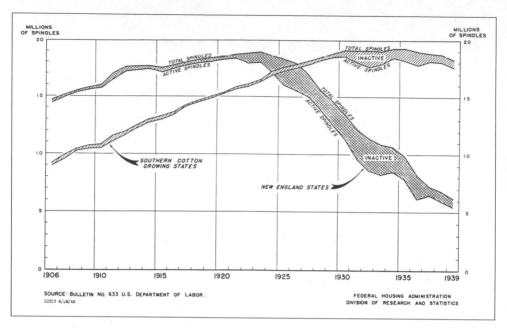

SOURCE: BULLETIN NO. 633 U.S. DEPARTMENT OF LABOR.

FEDERAL HOUSING ADMINISTRATION
DIVISION OF RESEARCH AND STATISTICS

FIG. 21. SOUTHERN TEXTILES OVERTAKE NEW ENGLAND
(Graph from Federal Housing Authority, Division of Research and Statistics, *Charlotte, NC: Housing Market Analysis* [1940], p. 27)

fourteen mills with a combined total of 77,218 spindles and 958 looms.[5] A few of these plants stood at rural whistlestops such as Cornelius or Huntersville or Pineville, but most gathered close to the outskirts of the Queen City. During the next thirty years nine more cotton factories appeared, putting a total of 196,834 spindles and 4,992 looms at Charlotte by the mid-1920s, an increase of more than 250 percent and 520 percent, respectively.[6] The factories actually within the county were only part of the story, however. Even more mills dotted the railroads that reached into the surrounding piedmont, creating a vast Southern textile belt extending all the way from Danville, Virginia, southward into South Carolina and Georgia. "One half of the looms and spindles in the South are within one hundred miles of this city," exclaimed D. A. Tompkins at the start of the 1900s.[7] By 1927 textile production in the South officially surpassed that of the long-established New England region, putting Charlotte at "the center of a textile manufacturing territory having 770 mills . . . and consuming more cotton than any other section of the world."[8]

Textile prosperity in turn spawned innovations in cotton marketing, mill financing, and motive power. "The increased mills in the Piedmont region naturally increase the importance of Charlotte as a cotton market," remarked

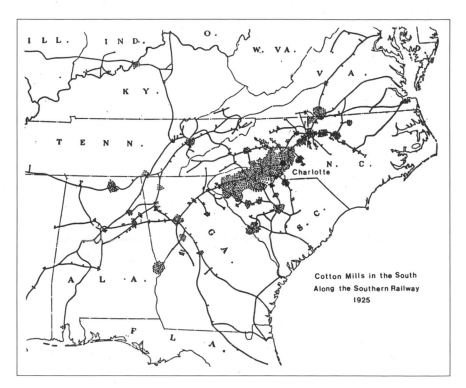

FIG. 22. CHARLOTTE AND THE PIEDMONT TEXTILE REGION
Most cotton mills in the Southeastern United States clustered along the Southern Railway, "The Main Street of the South." Charlotte, right on the Southern's trunk line, was strategically located near the center of the textile belt. (Map adapted by William Huffman from Potwin, *Cotton Mill People*)

the newspapers in the late 1890s.[9] "A great deal of cotton [is now] shipped here from Mississippi, Alabama and Georgia to the local mills."[10] In 1898 a group of merchants erected the Charlotte Bonded Warehouse, a sprawling concrete structure beside the railroads between Poplar and Graham Streets near Twelfth Street.[11] The affordable, secure cotton storage facility allowed Charlotte men to trade even more aggressively. "[Cotton] prices in Charlotte are above those in New York," the *Observer* cheered in 1899. "Charlotte is approaching the position of being a buying and not a selling market."[12] Such an achievement constituted a triumphant turning point. After almost a century exporting its crops, Charlotte finally had mills not only to spin its own cotton but to make money from others' cotton as well.

The city's vibrant economy now began to attract serious outside investment for the first time. Where mills into the 1890s had been financed one at a time by local men, entrepreneurs now began assembling chains of factories and selling stock as far away as New England.[13] Several Northern textile magnates seeking greener pastures arrived in the city to form partnerships with local men, creating institutions such as the Chadwick-Hoskins mill chain and the Charlotte National Bank (a predecessor to today's mammoth NationsBank). The clustering of mills around the city also caught the eye of other kinds of investors. In the 1900s millionaire cigarette manufacturer James B. Duke from Durham, North Carolina, chose Charlotte as the locus for a major experiment with the new technology of electricity. He bought up waterfall sites along the Catawba River nearby and set his engineer William States Lee to work at the task of making hydroelectric power commercially feasible. In 1904 Catawba Power Company (today Duke Power, one of America's largest utility companies) began offering electricity to customers in Charlotte, and soon its lines carried kilowatts throughout the piedmont, reinforcing the region's attractiveness for industry.[14]

Even before Duke, Charlotte was a powerful magnet for textile-related businesses. "We have in Charlotte seven machine shops . . . [including] four firms who will design, construct and equip a cotton mill complete for a given price," bragged D. A. Tompkins shortly after the turn of the century. "Charlotte is the only place in the United States where such a contract can be made."[15] Cole Manufacturing produced the agricultural implements that farmers used to plant the cotton crop, and Margolis Bagging and Ties made the wrapping materials to ship it to market.[16] The Southern Cotton Seed Oil Company offered housewives Snowdrift Hogless Cooking Fat, a vegetable shortening refined from cotton seed.[17] From leftover cotton lint and broken ends of fiber too small to spin, local processors such as Barnhardt Manufacturing and South Atlantic Cotton Waste made mattresses and upholstery stuffing.[18]

The cash generated by the mills and textile-related prosperity allowed Charlotteans to pursue a notable degree of diversification. Savvy tradesmen worked to make the city in every way the kingpin of the piedmont industrial region. They incorporated banks to attract the deposits of surrounding mill men and talked the Federal Reserve into opening its master bank for the region in Charlotte. They pushed a Good Roads Movement that created a radiating web of highways so that horse-drawn cotton wagons and, later, gasoline-driven trucks and autos could come and go easily. They promoted construction of factories to make consumer goods, ranging from locally originated Lance snack crackers to Model T Ford automobiles; a 1926 survey showed 141 Charlotte manufacturers producing a total of 81 different commodities.[19] And they undertook to wholesale all the humdrum day-to-day things needed in all the region's bustling mill communities, sending out an army of salesmen each week to visit small-town retailers and write up orders for Buick cars and RCA Victrolas and cool bottles of Coca Cola. "Every factory village planted adds to the income of our wholesale merchants," chortled the *Charlotte News* in 1903.[20] Other Carolina cities vied to fill textile needs and provide wholesale services—Winston-Salem, Columbia, Greenville, and Spartanburg—but none proved more successful than Charlotte. By the 1920s, if you went to a movie or wrote a check or bought a bottle of cough syrup anywhere from Charleston to Raleigh, you were probably doing business indirectly with some resident of the Queen City.

WORKING-CLASS INFLUX

Families flooded into Charlotte in search of jobs, pulled by the surging urban economy but also pushed by hard times in the countryside. Droughts and plummeting international cotton prices racked Southern agriculture around the turn of the century. Many farmers fell into debt, then lost their land altogether and became tenants laboring in rented fields. "In the Piedmont counties from which most mill workers came, a third more farmers tended someone else's land in 1900 than in 1880," according to a recent study. "By 1900, . . . more than half the farmers in the counties around Charlotte were tenants."[21] As hard times persisted, more and more rural people abandoned tenant farming and looked for better opportunities in town. Often that meant working in a cotton mill. Textile hands comprised the biggest segment— roughly one-third—of Charlotte's working-class white population during the 1900s–1920s.[22] Next most numerous were members of the building trades. The task of constructing the fast-growing city constituted a major industry in its own right, and Charlotte's corps of carpenters, brick masons, and painters almost matched the number of textile mill employees. A third important blue-collar group were the metal workers and machinery men who worked for the plants that made machines for the cotton industry. "Thousands of white tenants, who used to live [on farms] in piedmont North Carolina, are now laboring in the cotton mills, the foundries, the machine shops and for building contractors in the towns," noted the *Charlotte Observer* in 1906. "The short crop this year will drive thousands more of them to the cities, towns and villages."[23]

As Charlotte's working-class population grew, its members showed less and less willingness to bend docilely to the dictates of business owners. Mass actions by dozens of workers had been virtually unknown in the preindustrial era. Now, though, it seemed that hardly a year went by without some group of operatives angrily and openly defying the will of their bosses. Forty-five employees walked out at the Louise Mill in 1897.[24] One hundred struck the Charlotte Clothing Company in 1900.[25] Some 150 deserted the Highland Park Mill the same year.[26] Bricklayers walked off the job at a public school site in 1900, and Louise millhands went out again in 1904.[27] In 1905 typographers rose up at local newspapers, machinists vacated the D. A. Tompkins company, and messengers struck Western Union.[28] Owners usually broke the strikes in a day or two, simply hiring new hands, but the walkouts remained a disturbing phenomenon. They indicated not just discontent with particular working conditions but an underlying social discord. Problems at the Charlotte Clothing Company, for instance, came to a head because the white-collar owner had "used profane language in the presence of the female employees." When "objection was raised to his speech, he said, 'There are no ladies working here.' "[29] The blue-collar "men and women alike resented this language," reported the *Charlotte News*. "The strike was a protest against that remark" and what it implied about upper-class views.[30]

Indeed, laborers had every right to feel touchy about matters of respect. Prosperous citizens betrayed open disdain for millhands and their families. Workers, said one established Charlottean, fully deserved the "common phrases which we often hear on our streets": textile "trash" and "the ignorant factory set." She continued, "Mill operatives are responsible themselves for the disgrace that seems to rest upon them."[31] Sniffed another writer, "With this class little can be done to elevate the parents: the hope lies with the children."[32] Several influential individuals, among them merchant Samuel Wittkowsky and physician J. B. Alexander, spoke pointedly about the ridiculousness of allowing such people—even if they did pass the literacy test—to vote. It just did not seem proper, wrote Alexander in 1902, that anyone "not owning a dollar or supporting a good name, can have an equal vote with him who furnishes work for hundreds of operatives."[33]

The Reverend Gilbert T. Rowe of the prestigious downtown Tryon Street Methodist Church most cuttingly voiced the elite's misgivings. "Any sudden industrial movement carries with it grave problems, and the South realizes that the cotton mill has brought new questions to be settled," Rowe sermonized in a 1903 newspaper column. The new class of millhands showed chronic deficiencies of character, he charged, particularly in matters of religion. "Motives of mere respectability and good form do not influence people at a mill," complained Rowe.

> At present the majority of mill people do not attend church. . . . A reason frequently given by mill people for their failure to go to church is that they don't have clothes good enough to wear and that they would be laughed at. This is in part the truth. There are some people, who claim to be cultured, that are contemptible and mean enough to laugh at people in humbler circumstances. But the greater part of the trouble here lies with the mill people themselves, and the fault lies not so much in the quality of clothes as in the taste with which they are gotten up. . . . Enough money is spent on their clothes, but many mill people have poor taste, and they know it.[34]

These shortcomings only pointed to graver flaws, Rowe asserted. "It is thought by some men that culturally a peculiar type is being developed . . . [that] the class being produced by mill conditions today are in danger of becoming really inferior, because . . . work required in the mill is mechanical and easily learned, and most of the laborers tend to become merely a part of a machine during working hours." Such a Darwinian scenario might indeed be unfolding, said Rowe, since it was "the weaker element" that was being "drawn out of the rural sections and gotten together in the towns." Whatever the case, the minister counseled his wealthy parishioners, a firm "benevolent paternalism" should "be exercised over them."

Concerns about public health intensified the elite's perception of factory workers as threatening and unruly strangers. At the turn of the century, middle-class Americans were just discovering the germ theory of disease and starting to understand how contagious illness spread.[35] Prosperous Charlotteans began to recognize that the clusters of mill housing, such as those around the Victor and Alpha factories, afforded virulent breeding grounds for sickness—sickness that could potentially invade white-collar homes. "Any contagion spreads through the mill population like a prairie fire," worried Rowe in his newspaper column. "Many of them have a pallor peculiar to the cotton mill. They fall easy victims to consumption and other lung and throat diseases."[36] Concerned citizens might have blamed such problems on the exhausting sixty-hour workweeks in the lint-filled air of the mills or on the fact that the muddy-streeted mill villages usually lacked basic public facilities such as pure water and municipal sewers. Instead, they blamed the millhands themselves. "At first sight this fatality would appear to be the result of oppression and adverse conditions, but close observation shows that such is not the case," asserted Rowe. "The weak physical condition of most operatives is due to carelessness, . . . lack of physical exercise," and a lazy "fondness for embalmed [canned] food."[37]

A 1900 smallpox outbreak illustrated how class tensions and public health concerns intertwined. Following several reports of smallpox among poor black visitors to the city, officials decided to launch a vaccination campaign.[38] Doctors first visited the black and white public schools to implement the new and frightening technique of inoculation. With a sharp knife, they scratched children's arms and gave them a mild form of the disease. Recipients would experience flulike symptoms for several days but then be immune to any stronger strains of the disease. After vaccinating the city schools, the team moved next to the city's mill villages. There they met with resistance. At the Victor Mill two families asked to avoid inoculation on the ground that they had "been unwell for some time and . . . feared that [their] health was not sufficient to undergo the trying ordeal of vaccination."[39] Officials promptly jailed the scofflaws, including a mother and her four-year-old boy. The next day the doctors advanced upon the Gingham Mill, accompanied by the police chief and a squad of officers. "Just as soon as Chief Orr made his appearance in the mill the scramble begun [sic]. Men, women and children made for the doors and windows, and . . . like sheep scattered to pastures new," wrote a reporter. Nothing would coax them to return until the officials "with their knives and virus" departed.[40]

To white-collar Charlotteans such resistance to health regulations simply confirmed sharpening suspicion of "the more ignorant classes," but distrust stirred by the episode cut both ways.[41] Millhands boiled with anger at white-collar unwillingness to listen to legitimate concerns, and even more they took offense at being specially targeted by city officials. " 'O, the mill hands are so filthy and degraded now,' so they say by their actions," wrote one furious worker to the News.[42] "What officer or set of officers would dare to enter the homes of any of Charlotte's leading men or bankers and drag their wives to prison under the same circumstances as [Victor millhand] Mrs. Helms? Not one," maintained a second writer.[43] "There are numbers of people up town who have not been vaccinated and say they are not going to be. Clerks, bookkeepers, agents of various kinds, and other business men and professional men—men who are daily mingling with promiscuous crowds," complained another letter. "If the officers will commence at the square and vaccinate everybody engaged in public service within the limits of the town, then I think

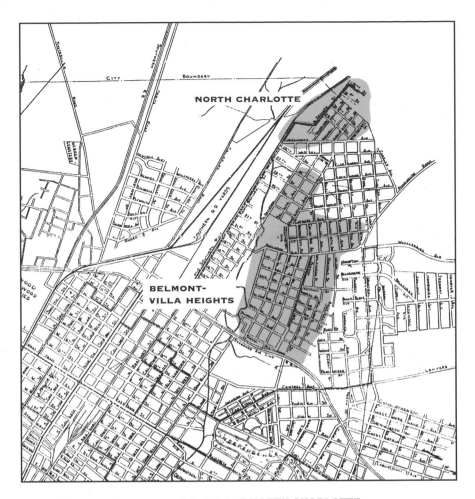

FIG. 23. BELMONT–VILLA HEIGHTS AND NORTH CHARLOTTE
The Belmont–Villa Heights district and the North Charlotte area emerged as Charlotte's largest blue-collar residential neighborhoods in the years immediately after 1900. (Base map: City of Charlotte, 1925)

I can say with surety that when they get to the mills there will be no need of pistols or dogs."[44]

In such a charged atmosphere Charlotte's "better classes" stepped up efforts to put physical distance between themselves and the factory population. Back in 1881 the initial Charlotte Cotton Mill had located its plant within sight of the town's poshest residences. In 1889 and 1891 subsequent mills had built clusters of housing, but millhands had still mostly shopped and worshiped in town. Now, though, urged the Reverend Gilbert T. Rowe solicitously, "at this period in the development of mill people it seems to be better to allow them to . . . form a class to themselves." Blue-collar folk, if set firmly apart, would "do better than where mill people and others are mixed promiscuously," he justified. It would be best for everyone concerned "if this tendency to become a class is not resisted, and churches and schools are provided to these people, all to themselves."[45]

BELMONT–VILLA HEIGHTS

As platted by its founders in early 1896, the subdivision called Belmont Springs bid fair to become a second Dilworth. Lying just north of Charlotte, the land draped picturesquely over the brow of a hill offering a handsome view back toward downtown, and a delightful spring bubbled forth just below the crest. Five prosperous local investors bought the "beautifully studded tract" in 1891 the very same month that Edward Dilworth Latta opened Dilworth on the opposite edge of town, and they set forth to create "an attractive resort" that would emulate his project on a smaller scale.[46] Belmont Springs experienced delays, perhaps due to competition from Dilworth or because of the nation-wide 1893 depression, but in April 1896 Belmont's promoters filed a formal plat map showing the neighborhood they envisioned.[47] They mapped out a grid of broad, straight avenues (including present-day Belmont Avenue) that, like Dilworth's, ran slightly out of kilter with the streets of Charlotte. In the western portion of the neighborhood, they included a landscaped park surrounding the natural spring and spilling down to the banks of Sugar Creek. A winding drive, a romantic footbridge, and abundant greenery recalled the naturalistic artistry created across town by Latta's landscape architect Joseph Forsyth Johnson.

As with Dilworth, rail lines ran close by and factories shared the immediate vicinity of the proposed Belmont Springs development.[48] The trackage soon to be purchased by the Seaboard Air Line paralleled the subdivision's south-ern border. The Southern Railway mainline lay to the west just a short dis-tance beyond Sugar Creek.[49] Several industrial concerns already lined the Southern track, marching outward from downtown. The Alpha Mill and its mill village (one of the city's three cotton mills constructed back in 1889) stood at Twelfth Street (see fig. 14).[50] Just beyond was the 1891 Highland Park Com-pany textile factory, better known as the Gingham Mill in recognition of the popular checked fabric it produced.[51] A scattering of factory cottages stood near the Gingham Mill on Brevard Street, Caldwell Street, and Davidson Street, three downtown avenues that had been extended outward in the time-

FIG. 24. MAP OF BELMONT SPRINGS, 1896

Developers' early plans for Belmont Springs suggested it would resemble Dilworth, with both adjacent industry (Louise Cotton Mill, lower right) and also white-collar homesites overlooking a naturalistic park. (Source: Mecklenburg County Register of Deeds Office, deed book 112, p. 8)

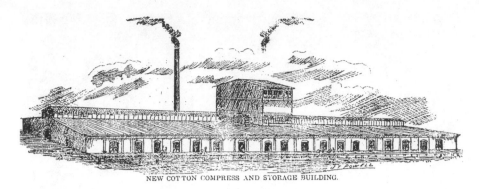

NEW COTTON COMPRESS AND STORAGE BUILDING.

FIG. 25. CHARLOTTE COTTON COMPRESS, 1899
The cotton compress, located along the Southern Railway on North Brevard Street, was "one of the largest and best compress and warehouse structures in the South," according to the *Charlotte News*. Over 600 feet in length, housing a steam-driven, 125-ton press at its center, the facility functioned as a key part of the city's cotton economy. (Source: *Charlotte News*, August 17, 1899)

honored fashion. Next up the railroad came the imposing Charlotte Cotton Compress. Its two-story tower held a gigantic steam-powered machine to compact cotton bales, which could then be stored in the long brick warehouse wings that extended 700 feet along the railway track. Opened in the early 1890s, the huge facility soon employed "sixty colored men" and eventually supplanted Charlotte's older downtown cotton Wharf.[52]

In addition to this industrial corridor already in existence just across Sugar Creek to the west, Belmont Springs's promoters anticipated construction of a textile mill immediately east of their subdivision. The 1896 Belmont Springs plat map showed the adjacent land of the Louise Cotton Manufacturing Company, chartered early that year by respected wholesale merchant H. S. Chadwick and lovingly named after his socialite wife. By November 1896 newspapers reported the two-story brick walls complete and the tin roof being installed.[53] Machinery arrived the following spring, and announcements soon celebrated the production of the mill's first cloth. "The 45 tenement [rental] houses which the Louise Mill is erecting are about completed," noted the *Charlotte Observer*, " 'Louise' will be a pretty mill town."[54]

The notion of a pretty mill town next to white-collar houses had seemed quite reasonable in 1891 when Latta launched Dilworth with its industrial corridor, and Belmont Springs promoters considered it no handicap as late as the spring of 1896 when they filed their plat map. But subsequent events severely battered that confidence. In the fall of 1896 blue-collar whites at

Charlotte's mill boxes cast their vote decisively for Populism, serving notice that they stood willing and able to act in opposition to white-collar interests. In November 1897 workers struck the new Louise Mill over wage cuts, Charlotte's largest walkout to that time.[55] In early 1900 the Gingham Mill became the site of the well-publicized resistance to smallpox vaccination, and cases of the disease subsequently surfaced both there and at the Louise Mill.[56] That March newspapers carried a brief story of a drunken and evidently disgruntled millhand who broke into the Louise factory late one night and shot it up with a revolver.[57] The following winter a rash of suspicious fires culminated in destruction of the company superintendent's house.[58]

The tensions took a toll on Belmont Springs. In such a climate, white-collar Charlotteans no longer felt comfortable living next to a mill village. Over in Dilworth there was enough momentum—lots sold, houses started, and trolleys running—to overcome this change in white-collar tastes, and Latta's suburb was large enough that white-collar buyers after the late 1890s could locate at some distance from the South Boulevard factory corridor. Belmont Springs was much smaller, however. Almost every lot in the district lay within a couple of blocks of either the Louise Mill or Gingham Mill workers' housing. And in Belmont Springs few, if any, white-collar buyers had yet invested in house lots. The promoters formally recognized the turnabout in 1900. They gave up their dream of a landscaped park and instead replatted its land as additional house lots. At the same time, the name "Springs" disappeared; the district became simply "Belmont."[59] The "beautifully studded tract" would now develop as the nucleus of Charlotte's first sizable working-class neighborhood.

During the next ten years a crazy-quilt of additional small subdivisions stitched more streets onto Belmont. Villa Heights, East End, Sunnyside, and Phifer Heights each had different developers.[60] Each got slightly different street patterns, as promoters strove to adapt grid arrangements to the shape of their particular pieces of land. But for all the confusion when viewed on a map, at ground level similar building types and similar income levels knit the neighborhood into a seamless whole known as Belmont–Villa Heights. One-story houses built of wood in a mixture of Victorian and Bungalow styles, smaller and less architecturally ostentatious than dwellings in Charlotte's white-collar suburbs, covered the district. Except for the look-alike rows of textile cottages near the mills, most structures in the neighborhood appeared to be constructed one at a time, each to its own design. Charlotteans never built any of the densely packed, multistory brick tenements that crowded blue-collar districts in the North; nearly all Belmont–Villa Heights dwellings

FIG. 26. BLUE-COLLAR HOUSING IN BELMONT–VILLA HEIGHTS
Houses throughout the Belmont–Villa Heights area—such as these on Allen Street—are generally one-story frame structures with broad front porches. Architecture is a blend of Victorian and Bungalow influences. (Photograph by author, March 1993)

were single-family, each set comfortably back from the street, with a cool front porch where neighbors visited and caught the breezes in those evenings before the invention of air conditioning.

The people who chatted on those porches mostly spent their days working with their hands. Charlotte city directories of the early 1910s, when the new streets had filled out enough to be listed for the first time, showed the overwhelmingly blue-collar character of Belmont–Villa Heights. The large majority of residents labored in one of three industrial occupations: millhand, machinist/metal molder, or overseer. Most of these employees walked to work at the nearby factories that bordered the district. A much smaller but still substantial number of men held jobs in Charlotte's building trades. The earliest inhabitants of Parkwood Avenue, for instance, were nearly all carpenters, bricklayers, or plumbers. Other streets usually had one or two such artisans.

Amongst the working-class houses, small businesses mingled casually, a common urban pattern in earlier times, but one dying out in pretentious white-collar suburbs. Belmont did eventually get a streetcar line in the 1910s, a track that ran down Pegram Street past the Louise Mill, where it hooked up with the Central Avenue line to downtown.[61] But blue-collar workers laboring ten to twelve hours per day, six days per week, seldom had the time, energy, or money to journey to the center city to shop. Grocery stores and other modest enterprises dotted the street corners throughout Belmont–Villa Heights. Examples that survived into the 1990s, thanks to brick construction, included the two-story Belmont Pharmacy building at Belmont and Pegram Streets; structures on Caldwell Avenue at Fourteenth Street that held a grocery, the Charlotte Day Nursery, and a labor union hall; and a row of stores at the end of the Pegram Street trolley line.[62] The families who originally ran these businesses usually lived near their shops; they and their clerks comprised most of the small white-collar component of this otherwise blue-collar neighborhood.

In several respects, including this commercial intermingling, Belmont resembled working-class districts of the urban North, but there were also distinctively Southern differences. Charlotte had none of the jumble of immigrant groups that characterized Northern industrialization.[63] Only Southern-born whites lived in Belmont–Villa Heights. The absence of foreigners triggered two other differences. Northern working-class zones were often predominantly Catholic, the religion of most Eastern European immigrants, which put them sharply at odds with the Protestant religious culture of white-collar suburbia. In Charlotte both blue-collar and white-collar residents shared Southern Protestant beliefs, perhaps with more Baptist and Methodist evangelical emphasis among mill workers, compared with Presbyterian and Episcopal leanings among mill owners, but still holding essential practices in common.[64] Also, the factory neighborhoods of the North tended to retain some very wealthy men, usually immigrants who had risen rapidly in the world and chose to stay among their countrymen rather than depart for the suburbs. In Charlotte no wealthy individuals resided in blue-collar Belmont–Villa Heights.

NORTH CHARLOTTE, TEXTILE "SATELLITE CITY"

While the Belmont area developed as a working-class district largely through happenstance, a collection of variously intended projects that came together as Charlotte's first large blue-collar neighborhood, North Charlotte sprang into being designed from the start as a self-contained factory community. Half a dozen textile-related industries, more than 200 mill-owned cottages aligned in neat rows, a section of overseers' houses, a park, plus a full-fledged downtown made North Charlotte a veritable "satellite city" of Charlotte. The carefully planned 1903 design embodied the Reverend Gilbert T. Rowe's advice that mill people should be provided with their own churches and schools and set apart to "form a class to themselves."

North Charlotte began as the brainchild of William E. Holt, Jesse S. Spencer, and Charles Worth Johnson, founders of Charlotte's earlier Gingham Mill. Holt had deep roots in the Carolina textile industry. His father had created the legendary Alamance Plaid Mills near Burlington that introduced the South's first textile dyes and machine-woven cloth in the 1850s, and the elder Holt had also made investments in Charlotte, including creation of the city's Commercial National Bank in 1874.[65] Young William Holt took up the family business, starting mills of his own in Burlington and Lexington before turning attention to the booming Queen City. With Charlotte financier Jesse Spencer, a longtime Holt associate who headed the Commercial National Bank, William created the Highland Park Manufacturing Company to launch the Gingham Mill in 1891.[66] To actually run the operation, the men brought in as partner a hard-driving, youthful manager named Charles Worth Johnston. A farmer's son, Johnston had started work as a store clerk in a Mecklenburg hamlet, married the storekeeper's daughter, and before he was far into his twenties launched the Cornelius Cotton Mill.[67] Johnston proved such a spark plug at the Gingham Mill that Holt and Spencer agreed to back him in assembling a chain of factories. Soon the trio owned the Anchor Mills at nearby Huntersville and Highland Park #2 in neighboring Rock Hill.[68] Emboldened by success, they began preparing an even more ambitious scheme for Highland Park #3.

In the North at the turn of the century the notion of industrial satellite cities was just coming into popularity among businessmen. The ever-larger factories of the era needed abundant land and easy railroad access, both of which could be had cheaply at the urban rim. As importantly, industrialists sought to pull employees away from the distractions of the city. "Contact with workers in other factories, with whom they might compare work conditions and wages, is much less frequent," noted a 1915 book on the phenomenon.[69] The era's first widely publicized experiment, the town of Pullman outside Chicago, gained notoriety in 1894 when its workers staged a bitter strike protesting wage cuts and high rents. But Pullman's problems did not deter a wave of other industrialists from launching less heavy-handed projects during the late 1890s and 1900s, including Ivorydale and Norwood at Cincinnati, Agro southwest of Chicago, West Nashville outside the capital of Tennessee, and ultimately United States Steel's sprawling town of Gary, Indiana.[70] The time seemed ripe in the early 1900s to bring such a development to Charlotte. First, the South was enjoying perhaps its greatest mill-building boom; North Carolina's number of spindles would jump 140 percent in the decade.[71] Second, Dixie possessed its own model for self-contained industrial communities: the mill village idea abandoned long ago in New England remained vital in the piedmont textile belt. Third and most crucially, the political and labor unrest of the 1890s made the idea of setting workers off from the city seem a highly desirable concept.

Holt, Spencer, and Johnston possessed the deep pockets and the energetic vision required for such a project, and in 1903 they set to work on plans for North Charlotte. From the estate of an antebellum planter they purchased 102 acres of farmland along the Southern Railway mainline.[72] The tract lay well beyond the limits of existing settlement, a full mile north of the Belmont–Villa Heights neighborhood. They also desired adjacent acreage that happened to hold the Mecklenburg County poorhouse plus a brand new Charlotte municipal reservoir and pumping station just completed in the 1890s. Thanks to Holt and Spencer's money and connections this proved no obstacle; water officials compliantly agreed to vacate the watershed.[73] With land assembled, the promoters hired Charlotte textile architect Stuart Cramer to draw blueprints for the Highland Park #3 cotton factory and the surrounding industrial town. At that moment Cramer ranked as Charlotte's up-and-coming mill engineer, a protégé of D. A. Tompkins who had recently launched his own firm in competition with his mentor. Cramer would become internationally known for important innovations in heat and humidity control for the cotton industry, and today he is widely credited with coining the term "air conditioning."[74] At North Charlotte the promoters encouraged Stuart Cramer to create a state-of-the-art textile facility.

Cramer's Highland Park #3 mill sparked excitement from the first. The two-story spinning building and the one-story weaving building together would "employ over 800 operatives and will have 30,000 spindles and 1,000 looms. The Gingham Mill, which is considered a large plant, has only 300 operatives," the *Charlotte Observer* marveled as construction commenced.[75] Stuart Cramer made the factory an architectural and mechanical showcase.[76] The complex's front proudly overlooked the Southern Railway mainline; Cramer designed a commanding four-story tower topped by a castle-like parapet with circular windows, sure to catch the eye of every railroad passenger steaming into Charlotte. The back of the facility faced present-day Davidson Street, and there Cramer arranged a separate cotton warehouse and gin (with an elaborate pneumatic cotton-handling apparatus) so that Highland Park #3 could

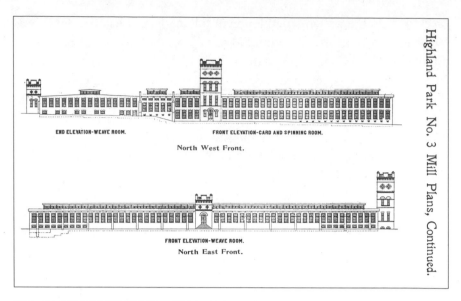

END ELEVATION-WEAVE ROOM.   FRONT ELEVATION-CARD AND SPINNING ROOM.

North West Front.

FRONT ELEVATION-WEAVE ROOM.

North East Front.

FIG. 27. HIGHLAND PARK #3 MILL, 1903
Charlotte textile architect Stuart Cramer proudly published extensive drawings of the
Highland Park #3 mill. The northwest front, with its commanding tower, faced the busy
mainline of the Southern Railway. (Source: Cramer, *Useful Information for Cotton Manufacturers*, vol. 3)

buy raw fiber directly from farmers. The most exciting aspect of Cramer's
engineering was his choice of motive power. Highland Park #3 would run
not on steam but on electricity, the first textile factory in North Carolina
constructed expressly for the new technology.[77] No commercial supplier of
current existed—James B. Duke had not yet launched Catawba Power—so
Cramer designed a handsome brick generator building where a massive Westinghouse steam engine generated electricity that passed along lines to the old
Gingham Mill, new Highland Park #3, and the rest of North Charlotte.[78] For
several years the Highland Park #3 mill would be among the half-dozen
largest textile facilities in the state, and by 1907 its proprietors would boast that
"in production of staple ginghams" the plant ranked "third of all the mills in
the country. The big Amoskeag and Manchester mills at Manchester, New
Hampshire, are the only ones in America which surpass it."[79]

Around Highland Park #3 Cramer set aside additional industrial sites that
North Charlotte's promoters sold to five smaller concerns. The Duke tobacco
family, diversifying into textiles, constructed the Mecklenburg Mill in 1903
in partnership with Charlotte businessmen.[80] Adjacent rose the 1913 Johnston Mill, solely owned by Highland partner Charles Worth Johnston.[81] The

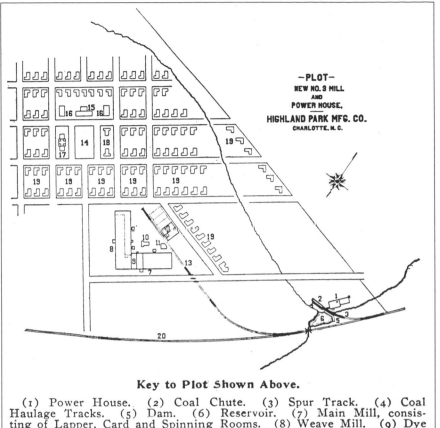

Key to Plot Shown Above.

(1) Power House. (2) Coal Chute. (3) Spur Track. (4) Coal Haulage Tracks. (5) Dam. (6) Reservoir. (7) Main Mill, consisting of Lapper, Card and Spinning Rooms. (8) Weave Mill. (9) Dye House. (10) Transformer House. (11) Boiler House for Heating Plant. (12) Cotton Storage Warehouse. (13) Spur Track. (14) Village square. (15) Hotel. (16) Stores. (17) School. (18) Churches. (19) Tenement Houses. (20 Main Line Southern Railway.

Only a hundred or more tenement houses are shown on the plot, the remainder being located along the brow of the hill to the Eastward. The open space left in front of the weave room is for future extensions to the plant.

FIG. 28. HIGHLAND PARK #3 MILL VILLAGE, 1903

Stuart Cramer's 1903 design for Highland Park #3 included a completely self-contained workers' community. This plan shows the mill and electric powerhouse near the railroad, plus houses, stores, churches, and a school. The stores and churches were actually built in a somewhat different arrangement, but the vision of a self-contained village was realized. (Source: Cramer, *Useful Information for Cotton Manufacturers*, vol. 3)

New Jersey-based Larkwood Silk Hosiery Company added a knitting plant in 1926.[82] Grinnell Manufacturing (also known as General Fire Extinguisher) arrived from New England in 1906, offering building-wide sprinkler systems that became standard equipment in textile factories across the piedmont.[83] South Atlantic Cotton Waste, a large concern that recycled lint and other mill byproducts, rounded out the district's textile-related enterprises.[84] Together the humming cluster of factories made North Charlotte almost instantly one of Mecklenburg's biggest employment centers.

The Highland Park Company and the Mecklenburg Mill housed much of their large workforces in company-owned quarters. Stuart Cramer's carefully drawn blueprints for Highland Park #3 showed six streets of mill cottages immediately adjacent to the factory. "There will be 80 houses in the mill town and they are going up at the rate of a dozen a day," a newspaper reported in June 1903.[85] The corporation added fifty more dwellings late in 1906 and still more during the 1910s or 1920s. All of the cottages used look-alike designs featuring pine clapboards, gable roofs, and broad front porches—traditional homey touches familiar to families fresh off the farm. Beyond Cramer's streets the Mecklenburg Mill soon added more rows of cottages in similar style, a total of over fifty dwellings on avenues with textile-themed names such as Warp Street and Card Street. A 1919 press release in the *Southern Textile Bulletin* spoke glowingly of the Mecklenburg Mill community's rural comforts:

> Each cottage has a large space for a vegetable garden and many fine vegetables are raised in both summer and winter, also a good quantity of beans, peas, corn, etc., are canned in the summer. There is a piggery where the mill community keep their hogs in a segregated spot, and many hundreds of pounds of pork is raised each year. Of course there are some chickens in the village but these are not encouraged for they are always liable to get out and do damage in the gardens. There are quite a number of cows that furnish plenty of milk and butter, and these are kept in perfectly sanitary stables away from the houses. The employees manifest considerable civic pride in keeping their village and their homes in a neat clean manner.[86]

North Charlotte's third residential section, located just east of the two mill villages, had a decidedly less rustic atmosphere. In partnership with veteran suburban developer Edward Dilworth Latta, Charles Johnston and William Holt chartered the North Charlotte Realty Company in 1906.[87] The company platted a grid of handsome avenues (including Holt Street and Spencer Street) with modest house lots for sale close to the mill villages and larger ones available further away. Latta arranged for a trolley line to serve the subdivision, running out Brevard Street and Davidson Street from downtown past the mills, then swinging east along Thirty-Sixth Street into the heart of the new district. The result was a small area of houses that looked much like the white-collar streetcar suburbs then springing into existence elsewhere around Charlotte. Most residents, though, did not commute downtown but, rather, worked as upper-level employees in North Charlotte enterprises. S. A. Abbey, for instance, served as a superintendent at General Fire Extinguisher and walked home each evening to a fine two-story Victorian house with Doric porch columns and art-glass windows. Such a house would have fitted nicely into suburban Dilworth; in North Charlotte its stylish design and two-story massing contrasted sharply with the one-story workers' cottages nearby, helping to emphasize and reinforce Abbey's status as a white-collar superior.

While the carefully planned industrial layout and extensive provision of housing clearly marked North Charlotte as something new on Charlotte's landscape, the district's boldest attribute was its downtown. Stuart Cramer's initial design for the Highland Park #3 mill village included a full-blown town square: a central park surrounded by two stores, a pair of churches, a hotel, and a school (see fig. 29). The hotel went up immediately in 1903 (and still stands on Alexander Street), a two-story, Colonial Revival structure where salesmen, machinery installers, and others on mill business could lodge.[88] The rest of the town square evidently did not materialize according to Cramer's plan, but the idea of a commercial hub was not abandoned. At the corner of Thirty-Sixth Street and Davidson Street, where the trolley turned and near where the three residential sections came together, a thriving "millhand main street" sprang into existence. Two blocks of brick business buildings, one and two stories tall, were filled with a barber shop, a drugstore, a dry goods emporium, a lunchroom, a doctor's office, and five small groceries by 1929.[89]

A sizable complement of institutional facilities reinforced the district's sense of self-containment. Most millhands attended either North Charlotte Baptist Church or Spencer Memorial Methodist Church, both built on land provided by the Highland Park Company.[90] A hall above Hand's Pharmacy offered space for fraternal groups and other types of meetings.[91] The former county poorhouse on Thirty-Sixth Street became the centerpiece for a community park. Known as Electric Park, it included a pond, a baseball diamond, picnic facilities, and a branch of the national YMCA that provided classes and organized recreation for residents.[92] In 1936 Charlotte Fire Station No. Seven opened in the heart of the business district on North Davidson Street.[93] The building resembled two others built about the same time in the white-collar neighborhoods of Eastover and Wesley Heights—with one interesting difference. The North Charlotte facility included a two-cell jail at the rear, in which constables could lock up millhands should they get disorderly.

North Charlotte and Belmont–Villa Heights comprised the largest of the new blue-collar districts that appeared in Charlotte after 1900, but they were not alone. Another informal collection of blue-collar streets much like Belmont–Villa Heights accreted in the town's Third Ward area around South Graham Street, West Morehead Street, and Cedar Street in the vicinity of the early Victor mill village. West of Charlotte, a second satellite city slightly smaller than North Charlotte sprang up around the new Chadwick and Hoskins textile mills, a neighborhood known today as Thomasboro.[94] Where once workmen had mingled salt-and-pepper fashion throughout the landscape of Charlotte, now increasingly they were physically segregated—in the words of the Reverend Gilbert Rowe—"to form a class to themselves."

For blue-collar families, that segregation could have some positive aspects. In the 1970s, University of North Carolina students interviewed longtime North Charlotte residents as part of research for the prize-winning book *Like a Family: The Making of a Southern Cotton Mill World*. Interviewees recalled a proud and tight-knit community, a place where most families kept chickens or pigs, canned the produce from their own gardens, and shared what they could with neighbors in times of need. "I guess there were two hundred houses on this village, and I knew practically all of them from a kid up," Hoyle Mc-Corkle remembered. "It was kind of a cliché: You grew up here and you knew everybody. It had its bad points; we didn't make too much money, I know my father didn't. But like I said, it was kind of one big family and we all hung together and survived. It was a two-hundred-headed family. Everybody on this hill, we looked after one another."[95]

Positive recollections, though, mixed with memories of tough working conditions and derisive second-class treatment. In 1919, during the economic recession following World War I, Highland Park cut pay and reduced operations to four days a week. One hundred and fifty employees launched a three-month strike that temporarily succeeded in winning resumption of a full workweek.[96] Millhands struck briefly again in 1921 and 1923, and in 1934 they participated actively in the General Textile Strike that swept the entire piedmont mill belt.[97] Even more than such organized actions, the interviewees at

Negro Property

If you are interested in cheap renting property that will make a good

INVESTMENT.

We can sell you a well located lot 99x136 on corner of 1st and McDowell St., room for half a dozen houses for only

$7[illegible]0,00

Abbott & Stephens,

PIEDMONT BUILDING, - CHARLOTTE, N.

A Good Investment

Corner Phifer and Alexander Streets,

FOR $1 500

A good 4 room house and barn, renting for $120 a year, on lot 198x198. By spending an additional $1400 on the property you can realize 18 per cent on the investment. This property is just outside of city limits and in white neighborhood entirely. House is only 3 years old and situated between the Louise, Gingham and Alpha Mills and will always rent.

Can be bought on easy terms.

REESE & BRICE,

Real Estate and Insurance.

Corner 5tn and Tryon Streets. Charlotte, N. C

FIG. 29. REAL ESTATE ADS, 1901

On the heels of the "political and social confusion" of the 1890s, Charlotte real estate dealers began identifying some properties as intended specifically for rental to blacks or millhands. (Source: *Charlotte News*, February 7, 25, 1901)

North Charlotte recalled how it felt to be set apart from the city. "Back in them days cotton mill people was about the lowest class of people there were. They called them linthead. That's right, that's what you'd hear—linthead," said George Shue.[98] Explained Ada Mae Wilson, "There was different classes of people that lived in different directions" in Charlotte. The "real highfalutin people" resided in the fashionable suburbs of Dilworth and Myers Park. "But we was trash out here; we was poor white trash because we worked in the mill. We didn't have white-collar jobs, as they called them, like working in a bank or the stores and things like that. 'Poor white trash' they called us. They thought we ought to wear brogan shoes to church."[99]

That sense of hurt felt by blue-collar whites, however, was mild compared with what Charlotte's African American citizens experienced during the era of sorting-out.

CHAPTER 5

CREATING BLACK

NEIGHBORHOODS

It seems to be a principle of life that when people become rich they
suddenly develop an aversion to poor white folks and to negroes.
—Charlottean H. M. Wilder, 1906

ALTHOUGH Southern urban historians once believed that separate black and white neighborhoods sprang into existence fully formed immediately after the Civil War, recent in-depth studies of particular cities suggest that patterns of racial segregation changed considerably over time. Scholars in Atlanta, Houston, Charleston, Louisville, and other communities have discovered a persistence of racial intermingling for twenty years or more following Emancipation.[1] With the anger unleashed by the upheavals of the 1890s, segregation abruptly intensified. In the years immediately after 1900, self-contained African American neighborhoods coalesced in city after city, frequently even including a "black main street" separate from the white downtown. These neighborhoods did not yet congregate in a single "black side of town," as they would later. But the change from earlier arrangements was dramatic, adding up to—in the words of one historian—a "startling reordering" of residential patterns.[2]

Charlotte experienced just such a reordering during the opening years of the twentieth century. The tensions of the 1890s, particularly the rhetoric of white supremacy, supercharged racist emotions among whites, who now sought to buttress their social position by instituting a strict Jim Crow system of separation by race.[3] In some Southern cities, leaders went so far as to write racial zoning into law in the years after 1900.[4] In Charlotte the strategies were less formal but no less effective. White property owners offered blacks opportunities for improved housing in specific sections of the city, erecting clusters of shotgun dwellings for renters and even opening a streetcar suburb for African American homebuyers. At the same time, opportunities vanished elsewhere. Downtown interests shunned black storekeepers, neighbors pressured landlords to evict black tenants, and in the suburbs developers inserted restrictive covenants into every lot deed forbidding ownership or residence by anyone of the "colored race."

This strategy of directed opportunity proved quite effective in producing hard-edged black neighborhoods throughout the city by the 1910s. Four districts of Charlotte, two on the east side and two on the west side, provide case studies of the impact of Jim Crow on the urban landscape. In First and Second Wards just east of downtown, longtime patterns of residential intermingling vanished, and a black business district sprang into existence. At the city's western edge, the rim village of Biddleville became the nucleus of another African American district, which by the 1910s would include the black streetcar suburb known as Washington Heights.

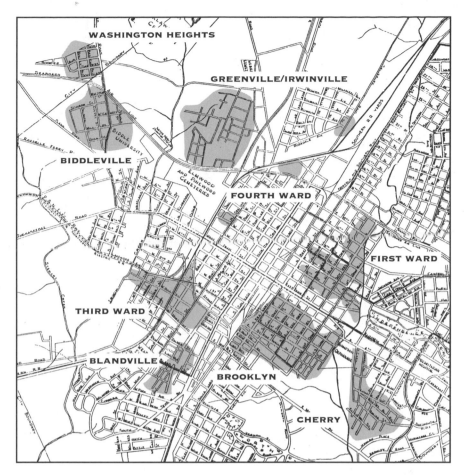

FIG. 30. BLACK NEIGHBORHOODS, CA. 1917

Black neighborhoods could be found on every side of the city in the 1910s. Within the grid of Charlotte's original four wards, the largest African American area was Brooklyn in Second Ward, where a veritable black main street was taking shape. First Ward and Third Ward (West Morehead Street area) also had sizable black districts, and a small one could be found around Sixth and Graham Streets in Fourth Ward. Beyond the original grid, several old rim villages were now urban neighborhoods: Blandville, Cherry, Greenville/ Irwinville, and the college community of Biddleville. Out beyond Biddleville lay the city's new African American streetcar suburb, Washington Heights. (Sources: John Nolen, "Civic Survey, Charlotte North Carolina: Report to the Chamber of Commerce, 1917," box 23, Nolen papers; base map: City of Charlotte, 1925)

The term "Jim Crow" had been around since at least the minstrel show craze of the 1820s and 1830s, when a white actor named Thomas D. Rice toured the country performing in blackface with a dance and song called "Jump Jim Crow."[5] By the mid-nineteenth century "Jim Crow" had entered the language as a derogatory term for things African American. Jim Crow segregation laws came more slowly. After the Civil War, black and white religious congregations often split, and as public schools began to appear, they, too, were usually separated by color. In a surprising number of situations, however, the two races continued to share space in Southern cities. In train stations, in parks, on streetcars, and elsewhere blacks and whites coexisted side-by-side, until the whirlwind of the 1890s. In its wake the phrase "Jim Crow" came to connote a rigid system of physical separation written into the rule books and legal codes of the South.[6]

In Charlotte the trend appeared first in the train stations. For a full generation following the Civil War, black passengers and white passengers had mingled freely in the city's railroad depots. Then in October 1893, just as elite whites were beginning to worry about black participation in Fusion politics, newspapers carried stories of a minor and quite unrelated incident at the Richmond & Danville terminal. A number of African American college students from Biddle University gave a noisy send-off to students traveling to the sister school of Scotia Seminary at Concord and failed to respond with proper deference when a white conductor attempted to quiet them. The *Charlotte Observer* seized the episode as pretext to lash out against African Americans in general. The paper scolded blacks as a disrespectful race who, "particularly on gala occasions, . . . make themselves offensive to the whites about them by loud talking and such characters of misbehaving."[7] The only solution to such chronic insolence, the paper thundered, was for the railroad to designate separate black and white waiting areas. The Richmond & Danville management complied.

As rumors of political alliance between Populists and the black voters of the Republican Party became reality, efforts to physically separate white and black travelers increased. In 1895 Charlotte's African American *Star of Zion* newspaper noted in dismay that the "Seaboard Air Line has . . . had signboards placed over its station room doors bearing these words: 'For White People,' 'For Colored People.' "[8] The following year the U.S. Supreme Court declared that racial separation on America's railroads was indeed constitutional; the decision in the case *Plessy v. Ferguson* became a precedent for "separate but equal" treatment of African Americans in every aspect of life.[9] Emboldened, Charlotte leaders stepped up efforts at separation. When the Southern Railway Company erected its grand 1906 station on West Trade Street, it put a four-foot-high iron fence between the white and colored sections. Whites complained loudly that even this was not enough. The company tore out the fence and substituted a stout floor-to-ceiling wall fully dividing the races.[10]

Segregation also increased markedly in government buildings and in parks. "SEPARATE BIBLES RECOMMENDED: The Color Line to be Drawn in the Courthouse and on the Books," headlined the *Charlotte Observer* on July 21, 1899. New regulations specified that henceforth "the two races be seated and kept separate and apart in the courtrooms and that there be no mixing of the races in the court room, and that a separate Bible be provided for the races to kiss when they are sworn as witnesses."[11] In 1903, when Edward Dilworth Latta announced that his Four Cs company would erect a modest picnic pavilion for black citizens at the end of its Biddle University trolley line, he noted that "the negroes have absolutely no place for recreation or to hold meetings of any kind. The white people have the county court house, Academy of Music, the fair grounds and other places, but the colored race is debarred from these places."[12] Latta's motivation in building the pavilion was not particularly philanthropic; he was under pressure from whites to get black people out of Latta Park. Since the creation of the Dilworth pleasure ground in 1891, whites and blacks had amicably shared its wooded groves for picnics and meetings. White newspapers had reported enthusiastically on the games played by black baseball teams there, and white and black worshipers had gathered together to hear the same preachers at religious revival meetings.[13] In May 1903, just as the summer season was about to begin, the peaceful coexistence ended. It would be "unpleasant, to say the least," rumbled the *Observer*, "for the white people of the community to mingle with, even to the least extent, the negroes at Latta Park another summer."[14] In 1905 park segregation became a matter of municipal law. When Charlotte opened its first city-owned recreation ground that year, Independence Park, the Board of Aldermen passed an ordinance specifying that "no colored person shall be allowed except as nurses to white children."[15]

Leading citizens pushed to force such separation even further. Charlotte papers carried news of places such as the city of Canton and the counties of Mitchell and Madison in North Carolina, which claimed to have expelled all black residents.[16] Continuing the racial drumbeat begun in the 1890s, the

Observer applauded Carolina author Thomas Dixon for his starkly racist play *The Clansman* and ripped President Theodore Roosevelt for professing to "see no difference between negroes and whites save as to color of skin."[17] In 1906 front pages exploded with news of a full-blown race riot in Atlanta. Stirred by rumors of assaults on white women, white mobs rampaged through the city, looting and burning black properties and attacking every African American they saw. Four prosperous black leaders lost their lives, and authorities had to virtually shut down the city for several days until whites could be brought under control; but not a single rioter ever stood trial.[18] To wealthy Charlotteans the behavior of Atlanta's unruly whites simply offered another excuse to further segregate African Americans. "The feeling between whites and blacks is undoubtedly growing more acute and it behooves us to use every reasonable precaution to prevent trouble such as they are now having in Atlanta," said an *Observer* letter writer. "One thing which might be done here to very greatly lessen the danger of trouble would be to have separate compartments for the races in the street cars," he went on. "I am a constant patron of the street cars and I have observed lately that the negroes are making themselves more and more objectionable to the white passengers by their insolent behavior."[19] On March 9, 1907, the state of North Carolina passed legislation requiring segregated seating on all trolleys and interurbans throughout the state.[20] Henceforth on mass transit (including buses, when introduced), black Charlotteans would sit in the back and whites would sit in the front.

African Americans protested the sharpening spatial segregation, but to no avail. "They ought to be disregarded by all decent people," stormed the *Star of Zion* when the first "White" and "Colored" signs appeared at the Seaboard depot in 1895.[21] In 1903 the *Star* rebutted those persons "who are telling the white men of the South that the Negroes are with a few exceptions satisfied with Jim Crow cars and disfranchising laws." Such speakers, said the paper, "are lying, and the white men know it. Who can be satisfied to be humiliated?"[22] When streetcar segregation went into effect, Charlotte's African American ministers staged a short-lived boycott. Other blacks displayed their feelings more directly. The *Charlotte News* reported that a black rider named Joe Robinson was fined $20 and made to post a $500 bond for cursing the conductor and refusing to move to the rear of a Dilworth-bound trolley.[23]

Charlotte's African American elite, who had so recently enjoyed at least a modicum of influence with white leaders, found themselves totally without power to slow the advance of Jim Crow after 1900. Even former allies within the Republican Party felt no incentive to pay attention to a group disfranchised at the ballot box. The realization stung Charlotte's black "better class," ambitious and accomplished men and women such as contractor William Houser, school principal Isabella Wyche, Biddle University president D. J. Sanders, AME Zion bishop Thomas Lomax, and Spanish-American War colonel C. S. L. A. Taylor.[24] Jim Crow cared not how you had served your country or improved your community. If you had black skin, you now rode in the back of the streetcar.

The most successful member of the city's black leadership, Dr. J. T. Williams, expressed the mounting frustrations clearly. Williams had arrived in Charlotte as a schoolteacher in 1881, passed the first state licensing exam to become one of North Carolina's earliest black physicians in 1886, and served two terms as city alderman from Second Ward.[25] In 1898 his political activities caught the eye of President William McKinley, who appointed him U.S. consul to Sierra Leone. Overseas in the service of his country from 1898 to 1905, Williams looked on in dismay at disfranchisement and the rising Jim Crow tide.[26] In 1905 he wrote friends in Charlotte: "I have learned more of the mercantile brand of trade since being out here than I ever thought it possible to acquire. And the more I see of it, the more thoroughly I am convinced that it is what we in the States need to give us power." Continued Williams, "It appears that though late we as a race are beginning to learn the fact from bitter past experience that money will accomplish what legislation will not."[27]

FIRST WARD: CREATION OF A BLACK NEIGHBORHOOD

First Ward, the center city district where we took our imaginary walk via the 1876 city directory and Beers map (see Chapter 1), provides a good place to follow the creation of a black neighborhood around the turn of the century. The 1876 data, together with similar snapshots for 1889 and 1910, show the shifting racial geography of the district.[28] Close examination of a sample of ordinary and elite houses provides insights on the process of change. The strategy of directed opportunity—particularly providing new rental housing in certain parts of the Ward while eliminating it in others—transformed a salt-and-pepper racial arrangement into a pattern of sharply defined black clusters by the 1910s.

During the 1876–89 period, changes in First Ward land use remained minor. Back in 1876 the ward had possessed a substantial African American population scattered almost randomly throughout the district (see color fig. 1). Black residents could be found next to whites on nearly every block in the district; only three block fronts were all black. By 1889 this virtually patternless arrangement was giving way to what geographer John Radford, in his study of Charleston, has called "micro-segregation."[29] Charlotte's 1889 directory data showed most First Ward block fronts as either all-black or all-white. But beyond that, the degree of separation was minor. Black block fronts alternated with white ones in almost random order. Only a single block in the ward had African American houses on all four sides. Throughout First Ward, for every row of three or four black cottages, there was a row of three or four white cottages around the corner, just up the road, or even across the street.

Between 1889 and 1910 change accelerated dramatically (see color fig. 2). Microsegregation vanished, to be replaced by a pattern of sizable black clusters. African American dwellings concentrated along First Ward's three lowest-lying avenues: Sixth Street, Eighth Street, and Tenth Street. Blacks supplanted whites in several places, such as on Eighth between Davidson and Myers Streets. More surprisingly, whites moved into some previously black block fronts, especially on Fifth Street, which now became entirely white.[30] Only one avenue retained any remnant of random alternation; one could still walk down Seventh Street and pass block fronts of white houses alternating with block fronts of black dwellings. Otherwise, randomness had disappeared. The distance between the races was still modest by today's standards; both blacks and whites continued to live in First Ward. But in place of the salt-and-pepper mixing of 1876, discrete black and white areas were clear by 1910, alternating like patchwork squares in a quilt.

White real estate investors operated as the active agents in this transformation. Many of the dwellings that made up First Ward's new African American clusters were shotgun houses erected in groups during the decade following 1900. Architectural historians define the "shotgun" as a narrow, one-story cottage with two or three rooms lined up one behind the other. A shotgun house had no hallway; if someone shot a gun through the front door, the bullet would pass through every living space. Some scholars now believe that the layout had roots in African American tradition, as a folk house-type carried by immigrants from Haiti to New Orleans around 1800.[31] By the time the shotgun reached North Carolina a century later, however, it had become simply an economical arrangement for rental quarters. After 1900 white investors began building shotgun houses by the score in Charlotte's emerging black neighborhoods.

John G. Hood developed the largest such project in First Ward. A wealthy white man who owned a downtown department store and resided in a hand-

FIG. 31. HOOD'S SHOTGUN HOUSES, FIRST WARD
Long, narrow shotgun houses characterized districts built for rental to African Americans after 1900 in Charlotte. Houses in this photo—looking up East Sixth Street from North Davidson Street in First Ward—were developed in 1902 by white department store owner John G. Hood. (Photograph from the 1950s, courtesy of the Robinson-Spangler Carolina Room, Public Library of Charlotte and Mecklenburg County)

some house on North Tryon Street, Hood purchased a half-block of vacant land on East Sixth Street in 1902 and filled it with shotgun cottages.[32] To maximize the number of dwelling lots, Hood carved a dead-end alley into the heart of the block. Only one or two such alleys had shown up on the 1877 Beers map of Charlotte; in 1910 they would be a defining characteristic of the city's black neighborhoods. By the time Hood finished work, his property held twenty-seven shotgun houses, crowded ten feet apart in close-packed rows, with front porches touching the street. Hood built his cottages cheaply, for maximum short-term return. Five years after completion, he sold the project to a real estate firm headed by two fellow department store owners, J. H. Little and William Henry Belk. The twenty-seven houses, plus twenty-two undeveloped lots, changed hands for just $13,500.[33] By comparison, a single new house in Charlotte's emerging white-collar suburbs cost around $3,000 to $4,000. After harvesting rents for a few years, Little and Belk in turn sold the property to another investment group.

Most of the people who first rented Hood's shotguns in 1902 found employment as unskilled laborers or in what would now be called the service sector.[34]

FIG. 32. MAKING A SHOTGUN HOUSE A HOME
(Courtesy of the Robinson-Spangler Carolina Room, Public Library of Charlotte and
Mecklenburg County)

Richard Dratford worked as a laborer for a coal and wood dealer. Charles Coletrain shoveled coal as a fireman for the Orient Mill, one of the few jobs open to blacks at the cotton factories. Lee White acted as porter at the New York Life Insurance Company office; many Charlotte businesses employed such a man to run errands. Women headed several of the households in Hood's shotguns. Hattie Brown served as a cook; Lizzie Watson was one of many listed as a nurse, which in this era meant a caretaker of small children; Amanda Nichols, Juno Wallace, and Annie Johnson all worked as self-employed laundresses, taking in washing for white families. This limited roster of occupations—laborer, porter, cook, nurse, laundress—represented the bulk of job opportunities for African Americans in Charlotte during the early twentieth century.

For such hard-working men and women, Hood's shotguns likely represented quite desirable housing in 1902. By constructing rows of fresh dwellings specifically for blacks, developers implicitly honored the rising economic power of Charlotte's African American community. Two or three new, clean rooms to live in, with a shady and inviting front porch, constituted attractive quarters in a city where black laborers had previously often found only shacks and shanties to rent. Later, as years of absentee landlords took their toll, shotgun houses would lose all appeal among black Charlotteans. In the 1900s, though, Hood and other investors had no trouble keeping such projects fully rented.

A further indication of the initial desirability of First Ward's new shotguns was the presence of elite African American residents nearby. Some, like Thad Tate, had built their handsome houses in the hopeful years of the late nineteenth century, when First Ward remained a completely integrated district. Tate's elegant brick Italianate-style dwelling stood on Seventh Street near Caldwell, still an integrated block in 1910. Tate reigned as the era's major spokesman for black Charlotte, a position facilitated by his ownership of the swank downtown barbershop where local white leaders came for haircuts. Among Tate's successes was convincing Cameron Morrison, the Charlottean who served as North Carolina governor in the 1920s, to create the state's first reform school for black youth. Morrison Training School near Rockingham gave juvenile delinquents an alternative to chain gang labor. Thad Tate and his wife, Mary, raised ten offspring in their Seventh Street house, and neighbors fondly referred to the ensemble as "The Dozen Family."[35] When a row of shotgun cottages went up immediately behind the residence in the 1900s, the Tate household made no move to leave.

FIG. 33. THAD TATE RESIDENCE, FIRST WARD
This photograph, taken sometime around the turn of the century, shows the handsome
brick dwelling of Thad Tate, one of Charlotte's leading black citizens, on Seventh Street
in First Ward. (Courtesy of the Robinson-Spangler Carolina Room, Public Library of
Charlotte and Mecklenburg County).

Other elite black dwellings joined Tate's in First Ward around the turn of
the century, many clustering on North Myers Street near Little Rock AME
Zion Church. *Star of Zion* publisher and AME Zion bishop George Wylie
Clinton commissioned the largest house, a two-story Colonial Revival manse
with a columned porch that wrapped around three sides. Neighbors recalled
the Clinton house as the neighborhood's elegant social center, with a yard-
man and a cook. Marie Clay Clinton, the bishop's wife and an alumnae of the
famed touring Fisk Jubilee Singers, presided over receptions and classical music recitals. "It's just like yesterday almost. I can see her," reminisced former
neighbor Thelma Colston McKnight years later. "She would be dressed so
fine, getting in that horse and surrey and driving off."[36] Just four doors from the
elegant Clinton home stood a row of shotgun houses.

At the same time that developers provided African Americans with opportunities to rent or buy in one part of First Ward, in other sections of the district
black people now found themselves distinctly unwelcome. Around North
College Street close to North Tryon Street, blocks that had once held scatter-
ings of African American residents became increasingly all-white. In 1906, for

instance, white citizens complained to the health department about a well that served six cottages rented by black families on Eighth Street near College Street. The location stood outside the emerging black neighborhood, and that was the real reason motivating the complaint, suspected the owner, an established white patrician named H. M. Wilder. Neighbors wanted "to destroy the property and run out the tenants, who are negroes, from the midst of the 'nouveau riche,'" he charged. "It seems to be a principle of life that when people become rich they suddenly develop an aversion to poor white folks and to negroes."[37]

SECOND WARD: BECOMING BROOKLYN

During the years that First Ward sorted out into separate black and white sections, other African American neighborhoods coalesced within each of the center city's four wards (see fig. 31). In Fourth Ward two small clusters appeared, one near Seventh and Graham Streets, and the other at the north end of Poplar Street. A bigger cluster formed in Third Ward around Clinton Chapel AME Zion Church, extending along the district's railroad tracks. Charlotte's largest and most important black neighborhood sprang into being in Second Ward. Nicknamed Brooklyn, it became a veritable city within the city during the years after 1900, with a full complement of community institutions, including Charlotte's black main strect.

Before 1900 Third Ward rather than Second Ward seemed the logical candidate to become the hub of black Charlotte. With higher and better-drained land, Third Ward attracted leading African American churches, academies, and affiliated institutions following the Civil War. Along with Clinton Chapel, which represented the region's strongest black-run denomination, Third Ward also contained Charlotte's First Baptist (Colored) Church as well as the Episcopalians' black "mission church," St. Michael and All Angels.[38] One private black educational institution, the Peabody School, opened in 1870 and numbered among its teachers the young Charles Chesnutt, who later became America's first celebrated African American novelist.[39] A second important academy debuted in 1883 when St. Michael's launched its Training and Industrial School.[40] St. Michael's also fostered creation of the Good Samaritan Hospital in Third Ward in 1891. Its solid brick edifice on West Stonewall Street near Mint Street ranked among the earliest black hospitals in the South.[41]

Despite having religious and service institutions, Third Ward lacked a

FIG. 34. GOOD SAMARITAN HOSPITAL, THIRD WARD
Good Samaritan Hospital was Charlotte's black hospital from the late nineteenth century
through the 1950s. Located at West Stonewall and South Mint Streets, Good Sam formed
an anchor for the African American community in Third Ward. (Photo ca. 1900 from
Protestant Episcopal Church in the U.S., *Church's Work among Negroes*; reproduction
courtesy of the North Caroliniana Collection, University of North Carolina, Chapel Hill)

major civic component: a business district. Indeed, thirty years after Emancipation, none of Charlotte's wards possessed a noticeable black commercial
concentration. Most black businessmen into the 1890s located their enterprises right downtown, among those of whites.[42] African American shops appeared particularly in the area around the cotton wharf, with its building stock
of small storefronts and its steady trade of farmers coming in from the country.
In the 1897 city directory, for example, the north side of the 200 block of East
Trade Street held the Queen City Drug Company store owned by J. T. Williams, doctors' offices for Williams and for another black physician named
M. T. Pope, the moneylending operation of "colored financier" J. T. Sanders,
Smith & Hall's ice cream parlor, J. J. Guerard's barber shop, W. P. Weather-
spoon's candy kitchen, plus the offices of black lawyer J. S. Leary and two
black-owned insurance companies.[43] The block was by no means exclusively
African American, however. It held fully as many white enterprises as black,
including several retail and wholesale groceries, restaurants and saloons, a
meat market, a furniture store, and the offices of prestigious white economic
leaders such as cotton buyer J. H. Sloan.

The tendency for black enterprises to locate among white businesses down-

FIG. 35. MYERS STREET SCHOOL, SECOND WARD
Neighbors called Myers Street School the Jacob's Ladder School, a testament to both its
uplifting power and its spindly exterior stairs. Established in the 1880s, the facility became
the nucleus of a thriving black neighborhood in Second Ward—or Brooklyn, as the area
became proudly known. (Courtesy of the Robinson-Spangler Carolina Room, Public Library of Charlotte and Mecklenburg County)

town was underscored in 1894 when AME Zion officials moved the denomination's publishing house to Charlotte. Bishop Thomas Lomax chose a two-
story commercial structure at 234 South College Street and remodeled it as
the Varrick Building, in honor of an early leader of the denomination. The
structure held printing presses and publication offices as well as rental space
for other black businesses.[44] Despite this considerable investment, the AME
Zion Publishing House's tenure downtown was brief. Before the 1900s were
out, it would depart for a new black business district in Brooklyn.

Second Ward's metamorphosis from a humble district of rude cabins
known as Logtown into the neighborhood proudly called Brooklyn seems to
have begun slowly in the late 1880s.[45] White Republican landowner W. R.
Myers gave land in Second Ward at Myers and Stonewall Streets for construction of Mecklenburg County's first black graded school building in 1886.[46]
The Myers Street School, a wood-frame, two-story structure with spindly
exterior stairs leading to the upper classrooms, was not much to look at. But

parents affectionately nicknamed it the Jacob's Ladder School and filled it with children. For many years no other such graded facility existed in the county, and ambitious families often moved into town to get schooling for their youngsters. "There are but thirty-six more white children of school age, than colored children, in the city," noted Charlotte officials already in late 1887. "This is probably explained by the fact that large numbers of colored children come here from the country to secure the benefits of the free graded school."[47]

As up-and-coming families boosted the population, the name "Logtown" seemed less and less appropriate. By the late 1890s two of Charlotte's five black meeting halls were located in the district, and the city's leading black physicians, Dr. J. T. Williams and Dr. N. B. Houser, both owned homes there. In 1904 the city's black Brevard Street Library opened its doors in Second Ward, "the first free . . . colored library" in the South, according to the *Charlotte Observer*.[48] The facility came as an ironic side effect of sharpening municipal segregation; the famous steel millionaire Andrew Carnegie had just given Charlotte a grant to construct a white public library, and in order to justify barring black citizens from the new structure, city aldermen allocated a modest sum to build a separate black building. A distinguished board of six African American leaders, including Thad Tate and St. Michael's rector P. P. Alston, directed the Brevard Street Library, and black librarian Lydia Schenck took charge of daily activities, which included fund raising, since the city allocation included neither furniture nor books. African American citizens came together enthusiastically for a series of benefits, highlighted by baseball games in which local black dignitaries playfully paired off as the "Fats" versus the "Leans."[49] Such efforts forged an intense community pride. Newspapers of the day were full of news of the bustling Northern town of Brooklyn, just being annexed into New York City as a quasi-independent borough. The name "Brooklyn," with its progressive urban cachet and connotation of a town within a town, neatly fit the emerging neighborhood within Charlotte's Second Ward. No one knows who first suggested it, but by the 1900s black Charlotteans were proudly using the new moniker.[50]

Brooklyn took on its commercial aspect at almost the same moment. Soon after the white supremacy campaign of the late 1890s, city aldermen began threatening to remove African American businessmen from Charlotte's central business district. One official in 1902, for instance, singled out "the 'nasty little negro restaurants' on East Trade Street, declaring that they should be taxed so heavily they should have to leave the street."[51] It is not clear whether such proposals actually became policy, but the chilling climate was unmistakable. With whites closing off opportunities downtown, black entrepreneurs looked for locations elsewhere and soon settled on Brooklyn as a locale for business.

A fast-growing enterprise called the Afro-American Mutual Insurance Company inaugurated the move to Brooklyn. Incorporated by local businessmen led by Thad Tate, the Afro-American Mutual promised that "an Afro-American policy, by an Afro-American agent, made by Afro-American clerks, on an Afro-American husband[,] an Afro-American wife, or an Afro-American child, makes an Afro-American home independent in the hours of sickness or death."[52] Such words echoed proposals then being offered by many national black leaders, from Booker T. Washington to W. E. B. DuBois, who saw economic self-sufficiency as a means for African Americans to advance in the face of Jim Crow.[53] "Trade," as J. T. Williams had written from Africa, might yet "accomplish what legislation will not." The Afro-American Mutual's appeal to racial self-reliance, together with an affordable payment plan beginning at five cents per week, caught the imagination of black wage earners in Charlotte and the surrounding region. The business prospered, soon outgrowing its rented space on East Trade Street. In 1907 the company launched construction of a three-story building in the 400 block of East Second Street in the heart of Brooklyn, just around the corner from the Brevard Street Library.[54] To create the structure, the company hired black builder W. W. Smith. Smith had apprenticed with William Houser and had gained a reputation as a master mason and contractor for both whites and blacks, executing the brickwork on the 1902 Grace AME Zion Church on South Brevard Street, among other projects.[55] For the Afro-American Mutual, he not only handled construction but also drew the architectural design. The Victorian facade featured cream brick enlivened with arches, corbelling, and red brick trim. The company liked the result so much that it asked Smith to create a smaller edition for a branch office in Rock Hill, South Carolina.

The Afro-American Mutual's proud structure on Charlotte's Second Street became a beacon attracting businessmen to the opportunities of Brooklyn. Around 1910 the AME Zion Publishing House made the decision to leave downtown. It hired W. W. Smith to design new quarters at Brevard and Second opposite the Afro-American Mutual. The large, three-story building, again in Smith's trademark cream and red brick, became a commanding presence in the neighborhood.[56] Over the next fifteen years a dozen additional buildings sprang up in its shadow, providing space for more than thirty

Office, The Afro-American Mutual
Insurance Co., Rock Hill, S. C.

Home Office, The Afro-American
Mutual Insurance Company.
412 East 2nd Street.

Sickness is Sure to Come: Death Follows.

If you were taken Suddenly Sick to-night and die, WHAT THEN?

From five cents, (5c.) to twenty-five cents, (25c.) per week when you are
well, brings you from one dollar, ($1) to five dollars ($5) per week during
sickness and from fifteen dollars ($15) to seventy-five dollars ($75) at death.
Who in your family will need it first?

An Afro-American policy, by an Afro-American agent, made by Afro-
American clerks, on an Afro-American husband an Afro-American wife, or
an Afro-American child, makes an Afro-American home independent in the
hours of sickness or death.

A Busy Day in Home Office Afro-American Mutua
Insurance Campany.

FIG. 36. AFRO-AMERICAN MUTUAL INSURANCE

Construction of the three-story main office of the Afro-American Mutual on East Second
Street about 1907 marked the beginning of the exodus of African American businesses
from downtown Charlotte to the black main street within Brooklyn. Both the main office
(no longer extant) and the Rock Hill branch (still standing) show the distinctive brickwork
of black mason and architect W. W. Smith. (Source: Watson, *Colored Charlotte*; from the
collection of Queens College, Charlotte)

FIG. 37. SOUTH BREVARD STREET IN BROOKLYN, SECOND WARD
South Brevard Street became a major avenue of Brooklyn, Charlotte's leading black
neighborhood after 1900. At the left is the residence of Dr. J. T. Williams, teacher and
physician who served as U.S. consul to Sierra Leone in West Africa. Two doors beyond it
stands Grace AME Zion Church, founded by African American temperance advocates
and built by brick mason W. W. Smith. In the distance is Smith's Mecklenburg Investment Company Building, holding stores and offices of black professionals. (Photograph
from the 1950s or 1960s, courtesy of the Robinson-Spangler Carolina Room, Public
Library of Charlotte and Mecklenburg County)

enterprises. By the 1920s Brooklyn was home to black restaurants, grocers,
drugstores, barbers and hairdressers, shoemakers, undertakers, and the Palace
movie theater. Businesses filled the 400 block of East Second Street and
spilled down adjacent blocks of Second and around the corner onto Brevard
Street.[57]

With Thad Tate, J. T. Williams was a driving force in the upbuilding of
Brooklyn, and the range of his activities illustrates the district's vibrancy. In
1905, five months after his letter from Africa, Williams platted a section of
house lots along Hill and Vance Streets at the south edge of Second Ward, a
subdivision he named Williamsburg.[58] Most Charlotteans probably missed
the allusion—the widely publicized restoration of Colonial Williamsburg in
Virginia would not begin until the 1920s—but J. T. Williams must have taken
quiet pleasure in linking his project to a birthplace of American liberty. When
Williams left government service, he stepped up efforts at economic development. He served as a trustee of the AME Zion Publishing House when the
organization moved to Brooklyn. In the early 1910s he bought land next to the
Afro-American Mutual building and built a three-story brick structure called

the Hotel Williams, one of the few decent accommodations available to black visitors barred from white hotels by Jim Crow.[59] The Queen City Drug Company, which Williams had founded on East Trade Street, moved to a new building on South Brevard in the late 1910s.[60] Williams himself lived nearby at 205 South Brevard Street and in the early 1920s had his one-story home expanded into a fashionable two-story residence trimmed in the Bungalow style.[61] In 1921 Williams and Tate organized Charlotte's leading black professionals into a cooperative known as the Mecklenburg Investment Company. Doctors, dentists, and lawyers were finding it almost impossible to obtain downtown office space. "The businesses would have to go in some little place where there was just a little room, somewhere to be rented," recalled Tate's daughter. "You'd have to climb up some steps to get there. So that's when they decided to put up this building."[62] The group erected the MIC Building on Brevard at Third Street, designed by W. W. Smith with shops at street level, office suites above, and a meeting hall for fraternal organizations on the third floor. Today the edifice still stands, its exuberant cream and red brickwork recently restored as a reminder of Brooklyn's business heyday.

BIDDLEVILLE: FROM RIM VILLAGE TO URBAN NEIGHBORHOOD

As black neighborhoods coalesced within the four central wards of Charlotte, the expanding city also reached out to swallow up African American rim villages. Biddleville off West Trade Street, Greenville/Irwinville out North Graham Street, Dulstown along North Tryon Street, Myers Quarter (updated as Cherry in 1891) beyond East Trade Street, and Blandville near South Tryon Street had all begun as informal African American settlements in the nineteenth century.[63] Now all came into the city as nuclei for urban black neighborhoods. Biddleville survives as perhaps the best-preserved of those districts today, with village streets surrounded by later subdivisions, including Western Heights and Wesley Heights. Biddleville provides a case study of the process of change on the urban periphery.

Even before the Jacob's Ladder public school provided a magnet for the creation of Brooklyn, the institution of higher learning today known as Johnson C. Smith University was already attracting other prosperous African American families to Biddleville. Founded in Logtown in 1867 by Presbyterian missionaries with help from the federal Freedmen's Bureau and Philadelphia philanthropist Mrs. Henry J. Biddle, the school originally was called Biddle Institute, honoring the philanthropist's husband who had died in the Union army fighting for black freedom.[64] A year after classes began, white Republican landowner W. R. Myers donated a hilltop site west of the city, near where West Trade Street forked into two country roads leading toward Rozelles Ferry and Beatties Ford on the distant Catawba River. Salvaging lumber from the former Confederate naval yard downtown, school members erected a classroom building, a pair of professor's houses, and three small student cottages named Asia, Africa, and Australia. In 1871 the Reverend Stephen Mattoon, institute president, personally purchased fifty-five acres across Beatties Ford Road from campus and over the next forty-five years slowly sold it in small lots to African Americans who wanted to settle near the school.[65]

Biddleville and Biddle Institute prospered during the late nineteenth century. Initially the school offered mostly high school courses, a necessity since no black public high schools yet existed in the South. As more and more students mastered this "preparatory" work, the institution added college classes and in 1876 changed its name to Biddle University in recognition of the advance. In 1885 Dr. George E. Davis became the school's first black professor, and in 1891 the Reverend Daniel J. Sanders took charge as its first African American president.[66] Brick buildings replaced the initial wooden ones. Most notable were the ornate Victorian 1884 classroom/auditorium/office structure called Biddle Hall, whose soaring clocktower could be easily seen from downtown Charlotte, and the 1895 Carter Hall, whose delicate woodwork and brick corner turrets were constructed by the students themselves.[67] Biddleville grew, too. Other white landowners offered land adjacent to the Mattoon plat, and by the 1890s the village extended along the west side of Beatties Ford Road all the way from West Trade Street to Mattoon Street at the Seaboard Railroad (Brookshire Freeway route today). A map of the village in 1892 showed three rows of houses along what are now Solomon Street, Campus Street, and Beatties Ford Road.[68] This linear arrangement was a striking feature of all Charlotte rim villages; no houses appeared on the cross streets. The lines of cottages called to mind the rows of cabins seen in slave quarters on some antebellum plantations. Whether the layout represented a pattern learned in slavery days or came from some other source, it was noticeably different from the around-the-block form favored in white neighborhoods.

By the late 1880s Biddleville was already beginning to take on urban attributes. The 1889 Charlotte city directory, the first to cover the district, showed nearly 200 adults living in Biddleville. The settlement had its own churches, cemetery, and grocery store. Many residents listed their occupations as teacher or student at the college or as farmer, evidently journeying out to surrounding fields each day. Slightly over half of Biddleville inhabitants, however, indicated urban employment. A considerable number worked as laborers and laundresses. A smaller but still sizable percentage held more skilled positions: blacksmith, brick mason, carpenter, chambermaid for cotton man Robert M. Oates, and butler at the downtown Buford Hotel. Such men and women had to walk two miles or more each day to hold jobs in Charlotte yet live near the university. Biddleville in 1889 was in some respects a village, yet also part of the city.

Urban ties strengthened as the twentieth century dawned. The university continued to grow, thanks to energetic president Henry L. McCrorey, who secured grants from industrialists Andrew Carnegie and James B. Duke for important new structures during the 1910s and 1920s.[69] A wealthy Pittsburgh widow named Jane Berry Smith became the institution's lead donor in these years, endowing eight additional buildings, and in 1923 McCrorey gratefully rededicated the school as Johnson C. Smith University to honor her deceased husband. The university's growing intellectual offerings increased Biddleville's attraction among Charlotte's black strivers. Extension of streetcar service along West Trade Street to the foot of the college hill in 1903 facilitated commuting, and in 1906 the Four Cs laid tracks all the way to "the top of the hill, opposite Biddle University."[70] Telephone service arrived about the same time, an indication that the district possessed numerous potential customers willing to pay for contact with the center city.[71] By the 1910s many Biddleville residents commuted into town, notably a contingent of public school teachers led by the principals of Second Ward High and First Ward's Alexander Street School. Napoleon Brown, raised the son of a Baptist deacon in the neighborhood a few years later, remembered it as a most desirable address: "When you said you lived in Biddleville, that was it!"[72]

Not only did Biddleville become firmly connected to Charlotte, but new subdivisions also sprang up encompassing the old village. A gaggle of white-owned houses known as Seversville had long stood just below the university on the south side of West Trade Street. In the 1890s, as the fashion for suburban living took hold in Charlotte, developers began to buy up the surrounding farmers' fields and carve them into streets and house lots. Seversville grew with the addition of Bruns, Auten, and Duckworth Streets. In 1893 Western Heights filled a triangular tract just north of West Trade Street adjoining the university. During the 1910s Wesley Heights pushed south from West Trade all the way to West Morehead Street, including South Summit Avenue and Grandin Road.[73] In the 1920s Roslyn Heights appeared in the triangle between

FIG. 38. JOHNSON C. SMITH UNIVERSITY CAMPUS
This postcard view, probably from the late 1920s, shows the campus of Johnson C. Smith University (originally Biddle Institute), which formed the heart of Charlotte's Biddleville neighborhood. On the left is Biddle Hall, erected in the 1880s. In the background stands the Carter Hall dormitory, constructed by students at the turn of the century. To the right is the Carnegie Library, built with aid from industrialist Andrew Carnegie in 1911. (Courtesy of the Robinson-Spangler Carolina Room, Public Library of Charlotte and Mecklenburg County)

West Trade and Rozelles Ferry Road.[74] The projects added streets and traffic to the old West Trade Street/Beatties Ford/Rozelles Ferry Road intersection, until people took to calling it and the surrounding area by the urban name "Five Points."

Surprisingly, despite location next to the black university, the Five Points subdivisions did not fill initially with African Americans. Every one of the new streets held white homebuyers. The suburbs' fate over the years offered vivid evidence of the drawing and redrawing of the color line in Charlotte.

Western Heights, the first to develop, experienced the greatest changes. White real estate developer W. S. Alexander launched the project in 1893, almost contemporaneously with Dilworth across town and well before the full fury of white supremacy.[75] From the first, Alexander clearly expected that both whites and blacks would buy lots in the district, which lay along the university campus on one side and bordered West Trade Street a reasonable walk from downtown on the other. Indeed, lot purchasers the first year included one black person and half a dozen whites. In the second year, "colored financier" J. T. Sanders purchased a number of lots for resale, and whites kept buying, often on the same streets and blocks.[76] During the late 1890s and 1900s, however, the subdivision began to sort out along an informal color line. By the time the city directory started covering the district in the 1910s, white families lived on Western Heights's lower blocks off Trade Street, while black families lived on the upper blocks next to the university. A memoir written by Mamie Garvin Fields, a schoolteacher who moved into 206 Flint Street in 1914 with her brick mason husband, provided a picture of African American life in the up-and-coming suburb:

> The people we knew were progressive. They believed in education, and they believed in buying property. Especially, they wanted to own their own houses. Some built other houses too, for an investment, which is how we got the first house we lived in together. I kept hearing about a fine, new development where Negroes were building, and about one little cottage in particular. A certain Professor Douglass, who taught at Biddle University, was building a cottage to rent out. . . .
>
> That little cottage was the perfect "honeymoon house." Looking in through the windows, we saw a parlor, dining room, kitchen, and two bedrooms, all on one floor—just enough room for a young couple and any guest we wanted to have. . . . Set back from the street, it had a good-sized yard in front and a planted path leading up to the door, which was between two windows with flower boxes. Very romantic, like a picture out of a magazine. . . .
>
> White people lived very near. . . . Most of the blacks close around us had more education. They told me to be careful of the white neighbors, because although they might stop to say something nice about the corn you had growing in your garden, yet still they called themselves better than you. And they might say "Howdy-do" at your door, but they would notice what you had, and some were begrudgeful, so look out for the white neighbors.[77]

The mid-subdivision color line proved too informal as Jim Crow came into full flower. By the 1920s Western Heights had become entirely African American. In the course of the transition, speculators snapped up the remaining vacant lots and filled out the neighborhood with shotgun houses.[78]

While Western Heights became all-black, the rest of the Five Points area remained white for decades—a striking illustration of the patchwork pattern of residence seen throughout Charlotte during the first half of the twentieth century. West Trade Street, with its busy traffic, evidently provided enough of a barrier to make whites comfortable. Distance from black areas was a factor, too. Roslyn Heights, closest to black Biddleville, developed with small and cheaply built cottages mostly inhabited by blue-collar whites. Wesley Heights, somewhat farther away, filled with larger houses owned by white business owners and managers, a fashionable white-collar neighborhood similar in every respect to the other streetcar suburbs then appearing around Charlotte. Not until the 1960s would the Trade Street color line break and Biddleville–Five Points become a single all-black neighborhood.

WASHINGTON HEIGHTS: BLACK STREETCAR SUBURB

Mamie Garvin Fields, happy in her honeymoon cottage in Western Heights, represented the vanguard of a small but energetic African American middle class in Charlotte. In 1915 local strivers compiled *Colored Charlotte: Published in Connection with the Fiftieth Anniversary of the Freedom of the Negro.*[79] The lavishly illustrated booklet celebrated accomplishment in the face of Jim Crow. "Other people have been and are still diligent in advertising our short-comings," explained Bishop George W. Clinton in the introduction, "and if we would counteract these damaging influences we must be no less zealous in collecting and publishing our best achievements." Tables set forth impressive statistics: African Americans owned 805 homes in the city, 144 businesses, and over $1 million in taxable property. Pictures filled the pages—of black businesses such as the Afro-American Mutual Insurance Company and the AME Zion Publishing House, of dozens of black-owned homes in Brooklyn and elsewhere throughout the city, of the Brevard Street Library and the Myers Street School, of ministers and churches and social organizations, and of black leaders, including J. T. Williams, Thad Tate, Col. C. S. L. A. Taylor, newspaper publisher W. C. Smith, and "Lawyer J. T. Sanders, the Colored Financier of Charlotte who owns and operates three Drug Stores, one Barber Shop, one Restaurant, one Hotel, one News Paper, Moving-Picture Building and large Real Estate Business,"[80] *Colored Charlotte* emphasized that such well-known individuals represented only a small part of the trend toward self-improvement. Below the black elite of doctors, lawyers, religious leaders, and businessmen there was a growing black "middling" group. These included the city's thirty-nine public school teachers, fifty-five carpenters, eighty brick-layers and plasterers, proprietors of twenty-four black-owned grocery stores, railway employees, and ministers of the smaller churches. Also in this group were the cream of the city's service workers: domestics for wealthy families, hotel workers, and those laborers and drivers who won long-term employment with a particular firm.

Such middling black citizens were often not as wealthy as Charlotte's white middle class, but they shared many of the same values and desires.[81] Like Mamie Garvin Fields they "were progressive" and "believed in buying property. Especially, they wanted to buy their own homes." Through hard work and careful saving they could afford the down payment for a modest house lot and the nickel fares for a daily trolley commute. To a family who had worked its way up from penniless ex-slavery in two generations, a house in the suburbs represented an exciting dream.

In 1912 the white real estate developer W. S. Alexander, having discovered this market in Western Heights, set out to reap its full potential by creating a full-fledged African American streetcar suburb called Washington Heights.[82] He purchased a tract of farmland half a mile beyond the university, along the west side of Beatties Ford Road, and hired African American real estate agent C. H. Watson to help develop the new district. The suburb's appellation paid homage to the famous advocate of black uplift, Booker T. Washington, and his name also graced Booker Avenue, the district's broad and gently curving central boulevard. The other main streets commemorated local African American leaders. Davis Avenue and Douglas Street honored Biddle professors George E. Davis and R. L Douglas. Tate Street celebrated businessman Thad Tate. Sanders Street took its name either from pioneering black university president Daniel J. Sanders or from "colored financier" J. T. Sanders. A glen called Lincoln Park (never built) was planned for a hollow near the end of Booker Street.[83] Soon advertisements touted:

> WASHINGTON HEIGHTS, the beautiful Negro suburb, about two miles from the heart of the city, with streetcars running through it. It is high and dry, being the highest point around Charlotte. It has beautiful streets convenient to churches and schools. In this suburb is to be found some of the best people and some of the handsomest homes to be found in any part of Charlotte. Persons planning to locate in Charlotte would do well to see "Washington Heights" before buying else-where. In this place are to be found some beautiful lots for sale on very easy terms and at a very low price.
>
> For further information write, C. H. WATSON, 412 E. Second Street.[84]

In addition to ordinary profit motives, W. S. Alexander had another reason to create a black suburb: its opportunities would direct African Americans away from the lily-white Elizabeth Heights subdivision he was completing on the opposite side of town. He told the white newspapers, "Washington Heights will be for the colored race exclusively, and will mean to them what such suburbs as Myers Park, Elizabeth Heights and Dilworth mean to Charlotte. The developers propose to cause Washington Heights to be a place of tone and character."[85] Alexander's careless contrast between "the colored race" and "Charlotte" spoke volumes about white attitudes in the Jim Crow era: to white leaders, black people were simply not part of the citizenry. African Americans likely winced at the verbal slight, but they welcomed Alexander's "place of tone and character" and the opportunities it offered for suburban home ownership.

Buyers eagerly snapped up Washington Heights's 200 house lots, with more than 40 changing hands during the first two years alone.[86] Parcels each measured 50 feet wide by 150 feet deep, a standard size in other Charlotte suburbs. Alexander pegged prices a bit below those in white districts, where lots usually sold for $500 and up. Washington Heights lots ranged from $500 right on the Beatties Ford Road streetcar line to as little as $300 on Tate Street, a two-block walk from transit. As in most streetcar suburbs of the day, the farther one had to walk from the trolley, the less one paid for property. Buyers largely came from the black middle class. Among the first purchasers was J. M. Springs, who with his wife, Bessie, operated a tailoring and cleaning shop downtown on College Street. Announced the *Star of Zion*, "Mr. and Mrs. J. M. Springs who have for sometime occupied rooms in the William's Hotel moved into their newly built and modernly equipped home on Washington Heights this week. Congratulations."[87] Early neighbors included prominent businesswoman Lethia Jones, who operated Charlotte's first beauty salon, a downtown establishment serving white clientele.[88] Jones purchased four Washington Heights lots and built rental houses on three of them, reserving the fourth for her own home. Other investment-minded buyers bought parcels for rental or resale while continuing to live elsewhere. University professors Rev. Yorke Jones and R. L. Douglas, Brooklyn grocer W. M. Williams, and Third Ward barber Eli Jewell, for instance, all held lots in absentia. The largest such buyer was black real estate professional I. D. L. Torrence, who headed a company called Progress Investment Realty. Over time Torrence and various partners acquired thirteen Washington Heights parcels and erected houses for rental.

By 1931, when city directories first listed Washington Heights streets, the subdivision had become a substantial neighborhood of over 160 households. *Star of Zion* editor Rev. W. H. Davenport resided in the district's largest dwelling, a two-story brick house at 1223 Beatties Ford Ford. Leading physician Dr. N. B. Houser lived close by on Beatties Ford, and important residents on adjacent streets included Luther Howard, bell captain at the elegant new Hotel Charlotte, and Samuel Peterson, headwaiter at the downtown Stonewall Cafe. At least half a dozen ministers commuted to parishes in all parts of Charlotte, among them Rev. P. R. Washington, who pastored Stonewall Baptist Church in Brooklyn. A number of residents worked for the Southern Railway, an important source of secure jobs for African Americans amid the tough times of Jim Crow: John Lyles, who owned one of the suburb's few two-story houses, porter L. C. Boger, machinist helper M. L. Dunham, and cashier J. C. Nelson.

Interestingly, this neighborhood of "tone and character" did not exclude unskilled blue-collar individuals. The tendency of the wealthy to separate themselves from poorer citizens was not nearly as evident in black Charlotte as it was in white Charlotte in this era. Many Washington Heights renters described themselves in the city directory as "laborer," "maid," "driver," or "helper." So did some owners, such as laborer William Lindsay at 2228 Sanders Street and Buick dealership helper Gaither Alexander at 2221 Booker Avenue. While the suburb did hold many unskilled residents, it had no shotgun houses, those cheap rental dwellings so common in downtown neighborhoods. Throughout Washington Heights, wooden one-story cottages trimmed in simple but fashionable Bungalow style defined the streetscape.

Though smaller than Brooklyn, Washington Heights could boast a considerable range of community institutions. Residents formed the Washington Heights Community Club, one of Charlotte's first neighborhood organizations, and included among its activities the fund raising for a day nursery and kindergarten to serve working mothers. While Lincoln Park remained unbuilt, promoter C. H. Watson did create a picnic pavilion for African Americans elsewhere along the streetcar line by 1915.[89] Watson also launched development of an adjoining subdivision east of Beatties Ford Road initially called Douglassville, which university president H. L. McCrorey eventually brought to fruition as McCrorey Heights. As the neighborhood filled out, it got its own small shopping district. A cluster of stores, which residents today still refer to as "The End," sprang up where the trolley terminated on Beatties Ford Road near Booker Avenue, providing a commercial hub for the blossoming African American suburb.

In the years from the late 1890s through the 1920s, then, Charlotte's black neighborhoods—like its blue-collar white districts—became increasingly well defined. Near downtown in First Ward, Second Ward, Third Ward, and Fourth Ward, African American enclaves developed hard edges, and in Second Ward's Brooklyn black investors built their own separate main street. At the edge of the city, as land began to be sought after by white suburbanites, Charlotteans gradually worked out where the color line would run. Predominantly white subdivisions surrounded the old rim villages such as Biddleville. For the historian the most interesting of those subdivisions is surely Western Heights, with its mix of black and white lot buyers in the early 1890s giving way to distinct black and white sections a few years later—yet another indication that the 1890s represented a watershed in white-collar white thinking about what constituted "a good place to live." Among themselves, African Americans seemed to make little class distinction in arranging dwellings. George W. Clinton, J. T. Williams, and Thad Tate continued to live among poor residents in the center city, and suburban Washington Heights held the unskilled as well as members of the black elite. In many ways this tendency resembled the immigrant enclaves of Northern cities, where economically successful individuals often stayed on in the old neighborhood.

White property owners subtly forged the new pattern of hard-edged black districts by closing off opportunities in certain areas while opening possibilities in others. Black renters who found themselves unwelcome in the area of H. M. Wilder's cottages in First Ward learned they could lease new shotgun houses in emerging African American enclaves elsewhere in the district. Black businessmen facing increasing discrimination downtown discovered that opportunities were open to build in Brooklyn. Black prospective homebuyers who saw doors close in most suburbs (as the next chapter describes in more detail) were gratified to read advertisements calling them to Washington Heights. This process of directed opportunity operated informally, through the ad hoc decisions of numerous individual property sellers and land developers. The result was the patchwork of black and white neighborhoods alternating across the landscape, rather than a single discrete African American ghetto.

A few big-thinking real estate entrepreneurs, though, envisioned just such an extreme pattern of segregation. The same 1912 article that announced W. S. Alexander's Washington Heights project also carried the striking suggestion that "the solution of the question of housing the colored population for the best interests of all concerned is afforded by sites west of the city, where their educational center is already established." The idea of confining African Americans to Charlotte's west side was quite audacious, particularly in light of the vibrant development just then occurring east of downtown in Brooklyn. "The Second Ward is already populated by [blacks], many owning comfortable homes," the writer acknowledged. Nonetheless, he asserted, "farsighted men believe that eventually this section, because of its proximity to the center of the city, must sooner or later be utilized by the white population."[90]

It would be many years before Charlotte's white leaders found the mechanisms to make such rigid segregation a reality. In the meantime, as we shall see, real estate developers focused on the challenges of keeping undesirables—white as well as black—out of Charlotte's emerging white-collar suburbs.

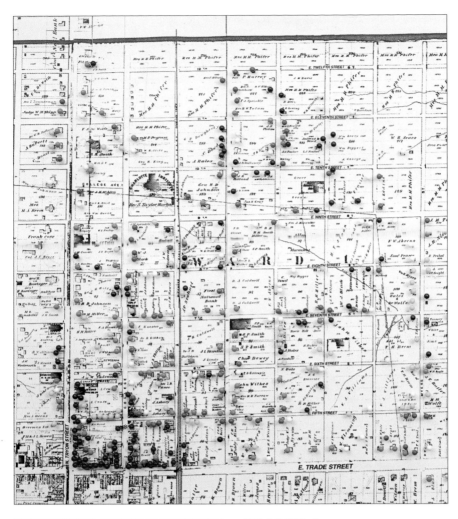

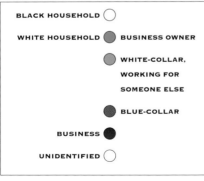

BLACK HOUSEHOLD ○

WHITE HOUSEHOLD ◐   BUSINESS OWNER

◐ WHITE-COLLAR,
WORKING FOR
SOMEONE ELSE

● BLUE-COLLAR

BUSINESS ●

UNIDENTIFIED ○

COLOR FIG. 1.

RACE AND OCCUPATION IN A
PORTION OF FIRST WARD, CA. 1875

First Ward made up the northeast quarter
of the city. Red dots at the lower left
indicate Charlotte's central business
district. Elsewhere there is surprisingly
little pattern to land use. Blacks and
whites of all classes lived intermingled
throughout the ward. (Sources: 1875–76
city directory, 1877 Beers map; base map:
1877 Beers map)

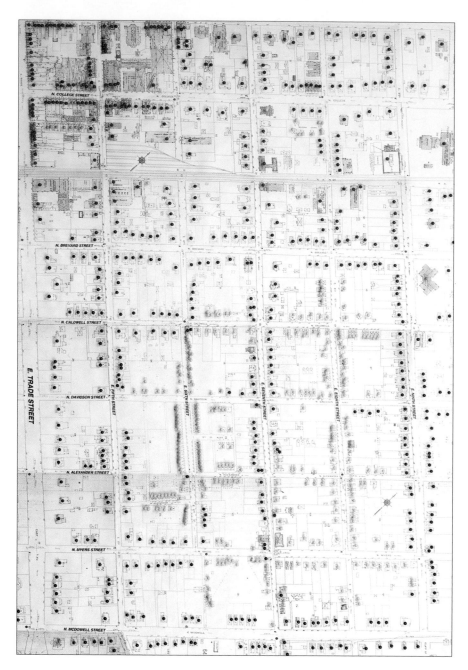

BLACK HOUSEHOLD ○

WHITE HOUSEHOLD ◔

BLACK-RUN BUSINESS ◑

WHITE-RUN BUSINESS ●

COLOR FIG. 2.

RACE IN A PORTION OF FIRST WARD, CA. 1910

By 1910 the racial intermingling of First Ward had disappeared, replaced by sharp-edged black and white districts. (Sources: 1910 city directory street list, 1911 Sanborn Insurance Map; Base map: 1911 Sanborn Insurance Map)

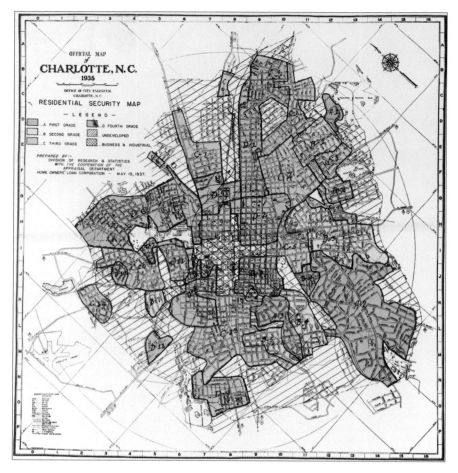

COLOR FIG. 3. FEDERAL HOLC REDLINING, 1937

The HOLC's credit-risk maps reinforced Charlotte's tendency to grow south and east. Only the wealthiest areas were given the best rating (green), and only white-collar white districts received the second-best designation (blue). All neighborhoods with blacks or large numbers of blue-collar renters, in contrast, were coded red, indicating highest risk. This "redlining" meant that after 1937, residents at Charlotte's north and west found it increasingly difficult to obtain house loans. (HOLC "Residential Security Map," 1937, National Archives, Washington, D.C.)

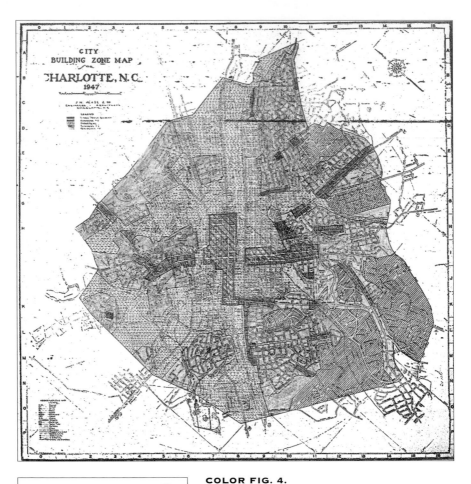

SINGLE-FAMILY RESIDENCE ⬤

MULTIFAMILY RESIDENCE ⬤

CENTRAL BUSINESS DISTRICT ◐

NEIGHBORHOOD BUSINESS ⬤

INDUSTRIAL ◯

COLOR FIG. 4.

BUILDING ZONE MAP OF CHARLOTTE, 1947

Charlotte's 1947 zoning map further reinforced the tendency for the well-to-do to locate in the southeast. Despite the fact that at least one white-collar area existed off West Trade Street (Wesley Heights), only eastside neighborhoods were protected by single-family zoning. Many African American areas, most notably Brooklyn on the east side, were zoned industrial to encourage developers to buy existing homes and demolish them for other development. (*Charlotte News*, January 25, 1947 [color added to enhance clarity])

CHAPTER 6

CREATING WHITE-COLLAR NEIGHBORHOODS

[Charlotte's newest] swell residence suburbs are Piedmont Park and Elizabeth avenue. In these places the lots are sold on condition that the houses to be erected shall not cost less than a specified sum, and as a result only handsome residences are built. There are various other [unrestricted districts], such as Villa Heights, Belmont Springs and East End, where the workingman can buy a home.

Charlotte Observer, May 20, 1903

A HIGH CLASS RESIDENTIAL SUBURB: Myers Park, adjoining Charlotte, North Carolina, is a new suburb created along distinctive lines designed aright from the first and influenced only by the best practice in modern town planning.

John Nolen, *New Towns for Old,* 1927

WHITE-COLLAR white Charlotteans now headed to the suburbs. The innovation that Edward Dilworth Latta had tried to introduce in the early 1890s, with limited success, abruptly caught on around the turn of the century. "The suburbs of Charlotte at all points of the compass are being improved," newspapers declared in 1900. "The future residential population of the town will live, for the most part, in the suburbs."[1] From Wesley Heights and Woodlawn on the west, to Wilmoore and Dilworth on the south, to Elizabeth and Myers Park on the east, to The Plaza on the northeast, a halo of new single-class, white-collar neighborhoods surrounded Charlotte during the years immediately after 1900. Compared with earlier extensions of the city, these suburbs embodied a very different conception of "a good place to live."[2] Previously, from the town's founding through the creation of Dilworth, prosperous citizens had lived on blocks that intermingled residents of all incomes, admitted black people as well as whites, and often included both workplaces and houses. After the 1890s that tolerance for diversity evaporated. Affluent buyers showed a decided preference for residential areas away from African Americans and, as critically, away from factories and workers.

Charlotte's developers now looked for ways to insulate suburbs from the hurly-burly of the city. Subdivision streets became increasingly separate from the urban grid. Restrictive covenants inserted into deeds legally barred certain land uses. Suburbanites adopted new styles of architecture distinct from those in older parts of the city. Planners were hired to guide the development of suburban parks and then of entire neighborhoods whose designs consciously turned their backs on the rest of the community. Two early twentieth century white-collar developments illustrate these tendencies. The 1899 Piedmont Park subdivision in the Elizabeth neighborhood introduced deed restrictions to Charlotte and also fostered creation of the city's first public park, which launched the career of nationally important planner John Nolen. The 1911 neighborhood of Myers Park, a landmark work by Nolen, was the finest of a series of professionally planned enclaves that redefined elegant living for Charlotte's elite during the 1910s and 1920s.

PIEDMONT PARK: INTRODUCING THE EXCLUSIVE NEIGHBORHOOD

On May 20, 1891, the very day that auctioneers launched lot sales in Dilworth, Charlotte newspapers excitedly announced "Another Suburban Villa. . . . Dilworth to Have Rival."[3] Real estate developer W. S. Alexander and a group of partners had taken options on several tracts of land out East Trade Street

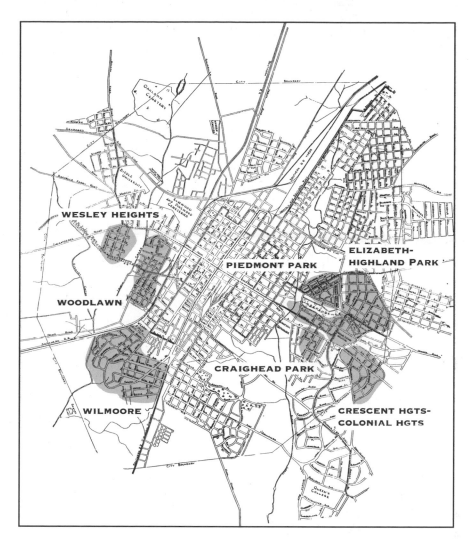

FIG. 39. EARLY SUBURBS DEVELOPED FOR WHITE-COLLAR WHITES
After Dilworth in 1891, there came a pause in Charlotte's suburban development. Then,
starting with Elizabeth in the late 1890s, Charlotte sprouted a series of suburbs intended
for white-collar buyers, located on the east, south, and west sides of town. (Base map: City
of Charlotte, 1925)

east of town, an area of rolling hills around the city's main reservoir (today
Independence Park). They hoped to cash in on the wave of enthusiasm for
suburban living apparently being generated by Latta's lavish promotional
machine. When Dilworth lot sales fizzled, however, Alexander was forced to
put his plans on hold for half a decade. In 1896 he devised a strategy to get
things rolling again. He donated a hilltop site to Elizabeth College, a Lu-

theran school for women, which constructed an imposing two-story brick building and began classes the following year.[4] The institution aimed its offerings at the daughters of the Carolinas' growing white-collar elite, providing academic courses plus conservatory training in art, piano, voice, and violin. "Director of Music a Leipzig graduate of International reputation," trilled advertisements. The college's suburban campus would shelter young ladies from urban strife, the ads assured, and provide them with the wholesome benefits of Nature: "Location unsurpassed, twenty acres of park campus overlooking the city . . . free from dust, smoke, noises, etc., with pure upland country air, surrounded by song birds and the beauties of nature."[5] Bolstered by this white-collar institution in its midst, Alexander's hillside took on fresh desirability. By the mid-1900s he and other developers had laid out half a dozen subdivisions in the vicinity, creating the neighborhood today known as Elizabeth.[6] The most innovative of the subdivisions was one called Piedmont Park. Its name would eventually fade from popular memory, becoming merely part of Elizabeth, but its design nonetheless made broad and lasting impacts on Charlotte's landscape.

As so often in Mecklenburg history, the company that created Piedmont Park combined old money with newly arrived youthful energy. Senior partner Walter Brem ranked as one of the town's leading insurance men, while B. D. Heath had made his fortune as a cotton trader, then founded the Charlotte National Bank.[7] Junior partner F. C. Abbott, by contrast, had just come to town from Connecticut and hoped to make a living as a real estate broker— still something of a novelty as a full-time profession.[8] George Stephens, youngest member of the foursome at age twenty-six, brought a particular zest for fresh thinking. Born near Greensboro, he had won fame as an athlete at the University of North Carolina, not only leading the baseball team to a championship but also making his mark in the fledgling sport of football.[9] Football was still solely a running game in those days; but in one memorable 1895 contest a desperate teammate heaved the ball, and Stephens snatched it to win the day. "The lad who caught it ran seventy yards for a touchdown! I had seen the first forward pass in football," wrote football great John Heisman, who happened to be in the stands that day. Heisman pushed to add the invention to the official rulebook, and the forward pass revolutionized the sport.[10] After graduation Stephens carried that innovative spirit to Charlotte, where he quickly forged a partnership with newcomer Abbott. The pair moved eagerly into the business of buying and selling houses—introducing the first "For

Sale" signs seen in the small city—and soon sought backing from Brem and Heath to initiate a real estate development of their own.

Stephens and his partners purchased eighty-six acres of farmland owned by W. R. Myers, a trapezoid-shaped tract that lay northeast of the city's edge. One side of the property bordered Monroe Road (Seventh Street Extension), a country road leading to the neighboring courthouse town. Angling northeastward from Monroe Road and cutting through the center of the land ran another old country highway, Lawyers Road, which had once taken barristers to the colonial legal center of Wadesboro. To lay out the avenues of their subdivision, the developers hired local civil engineer C. A. Spratt, and the street plan he devised became the first of Piedmont Park's innovations.[11]

The plat map that Spratt filed in 1900 signaled the final demise of Charlotte's long tradition of community planning. For a century and a half, every extension of the city had respected the original grid arrangement of streets. Even after developers took over from local government the task of laying out new avenues in the 1890s, streets had tended to pay heed to the grid. Some of Dilworth's rectangular blocks matched up with streets in Second Ward. W. S. Alexander's handsome Elizabeth Avenue extended existing East Trade Street. But Piedmont Park broke with that pattern completely. Spratt did use straight avenues—including present-day Sunnyside, Jackson, and Louise—but he blithely aligned them with Lawyers Road rather than with any urban street. On a city map Piedmont Park stuck out like an oddly angled sore thumb. Stephens and his partners did not care. The arrangement made the most profitable use of their tract and allowed them to utilize Lawyers Road as a broad central boulevard, which they renamed Central Avenue (today a major thoroughfare extending for miles through Charlotte's east side).[12] As importantly, the street plan served, by its very angularity, to set the new subdivision off from the city.

Along with street arrangement, the developers employed a second and more powerful innovation to reinforce the sense of separation. In 1901 Stephens and his partners introduced to Charlotte the practice of writing restrictive covenants into every lot deed, explicitly spelling out acceptable uses. "This conveyance is made," ran a typical Piedmont Park deed, "upon the condition that no owner of said real estate shall at any time hereafter . . . erect any structure except a dwelling house which shall cost not less than 1500 dollars, and no owner of said real estate shall permit any building erected there on to be used for any other purpose than dwelling. . . . [Further,] no part

FIG. 40. PIEDMONT PARK PLAT MAP, CA. 1900

This plat map—the legal document establishing street and lot arrangement—bore the label "Piedmont Park, Charlotte Suburb." It featured a small park (later incorporated into Independence Park) in a ravine near the center of the development. For the first time in the city's history, streets were arranged merely to best fit the available land, with no regard for the earlier urban grid. (Source: Mecklenburg County Register of Deeds Office, deed book 146, p. 206) of said real estate shall ever be owned or occupied by any person of the Negro race."[13] In this era before the invention of zoning, such covenants comprised the most effective legal tool available to exclude land uses deemed undesirable by white-collar citizens. The words hammered home three essentials of the sorted-out city. They announced the splitting of work and residence: the land would hold only dwellings. They announced the segregation of whites and blacks: African Americans could neither own nor rent. And they announced the separation of prosperous residents from poorer ones: families who could afford a $1,500 house would be protected from those who could not. "The restrictions on buildings are severe, the kind and cost of homes being looked after very carefully," applauded a brochure published by Charlotte business boosters soon after the deeds went into effect. The strategy, the brochure went on, "offers especial attractions to the man of affairs . . . the best population of Charlotte."[14]

The notion of deed covenants came as part of what historian Robert Wiebe has called the "search for order" that accompanied industrialization in America.[15] Covenants promised predictability in an increasingly fast-changing world. On one level they protected economic investment. Just yesterday the center city had been the fashionable place to live; today the favored locale was the suburb. Restrictions eased the homebuyer's nagging fear that today's suburb might become tomorrow's slum. On a deeper level the covenants provided a bulwark against a society that seemed to be growing more and more topsy-turvy. In such a district the "best population" would suffer no intrusions from people who did not "know their place." A restricted neighborhood would be, very literally, exclusive—a place that excluded.

By the time covenants showed up in Piedmont Park, the practice had been popular among the well-to-do in America's busiest industrial and commercial centers for half a century. The deed covenant technique probably arrived in the United States from England, the cradle of the industrial revolution, where posh districts such as London's Regents Park had featured restrictive covenants since at least the 1810s. By the 1850s American businessmen were using them to create elite enclaves in places such as St. Louis and Kansas City. Landscape architect Frederick Law Olmsted adopted the tool in 1871 for his Riverside neighborhood outside Chicago and incorporated it in most of his firm's subsequent designs. By the 1890s deed restrictions were in common use from Boston's Brookline to Baltimore's Roland Park to Chicago's swank North Shore neighborhoods.[16]

Now deed restrictions came to the small city of Charlotte. The timing spoke volumes about the changing social atmosphere of the town at the turn of the century. Before the Populist challenge of the 1890s, blacks and workers had not seemed especially threatening to those higher up in Charlotte's social pyramid. Edward Dilworth Latta had set minimum house cost requirements for lots along the grand Boulevard in Dilworth in 1891, but otherwise he welcomed buyers of all income levels and put no restrictions on the rest of Dilworth's avenues. The idea of excluding black people had seemed too strange even to propose. Latta had planned streets for blacks in one part of his subdivision and had sold land for an African American church elsewhere in the neighborhood. Ten years later, attitudes had clearly changed.

Once introduced in Piedmont Park, deed restrictions spread rapidly through Charlotte's other new neighborhoods. After 1901 virtually all developers of subdivisions aimed at white-collar buyers wrote racial and house cost clauses into their deeds.[17] The practice became so popular that it even showed up, with modifications, in blue-collar and black districts. By 1912 deeds in working-class Villa Heights prohibited black inhabitants; nothing was said about minimum house costs. Conversely, deeds issued the same year in Washington Heights, the African American suburb "of tone and character," set modest requirements for construction investment but made no restrictions concerning race.[18]

A PUBLIC PARK FOR A CENTERPIECE

Along with its break with the urban grid and its adoption of deed restrictions, Piedmont Park also introduced Charlotte to new thinking in the provision of public parkland. A nationwide movement toward urban parks had been building for decades in America, sparked by Frederick Law Olmsted's creation of Central Park in New York City during the 1860s.[19] In Charlotte, city fathers had long maintained Settlers Cemetery behind First Presbyterian Church as a bit of green space in the heart of downtown and in the 1850s had opened picturesque Elmwood Cemetery at the west edge of Fourth Ward.[20] But parks were another matter. When a group of women asked the Board of Aldermen to finance a city park in 1876, the board could see no point in such frivolous expense.[21] Edward Dilworth Latta took matters into his own hands in 1891, introducing Charlotteans to the joys of park-going with his privately created Latta Park. Efforts to sell the completed glen to the city ran into a storm of opposition, however.[22] Many tradition-minded politicians still thought that government should stay out of the recreation business, no matter what the trend elsewhere. Other opponents rebelled at using public money to provide an amenity to a suburban developer; in the Populist atmosphere of the 1890s, buying Latta Park seemed too much like a city subsidy for the wealthy Charlotte Consolidated Construction Company investors. There matters stood when George Stephens, W. S. Alexander, and others commenced work on the creation of the Elizabeth area.

Stephens and his associates knew that, in the wake of Dilworth, they would have to provide attractive parkland if they wished to lure white-collar lot buyers. The city reservoir near Seventh Street and the campus of Elizabeth College at the top of the hill could satisfy some of this requirement, but neither was really a park. W. S. Alexander worked a small bit of parkland into his Elizabeth Heights subdivision, building Park Drive in 1903 in a curve around a spring that trickled down to the city reservoir.[23] George Stephens incorporated a similar plot into the Piedmont Park plat, a tree-shaded hollow that dropped from Sunnyside Avenue to the reservoir's edge.[24] Setting aside land was fairly painless; such low-lying ground would be difficult to sell as house lots. Actually developing the properties into parks was another matter, though, a costly investment for private developers.

Then, in 1904, the city announced plans to abandon its Elizabeth reservoir in favor of a bigger facility west of town, and the eastside real estate men saw their opportunity. Enlisting support from leading Charlotte booster D. A Tompkins and securing letters from mayors of other municipalities "commending parks as essentials to city life," the promoters approached the Board of Aldermen and proposed a deal.[25] Alexander, Stephens, and associates would donate to the city their small park sites adjoining the old reservoir if the city would drain the lake and develop the whole ravine as a spacious municipal recreation ground. The deal faced none of the opposition that had blocked acquisition of Latta Park a decade before. The prospect of getting such a symbol of urban progress without spending an additional penny on land won the frugal conservatives who had balked at the Dilworth proposal. More importantly, Charlotte's political climate had changed greatly since the 1890s. White-collar voters now securely controlled the ballot box. This time no one complained that the park might represent a subsidy to wealthy suburban developers and their upper-class customers. Nor did any politician point out that this "public" park was located far from the center of town in the midst of a neighborhood that barred most Charlotteans from buying homes. On August 1, 1904, the Board of Aldermen announced the creation of Independence Park.[26]

To guide the new facility, the city created the Charlotte Park and Tree Commission and appointed George Stephens as its executive secretary. Stephens energetically wrote to the American Civic Association and to the recently founded program in landscape architecture at Harvard University, seeking a professional park designer who might fit the commission's slender finances. Letters came back singing the praises of a Harvard student named John Nolen. The young man lacked experience—he was just completing his last year of coursework—but his vision and energy seemed to mark him as someone who would make a major impact on the new profession of city planning.

John Nolen burned with a desire not merely to plan beautiful landscapes but to reform urban life. Born the son of a Philadelphia carpenter in 1869, he worked his way through the University of Pennsylvania's prestigious Wharton School majoring in economics and public administration.[27] His education brought him into contact with the ideas of the generation's Progressive reformers, led by men and women such as muckraking journalist Lincoln Steffens and social work pioneer Jane Addams, who urged America to recognize and remedy its urban ills. Upon graduation Nolen took charge of the Society for the Extension of University Education, a "people's college" that brought college classes to urban workers. In the course of that work he discovered the field of city planning and slowly became convinced that this new profession might offer a more effective way for him to improve urban conditions. A visit to Europe's Garden City experiments in 1900 particularly intrigued him. The Garden City idea, formulated in England during the 1890s, proposed medium-sized towns as an alternative to the unmanageable metropolis. Carefully planned and surrounded by belts of green fields and parks, such communities could combine the best features of city and country.[28] Nolen returned to the United States, quit his job, and—at age thirty-three, with a wife and two children—went back to school. No university in America yet offered a city planning degree, so Nolen enrolled in Harvard's School of Landscape Architecture. When George Stephens's invitation to visit Charlotte arrived on Nolen's desk, it promised the very means to put his learning to work. Charlotte was a small community poised on the brink of growth, a place ready for change and improvement. Right now the Park and Tree Commission might think it merely wanted a park, but in the hands of a skillful educator that desire could lead to bigger things. Nolen convinced his professors to forgo final exams so he could catch a train south. "Definite Engagement for Charlotte, N.C.," he wrote excitedly in his diary on May 29, 1905, "First important landscape work."[29]

During the next ten years Nolen visited the city often, advising on Independence Park and cultivating a growing portfolio of other projects. The city had no real budget for creating and carrying out a full-scale plan for Independence Park, it turned out, so Nolen gamely worked piecemeal, contributing planting ideas, designs for drives and pathways, and so on, as finances permitted.[30] No drawings survive in Nolen's papers at Cornell University, but the natural-seeming scattering of trees throughout the park today is likely a legacy of the designer's naturalistic philosophy. At the same time Nolen also offered advice on the landscaping of Settlers Cemetery and the grounds of the old U.S. Mint downtown, both of which had been placed under the Park and Tree Commission's purview. Sketches that survive for the cemetery show a planting scheme of cedars, oaks, and evergreens and advise the addition of curving paths to make the burial ground a pleasant downtown park.

Nolen used each Charlotte visit as an opportunity to stir citizen enthusiasm for planning—"missionary work," as he confided in a letter to George Stephens. On several occasions he brought boxes of glass slides and arranged to have Stephens provide a "magic lantern" (the wondrous new technology of the day) for illustrated public lectures. "Standing to one side of the darkened room, as picture after picture was thrown on the wall," the designer beguiled Charlotteans with the possibilities of "Outdoor Art," "Parks and Playgrounds," home landscaping, and entire city plans. "He possesses the faculty of making others see as he does," marveled the *Observer*, which printed complete texts of the speeches.[31] Among slides of famous American sites and ancient European landmarks, Nolen mixed more and more views of his own projects. Monthly he was winning major commissions across the United States: park designs for Savannah, Georgia, and Madison, Wisconsin; campus layouts for Smith College in Massachusetts and Queens University in Ontario; and city plans for Roanoke, Virginia, for Montclair, New Jersey, and for San Diego, California.[32]

Nolen also used the Independence Park trips to develop individual working relationships with key movers and shakers in Charlotte. On an early visit George Stephens talked F. C. Abbott into hiring Nolen to prepare a landscape scheme for the grounds of Abbott's handsome home on Central Avenue. Affluent lot buyers in Elizabeth and other suburbs admired the results. A professionally designed setting offered a badge of elegance, bringing the sheltering benefits of Nature to one's very door. Soon Nolen carried a fresh stack of such commissions each time he boarded the train back to his office in Harvard Square.[33] The strongest convert to Nolen's missionary zeal was George Stephens himself. Something about Nolen's message of progress and beauty deeply touched the young real estate man, and Stephens came to believe

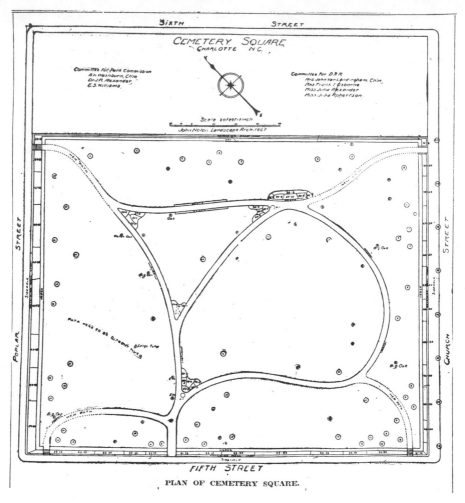

PLAN OF CEMETERY SQUARE.

FIG. 41. NOLEN SKETCH FOR CEMETERY SQUARE, DOWNTOWN
Young John Nolen, soon to become one of America's leading city planners, began his career in Charlotte, where he provided designs for the Park and Tree Commission. Nolen's drawings for Independence Park are lost, but this early sketch for the commission's Cemetery Square (Settler's Cemetery on West Fifth Street, downtown) shows his enthusiasm for naturalistic planning. (Source: *Charlotte Observer*, May 7, 1906)

fervently in the vision of cities planned with nature. In 1910 Stephens hired the designer to help create Kanuga Lake in the North Carolina mountains near Hendersonville, a sprawling, 1,500-acre, private-membership resort.[34] Before long he would invite John Nolen back to Charlotte to create not just a park or a house lot but an entire neighborhood.

Residents who moved out to Piedmont Park and the surrounding Elizabeth neighborhood during the 1900s and 1910s inhabited a white-collar world. Fathers commuted downtown each morning on the streetcar to work and came back each evening to dinner. During the daylight hours the suburb was a place of women and children playing on the grassy lawns, roller-skating on the smooth cement sidewalks, visiting Independence Park, or resting on cool, shady front porches. In the early years not even neighborhood stores disturbed the purely residential character of the suburb.[35] This represented a marked contrast to the numerous corner groceries found in blue-collar districts. White-collar housewives had the time to travel downtown on the trolley—or send their maids or housemen—to shop at the grocery and dry goods establishments near the Square, which sent out delivery wagons to the suburbs each afternoon. Not until well into the 1920s would drugstores and small food markets begin to show up in Elizabeth. While shops remained rare, churches formed almost immediately. St. Martin's Episcopal opened in 1912, Hawthorne Lane Methodist began in 1915, and Caldwell Presbyterian followed not long after, each splitting off from downtown institutions to form purely white-collar suburban congregations.[36]

In these early subdivisions the wealthiest families lived on the main boulevards, a continuation of patterns seen in nineteenth century Charlotte. On Piedmont Park's Central Avenue, large residences of notables such as banker B. D. Heath, factory owner E. A. Cole, and department store founder J. B. Ivey proclaimed their prosperity for all to admire. Elsewhere in Elizabeth, showplace streets included the trolley routes of Elizabeth Avenue, Clement Avenue, and especially Hawthorne Lane. Two of Hawthorne's early mansions still command the hillcrest today: the 1914 house designed for James Staten, manager of the Little-Long Department Store, and the 1918 edifice erected by William Henry Belk, founder of the far-flung Belk department store chain.[37]

Off the boulevards, more modest but still substantial dwellings lined the side streets. Many housed middle managers, such as Curtis Mees on Louise Avenue, who worked as chief of the design office at Duke Power, or Zebulon Vance Linker on Seventh Street, who served as assistant superintendent of the Charlotte Post Office. Others held the owners of Charlotte's smaller businesses, residing near the leading Belk and Ivey families much as their shops clustered in the shadow of the downtown department stores. Examples included Tryon Street jeweler Charles Elam on Seventh Street, Queen City Cycle Company proprietor James Pickard on Beaumont Avenue, and print shop owner George Dooley on Louise Avenue. Two other common side street occupations were bookkeeper and—that mainstay of this wholesaling city—traveling salesman.

Elizabeth's houses mostly went up one or two at a time. A homeowner might purchase a lot, contract with an architect or a builder, and have a house constructed for himself. Or a builder might buy a lot or two and erect a couple of dwellings to sell on speculation. Real estate promoters, too, often purchased groups of parcels and had "spec" houses constructed for sale and, quite often, for rental. The promoters showed little territorial jealousy; F. C. Abbott, for instance, advertised dwellings for sale and rent on W. S. Alexander's Elizabeth Avenue, and other entrepreneurs in turn put up houses in Abbott's Piedmont Park. The variety of builders in the Elizabeth district gave the neighborhood a pleasing diversity of house designs.

At the same time, though, Elizabeth's architecture embodied shared aesthetic assumptions that assured the neighborhood a distinctly suburban appearance.[38] Unlike mill villages and black districts, where houses often sat close to the road, white-collar dwellings were twenty to thirty feet from the street. Front lawns with purely ornamental plantings proclaimed the owner's prosperity and signaled his appreciation of Nature.[39] Further, white-collar residences were substantial and up-to-date. Proper suburbanites demonstrated their educated taste and wealth by building only in the most current modes. There were no shotgun houses, of course, or any examples of the sort of traditional one-story cottages seen in mill districts, or even much of the Queen Anne Victorian architecture so prevalent in the center city.

America around 1900 was turning away from Victorian exuberance. The elaborate shapes and colors that characterized the Victorian style now seemed too vain and loud, out of place amidst the calm efficiency of the Progressive era. National architectural journals in the 1890s abandoned long-popular Victorian conventions and began to counsel against the practice of drawing ornament from an eclectic array of historic eras, against designing complicated rooflines, and against using asymmetrical massing, elaborate window treatments, and multihued paint schemes.[40] Even newspaper columnists such as the nationally syndicated humorist Bill Nye joined the chorus, mocking Victorian architects for their seeming propensity to "throw in odd windows nobody else wanted, then daub it up with colors they have bought at an auction and applied to the house after dark with a shotgun."[41] In place of such chaos suburbanites now embraced simpler styles that promised more efficient living and also often harked back to the seemingly calmer, more orderly society of preindustrial times.

The first post-Victorian mode to win popularity in Charlotte's suburbs was the Colonial Revival, a style that carried powerful resonances among the Southern elite. Charlotte's rising young architect C. C. Hook introduced the fashion in 1894 with a house on The Boulevard in Dilworth, and it quickly became a favorite among suburbanites. A Colonial residence represented a refreshing departure from Victorian extravagance: a symmetrical rectangular form under a simple hip or gable roof, with plain brick or clapboard walls and understated, classically inspired trim. As Hook explained in a newspaper story, "[The] striking feature of the house will be its simplicity of design and convenience of arrangement. The so-called 'filigree' ornamentation will not be a consideration, and only one true design will be carried out and thus give Charlotte another new style."[42] Colonial architecture not only looked straightforward and convenient but also embodied a strong message about the proper order of Southern society. "In antebellum days when a home was built of any pretensions the owner and designer as a rule was an educated gentleman of refinement," Hook wrote in 1903, "and being familiar with the classics and having other colonial work as models took pains to preserve the proper proportions and details." The decline in popularity of classical and colonial forms during the latter half of the nineteenth century, Hook felt, offered yet another indication of how the South's social pyramid had turned wrong-side-up: "[With] things being reversed in general we find a greater reversal in architecture than in any other sign of the times. Why was it? Because the illiterate and unrefined being new to wealth desired display more than purity, and the cultured and once-wealthy were either too poor or too busy." Now, having repelled the Populist challenge of the 1890s, "gentlemen of refinement" were regaining control of society. "Out of all this chaos," Hook concluded happily, "we again have a revival of the colonial."[43]

Such reasoning pleased Charlotte's white-collar business owners. Most were men of newly made wealth, if truth be known, but living in a Colonial home put them in company with the South's historical leaders. Colonial Revival dwellings became quite fashionable along Elizabeth's main boulevards. Banker and partner in the Piedmont Park development B. D. Heath employed the style for "Heathcote," his mansion on Central Avenue begun in

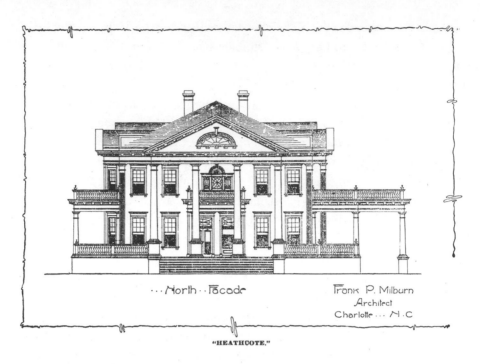

North · · Facade   Frank P. Milburn
Architect
Charlotte · · · N · C

"HEATHCOTE."

FIG. 42. SUBURBAN ARCHITECTURE: COLONIAL REVIVAL
This early example of the Colonial Revival style was designed for banker and real estate developer B. D. Heath on Central Avenue at Louise Avenue. (Source: *Charlotte Observer,* September 19, 1899)

1899.[44] The neighborhood's grandest surviving Colonial examples today are the James Staten mansion and William Henry Belk mansion on Hawthorne Lane, the latter designed by C. C. Hook himself.[45]

At almost the same time that the Colonial Revival achieved popularity, the Rectilinear style (sometimes called the Four Square style) arrived in Charlotte.[46] The Rectilinear shared the Colonial's impatience with Victorian fussiness but took it one step further. Rectilinear designs abandoned virtually all historic ornament and instead featured clean surfaces and plain trim. Architectural historians once assumed that Rectilinear houses were built by people too poor to afford something with "style." As historic preservationists have cataloged America's buildings, it has become clear that such houses were erected by wealthy individuals who could afford whatever architecture they desired. In Charlotte, men who chose the style were often entrepreneurs involved in creating new businesses. The stripped-down Rectilinear style embodied the zest for efficiency that Progressive businessmen held dear.

Charlotte's earliest major Rectilinear house stands on Piedmont Park's

FIG. 43. SUBURBAN ARCHITECTURE: RECTILINEAR
Prosperous downtown merchant Charles W. Parker commissioned this dwelling on suburban Central Avenue in 1904. The house was among the first in Charlotte in the new efficient-looking Rectilinear style (also known as Four Square). Its simple massing and restrained, geometric ornament represented a marked contrast with the florid forms of the older Victorian style (compare with fig. 19). (Photograph by author, March 1993)

main boulevard. The dwelling at 901 Central Avenue was completed in 1904 for Charles W. Parker, a self-made storekeeper who founded the Parker-Gardener Company, a major downtown concern selling furniture and, later, musical instruments.[47] Parker's house was a two-story cube with a pyramid-like hip roof and a one-story porch across the front. The interior had four bedrooms upstairs and an entry hall, parlor, dining room, and kitchen downstairs. The front door and entry hall were not located symmetrically, as in the Colonial Revival, but off to one side. The trim of the house also broke explicitly with historic precedent. Everything was geometric: wide eaves with no brackets or other ornament, grooved siding punctuated by plain vertical boards, diamond-shaped window panes, and square balusters supporting the porch railings. Even the columns flanking the fireplaces inside were turned on a lathe in a such a manner as to emulate no historic form. A full-page photograph of Parker's modern dwelling graced the 1905 book *Art Work of Charlotte, North Carolina*, which celebrated the city's finest residences.

Joining the Colonial and Rectilinear modes was the Bungalow style, which reached Charlotte around 1910. Like the other post-Victorian styles, it re-

FIG. 44. SUBURBAN ARCHITECTURE: BUNGALOW
Charlotte architect F. L. Bonfoey made a specialty of the rustic new Bungalow style, marked by broad porches and low, spreading roofs. This row of 1910s Bungalows on East Eighth Street includes the boyhood home of big band star Hal Kemp. (Photograph by Peter Wong, spring 1997)

nounced elaborate geegaws in favor of simplicity, in this case with a strong rural flavor. The basic form came from preindustrial British India, where a "bangla" was a "low house with porches all around," a back-country dwelling. Builders in California took hold of the idea at the end of the 1890s, and it swept across the United States during the next decade. Bungalow designs hugged the ground, the exact opposite of Victorian accentuation of height. The roof became the most prominent feature of the design, a sheltering sweep that usually extended its eaves well out from the dwelling's walls. A Bungalow often included two floors, but from the street the sloping roof always made it appear to be a low, one-story cottage. Bungalow decoration looked rustic; heavy, plain rectangular posts and planks were the antithesis of Victorian, machine-turned ornament. Completing the "hand-hewn" theme, architects often specified wooden shingles on the outside walls and used natural stone boulders to build up the chimneys and porches. To suburbanites desiring escape from the city, the Bungalow stood for woodsy serenity.[48]

Elizabeth quickly became a veritable "Bungalowland," in the words of developer W. S. Alexander. His 1911 advertisements perfectly caught the architecture's antiurban appeal, extolling the cozy charm of the "unpretentious bungalow, stowed away under gigantic pines, with low gabled roof, and vines clinging about the door, with a warmth of sunshine and noise of laughter within, [a place to] be happy, and be content, for it is home. . . . Some evening when your day's work is over stroll out Elizabethway, wander over to our 'Bungalowland' and seriously consider one of these steppingstones to someone's future happiness, one of these bungalows in the pines."[49] The neighborhood's best collection of Bungalows lines East Eighth Street from Louise Avenue to Hawthorne Lane. The half-dozen houses all went up around 1911, probably designed by F. L. Bonfoey, a Charlotte architect who made a specialty of the style.[50] Early owners included white-collar householders such as lawyer A. B. Justice, factory manager Jay Hirshinger, and Southern Railway bridge engineer T. D. Kemp Sr., whose son Hal Kemp went on to national fame as a big band leader in the 1930s.[51] Today the spreading roofs, wood-shingled walls, and spacious porches set well back from the street still offer a homey welcome.

A PATCHWORK PATTERN OF NEIGHBORHOODS

For all their success in luring white-collar residents, Piedmont Park and the other subdivisions in the Elizabeth area of Charlotte's east side had plenty of competition. During the initial wave of enthusiasm for suburban living after 1900, it was not at all clear where the city's "best neighborhood" might develop. Anywhere that promoters could get hold of land on the city's rim, they laid plans for white-collar subdivisions. The practice seemed quite logical in light of previous residence patterns. The existing houses of elite Charlotteans were found equally at all four directions of the compass, along East Trade, West Trade, North Tryon, and South Tryon Streets. The practice also made sense in terms of transportation technology. White-collar suburbs depended on trolley connections to downtown, and streetcar tracks could be laid most cheaply into areas closest to existing population—a constraint that encouraged development immediately adjacent to the densely built-up city rather than extending out in one particular sector.

During the 1900s developers launched white-collar subdivisions in almost every direction (see fig. 40).[52] To the southeast appeared Craighead Park (including Torrence and Baldwin Avenues) and Colonial Heights/Crescent Heights (with half-circle Crescent Avenue). South of town the original Dilworth suburb now filled out, and southwest of it F. C. Abbott purchased the former Wilson and Moore farms to create Wilmoore (with main avenue West Boulevard). On the city's west side, promoters platted Wesley Heights (Summit Avenue and Grandin Road) and Woodlawn, touted as "the nearest suburb to the business part of the city, yet none is prettier" (considered part of Third Ward today). The only part of Charlotte's rim without a suburb by 1900 was the north side, where the Southern Railway and its growing industrial corridor took up much land, and where the tracks of the Seaboard Railway crossed North Tryon Street and slowed easy travel. Elsewhere all around the city, new subdivisions attracted populations of white, middle-class homebuyers.

While Charlotte circa 1910 thus had no sector of white-collar neighborhoods stretching out in one particular direction, neither did suburbs form an unbroken ring around the city—another image that has been suggested by geographers. Blue-collar Belmont lay next to white-collar Elizabeth. The African American neighborhood of Cherry stood between white Craighead Park and Dilworth. Another black neighborhood and a factory district interrupted the ring to the southwest between Wilmoore and Wesley Heights, and so on. The same alternation was becoming a fact inside the city as well, with sharp-edged black and white districts appearing within each ward (as described in Chapter 5).

Rather than developing ring-shaped concentric zones or pie-shaped sectors, Charlotte was sorting out more on the pattern of a patchwork quilt. There were three types of "quilt blocks": blue-collar neighborhoods, white-collar neighborhoods, and black neighborhoods. The quilt blocks came in all shapes and sizes, each sharp-edged like a piece of fabric cut crisply with a scissor. As with the alternating piecework of a handsewn coverlet, any type of neighborhood might lie next to any other.

SUBURBAN PLANNING FOR CHARLOTTE

By the early 1910s most of the available land immediately adjacent to Charlotte's rim had been snapped up and platted for suburban development. Many house lots remained for sale within these neighborhoods, but demand among white-collar buyers ran so strong that some promoters now began considering the possibility of creating second-tier suburbs farther out from the city. Such a project would be expensive to launch. With the inner suburbs still not densely developed, extending trolley service even farther outward would be a costly proposition. A developer would have to mobilize considerable financial resources and, to hope to turn a profit, would need to create a product capable of luring Charlotte's wealthiest homebuyers.

During the 1910s three Charlotte developers attempted major second-tier suburbs. In 1910 textile manufacturer Paul Chatham, heir to the Chatham Woolen Mills at Elkin, North Carolina, teamed up with founders of the Charlotte Country Club to launch Chatham Estates near the club's golf course northeast of town.[53] In 1911 veteran developer Edward Dilworth Latta and his sons announced a large, up-scale extension of Dilworth south of the city.[54] The same year George Stephens, with help from the old-line Myers family, began work on Myers Park to Charlotte's southeast.

In each case, to increase appeal to the elite, the developers placed the project design in the hands of a professional planner. Leigh Colyer, a Charlotte-based garden designer, laid out Chatham Estates and landscaped its main boulevard, The Plaza. The famed Olmsted Brothers landscape architecture firm of Boston created Dilworth Road and adjoining new streets for the Lattas. And John Nolen returned to mastermind the glens and curving avenues of Myers Park. All three planners utilized the latest naturalistic techniques of landscape architecture. Instead of straight streets and square blocks they laid out curving avenues designed in harmony with the lay of the land. To enhance the experience of nature the planners specified extensive use of trees and shrubbery, giving the suburbs the look of romantic, semirural parkland. Neighborhood road systems became increasingly self-contained, opening onto city streets at a limited number of points. Main boulevards no longer held the finest homes; now the most prestigious residences would be tucked away on the side streets.

Together the work by Colyer, the Olmsteds, and Nolen during the 1910s made the small city of Charlotte a national exemplar of suburban planning. Elsewhere in the South, Joseph Forsyth Johnson's Inman Park and the Olmsteds' Druid Hills existed in Atlanta, and the Olmsted-created district of Roland Park flourished in Baltimore; but otherwise naturalistic neighborhood planning was virtually unknown.[55] Indeed, naturalistic suburbs remained rare anywhere in the United States. "Innovative communities like Llewellyn Park, Riverside, Lake Forest, and Roland Park . . . [had] adopted curvilinear streets in the nineteenth century," writes suburban historian Kenneth Jackson, "but the grid remained dominant in most suburbs until after 1900."[56]

Why did Charlotte so enthusiastically embrace this new fashion? Economics helped set the stage. City population grew 88 percent in the decade leading up to 1910, and real estate companies reported as much as 50 percent

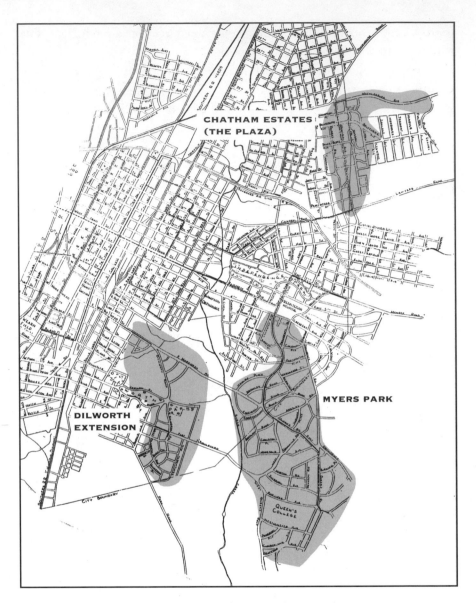

FIG. 45. SECOND-TIER WHITE-COLLAR SUBURBS, 1910S
In the 1910s developers pushed farther outward, creating a second tier of streetcar suburbs. To attract high-paying buyers (a necessity, due to the expense of extending trolley tracks), the promoters all sought help from professional landscape planners. Chatham Estates (part of present-day Plaza Midwood) was designed by Leigh Colyer, the extension of Dilworth was drawn by Boston's Olmsted Brothers, and Myers Park received the careful attention of John Nolen. (Base map: City of Charlotte, 1925)

FIG. 46. OLMSTED PLAN FOR DILWORTH, 1912
The Olmsted Brothers' 1912 design for Dilworth showed the existing straight streets and proposed curving avenues. Note the trolley line from downtown, at the left, and the "garden courts," cul-de-sacs north of Morehead Street that were proposed to create a barrier between Dilworth and the black Brooklyn neighborhood. North of Latta Park, only Dilworth Road was built as designed, but south of the park the Olmsted plan was carried out much as intended. (Courtesy of Olmsted National Historic Site, Brookline, Massachusetts)

annual return on investment, an atmosphere that made investors willing to experiment.[57] John Nolen's tireless evangelism also played a powerful role in making the possibilities of planning known to Charlotte developers. Nolen considered neighborhood plans the next logical step toward his hope of planning the city as a whole, and he made that point often in his repeated visits to the Queen City. The underlying reason for Charlotte's wholehearted adoption of suburban design, though, was the way that particular component of the Progressive urban planning vision fit the mood of the elite at that moment. Planning, as fostered by Nolen and his colleagues, promised a new era of order and beauty for America's cities. That order and beauty would be very different from the all-encompassing grid plans seen in colonial Philadelphia or nineteenth century Charlotte. Instead the new planning would create a city with a place for everyone and everyone in their place.

At the dawn of the twentieth century the planning profession was just blossoming into full flower in the United States, drawing nourishment from three intellectual streams of the day. One was the conservation movement, which promoted the idea that people needed contact with nature to counter-act the dehumanizing effects of urban industrial life.[58] Where once American frontiersmen had regarded the wilderness simply as an adversary to be con-quered, now citizens of an urbanized nation came to see nature as an asset to be celebrated, a turnabout neatly symbolized by the founding of the nation's first national parks under President Theodore Roosevelt during the 1900s. The City Beautiful movement offered a second intellectual current.[59] In 1893 the World's Columbian Exposition in Chicago had set a shining example of truly artistic urban form. Its white-columned buildings drew on the classical architecture of ancient Greece and Rome, as reinterpreted by the Beaux Arts school of France. The orderly promenades of the Exposition's White City stood in gleaming contrast to the dingy disorder of the real metropolis outside the gates, inspiring a call throughout urban America for artful public architec-ture and graciously designed civic spaces that would bring all citizens to-gether. The third intellectual current propelling planning was the wider Pro-gressive movement in the United States.[60] A once-rural country suddenly found itself a nation of huge cities facing tremendous technical and social problems ranging from the proper housing of workers to the most basic provi-sion of pure water. To deal with these challenges, Progressive activists called for the training and employment of new types of urban experts: professional city managers to systematize urban government, professional social workers to foster public health, professional civil engineers to create water and sewer systems, and professional city planners to guide overall urban growth. In this Progressive milieu, planning came of age as university-schooled specialists replaced the self-trained pioneers of the days of Frederick Law Olmsted Sr. In 1917 several of these young men, led by John Nolen and Frederick Law Olmsted Jr., founded the discipline's first professional organization, today the American Planning Association.[61] The group urged municipalities to give planners an active role in every aspect of physical development. Rather than hiring surveyors to extend streets, landscape architects to create parks, and so on in a piecemeal fashion, a city should employ a planner to devise a fully thought-out development strategy appropriate to the modern industrial era.

Basic to the Progressive vision of comprehensive planning was the notion that the city should be sorted out into separate districts.[62] John Nolen, Frederick Law Olmsted Jr., and most other Progressive designers hailed from the industrial centers of the Northeast and Midwest where blue-collar and white-collar neighborhoods had been a way of life for generations. In their experience, a mixed district was usually a district undergoing the awkward transition from one use to another. Planning for particular uses in particular areas, they believed, would enhance stability and give property owners peace-of-mind about their investments. Nolen, one of the profession's most prolific writers by the 1910s, expressed the ideal of separation eloquently in his articles and books.[63] He ridiculed backward communities where "there is no homogeneity of neighborhoods, no protection of any class," and he championed the new technique of zoning, whereby local governments took on the task of regulating land use "so as to differentiate neighborhoods and protect real estate values."[64] Zoning remained almost unknown in the United States before New York City adopted America's first comprehensive ordinance in 1916, and it spread only slowly for years thereafter. In the absence of such government regulations, Nolen urged the use of restrictive deed covenants, applauding "the unofficial separation" that restrictions had accomplished in "many of our American cities."[65]

Carefully defined single-class neighborhoods for each social group would comprise the basic building blocks of the planned city, Nolen wrote. Planners would create "segregated fine residence sections, free from objectionable features" to house the city's wealthiest residents.[66] As importantly, they would also design well-appointed neighborhoods for the non-elite. Nolen spoke approvingly of the blue-collar satellite cities that were growing up around factories at the edges of American metropolitan areas (see Chapter 4). He eagerly sought opportunities to design several such working-class communities, notably Neponset Garden Village for a building-materials maker outside Walpole, Massachusetts.[67] In the South Nolen envisioned similarly separate and desirable neighborhoods for African Americans. In plans for both Roanoke, Virginia, and Kingsport, Tennessee, he proposed creating a "Negro neighborhood . . . in marked contrast to the squalid 'Nigger-town' districts so common in Southern communities. Here colored people [will have] comfortable, new houses built for them, with modern improvements. In this section the playgrounds, schoolhouses and churches have been planned for in ways commensurate with the advanced standards set for the rest of the community."[68]

Inside each homogeneous neighborhood, protected from the social chaos of the modern city, citizens would enjoy an old-fashioned spirit of neighborliness, the Progressive planners believed. "Only in settled communities where a sense of personal responsibility among the people prevails can a genuine social life manifest itself," argued Nolen.[69] People would be able to let their barriers down—literally as well as figuratively. In his designs for such neighborhoods, Nolen urged that residents not build fences or walls in their front yards. The back yard and the house itself guaranteed privacy enough in a homogeneous district. "The seclusion of the private house may be understood to represent the personal qualities of the individual and the family," he wrote grandly, while "the street and the great out-of-doors assuredly stand for the brotherhood of man and its unity with all nature."[70]

This overarching vision of "the brotherhood of man," significantly, meant that single-class neighborhoods represented only one component of Progressive planning theory. The planner must also join the separate districts together into a unified whole. The ideal city would have an extensive park system, a carefully thought-out hierarchy of public spaces featuring a children's playlot at the heart of each district, then larger parks between each neighborhood, then "greenways" connecting all together in order to bring people into contact with one another in the enjoyment of nature.[71] At the center of town a handsome civic plaza on the City Beautiful model would provide the focus of public life, holding institutional buildings that attracted the whole population, such as the city hall, public library, and courts. A web of landscaped boulevards would radiate outward from this city center, joining it to the neighborhoods. Wherever possible these roads would be wide, tree-shaded "parkways," with trolleys running down a landscaped median. At the city's outer rim, Nolen presciently urged, another parkway should form "an encircling ring" wrapping around the entire town, "an indispensable contribution toward tomorrow's efficiency."[72] Skillfully employed, all these components—fine residence sections, comfortable blue-collar and black districts, park systems, boulevards, and public plazas—would unite a city's diverse peoples into a healthy and happy community. The Progressive planners often discovered, sadly, that this vision of unity proved much harder to implement than did the notion of insulated suburbs. Such would be the case in Charlotte.

MYERS PARK: CHARLOTTE'S GRAND PLANNED SUBURB

Myers Park, among Charlotte's three planned second-tier suburbs, did the most to redefine the city's landscape during the 1910s. Leigh Colyer's grassy boulevard The Plaza and adjoining avenues attracted important families to Chatham Estates, among them cotton broker Ralph VanLandingham and Methodist bishop John C. Kilgo. But problems with trolley connections slowed the neighborhood's growth by the middle of the decade.[73] The Olmsted Brothers' design for Dilworth went beyond Colyer's in its use of curving roadways, especially the elegant sweep of Dilworth Road. The Latta family, however, balked at the expense involved in the Olmsted proposals and never completely implemented the plans, but nonetheless the tree-shaded streets rapidly filled with gracious upper middle-class houses.[74] Alone, even with its transit difficulties, Colyer's Plaza might well have made northeast Charlotte the city's elite sector. Alone, even with the Lattas' penny-pinching, the Olmsteds' Dilworth extension would likely have directed development southward. But as it was, both efforts paled in comparison with the handsomely funded suburb of Myers Park taking shape southeast of town under the diligent direction of John Nolen.

Genealogy played a larger role than geography in the location and success of Myers Park. George Stephens, now finished with Piedmont Park and at the helm of his own Stephens Company, set his sights on a prime tract of land out Providence Road, the 1,005-acre farm owned by John Springs Myers, who happened to be Stephens's father-in-law.[75] Myers had been toying with the notion of suburban development for years. In the late 1890s he had planted trees and flowers around the farmhouse he maintained on the property and had encouraged a handful of other wealthy men to establish "country houses" nearby.[76] The 1898 Colonial Revival dwelling of Adolph Thies (544 Providence Road) survives in the 1990s as a reminder of this clustering of houses around "Myers' park." When son-in-law Stephens proposed extending the development and making the whole cotton farm a fashionable suburb, Myers was delighted. He offered Stephens the property on breathtakingly generous terms. The Stephens Company could take title to the land in sections as needed and make no payments until the lots sold.

Myers's generosity magnified George Stephens's already considerable resources. Free from the need to tie up large amounts of capital in land, he could devote cash to everything that would make Myers Park succeed. From other owners he bought 200 more acres, extending his property until it touched the existing Elizabeth neighborhood at Hawthorne Lane. To avoid the transit problems that plagued The Plaza, Stephens arranged from the start to subsidize regular trolley service into Myers Park. He paid the Southern Public Utilities Company to run its cars through the neighborhood every twenty minutes, and he helped lobby the city to build a railroad underpass on East Trade Street near College Street so that trains would not block streetcar movement from downtown. Stephens opened his wallet again to subsidize municipal utility service, hiring work crews to extend gas mains and city sewers and water out to his subdivision. He also specified that all Myers Park streets would be paved—a luxury not yet common within the city itself. Stephens even went so far as to purchase the *Charlotte Observer*, assuring abundant favorable publicity.[77] According to one project participant, the Stephens Company invested $600,000 in public improvements during the development's first decade, a staggering sum in that era.[78]

The wealth of resources also meant that the Stephens Company could give free rein to John Nolen. The eager Harvard student who had come to Charlotte to design Independence Park in 1905 had rapidly matured into one of America's busiest and most respected planners. By 1911 Nolen had already completed full-scale urban plans for cities from Roanoke, Virginia, to Madison, Wisconsin, to San Diego, California.[79] He had created one of the first plans for a state park system, for Wisconsin in 1909, and was becoming known for his campus designs, which would soon include a 1917 vision for the expansion of the University of North Carolina at Chapel Hill. During World War I he would design some of America's first federally funded housing projects, and in the 1920s his scheme for the new village of Mariemont outside Cleveland would win renown as one of the decade's best planned communities.[80] In addition to cofounding the American Planning Association, he helped create the American Society of Planning Officials and the National Housing Association and served as the first American president of the International Federation of Housing and Town Planning.[81] Upon his death in 1937 the *New York Times* would praise John Nolen as an "internationally known architect and pioneer in modern city and regional planning."[82]

In Myers Park Nolen set out to create a state-of-the-art example of the Progressive planned neighborhood, a project he later referred to proudly in books and articles as "a high-class residential suburb . . . designed aright from the first and influenced only by the best practice in modern town planning."[83] Nolen felt it essential to conceptualize a fully thought-out "unified" design for the entire 1,220-acre tract, even though it would take years to fill out as he planned. The scope was impressive not just by Charlotte standards. America's most celebrated large suburb of the decade was developer J. C. Nichols's Country Club District on the outskirts of Kansas City, advertised under the slogan "1,000 Acres Restricted." Myers Park would be one-fifth larger.[84] During 1911

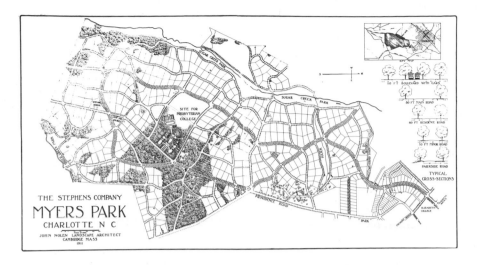

FIG. 47. NOLEN'S PLAN FOR MYERS PARK, 1911
A curving landscaped boulevard formed the main avenue of Myers Park, and abundant
parklands lined low-lying areas. John Nolen's winding street pattern conformed to the natural lay of the land and served to set the suburb off from the workaday grid of the city.
(Source: Nolen, *New Towns for Old*)

Nolen and his Boston staff drew plans to turn George Stephens's 1,200 acres
into a neighborhood of winding avenues, abundant parks, and gracious homes.

Nolen began his work with the street system, which he intentionally devised
to turn away nonresidents. "The street plan . . . in high-class residential tracts
demands the satisfaction of a sense of seclusion," he explained, "together with
the means for easy and convenient access to the broad world" for residents.[85]
Nolen discarded the old Charlotte grid pattern, referring derisively to "unnatural checkerboard streets on an undulating surface."[86] In its place he devised winding secondary roads that ignored existing city streets and instead fed
into a single main neighborhood boulevard. Nolen made the side streets
narrow and complicated, both for picturesque effect and to ensure seclusion.
"Not every street is a carrier of traffic," he observed. "Some merely lead to the
home."[87] The main boulevard, while offering "easy and convenient" access
for Myers Park residents, reinforced the neighborhood's isolation. Named
Queens Road/Queens Road West by Stephens, it began at Hawthorne Lane,
where an elaborate stone gateway "of singular beauty and lithic solidity"
alerted visitors that they were leaving the ordinary city and entering an exclusive realm.[88] The avenue then proceeded southward through the midst of the
suburb, with only two minor connections to outside streets (one at Providence

Road, the other at Morehead Street). In the southern half of the district the road looped back on itself, turning casual travelers around and pointing them back toward the suburb's main entrance. The loop arrangement had partly to do with the requirements of mass transit; a grassy median in the middle of the boulevard carried trolley tracks, and the loop route served to put every house in the district within a two-and-a-half-block walk of the streetcar. More importantly, the Queens Road loop fostered the desired sense of seclusion by making the entire Myers Park street system in effect a giant cul-de-sac.

Proposals for large house-lot sizes and provisions for elite educational and commercial facilities added to the neighborhood's exclusivity. Initially Nolen suggested that no Myers Park lot be smaller than one-half acre. Such a parcel size represented a major jump from the standard in other Charlotte subdivisions, where ⅙ acre, 50′ × 150′ lots were customary (the half-acre size did remain modest compared with affluent suburbs in older industrial areas, such as Detroit's Grosse Point or Chicago's North Shore, where families regularly marshaled the wealth to maintain estates of an acre and upwards).[89] Lack of large numbers of rich buyers in newly prosperous Charlotte forced the Stephens Company to hedge on the proposed minimum. Dartmouth Place and Amherst Place on the 1911 Myers Park plan included smaller, standard suburban lots, and as time passed Nolen's draftsmen redrew some other blocks to create additional middle-income parcels. Yet the average lot in Myers Park remained noticeably larger than that in less fashionable districts of Charlotte. Along with large lots, Nolen's drawings also showed educational institutions. The Horner Military School, an academy for young men, stood at the south edge of the suburb (later the site of the Myers Park Country Club), and in 1913 George Stephens enticed the women's school Queens College to relocate to a prime site in the heart of the neighborhood, where Nolen created an elegantly landscaped campus.[90] In addition to having its own schools, John Nolen believed that such a suburb should have its own shops, in order that housewives might avoid journeying downtown. At the Queens Road/Providence Road intersection his maps included a row of stores with automobile parking at the door, a complex that would have become of one America's earliest suburban shopping centers had it been built as planned.[91] The idea proved too far ahead of its time, though, and only a single modest shop was constructed, soon replaced by the Myers Park Presbyterian Church.[92]

While Nolen's street system and land use ideas emphasized self-containment, his proposals for community green space showed the Progressive planners' desire to both shelter and connect. A prototype children's playlot ap-

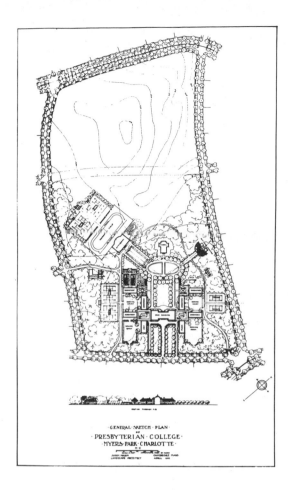

·GENERAL·SKETCH·PLAN·
of
·PRESBYTERIAN·COLLEGE·
·MYERS·PARK·CHARLOTTE·
N·C
JOHN·NOLEN   CAMBRIDGE·MASS
LANDSCAPE·ARCHITECT   APRIL·1915

FIG. 48. NOLEN'S PLAN FOR QUEENS (PRESBYTERIAN) COLLEGE

Queens (originally Presbyterian) College formed the centerpiece of John Nolen's plan for Myers Park. The gymnasium and chapel were never built, but most of the rest of the main buildings remain in much the same arrangement that Nolen designed. (Source: collection 2903, box 41, Nolen papers)

peared in the midst of one block of houses, a facility purely for neighborhood parents and accessible only by walkways running between the house lots.[93] Jack Myers's old landscaped front yard, bordered by Providence and Ardsley Roads, became another explicitly neighborhood-controlled park, owned by a self-perpetuating Myers Park Civic Commission made up of surrounding property owners.[94] Most of Myers Park's generous complement of parks, though, were less excluding. Throughout the suburb Nolen drew greenways along existing creek banks. He believed that developers should dedicate low-lying areas to public use, rather than selling them off as waste space at the backs of houses, a standard practice. This vision was realized with the building of Edgehill Park along a branch of Sugar Creek. Its grassy, tree-shaded banks are framed by the narrow twin roadways of Edgehill Road, one of the city's most beautiful drives today. Nolen urged that this greenway should extend

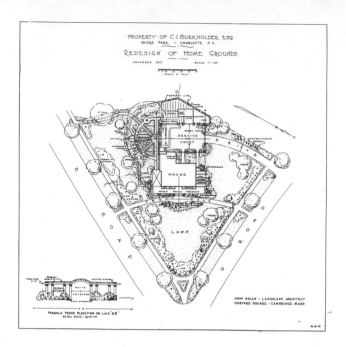

FIG. 49. NOLEN LOT PLAN, MYERS PARK

Developer George Stephens's commitment to planning was so strong that he arranged for John Nolen to provide landscape plans for lot buyers in Myers Park. These two examples, drawn by Nolen's protégé Earle Sumner Draper, show houses along Queens Road. Nolen believed that front yards should have no walls or fences, so that the landscape would flow together in parklike unity. Behind the houses are more private areas with gardens, garages

along the full course of Sugar Creek, connecting the neighborhood with Independence Park in Elizabeth and thence with other parks throughout the entire city.[95] Charlotte's showplace Freedom Park, created along Sugar Creek in the 1940s, fulfilled a tiny part of Nolen's greenway scheme, but most of the system, unfortunately, remained unbuilt.

Once streets, parks, and building locations had been decided, Nolen's Boston staff turned to the task of creating landscape plantings for Myers Park. This work was no less crucial than the overall design, since greenery constituted another powerful tool to reinforce the planner's social vision. When Nolen first saw it, the 1,200-acre tract consisted almost entirely of open fields with only two clusters of trees, one near Queens College and the other at J. S. Myers's old park. Nolen, however, desired to create a neighborhood that seemed to be set within a timeless forest, a tree-shaded retreat distinct from the hard-edged city. Under the direction of chief designer Phillip Foster, Nolen's office prepared cross-section drawings for five classes of streets, each showing

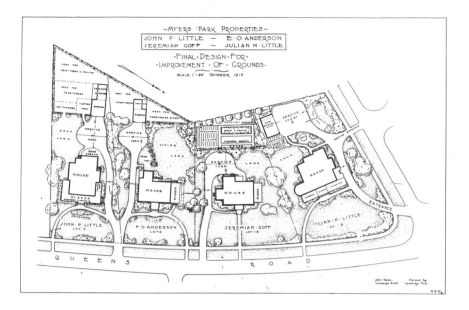

(many with servant's apartments), and often space for fruit trees and poultry—early owners evidently felt that moving to a "country home" should include such country activities as keeping chickens. Most house lots in Myers Park ran a half-acre in size. This was noticeably larger than in other Charlotte neighborhoods, though small in comparison with the rambling acreage of elite suburbs in wealthier industrial metropolises of the era—an indication of Charlotte's growing but still-modest economy in the 1910s. (Source: collection 2903, box 41, Nolen papers)

size and placement of trees, planting strips, and sidewalks adjacent to the roadways.[96] Additional blueprints illustrated landscape details; one for the Queens Road median and sidewalk area, for instance, used over two dozen species of flora to create a carefully orchestrated visual effect. Drawings listed all the plants with their precise Latin names; a gardener today would have little trouble re-creating the boulevard's original landscape.

Thanks to Stephens's impressive bankroll, John Nolen went even beyond the design of public spaces. The planner wrote landscape design guidelines into all Myers Park deeds. Along with the usual wording concerning race and minimum house cost, Myers Park restrictions included clauses aimed at encouraging beautiful greenswards along all neighborhood streets. The covenants mandated that houses be set well back from the road—forty to eighty feet according to the type of street—and forbade that any fences be erected in front yards to interrupt the visual flow of space. For dozens of lot buyers up to 1918, John Nolen's office went even further and "provided free a landscape plan showing a house with rooms best oriented to exposure, and the arrangement of driveways, walks, lawn areas and plantings."[97] The Stephens Company underwrote this custom service and also offered homeowners the materials and labor at cost to carry out the designs. Few suburbs anywhere in the United States could boast such thorough planning.

The high level of designer involvement continued as Myers Park construction began in 1912. In many fashionable suburbs planners would visit the site only a handful of times, initially to ascertain the lay of the land and then perhaps once or twice to inspect construction. Such was the case with Dilworth, where Frederick Law Olmsted Jr. sent his designer Percival Gallagher to Charlotte on two occasions, then came once himself. Even in the Olmsteds' much grander Druid Hills district in Atlanta most design work was done from the firm's New England office, with actual construction entrusted to the local developer. In Myers Park, by contrast, Nolen's office kept an employee on site at all times to supervise construction, make any necessary revisions to the overall plan, and prepare the landscape plans for individual lot buyers. In October 1915 a young man named Earle Sumner Draper, just graduated with a degree in landscape gardening from what is now the University of Massachusetts, arrived in Charlotte to take over the field supervisor job.[98] Draper's training had a clear impact on Myers Park's landscape, and his experiences in the neighborhood set him on the road to a noted career in planning. As soon as he arrived, Draper found himself caught up in a massive tree-moving effort.[99] Tobacco magnate J. B. Duke had just purchased a fifty-room mansion at the heart of Myers Park, and he expressed disappointment at the small size of saplings being planted along the neighborhood's avenues. Using foremen and special mule-drawn carts from Duke's estate in New Jersey, Draper and his crews moved hundreds of mature willow oaks and water oaks (ten to sixteen inches in trunk diameter) up from low-lying spots to line the new streets. The project's success won regional and national notice.[100] Almost instantly Myers Park's raw cottonfields became the forested glen that Nolen had envisioned.

Charlotte's New South elite flocked to build houses in the suburb. The very first lot buyers followed the old custom of locating their dwellings on the busiest and most visible streets. In 1912 furniture manufacturer H. M. Wade had a commanding house erected on Hermitage Road facing across J. S. Myers's old park toward busy Providence Road, and the same year hotelman J. M. Jamison commissioned a large stone villa right on the Providence highway.[101] Grain merchant Charles Moody erected a similar-sized mansion next door in 1913. Fairly quickly, though, a new pattern manifested itself. Myers Park's wealthiest citizens would locate not on Providence Road or even on the grand boulevard of Queens Road, but on the small secondary streets hidden away in the heart of the neighborhood. David Clark, who published the influential *Southern Textile Bulletin,* built at the corner of Queens and Hermitage Roads in 1914 but faced his house toward Hermitage Road rather than toward the Queens Road boulevard. George Stephens constructed a large house for himself the following year, tucked away on tiny Harvard Place. H. M. McAden, who headed Charlotte's First National Bank and controlled the textile town of McAdenville, commissioned leading local architect Louis Asbury to create one of the city's finest mansions in 1917, a Mediterranean-style dwelling hidden from the public eye on narrow Granville Road. No one better personified the move to the side streets than the engineer-entrepreneurs of James B. Duke's Southern Power Company. First came Norman Cocke, who built on Harvard Place in 1913. He eventually rose to head the utility, and today Lake Norman north of Charlotte is named in his honor. In 1915 three other top Southern Power officials built nearby. Company president E. C. Marshall's house looked across J. S. Myers Park at Providence Road, but the homes of executives Charles I. Burkholder and Z. V. Taylor were located farther back within the neighborhood, the former on Ardsley Road and the latter overlooking Edgehill Park. Taylor's site proved so attractive that James B. Duke himself bought the house shortly after its completion. Duke expanded the residence into a fifty-two room mansion, added acres of gardens and fountains, and used the estate as his Southern base when visiting from his main home in New Jersey to attend to his hydroelectric investments.[102]

The fine houses clustered in the quiet heart of Myers Park made the suburb a concentration of wealth and power not merely for the city but for the entire Piedmont region of the South. Duke, Marshall, Taylor, Cocke, Burkholder, and William States Lee, who bought the Stephens house on Harvard Place in the 1920s, constituted the top management of Southern Power and its successor Duke Power for nearly half a century. Under their leadership the company brought electricity to a broad swath of the Carolinas, developed industrial real estate, and operated urban transit systems throughout the region.[103] Rivaling the Duke Power men in importance was Myers Park's impressive roster of textile mill owners. R. Horace Johnston, proprietor of the factories at North Charlotte, resided in a Myers Park estate almost as impressive as J. B.

Duke's. Colonel Leroy Springs, the famed founder of Springs Mills, lived across the street. Members of many of the other major mill-owning families throughout the region—Cannon, Hanes, Erwin, Pharr, Stowe, Lineberger, Tanner, and Gossett—maintained homes in the suburb by the 1920s. To a very large extent these men controlled the economic destiny of North and South Carolina.

The architecture these residents chose reflected the latest suburban fashions. The 1910s saw some Colonial-style dwellings, most notably architect C. C. Hook's design for the J. B. Duke Mansion, and several houses in the no-nonsense Rectilinear mode, including the 1916 residence of David Ovens, hard-driving executive of the Ivey's Department Store chain and the man for whom Charlotte's municipal Ovens Auditorium is named. The favorite style in the 1910s in Myers Park was the Bungalow. George Stephens, Norman Cocke, C. I. Burkholder, and banker Charles Lambeth were among those who favored the rustic, wood-shingled look. It perfectly conveyed the adventure of moving into the countryside—"a country home on a city street," promised one Stephens Company ad—and it also gave the big houses a manly "hunting lodge" appearance.

In the 1920s, as Myers Park came to seem less remote and as national architectural fashions changed, Bungalow architecture fell from popularity, and the Colonial Revival and various European styles became favorites. The new styles continued to serve to set wealthy suburbanites apart from blue-collar folk, as a Chamber of Commerce brochure noted at the decade's end: "Cottage and bungalow types of homes"—comfortable but passé—"house the large majority of the working population, while hundreds of handsome homes of English, Italian, Spanish and Colonial types adorn the more expensive residential sections."[104] An example of 1920s Colonial Revival in Myers Park is the house that H. M. Wade built in 1928 to replace his original residence on Hermitage Road. Charles Barton Keen, the New York "society" architect responsible for the famed R. J. Reynolds mansion in Winston-Salem, gave Wade an elegantly stylized design in red brick with stately chimneys and attenuated white columns.[105] Perhaps the finest of Myers Park's outstanding collection of English designs is the Tudor Revival-style Lethco House on Roswell Avenue. Designed by Charlotte architect William Peeps, a native of England, it combines brick and stone and half-timbered stucco in baronial splendor. "Standing in even ranks beneath their great trees," writes a leading architectural historian, Myers Park's houses "recall individually the architecture of the great

Virginia planter or the English squire; as an ensemble they evoke a shared set of tastes, values and ambitions . . . a powerful sense of group membership."[106]

Specific details seen in Myers Park would continue to pop up in subsequent elite developments in Charlotte throughout the century: entry gates, landscape plantings, a bit of boulevard with a grassy median, and especially winding street systems calculated to thwart intruders. Nolen's design would exert considerable influence beyond the city as well, particularly through the work of Earle Sumner Draper, who stayed on after his apprenticeship and became a busy planner of some 250 curvilinear subdivisions all over the South.[107] Perhaps the neighborhood's greatest significance to the historian, however, is the way its form neatly summed up a period of swift and radical change in Charlotte's residential landscape. Twenty years earlier men with money had chosen prominent sites at the heart of town. Now they sought seclusion in the suburbs. By the late 1910s it was clear that Charlotte's "best residences" henceforth would be located away from main roads, sheltered amidst artful landscaping, protected by deed restrictions, and buffered by self-contained suburban street systems.

Thanks to George Stephens's support, John Nolen succeeded in Myers Park in realizing much of his vision of an exclusive "high class residential suburb" embodying "the best practice in modern town planning." Nolen would face greater challenges as he strove to make Myers Park the first step in a comprehensive city plan for Charlotte, as we shall see in Chapter 8. First, though, we will turn attention to the area that elite residents were leaving as they moved out to Piedmont Park, Myers Park, and the other new white collar suburbs: Charlotte's center city.

The . . . business buildings erected and in contemplation in Charlotte while adding to the general appearance of the City . . . also [offer] another indication of general prosperity and show the City's onward stride towards being one of the leading cities of the South. Skyscrapers are gradually rising here.

—The Story of Charlotte, Illustrated, 1915

THE SAME YEARS of the early twentieth century that witnessed the rapid sorting-out of Charlotte residential areas also saw major changes in the central business district. Downtown grew dramatically in size, driven both by the growing city population and by a business economy that generated more and more white-collar jobs. Organization of land uses sharpened noticeably during the 1900s–1920s. Businessmen increasingly clustered particular types of enterprises into zones: a provision district catering to blue-collar shoppers, a fashionable row of genteel ladies' apparel stores, and other distinct areas for doctors, for cotton brokers, for motion picture distributors, and so on.[1] Most visibly—and most remarkably for this small town (46,000 people in 1920)— South Tryon Street took shape as a "financial canyon" of skyscrapers whose symbolism explicitly echoed New York City's Wall Street. As elsewhere in the New South city, the forms that Charlotteans chose for this evolving downtown had much to do with the way they viewed society.

GROWTH OF COMMERCE

The years immediately after 1900 witnessed explosive growth in Charlotte's central business district. As the town mushroomed from fewer than 20,000 citizens in 1900 to more than 82,000 in 1930, businesses crowded around the crossroads at Trade and Tryon Streets. Residences—a familiar sight in the heart of the community only a generation earlier—disappeared completely within the downtown commercial core. "The second and third floors of the First National Bank Building, which have always been used as a residence, will be converted into office rooms," reported the *Charlotte Observer* in 1897.[2] Transportation patterns of the era helped focus all the city's commercial energy directly on the blocks surrounding the Square. With no interstate highways or bypasses in those days, every country lane in the vicinity funneled its traffic onto Trade and Tryon Streets. The Southern and the Seaboard Railroads and the Piedmont & Northern interurban let off their passengers downtown. Charlotte's streetcar system intensified the crush. In a marvelous maze of steel rails and overhead wires, all trolley lines from every corner of the city converged upon the Square. "Through Independence Square, the center of the city, 1,640 [trolley] cars pass every day," wrote an observer in 1924.[3] Such traffic made the intersection an unparalleled coming-together place. White housewives in from Myers Park for lunch and shopping, black ministers from Washington Heights on their way to Second Ward churches, factory hands from South Boulevard industries going back home to Belmont–Villa Heights, and clerks hurrying from Elizabeth Bungalows to downtown offices all met at Trade and Tryon. Retailers and employers of every sort vied to locate enterprises close to this pulsing stream. Shopkeepers dependent on walk-in customers, wholesale operations drawing visiting buyers, and even office managers wishing to attract white-collar employees from the suburbs all saw great advantage in being close to the Square. Charlotte's downtown, which had extended little more than a block from the intersection in the nineteenth century, now expanded exponentially. By the end of the 1920s a visitor stepping off the trolley at the Square could stroll through an area covering more than twenty blocks with an unbroken streetscape of nothing but business buildings.

That streetscape did not merely hold more businesses than before; it included whole new categories of economic enterprise. Chain stores, a fresh trend nationally, appeared in growing numbers after 1900. Tennessee-based S. H. Kress opened the city's first "dime store" in 1904, followed by Woolworth, McClellans, and W. T. Grant.[4] By the 1920s chains competed with local merchants in nearly every category, from Thom McAn Shoes to Liggett Drugs to Sterchi Furniture.[5] Technological innovation accounted for other retail expansion. In 1906 and 1907 local impresario Colonel William A. Peters outfitted three downtown shops as "nickelodeons" where patrons could view just-invented motion pictures. By the late 1920s Peters's picture parlors would give way to opulent movie palaces operated by national theater companies, including the Broadway on South Tryon Street, owned by Warner Brothers, and the Carolina on North Tryon Street, owned by the Publix Corporation.[6] Automobiles entered the retail scene circa 1903 when downtown hardware dealer Osmond Barringer began selling Oldsmobiles. Barringer quickly found that he could also wholesale cars to sellers in surrounding mill towns, and he soon boasted the "state agency for White Steamers, Baker electrics, and Franklin and Oldsmobile gasoline machines."[7] By the 1920s most autos sold in the Carolinas would pass through Charlotte distributors, and Ford assembled Model Ts and Model As in a sprawling factory on Statesville Avenue.[8]

Indeed, distribution of all kinds of products now emerged as a mainstay of Charlotte's economy. Numerous concerns attracted by the city's rail connections and economic vitality launched new office/shipping operations in the center city. Nabisco, pioneering the concept of brand-name bakery products for the national market, chose a First Ward site at the edge of downtown for its regional bakery and distribution center in the 1920s.[9] A major Southern rival, Lance Incorporated, got its start in a coffee-roasting establishment at Fourth and College Streets in 1906 before moving to a large suburban baking plant.[10] The Great Atlantic and Pacific Tea Company, better known as A&P, erected a four-story warehouse and corporate office downtown in 1926 to serve its growing brood of grocery stores in the region.[11] The Baltimore Victor Talking Machine Company rented upstairs quarters on South Tryon for use as a wholesale showroom for its radios and Victrola phonographs. In the 1930s that space would be used as a field recording studio by RCA Victor engineers who captured on disc dozens of important country, blues, and gospel musicians, including the father of bluegrass music, Bill Monroe.[12]

Along with the retailers and wholesale distributors, new kinds of office operations also bolstered downtown's white-collar workforce. Mill owner R. Horace Johnston provided one example when he commissioned construction of the Johnston Building. In the early days of the textile industry, mill men had often done their managerial work out of a room in the factory or an office on the grounds. As the Southern cotton mills now progressed into their second generation of prosperity, executives often migrated downtown. Horace Johnston, son of Charles Worth Johnston and heir to the factories his father had developed at North Charlotte, moved into his skyscraper on South Tryon Street in 1924.[13] The showy sixteen-story tower designed by New York City architect William Stoddard held not only Johnston's headquarters but also suites for textile trade associations, mill machinery salesmen, insurance company representatives, and other white-collar enterprises that had grown up to serve the piedmont manufacturing region.

Banks comprised the most visible component of the explosion in office work. Back in the nineteenth century, lending had occurred largely informally as men of property advanced cash to their neighbors. Those formal financial institutions that did exist had few employees, often just the banker himself and a cashier. Around 1900, however, a transformation took place as men grown wealthy in textiles and real estate development turned to banking to put their money to work in more diverse projects. Many of the institutions that would make North Carolina the banking center of the Southeast by the 1990s took root in this turn-of-the-century boom. Real estate developers F. C. Abbott and George Stephens created Southern States Trust in 1901, soon reorganized with the addition of textile entrepreneur A. J. Draper as American Trust.[14] American Trust would eventually merge with the city's older Commercial National Bank (controlled by the Holt textile clan) to form North

TABLE 5. Charlotte's New South Banks, 1865–1930

Bank	Date Founded	Descendant in 1990s
First National Bank	1865	*
Commercial National Bank	1874	NationsBank
Merchants & Farmers National Bank	1875	*
Charlotte National Bank	1897	Wachovia
Southern States Trust/American Trust	1901	NationsBank
Union National Bank	1908	First Union
Independence Trust Company	1912	*
Citizens Bank	1914	First Citizens
Charlotte Morris Plan Bank/Bank of Charlotte	1918	
Fifth Street Industrial/City Industrial/City Savings	1920	
Industrial Loan & Investment Bank/Bank of Commerce	1922	
Industrial Bank of Mecklenburg	1923	*
Federal Reserve Bank	1927	still in operation

* failed in depression of 1930s

Source: Blythe and Brockmann, *Hornets' Nest*, pp. 303–9.

Carolina National Bank—today the national powerhouse NationsBank. Its main contemporary rival, First Union of Charlotte, dates back to the Union National Bank founded in 1908.[15] Two other leading Carolina institutions also have progenitors in turn-of-the-century Charlotte. The Charlotte National Bank of 1897 became a major part of modern-day Wachovia, and Citizen's Bank of 1914 contributed to the creation of today's First Citizens. Confirmation of the city's rise as a banking center came in 1927 when Charlotte succeeded in luring a branch of the Federal Reserve Bank. The Queen City offered a logical spot for the bank's operations serving western North Carolina and upcountry South Carolina, a Reserve official wrote, since the city already possessed "more banks, capital, deposits and resources than any other city in North Carolina."[16] The Federal Reserve branch maintained the cash reserves of area banks and made loans to them, moved currency and coins in and out of circulation, and provided swift interbank check clearing, which gave Charlotte an additional financial edge over other cities in the region. In all, between 1897 and the end of the 1920s, ten new banking institutions opened their doors in Charlotte, each adding a workforce of loan officers, tellers, accountants, and managers to the bustle of downtown.

While business growth pushed residences out of the downtown proper, the center city did still retain a sizable residential component. Beyond the edges of the business district, dwellings continued to line the streets of Charlotte's original four wards (the area from McDowell Street to Graham Street within today's inner expressway loop). The character of these avenues shifted as population intensified and suburbia drew away particular social groups.

With the rise of Charlotte's white-collar suburbs, affluent families largely ceased building new single-family dwellings in the old central wards after the 1900s. Trade Street and Tryon Street, the town's most sought-after residential addresses in the late nineteenth century, gradually faded in desirability, retaining some prestige only as long as the couples who had taken up residence there before 1900 remained alive. Old-line churches helped preserve a certain sense of stability. First Presbyterian Church on West Trade Street, St. Peter's Episcopal on North Tryon, and St. Peter's Catholic on South Tryon continued to occupy structures erected in the nineteenth century. Other congregations joined them immediately after 1900, when land was just becoming available on the main avenues but it was not yet clear that most parishioners would soon be in the suburbs. First Baptist Church (1908) and First Associated Reform Presbyterian (1910) on North Tryon Street and Tabernacle Associated Reform Presbyterian (1911) on East Trade contributed an air of elite desirability to the old avenues, but change continued nonetheless.[17] One battle over street names symbolized the transition. In 1895 wealthy homeowners on East Trade below Brevard Street petitioned to have their street renamed East Avenue.[18] The linguistic device was intended to set the still-residential portion of the street apart from the expanding commercial section near the Square. Before long, however, business structures and government buildings began supplanting houses even in the East Avenue blocks. In the mid-1920s the name reverted to East Trade Street.

The decades after 1900 did witness some new white-collar residential construction in downtown Charlotte in the form of apartments. The United States experienced a vogue for apartment living beginning in the late nineteenth century.[19] Though critics cried that the new mode would spell the end of traditional family life, middle-class urbanites flocked to live in stylish multi-family dwellings. Landlords often included the latest inventions in household comfort—full bathrooms, electric kitchens, garbage incinerators, and vacuum cleaning apparatus—to distinguish the apartments from the older and decidedly unpopular tenements of the big-city poor. In Charlotte, where land remained inexpensive, apartments arrived comparatively late. In 1900 the *Observer* suggested that the city's growing number of young white-collar workers might constitute a market for apartment living.[20] Three years later the paper carried a drawing of downtown's first such structure, the elegant Graham Apartments then under construction on North Tryon Street between Sixth and Seventh Streets (site of Discovery Place museum today). Architecturally the Graham was a two-story row of townhouse-type rental units solidly executed in brick and stone in the latest Victorian style. The spacious quarters were clearly aimed at the well-to-do, an appeal reinforced by the Graham's address among the older estates on long-fashionable North Tryon.[21]

The apartments that followed the Graham usually occupied similar sites—convenient to downtown on streets just beginning to lose desirability for upscale, single-family houses. North and South Tryon proved particularly popular (see fig. 51), as did North Church Street one block over in Fourth Ward.[22] Developers soon settled on a standard plan: a three- or four-story structure with apartments on each floor lining a central hall running back the length of the building. Ornament enlivened the street facade, which was often crowned with a panel delineating the apartment's name. The Frederick, for instance, which still stands on North Church Street, took its name from its developer, Fred Casey. In April 1927 he announced construction of the three-story structure with "eleven living apartments, sixteen single rooms with bath, and seven pairs of rooms with bath," featuring refrigerators and dishwashers in each unit.[23] Among the Frederick's tenants in its first decade was the young newspaperman W. J. Cash, who lived there while writing editorials for the *Charlotte News* and completing his acclaimed book *The Mind of the South*.

New apartment buildings constituted just a small part of a noticeable increase in the density of land use in the center city during the early twentieth century. White-collar dwellings built prior to the suburban exodus were now cut up into multifamily rental units by their old owners or by speculators. Those houses that did remain single-family homes passed into the hands of less-affluent people. Center city residential streets became a mix of blue-collar rooming houses, homes owned by blue-collar families or older white-collar individuals, and apartments for young downtown store clerks and office workers. At the same time, the area grew as a location for commerce and manufacturing. "Back Lots Becoming Warehouse and Factory Sites," headlined the

Observer in 1899. "The ground in the rear of business blocks is beginning to be utilized. . . . Charlotte is learning to economize space as her larger and more populous sisters do."[24]

As land uses shifted and intensified, Charlotte's original four wards each took on different identities. In First Ward, as we saw in Chapter 5, an African-American enclave sprang into existence with the rise of Jim Crow. Its presence evidently discouraged investors who might have contemplated construction of upscale apartments, and as a result First Ward became increasingly a purely blue-collar district, with both black and white residents. In Second Ward the old black section expanded markedly after 1900 and whites departed, making the entire ward almost exclusively African American. Third Ward, meanwhile, absorbed the greatest business expansion. During the 1910s James B. Duke bought up the heart of the district to build headquarters for his Duke Power Company and Southern Public Utilities transit corporation, plus the terminal for his Piedmont & Northern interurban electric railway line.[25] Pockets of working-class cottages lingered, but by 1930 Third Ward was the most heavily nonresidential of the center city wards. Fourth Ward, by contrast, retained the most residential appeal. There the new apartment blocks on Church Street attracted downtown's only sizable white-collar population. Elsewhere in the ward, however, streets that had long held leading citizens fell from fashion, and once-proud Victorian houses became cheap rental quarters.

DISTRICTS FOR RETAIL, DISTRIBUTION, AND FINANCE

Changes in economics and fashion similarly reshaped the downtown business district. Charlotte's growing economy attracted new stores and offices, all of which vied to locate as close as possible to the vibrant transportation crossroads at Trade and Tryon Streets. Businesses of every type bid against one another for prime spots, and land use became denser as developers sought to pack more enterprises into the available acreage. Raw economics alone did not dictate the look of downtown's evolving landscape, however. Entrepreneurs often chose locations and architectural forms based on image as well as function.

A good place to begin examining the sorting-out within the business district is in the long-established shops of East Trade Street. In the nineteenth century the railroads and the cotton wharf had made East Trade the commercial hub of Charlotte, home to businesses of every type. Wealthy cotton brokers occupied genteel offices; general merchants bought cotton and sold all the supplies that visiting farmers might need for the year; black businesses (see Chapter 5) as well as white ones competed to catch the trade of country folk and townspeople of every class. As the twentieth century dawned, that casual intermingling declined. The old-fashioned dry goods store, with its wide variety of merchandise, was giving way to the new specialty store, which focused on one particular line. In Charlotte, specialized outfits such as Max's Men's Shop, Kirshbaum Furriers, and J. L. Staten Lingerie appeared. These new stores tended to depart from East Trade Street, leaving behind those businesses that carried on the old work of supplying basic necessities.

By 1907 East Trade was "center of the feed, provision and supply houses and wholesale grocery stores," a workaday shopping district.[26] Nearly all the city's full-line grocers located there, as did specialty markets such as the Acme Fish Company and the fruit stands operated by Charlotte's handful of Greek, Syrian, and Italian immigrants.[27] When farmers came in from the country, or when millhands journeyed downtown after the factories let out on Saturday, they often headed first to East Trade Street. The district became a prime site for businesses catering to clientele with limited pocket money: Biltrite Credit Shoe Store, the Convenient Payment Tire System, the Big Chief Medicine Company, and Uncle Sam's Loan Office. Black customers as well as whites shopped along East Trade. A few black-owned businesses, refusing to bow to pressures to relocate to Brooklyn, remained in the 200 block of East Trade, particularly in the mid-block alley known as Howell's Arcade.[28] White entrepreneurs often made a point of welcoming black trade along with whites, as when Colonel Peters opened the Star Nickelodeon in 1907 with seating for both races.[29] East Trade's constant throng of shoppers made the street the site of an informal curb market at harvest time, where farmers pulled wagons up to the sidewalk to sell produce directly to passersby.[30]

As East Trade Street took on the character of a provision district for the mass of Charlotteans, the "better class of businesses" moved out. The progression could be seen clearly in the city's department stores. Charlotte's earliest department stores all appeared initially on Trade Street and carried names that indicated their mass appeal: the Racket Store, the Beehive, and the operation run by William Henry Belk under the slogan Cheapest Store on Earth. Once established, though, Charlotte department stores strove to emulate elegant emporiums such as Macy's in New York and Marshall Field in Chicago. Belk initiated this upscaling when he commissioned architect C. C. Hook to erect a five-story tower with a distinguished stone and terra-cotta front next to his original modest Trade Street shop in 1911.[31] Belk's chief rivals, Efird's and

Ivey's, countered by leaving the East Trade district altogether and erecting elaborate premises on North Tryon Street in the 1920s.[32] Eventually Belk would buy out Efird's in order to get a foothold on North Tryon as well.

North Tryon, indeed, became the city's most elite shopping area by the 1920s. Leading businesses did not locate only there. Garibaldi & Bruns, the city's top jeweler, occupied a distinguished terra-cotta shopfront on South Tryon, for instance, and the stylish Art Moderne-style premises of the S&W Cafeteria stood on West Trade. But none of these blocks could match North Tryon in density of upscale shopping opportunities. In addition to the major department stores, the street held nearly all of the women's apparel shops catering to Charlotte's middle and upper class. Ladies could look for hats at New York Millinery and Gross Millinery, enjoy a beauty treatment at the Lucille Permanent Wave Shoppe, try on shoes at the Rose Marie Slipper Shoppe, or browse through the new dresses at Braus, Worth, Rice's, Purcell's, or Lucie Shops—just to name the stores in the block of North Tryon closest to the Square. Such clustering created an air of sales excitement à la the "ladies' miles" appearing in bigger cities. And amid predominantly feminine stores, a woman shopper enjoyed the comforting likelihood of mingling mainly with her social peers.[33]

Not all image-conscious businessmen chose spots close to the Square. As automobile dealers appeared in the city, they shrewdly sought to capitalize on the fading fashionability of the grand avenues leading out of downtown. The big old houses coming on the market included land adequate for a car lot, and the addresses still held enough glamour to make them desirable for dealers of such upscale goods as automobiles. Carolina Oldsmobile, for instance, built on North Tryon Street, while C. C. Coddington's elegant Buick showroom, designed by nationally renowned architect Louis Kahn, rose proudly on West Trade Street.[34] Similar considerations also made such locations ideal for a very different kind of new establishment: the funeral parlor. The city's first full-time mortician had arrived only recently, in 1887, promising to "conduct the business in regular city fashion."[35] To entice families away from the tradition of holding funerals at home, morticians favored prestigious, semiresidential locations. Charlotte's finest such establishment in the 1920s was the Hovis Mortuary on North Tryon Street. Its architecture, by leading residential designer William Peeps, reinforced the prestige of its address by employing the same Tudor Revival elements then in vogue for estates of the rich.[36]

Fourth Ward emerged as a center for professionalized medical care in this period. St. Peter's Hospital introduced the notion in the 1880s, and after the

FIG. 50. NEW LAND USES ON NORTH TRYON STREET
This block of North Tryon Street between Eighth and Ninth Streets illustrates the
changes in land use that downtown avenues witnessed during the first years of the twentieth century. Until the 1910s this block held elegant residences. Soon after 1910 houses
gave way to auto dealerships (Carolina Olds, at right), white-collar apartment houses
(Tryon House, center), and funeral homes (Hovis Mortuary, left). (Photograph by author,
March 1993)

turn of the century its red-brick complex at Sixth and Poplar Streets came to
anchor a veritable medical district in downtown's northwest quadrant.[37] Presbyterian Hospital started operation on West Trade at Mint Street in 1903, and
the Charlotte Sanitorium opened at Church and Seventh in 1907, joined in
the 1920s by the adjacent Charlotte Eye, Ear, and Throat Clinic.[38] One other
care facility, 1906 Mercy Hospital on the grounds of St. Peter's Catholic
Church on South Tryon, fell outside this quadrant. But the concentration was
otherwise strong enough to lure a major medical school to the Fourth Ward.
The North Carolina Medical College, whose handsome 1907 building still
stands at Church and Sixth Streets, functioned for several years as the only
such school in the state for white students.[39] Doctors clustered near the hospitals and college; city directories by the 1910s showed physicians' offices of
every description located above the stores on West Trade and North Tryon. In
1923 a number of such men pooled their resources and hired architect Louis
Asbury to design a Professional Building on North Tryon at Seventh.[40] The
eight-story tower, rising above surrounding structures with its distinguished

cream-colored brickwork, provided a strong visual image for the city's medical community, an important asset as Charlotte grew and physicians could no longer depend on word-of-mouth networks to bring in patients.

Clustering could be observed even in businesses that did not directly deal with the public. One such group were motion picture distributors, another of the regional wholesale operations attracted to the Queen City by the town's excellent transportation ties. "Charlotte's location and railroad facilities are such that the place lends itself as a logical city for film distribution and the distribution of theatrical supplies," explained the proprietor of one of the first such agencies.[41] Fox opened a facility with storage and shipping space and a screening room in 1921, followed by other major Hollywood studios, including Goldwyn and Paramount in 1923 and Columbia and United Artists in 1926.[42] "All national film companies maintain exchanges in Charlotte and the movie establishments of the Carolinas are served through this city. The aggregate volume of business transacted annually by these film exchanges is approximately $2,250,000," boasted Chamber of Commerce officials in 1929. "As a motion picture distribution center Charlotte has developed into one of the most important in the South."[43] The competing distributors vied to win the business of visiting theater owners, in town for the day, who moved from agency to agency previewing films and deciding which to book. To catch this trade, the film exchanges clustered tightly in a two-block stretch of South Church Street nicknamed Film Row.

Cotton brokers, too, coalesced into a highly identifiable district in this period. In the nineteenth century these men had scattered throughout the vicinity of the cotton wharf, where their offices intermingled with the restaurants and groceries serving visiting farmers. As East Trade Street sank in stature during the 1900s, brokers began seeking more prestigious surroundings. They found them in the Latta Arcade, an elegant two-story array of offices and shops under a glistening glass roof, developed by Edward Dilworth Latta on South Tryon Street in 1914.[44] So many brokers and allied professionals sought space in the building that in the 1920s Latta created a through-block extension known as Brevard Court. By 1929 virtually all the city's cotton merchants had left the provision district and taken up quarters in the Latta Arcade/Brevard Court vicinity. It was an image-conscious move. "The old sample hung from over a door by a string to indicate the office of a local cotton buyer on the street that was central to that business, has disappeared and the gold leaf sign on a plate glass front has taken its place," wrote a Charlotte booster in 1924.[45] Cotton traders now manipulated goods by telephone and

Charlotte, N. C.   Mecklenburg County Court House, showing Square, Independence Monument and New Office Building.

FIG. 51. 1897 MECKLENBURG COUNTY COURTHOUSE
Construction of a new county courthouse set the stage for the transformation of South
Tryon Street from residential to office use. The building went up in 1897 at the southeast
corner of Tryon and Sixth, then an area of dwellings. (Courtesy of the Robinson-Spangler
Carolina Room, Public Library of Charlotte and Mecklenburg County)

telegraph, rather than dirtying their hands dealing with actual bales on the
loading dock, and their new offices were intended to emphasize this white-
collar professionalism.

Such men considered the Latta Arcade an especially fitting address because it lay within the city's financial district, just then taking shape along
South Tryon Street. For well over a century of Charlotte's history, South Tryon
had been no more or less prominent than any of the other of Charlotte's four
principal avenues. Near the Square could be found the same mix of businesses as operated on North Tryon or West Trade or East Trade. Farther from
the Square stood the big houses of prosperous leaders, just as on those other
streets. Then, around the turn of the century, South Tryon's land uses began
to shift. The immediate catalyst was the construction of a new Mecklenburg
County Courthouse at South Tryon and Third Street in 1897, an elaborate
structure in the Neoclassical style with gleaming white walls and a shining
dome reminiscent of the U.S. Capitol. Immediately, a sharp-eyed entrepreneur erected a similarly styled building (minus the dome) across the street.[46]
Rising an unheard-of four stories, it held nothing but offices. Some rented to
lawyers needing space near the courthouse, a long-familiar pattern. But the

A 12122 South Tryon Street, Charlotte, N. C.

FIG. 52. OFFICE DEVELOPMENT BEGINS ON SOUTH TRYON
Within months of completion of the 1897 courthouse, an enterprising developer erected a
four-story office building across the street (left of postcard). In 1903 it was joined by the
elaborate mansard-roofed Trust Building of F. C. Abbott, a seven-story structure that
ranked as Charlotte's first office tower. With that, South Tryon Street's destiny as an elite
office corridor was set. (Courtesy of the Robinson-Spangler Carolina Room, Public Library of Charlotte and Mecklenburg County)

prime tenant was the Piedmont Fire Insurance Company, one of the rapidly
growing number of white-collar businesses springing up to serve the region's
bustling textile economy. The success of the Piedmont Building showed real
estate dealers that a market for office space existed in Charlotte. In 1899
Edward Dilworth Latta announced plans for a seven-story tower just up the
street, publishing grand drawings of a mansard-roofed skyscraper in the *Charlotte Observer*.[47] Latta's scheme failed to materialize, but in 1903 fellow developer F. C. Abbott adapted the plans to create the Trust Building at 212 South
Tryon.[48] Looming dramatically over the surrounding two- and three-story
buildings of downtown, it formed a mighty beacon for future development.

The Trust Building touched off a skyscraper boom that remade Charlotte's
downtown landscape during the next two decades. In 1909 the Independence
Trust Company bank completed construction of the Independence Building
at the Square.[49] Rising ten stories, the tower held the bank on its ground floor
and office suites for rental above. The Independence Building attracted attention across the South as the first structure in the Carolinas to employ the just-
perfected technology of steel frame construction. To make way for the tower,

TABLE 6. Downtown Charlotte's Tall Building Boom, 1900–1930

Year	Name	Address	No. of Stories	Architect	Fate
1903	Trust Building	212 S. Tryon	7	Hayden, Wheeler & Schwend	burned 1920s, replaced by Johnston building
1909	Independence Building	N. Tryon & W. Trade	10	Frank Milburn	demolished 1980s, replaced by Marriott Hotel
1911	Commercial National Bank	S. Tryon & W. 4th	11		demolished 1960s, replaced by BBT Tower
1923	Professional Building	N. Tryon & W. 7th	8	Louis Asbury	demolished 1990s
1924	Hotel Charlotte	W. Trade & Poplar	10	W. L. Stoddard	demolished 1980s
1924	Johnston Building	212 S. Tryon	16	W. L. Stoddard	extant
1926	Builders Building	314 W. Trade	7	M. R. Marsh?	renovated as Peace Building 1980s
1926	Wilder Building	S. Tryon & E. 3rd	10		demolished 1980s
1926	First National Bank Bldg.	S. Tryon	20	Louis Asbury	extant
1928?	Law Building	E. Trade	8		demolished 1990s, replaced by jail addition
1929	Mayfair Manor Hotel	N. Tryon & W. 6th	10	Louis Asbury	renovated in 1980s

poignantly, workmen razed the old wooden structure at the Square that banker and planter John Irwin had built back in the 1830s as his combined home and workplace (see fig. 10), a transition symbolic of downtown's remaking as a place solely for commerce. Once Independence Trust was installed within the granite-and-brick splendor of the Independence Building, other banks began coveting skyscraper addresses. Commercial National Bank erected a tower at South Tryon and Fourth Streets in 1911.[50] Desire for height apparently played a major part in the bank's calculations. The building was slim—just thirty-five feet wide—and elevators and stairs took up much of the space on each floor; but it did soar eleven stories and thus outrivaled the Independence Building.

In 1924 Merchants and Farmers Bank left its original building on East Trade Street to join the coalescing financial district on South Tryon, taking up the ground floor of the sixteen-story Johnston Building. Winner of the skyscraper competition was First National Bank. The bank now demolished its original 1860s building and erected a twenty-story tower in the first block of South Tryon in 1926, with a grand carved stone archway highlighting the entrance to the banking rooms. Unfortunately, the structure proved too great a strain on the institution's resources when the Great Depression arrived three years later; First National permanently closed its doors in 1930.[51]

With the clustering of skyscrapers along Tryon Street from the Square southward, Charlotte thus developed a highly visible financial corridor. Other organizations seeking prestigious addresses increasingly gravitated here, such as the city's Masonic lodges, which erected an ornate Masonic Temple in the mysterious Egyptian Revival style in 1915.[52] By the 1920s the demand for South Tryon quarters grew so great that developers could launch a skyscraper without first securing a prime tenant—the Wilder Building, completed in 1926.[53] South Tryon did not exercise a complete monopoly on tall buildings, of course. Local contractors pooled resources and constructed the seven-story Builders Building on West Trade Street to house their offices, and attorneys employed a similar sort of cooperative arrangement to erect the eight-floor Lawyers Building next to the county's new courthouse on East Trade.[54] The Hotel Charlotte rose on West Trade near the Southern Railway Station in 1924, and the smaller Mayfair Hotel appeared out North Tryon Street in 1929.[55] Those structures remained isolated, individual buildings, though, in contrast to the veritable canyon of skyscrapers taking shape on South Tryon Street.

The visual image of the South Tryon financial corridor was an important part of its reason for being. If mere proximity to one another had driven bankers, they would have done better to pick sites clustered tightly around one or two blocks, rather than array structures in a line a quarter-mile long. And if cost had been key, low-rise buildings would have made more sense; ample land existed within an easy walk of the Square. The financial corridor, however, offered intangible benefits more important than considerations of efficiency or economy. By lining their offices along South Tryon Street, the bankers provided a potent symbol of their community's collective economic power. By investing in skyscrapers, they signaled their modernity and their complete confidence that the city's future prosperity would fulfill such present expenditure. Explicitly, the image of a skyscraper-lined street linked Char-

FIG. 53. THE FINANCIAL CANYON

This 1930s postcard shows the "Wall Street of Charlotte," South Tryon Street. Despite the title, the view actually looks northward toward Independence Square (same view as fig. 52). The skyscraper on the right is the Wilder Building. Tall structures on the left include the Johnston Building, the Commercial National Bank tower, the First National Bank, and in the distance the Independence Building. (Courtesy of the Robinson-Spangler Carolina Room, Public Library of Charlotte and Mecklenburg County) lotte to the financial canyon then taking shape along New York City's legendary Wall Street. As early as 1915 local Chamber of Commerce brochures proudly displayed pictures of the "Banking District" and announced that "Skyscrapers are rising here"—an "indication of . . . the City's stride toward being one of the leading cities of the South."[56] By the 1920s, Chamber of Commerce literature and hundreds of color postcards carried photos of the financial canyon stretching southward from the Square, under the heading "South Tryon Street . . . Wall Street of Charlotte."[57]

The writer W. J. Cash, in his sharp-tongued opus *The Mind of the South* (1941), poked fun at the skyscraper boom of the 1900s–1920s while at the same time providing insight into its significance. Towers, he snickered, "were going up in towns which, characteristically, had no call for them—where available room was still plentiful, and land prices were still relatively low . . . where there was no immediate prospect of their being filled, unless by tenants willing to forgo a meal now and then to participate in such grandeur." Building skyscrapers in Charlotte was like putting a tuxedo on a pig, he wrote. Such a city "had little more use for them than a hog has for a morning coat."[58] That dig perhaps gave Charlotte's economy less credit than it deserved, but nonetheless the metaphor nicely caught the importance of image-making in the New South city. South Tryon Street by the 1920s was indeed Charlotte's tuxedo, an expensive article of formal dress worn to signal its wearer's wealth and refinement. Here one would not find the lower class shops of the provision district or even the prosaic offices of film row. South Tryon Street functioned as the showplace of Charlotte's white-collar wealth.

MOVING OUT OF THE CENTER CITY

With the specialization of downtown districts during the 1900s–1920s came a companion trend. If one looked closely, one could see certain types of land use quietly leaving the center city. As early as the 1900s, institutions controlled by upper-class families began relocating to the suburbs. The movement seems to have largely predated the automobile. Motorcars remained the province of wealthy weekend hobbyists well into the 1910s; Charlotteans had just 76 autos in 1906, 259 in 1912, and still only 1,737 in 1917.[59] The shift of churches, medical institutions, and other facilities started in the 1900s–1910s and picked up speed in the 1920s. Observed the *Charlotte News* in 1926, "The population is moving outward and taking the city with them."[60] This suburbanization had ramifications beyond the mere geographic relocation. By shifting functions into the suburbs, white-collar Charlotteans made it easier to remain aloof from people below their social strata.

Churches led the suburban move. Episcopal and Associated Reform Presbyterian congregations took root in Dilworth during the 1900s, and Elizabeth boasted its own Episcopal and Methodist sanctuaries by 1915.[61] These did not entirely supplant downtown churches. Established families still went downtown, and congregations even erected new center city sanctuaries as late as the 1920s. But, particularly when considered in light of facilities such as the Episcopalian Chapel of Hope near the Highland Park #1 Mill and the Methodist and Baptist churches in North Charlotte, it meant that the old ideal of a church as gathering place for the whole community was crumbling by the 1900s. White-collar suburbanites, if they chose, might now avoid blue-collar Christians on Sunday mornings much as they did the rest of the week.

Medical facilities also moved quickly toward suburbia. Almost as soon as Charlotte's medical district came into being downtown, it began to erode. In 1916 Mercy Hospital abandoned a cramped wooden building downtown in favor of a full-block site in suburban Elizabeth, erecting an elegant brick Tudor Revival structure.[62] Two years later, Presbyterian Hospital seized an opportunity to trade its original West Trade Street site for the recently vacated campus of Elizabeth College on Hawthorne Lane.[63] Suburban sites gave the hospitals abundant expansion space at a reasonable price. But the moves made the hospitals much more convenient to the Myers Park and Elizabeth homes of the trustees and physicians than they were to the majority of patients. This trend became even more pronounced two decades later when downtown St. Peter's Hospital closed in favor of a new, city-funded Charlotte Memorial Hospital in Dilworth, and physicians left the downtown Professional Building for a new Doctors' Building tower nearby.

In the 1920s, grocery stores joined the outward shift. Blue-collar areas such as Belmont and North Charlotte had always had little neighborhood groceries, while white-collar housewives had ridden the trolley downtown to patronize the better-stocked stores of the provision district.[64] When Piggly-Wiggly, one of the nation's pioneer grocery chains, arrived in Charlotte, it initially took space downtown in the time-honored pattern.[65] Soon, though, the chain began to forge outward in an effort to scoop up high-margin white-collar trade. Piggly-Wiggly's first branch outside downtown opened in 1923 at 123 Park Avenue, just off South Boulevard in Dilworth. By 1929 the list of Piggly-

Wiggly's Charlotte stores read like a roster of the city's most affluent southern and eastern suburban addresses: East Morehead Street, East Boulevard, and South Boulevard in Dilworth, Eighth Street at Pecan Avenue in Elizabeth, and Providence Road in Myers Park. No longer would suburban women need to brave the jostling throngs of country folk, laborers, and blacks who frequented the provision district downtown.

The most symbolically important institutions to locate out from the center city during the 1920s were Charlotte's public high schools. Citizens began discussing adding upper grades to the city's graded schools in 1906, with the particular purpose of giving boys the training needed for the white-collar jobs becoming available in textile management.[66] Proposals soon broadened to include girls, and in 1908 three additional grades were added to the eight-grade curriculum at existing North School in First Ward near downtown.[67] The experiment won over skeptics, and by the 1920s Charlotte was ready to build its first high school buildings. Three very different structures, officials decided, would be required to serve Charlotte's teenagers. Tech High School, which opened in 1922, trained the white sons and daughters of blue-collar workers in skills appropriate to the factory. It stood in Belmont–Villa Heights, in the midst of the new industrial corridor that had sprawled northward to North Charlotte. Second Ward High, which opened in 1923, served Charlotte's black youngsters. It rose in the heart of Brooklyn, the district that had become the city's major African American business and residential enclave in the era of Jim Crow. The system's jewel was white Central High School, completed in 1921. Located on Elizabeth Avenue, it was situated conveniently to the moneyed white-collar suburbs of The Plaza, Elizabeth, Dilworth, and Myers Park.[68]

The carefully differentiated educational aims and precisely chosen locations of Charlotte's first high schools summed up the great changes that had taken place in the New South city. The very need for such advanced education sprang from the new industrial economy that had supplanted traditional craft production—with its apprentice system of education—in the years since the opening of the Charlotte Cotton Mill in 1881. The three curricula symbolized the fact that Charlotteans increasingly saw society divided into separate groups: blacks, blue-collar white workers, and white-collar businessmen and professionals who controlled political and economic life. The sites of the new schools showed the extent to which these divisions were now indelibly woven into the very fabric of the city itself. No longer did people of all kinds live intermingled near the Square as they had only a generation earlier. By the 1920s Charlotte had clearly sorted out into a city of separate neighborhoods sharply defined by race and by class.

CHAPTER 8
THE LIMITS OF LOCAL GOVERNMENT

DEBATING ANNEXATION AND PLANNING

The social structure of [Charlotte] is extremely conservative, with well-understood class distinctions. . . . There is a hesitancy on the part of government officials to offer social services which would benefit the lower classes, and a strong prejudice against raising the tax rate to provide services which are thought unessential. —Harold and Kathryn Stone, *City Manager Government in Charlotte* (1939)

CHARLOTTE'S rapid physical enlargement during the 1890s to 1920s brought new issues to the fore in local politics. How would city government cope with demands for expanded services? What would be the relationship between the city and its increasingly disparate suburbs? What role should government take in planning for future urban development? Such questions were not unique to Charlotte. Explosive urban growth all over America made the nature of municipal government a major focus of Progressive era political debate. In the South, however, the particular makeup of the electorate in the wake of disfranchisement profoundly affected the way those questions were answered. Government organization, suburban annexation, and city planning emerged as political flashpoints in Charlotte as citizens sought to come to terms with their city's changing built environment.

GOVERNMENT EXPANSION, VOTER RESISTANCE

Well into the New South era, Charlotte leaders held proudly to the old-fashioned American tradition of volunteer government. In the nation's earliest preindustrial years, government had been largely a local affair, and most municipal activities had been carried on by the citizens themselves, taking brief time out from their other day-to-day tasks. Long after the Civil War, the Board of Aldermen in Charlotte continued to provide almost all of the city's few services with their own hands. They called neighbors together to take up shovels and patch the dirt streets; they personally collected and handed out firewood to the poor in cold weather; they took turns supervising the cemeteries and settling disputes at the cotton scales. The town's paid workforce consisted mainly of its eight policemen. As late as the 1880s, in fact, Charlotte felt no need for a city hall at all, making do with a rented office for the city clerk and a meeting room upstairs over a restaurant for the mayor and aldermen.

As the town developed into an industrial city, that simple and direct method of governance faced new challenges.[1] In 1887, to safeguard the growing investment in stores and manufactories, aldermen voted to replace volunteer fire companies with a full-time, professional fire department on the city payroll.[2] In 1888 the city issued its first street improvement bonds, taking on an unprecedented $50,000 debt in order to surface the busiest dirt streets with a gravel mixture known as macadam.[3] Gingerly, city fathers also moved into the business of providing water and sewer services. A New York firm in partnership with local investors had built a waterworks at Charlotte's edge in 1881 and laid pipe along main avenues to supplant the old reliance on individual wells. The system experienced continuous problems, however, including an annoying tendency for fish to get into the pipes. In 1896 the city issued bonds to buy out the private corporation and build a larger, publicly owned facility.[4] As water flowed more reliably out of local faucets, it became necessary to handle the streams of wastewater that disappeared down Charlotte drains. The city first installed sewers in the 1880s, expanded the system as part of the 1896 bond issue, and in 1899 passed an ordinance requiring all buildings in the most populated blocks of Trade and Tryon Streets to hook up. Over the next decade the system gradually extended to cover much of the town.[5]

As service added to service, aldermen's duties became more and more complicated. They now had to oversee bond repayments, keep up with developments in street-paving techniques, and master the fine points of sewerage. They struggled to pass wise judgment on municipal franchises for new technologies such as horsecars and trolleys, telephones (1883), and electric streetlights (1887).[6] They took on the work of operating a city crematory to dispose of refuse (1896), supervised a growing police force (which tripled in size to twenty-four men in 1901), and hired inspectors for public health and building construction.[7]

With the burgeoning growth in municipal activities, Charlotte taxpayers found themselves asked to dig into their pockets for construction of not one but two city halls in a period of barely thirty-five years. In 1891 the city gave up its old rented quarters and erected a monumental brownstone city hall with a soaring tower on North Tryon Street at Sixth Street.[8] Citizens grumbled but assured themselves that the costly edifice would outlast the ages. To their amazement the facility was outgrown within its builders' lifetimes. In 1927 the municipal offices moved a second time, into a commanding Neoclassical-style city hall whose building and grounds took up an entire city block on East Trade Street.[9] In retrospect such brick-and-mortar expansions may seem the inevitable consequence of population increases and new urban service technologies. But Charlotteans in the period did not see it that way. Voters argued strenuously over the proper nature of urban government and explored alternative ways to structure the work of City Hall. Could some system be found that would retain the tradition of volunteer leadership, yet also provide the growing amount of specialized effort required to run the town?

This debate in Charlotte took place within the wider context of the era of Progressive government reform in urban America. Massive industrialization and population growth were forcing all municipalities to cope with new problems in water supply, sanitation, streetlighting, paving, and a hundred other

FIG. 54. 1891 CHARLOTTE CITY HALL

This commanding brownstone edifice in the first block of North Tryon Street was Charlotte's first city hall. Previously business had been conducted out of rental quarters over a restaurant. Citizens were shocked by the expense of the 1891 building—and more shocked when the city outgrew it less than a generation later. (Courtesy of the Robinson-Spangler Carolina Room, Public Library of Charlotte and Mecklenburg County)

FIG. 55. 1927 CHARLOTTE CITY HALL
Construction of a second city hall in 1927 capped a period of intense debate over the expansion of municipal government and over enlargement of Charlotte's physical boundaries. Charlotte architect C. C. Hook designed the new structure. He set it well back from East Trade Street to form a "civic plaza," which soon also included a similarly Neoclassical-style county courthouse. (Hook's architectural rendering, courtesy of the Robinson-Spangler Carolina Room, Public Library of Charlotte and Mecklenburg County)

specialties. To compound the sheer technical challenges, cities in the industrial North were also absorbing waves of European immigrants, who possessed enough votes to swing elections. Unscrupulous political bosses took advantage of the situation, winning office by offering favors (a bucket of coal in cold weather or assistance in the event of eviction) to the needy newcomers. Once elected, bosses used their power over franchises and contracts to enrich themselves and rob the city. Such chaos brought forth the coalition of reformers known as the Progressive movement. Progressives campaigned for a more activist government that would provide services to improve the lives of urbanites of all classes and thus lessen the influence of the political bosses. They also experimented with ways to make government more structured and efficient, putting responsibility in the hands of professionally trained experts. Today the Progressive era is remembered for its pioneering accomplishments in social service realms such as child labor laws, public health regulations, and building codes requiring safe and sanitary residential construction. The Progressives are credited with creating modern bureaucratic urban government, in which elected officials set policy but then leave the day-to-day work of running the city to departments headed by full-time, college-trained specialists, often under the direction of a professional city manager.[10]

In the urban South, Progressive era accomplishments had a unique tilt. Southern cities, as historian David Goldfield observes, "generally avoided the social reform aspects of the movement but participated in political reform efforts."[11] Dixie voters showed little interest in uplifting the unfortunate, but they enthusiastically pursued the search for more efficient forms of municipal government. Indeed, two of the main American innovations in urban bureaucratic structure during the Progressive era originated in the small-town South. The commission plan, in which voters elected department heads directly, appeared in 1900 in Galveston, Texas. The city manager plan, in which elected officials hired a full-time administrator to coordinate municipal activities, debuted in 1908 in Staunton, Virginia.[12]

The lopsided character of urban Progressivism in the South, it may be argued, reflected the unique composition of the Southern electorate after 1900. Virtually all black people—one-third of the urban population in North Carolina—lost the right to vote following disfranchisement. After the seven-year grace period provided by the grandfather clause, the same literacy requirements and poll taxes applied to North Carolina whites as well. The regulations had the effect of keeping a sizable proportion of blue-collar urbanites, black and white, away from the polls. Voter turnout dropped dramatically all over the South, from 73 percent of adult males in the early 1890s to just 30 percent by the end of the decade of the 1900s.[13] Southern city politics became largely a white-collar affair. The only voices heard, reported historian Blaine Brownell in his survey of Dixie's cities in the 1920s, were those of the "commercial-civic elite."[14]

In short, the South lacked the political dialogue between blue-collar and white-collar interests that shaped Progressivism elsewhere in the United States. With blue-collar citizens casting few votes, politicians had little incentive to spend money improving the conditions at the bottom of the social pyramid. Conversely, there existed a strong political incentive to keep property taxes low, since a disproportionately large percentage of voters were property owners. As a result, politicians in the South—even more than in other sections of the United States—vied with one another to promise government efficiency and pare costs to the bone.[15]

In Charlotte, cost-cutting became the perennial campaign theme. Candidates seeking office routinely expressed horror at the city's bonded indebtedness, which topped half a million dollars by 1910. Using phrases plucked from big-city headlines, they hurled charges of corruption and painted lurid pictures of behind-the-scenes political "rings" bent on looting city coffers. In reality no such rings existed; the debt resulted purely from the rush to create paved streets, reliable water service, and effective waste removal. But reality was hard to believe for people who had grown up with the minimalist government of nineteenth century Charlotte. The root of the problem, some suggested, must be that the political structure was failing to put the best and most business-minded men into office. The trouble arose, other candidates said, because elected officials were becoming too caught up in municipal affairs, turning from wholesome volunteers into that dreaded and inherently corrupt species, the "professional politician."

In 1917 Charlotteans considered reorganizing the structure of their city government in hopes of finding the magic solution. A group of business leaders drew up a proposal that offered two innovations. In place of a board of aldermen dealing with city affairs as a whole, the voters would elect three commissioners, each of whom would head a specific department. One commissioner would take charge of finance and administration, another public works, and the third public safety. Voters could thus judge candidates on the basis of their expertise for a particular task. Combined with this organizational change was an electoral one. Charlotte would scrap its system of electing a candidate from each ward and instead would elect all candidates at-large from the city as a whole. The prestige thus given to a winner, proponents claimed, would entice the city's best-qualified businessmen to run for office. This, combined with the definiteness of responsibilities under the commission system, would reinvigorate the honored tradition of volunteer leadership.[16]

Though advocates pitched the at-large aspect of the proposal as a simple matter of prestige, much more lay at stake. Ward election ensured that each neighborhood of the city selected one of its own citizens to represent its particular interests. In a town increasingly sorted out along class lines, this system had guaranteed that blue-collar districts and white-collar suburbs both had some say in government. At-large elections would wipe out this safeguard. Poorer residents would lose power to wealthy downtown businessmen who could afford the cost of campaigning citywide. Denying neighborhoods the right to elect their own representatives, opponents of the 1917 proposal charged, would stifle democracy.

Proponents cheerfully acknowledged the point. Charlotte, they said, needed leaders "of substantial experience in handling business, upon whom is the stamp of character." Lesser men should be satisfied to be governed by their betters. "The way a city's affairs should be run," one advocate counseled paternally, "might well be likened to a prudent and impartial father of a family . . . [who] carefully considers all the needs, present and future of each member of the family and apportions the budget accordingly."[17]

When ballots were counted in May 1917, the at-large proponents' easy confidence proved justified. The referendum drew just 2,956 voters—a tiny fraction of the town's 40,000 citizens, but a typical turnout in the years after disfranchisement.[18] A look at the returns in two sample districts confirmed the identity of supporters and opponents. Ward Seven, made up of the wealthy white-collar Elizabeth and Myers Park neighborhoods, voted overwhelmingly in favor of the at-large commission proposal. Ward Five, composed of working-class Belmont and North Charlotte, voted to continue ward representation.[19] Blue-collar interests, already underrepresented on the voting rolls, could not muster sufficient ballots to save the ward system. The Queen City now adopted at-large elections and commission leadership.

Commission government, ironically, had absolutely no impact on the problems it was supposed to cure. Professional management still was needed; few competent businessmen actually proved willing to put aside their own businesses for two years or more in order to devote full time to administering a municipal department. And expenses continued to grow. Wealthy patrons continued to demand expanded municipal services, keeping bonded indebtedness high. Per capita cost of local government in the city jumped from $19.26 in 1917 to $40.38 by 1929. Compared with outlay in America's largest 146 cities, tax rates in Charlotte were still a bargain. Average per capita municipal spending in the United States went from about $35 to nearly $80 in the same period.[20] In an electoral environment that emphasized taxpayer saving, however, even Charlotte's modest growth seemed reason for alarm.

In 1929 the city underwent a second governmental reorganization. A self-appointed committee of "nine men occupied in real estate; four manufacturers; a physician; an accountant; and a public accountant"—all members of the elite Charlotte Country Club—urged a switch to the city manager form of government.[21] A full-time professional manager would be hired to supervise the departments, while a city council composed of volunteer politicians would guide policy. Significantly, the sole element of the 1917 system that the new proposal retained was the process of at-large election. "The better residential wards voted heavily in favor of the city manager plan, exclusive Myers Park expressing an eight-to-one preference," reported an approving observer. "Labor was the only organized group that opposed the work of the industrialists, real estate operators and bankers."[22] The city manager/at-large council plan would continue to operate in Charlotte with only minor modifications into the 1970s.

THE RISE AND FALL OF ANNEXATION AS AN ISSUE: THE DILWORTH DEBATE

Along with government organization, the annexation of suburbs emerged as a hotly contested issue in American cities in this period. Wealthy citizens who headed toward suburbia began to resist the expansion of municipal borders that would bring them back into the city. They wanted to focus their tax money on services that would benefit themselves rather than the entire metropolis, and also they feared losing political control to inner-city bosses. Starting with upper-crust Brookline outside Boston in 1873, affluent suburbs all over the United States took steps to incorporate themselves as separate municipalities independent from their parent cities.[23] By the 1910s resistance to annexation had become so strong that many major American cities found themselves without any avenue for further expansion, their borders completely choked by obstinately separate suburbs. In the South, though, antiannexation sentiment ran notably less strong. Many Dixie cities continued expanding their boundaries well into the late twentieth century. In Charlotte the history of early twentieth century debates over annexation suggests that the white-collar domination of urban politics played a key role in the Southern tendency.

Annexation arose as an issue in the Queen City considerably later than in many Northern municipalities. As long as the edge of town remained the province of poorer residents—much later than in the industrial cities of the North, as we have seen—annexation went on with virtually no debate. In 1877 and again in 1885 Charlotte expanded its borders almost without discussion. The single objection in 1885 came from a Democrat who worried that annexing the borderland's predominantly black settlements might add too many Republicans to the voter roles.[24] When annexation came up for consideration in 1906, however, the calm was shattered. By the 1900s Charlotte's periphery was no longer solely the province of the poor and powerless; this time the proposed expansion would take in the well-to-do suburbanites of the new Dilworth district. In long and vigorous debate the town's commercial-civic elite hashed out the pros and cons of bringing suburbs into the city, setting precedents that would last into the 1980s.

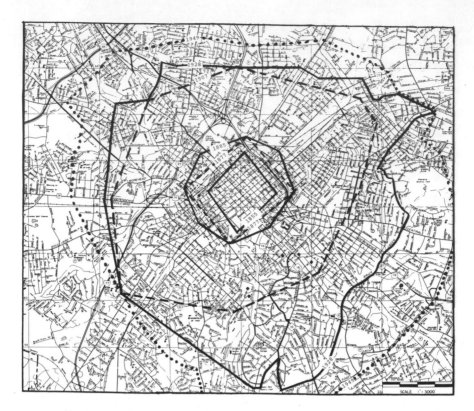

FIG. 56. CHARLOTTE'S EXPANDING BOUNDARIES
A compact and orderly grid of streets as late as the 1870s, Charlotte had become a swirling spaghetti bowl of separate subdivisions by the 1920s.

Dilworth residents themselves launched the discussion, impelled initially by a simple economic concern. Early in 1906 a rash of industrial fires broke out in the corridor of factories adjacent to the suburb's South Boulevard.[25] When shaken homeowners rushed to purchase fire insurance policies, they got bad news. Because their neighborhood lay outside the city limits and possessed no fire station, insurance companies would charge maximum premiums.[26] The solution seemed simple, a gathering of citizens decided. Dilworth should incorporate as a municipality and set about providing fire protection and other modern municipal services. "We will always do our trading in the city and patronize her institutions and help make her great," assured a spokesman for incorporation, "but the time has come when Dilworth must have fire and police protection."[27]

Once proposed, the idea of creating a self-sufficient city quickly gained momentum among suburbanites. Such a municipality could provide additional services: "We want our streets and sidewalks paved and the streets sprinkled in dusty weather."[28] At the same time the notion conversely held out hope of escaping the governmental "wastefulness" of Charlotte. "Dilworth objects to becoming a [annexed] suburb of Charlotte on account of the million dollars of indebtedness upon which the citizens of Charlotte are paying taxes," one advocate explained to the *Observer*. "The cry last night was 'Dilworth taxes for Dilworth improvements.'"[29]

Inside Charlotte, businessmen and real estate boosters listened to this rhetoric with alarm. In 1900 the Queen City had edged past Raleigh to become the largest urban center in North Carolina, a proud achievement and one sure to bring attention and draw additional business. But Charlotte's lead remained precarious. Not only did Raleigh continue to expand, but the piedmont tobacco towns of Winston and Salem would soon unite to create another major rival.[30] With an eye toward the 1910 census, businessmen had formed the Greater Charlotte Club in 1905, with the slogan Watch Charlotte Grow.[31] Loudest among those calling for a Greater Charlotte were the owners of undeveloped suburban real estate. Not only did they stand to benefit from any strategy that might draw more population, but also when their holdings came into the city, they would be able to get municipal aid in extending streets, sewers, and water mains.[32] If Dilworth should incorporate as a separate municipality, the Greater Charlotte expansion drive would be crippled.

The call by suburbanites for low taxes and more services, and the countervailing push by business boosters for a bigger city, were familiar salvos in battles over annexation everywhere in the United States. What happened after the two sides fired their opening shots, however, marked Charlotte as different from many American cities in the post-Brookline era. In a flurry of behind-the-scenes maneuvering, Charlotte's downtown businessmen convinced the Dilworth citizens to drop the notion of separate incorporation.[33] The reality of the situation was that the suburban leaders shared the sentiments of the Greater Charlotte boosters. Most were downtown businessmen themselves, and a number owned suburban land that they looked forward to developing as house lots. Since they and their white-collar friends in the city held firm control over local politics, they felt none of the fear of inner-city bosses that contributed to the drive for separate incorporation in Northern metropolises. In the summer of 1906 Charlotte newspapers abruptly ceased speculating whether Dilworth and other suburbs would be annexed and instead began discussing where the enlarged boundary would run.[34]

Deciding just how to redraw Charlotte's border provoked deeper conflicts, however. Advocates broke into three warring camps, each pursuing its own economic interest in a particular expansion scheme. Downtown businessmen mindful of the 1910 census, together with real estate developers interested in urban services, wanted the city to take in as much territory as possible. These men proposed that the new boundary be drawn as a circle two-and-a-half miles from Independence Square.[35] The second group consisted of farmers worried about paying city taxes under that proposal, in alliance with Highland Park Mill owner Charles Johnston and a small number of other owners of outlying factories, who also wished to avoid taxes. They called loudly for a border running only two miles beyond the Square.[36] The third camp was headed by Heriot Clarkson, a lawyer and former state legislator who ranked as the city's most powerful politician. Clarkson had been architect of a 1904 ordinance that prohibited the sale of liquor in Charlotte, an achievement that fulfilled a long-sought white-collar goal. Clarkson refused to consider anything greater than the two-mile line, fearing that if too many blue-collar voters from the outlying textile villages were brought into the city, his prohibition victory might be reversed.[37]

Resolution of the boundary question illustrated the power of the few over the many in Charlotte politics. Initially it seemed that the two-and-a-half-mile circle would carry the day, since its business proponents far outnumbered the other camps. The Charlotte Board of Aldermen overwhelmingly endorsed the businessmen's map and forwarded it for approval to the state legislature in Raleigh, where they received a series of humbling lessons in the exercise of power. The wealthy farmers who opposed the two-and-a-half-mile limit turned out to have great pull with particular members of the legislature. The legislative committee refused to consider the document as submitted, returning it to Charlotte for revision. The Board of Aldermen meekly redrew their line. The border would now be an octagon two miles in diameter but with V-shaped extensions to two-and-a-half miles at the north and south to take in the town's two busiest manufacturing corridors, North Charlotte and South Boulevard. The compromise would incorporate virtually all existing built-up areas while omitting most farmland. Everyone now seemed satisfied, except Charles Johnston and Heriot Clarkson. The northern V included part of the Highland Park #3 mill village, which would mean more taxes for Johnston and troublesome new blue-collar voters for Clarkson. The two powerful men traveled to Raleigh for an intense round of personal lobbying.[38] When the state legislature approved Charlotte's new city charter on March 7, 1907, the northern V had quietly been revised to leave out Highland Park.[39]

Charlotte leaders took several lessons from the 1906–7 extension battle. For one thing, the episode made it very clear that no matter what the fashion was in Northern cities, the Charlotte electorate favored suburban annexation. Only one other time would a well-to-do suburb consider separate incorporation. Just as federal officials were about to launch the 1920 census count, a group of Myers Park residents headed by developer George Stephens petitioned the city to extend municipal services to the sprawling suburb. Part of Myers Park already fell within the Charlotte limits, but Stephens was finding it impossible to subsidize fire, water, and sewers to the eighty or so homeowners beyond the line. If Charlotte did not act, Stephens threatened, Myers Park would incorporate and block the future southeastward expansion of the city.[40] Charlotte officials refused to be intimidated. Myers Park briefly incorporated as a village, but everyone realized there was no way that so few residents could finance the desired services. "The town tax rate is 0. No tax is levied, no police and fire department maintained, no schools constructed," chuckled the *Charlotte Observer* in 1922. The neighborhood gave up the bluff in 1924 and waited to be taken into the city.[41]

A deeper impact of the 1906–7 fight lay in the lessons it taught about getting things done in Charlotte. The episode showed that it simply did not pay to raise issues that divided the white-collar electorate. Such divisions might be worth risking in cities outside the South with their large blue-collar voting rolls; each side could strive to appeal to "the people." In the severely limited electorate of Dixie, however, the faction with the most wealth and the most pull in the state legislature was sure to triumph. To succeed in Charlotte a politician should work carefully to appease the economically powerful and build consensus in advance of any vote.

This political dictum could be seen in action in 1927 when Charlotteans, eager to pump up population figures for the next U.S. Census, made ready to annex the newest crop of suburbs. This time politicians took meticulous account of the wishes of the rich and well connected. The 1927 border could not avoid embracing Charles Johnston's Highland Park #3 mill and village in North Charlotte. But it courteously left out his Mecklenburg Mill and Johnston Mill. Likewise the boundary zigzagged sharply to exclude the Charlotte Country Club so that its influential members might be spared the inconvenience of paying extra property taxes as part of their dues. In Myers Park the line thoughtfully swooped southward to include all the residential area so that homeowners would gain the services they had so desired; taxpayers of the entire city would help pay for a new fire station, elementary school, sewers, and water mains. The Myers Park Country Club, though, would not be asked to pay any of those taxes, since a well-placed notch put it safely outside the border. "They made the line crooked as a dog's hind leg," complained one lone dissenting letter to the editor, "to leave the Myers Park Country Club outside the limits . . . [and] to leave outside the Johnston and Mecklenburg Mills . . . giving the fashionable club owners and the rich mill owners the privilege of voting before the lines were run."[42] With the adjustments quietly made in advance, Charlotte's white-collar electorate was able to speak as one voice. Where the earlier annexation had occasioned more than a year of battle, the 1927 proposal sailed through the city commission and state legislature, winning approval in a matter of weeks.[43] Without a large blue-collar electorate to provide a balancing force, the fashionable club members and mill men indeed held undisputed control of the reins of power in Charlotte.

NEIGHBORHOOD PLANNING, YES; CITY PLANNING, NO

Of all the proposals floated by American municipal reformers during the Progressive era, the one that Charlotteans seemed most predisposed to adopt was comprehensive urban planning. All across the United States during the 1910s and 1920s hundreds of municipalities undertook efforts to draw up city-wide plans.[44] Charlotte possessed ample precedents for climbing aboard the bandwagon. For one thing, the colonial tradition of grid planning, under which government planned the extension of streets for the entire city, had remained alive in the town much longer than in many other parts of the United States, well into living memory of the Progressive generation. Even more compellingly, Charlotte in the 1910s ranked as a national leader in the practice of neighborhood planning (that suburban subset of city planning). Thanks to the accomplishments of Leigh Colyer along The Plaza and the Olmsted Brothers in Dilworth, and especially to the evangelism of John Nolen and his protégé Earle Draper in Myers Park and related projects, Charlotte could boast a collection of planned suburbs unsurpassed in any small city in America. It seemed only a small step to extend that kind of thoughtful design to the community as a whole.

In 1916, with Myers Park well under way, planner John Nolen and his patron George Stephens decided that the time was ripe for the next phase of their campaign to bring city planning to the Queen City. Stephens lobbied the Board of Aldermen and the Chamber of Commerce and convinced them to split the cost of conducting a "civic survey" of Charlotte. Nolen's staff would carefully gather and map data on the existing city, creating the documents on which to base a city plan. To John Nolen the prospect of creating an overall design for the Queen City represented the fulfillment of a long-sought goal. "You will recall," he wrote privately to Stephens, "how my services began there with the parks of Charlotte, passed then to a consideration of private places, then to the campaign of lecturing and speaking . . . and finally to the preparation of the plan for Myers Park. All of this work was done without much, or any profit, some of it at a direct loss. In other words I was a missionary."[45] Charlotte's city plan would be a jubilant harvest after long labor in the vineyards.

Completed in September 1917, the civic survey not only summarized existing conditions but also went on to offer a preliminary sketch suggesting what a city plan for Charlotte might look like.[46] A downtown "civic center" on West Trade Street would hold all the city's municipal buildings and provide a focal point for public life. Selected streets would be widened to better connect the center city to the suburbs and mill districts. To facilitate street widening, a building code would dictate that new structures must be set back from the existing roadways. The plan recommended that the city fund additional parks on the north and west sides to balance the existing Latta Park, J. S. Myers Park, and Independence Park to the south and east. In addition, it suggested extensive greenways along all the town's creeks, and it drew a system of picturesque parkway drives on the creek banks to link all of Charlotte's neighborhoods. At the city's rim, just beyond Dilworth, Washington Heights, Belmont, and Elizabeth, a belt road would encircle the entire town.

Nolen's proposal, in short, sought to knit the city together. Homogeneous elite neighborhoods, such as the one he had planned in Myers Park, were an important component of the ideal city but should not be isolated from the larger civic fabric. Public outlay should provide parks in areas too poor to finance such amenities themselves. All parks should form a network of greenways that everyone could share. Likewise, the boulevards and belt road would give anybody easy access to any part of town. The park system and the boulevards would converge on the central civic plaza, bringing people together from every neighborhood.

The proposal fell on deaf ears. Charlotte's leaders saw no need for such connective tissue; boulevards and greenways seemed a frivolous thing for a municipality to spend tax dollars on. Months before the civic survey appeared, Chamber of Commerce members began grumbling about Nolen's "radical changes" and "impractical" staff.[47] When Nolen requested additional funds to flesh out the preliminary sketch into a full city plan, the chamber refused. No more money would be wasted. Charlotte's businessmen set the survey aside virtually without opening it.[48] In the 1920s local leaders did create a civic center similar to Nolen's suggestion, erecting a new city hall and county courthouse in a grassy plaza on East (rather than West) Trade Street. But they took no interest in Nolen's larger vision of a city of neighborhoods joined together with a system of parks, broad boulevards, and a belt road.

Charlotte remained obstinately without a city plan throughout the entire booming first half of the twentieth century. During the 1920s Nolen watched sadly from Boston as Charlotte's creek banks were cut up into backyards and as expanding development made the possibility of crosstown and belt highways more and more expensive. "I think Charlotte is slipping so far as city planning goes," Nolen wrote to chamber official Clarence Kuester in 1924. "There are examples in the city of errors that are costly and more or less irremediable. Other errors will follow without a city plan."[49] In 1930 an eager city manager, new to Charlotte and imbued with Progressive ideals, hired a New Jersey consultant named Herbert Swan to draw up a zoning map and master plan. Real estate leaders and businessmen rose in angry opposition led by F. C. Abbott, "dean of Charlotte's real estate dealers" and former partner of George Stephens, who attacked the proposal as "a serious damage to all property owners." City council not only shelved Swan's work before it was completed but fired the city manager for good measure.[50] Not until after World War II would Charlotte adopt a comprehensive plan. Ironically, its proposals would closely resemble John Nolen's 1917 concepts, despite the fact that thirty years of growth made implementation much more difficult and costly.

The failure of Nolen's city plan proposal in 1917 marked the beginning of the end of professional planning in Charlotte. Five years later George Stephens departed for retirement in the mountains of Asheville, North Carolina (where he convinced local leaders to hire John Nolen to devise an Asheville city plan, which won national acclaim as model of small-town planning).[51] Without Stephens the drive for planning in Charlotte lost momentum. The change could be seen even in Myers Park, where the Stephens Company quietly moved away from its founder's costly commitment to professional planning and extensive landscaping. About 1926 the company dropped connections with Nolen's disciple Earle Draper and put a stolid civil engineer named Wilbur Smith in charge of laying out new blocks.[52] In some places, such as Wellsley and Sherwood Roads, Smith implemented Draper's proposals exactly, but more often he straightened and simplified street design to squeeze in more middle-income lots. In the mid-1930s a young real estate booster named E. C. Griffith took control of the undeveloped remainder of the Myers Park project. As he completed the suburb, the economy-minded developer jettisoned key elements of Nolen's design. Griffith omitted Queens Road's distinctive grassy median when he finished the boulevard loop, and he built arrow-straight Kings Road along Sugar Creek, selling off John Nolen's proposed creekside greenway for house lots.[53]

A last hurrah for professional planning in Charlotte came with the creation of the Eastover neighborhood in 1927. Sited across Providence Road from Myers Park, Eastover became the city's first white-collar district with no trolley connections, a prestigious "automobile suburb" for the elite.[54] Its location definitively marked the southeast—rather than south or east or northeast—quadrant of the city as Charlotte's most fashionable address. The neighborhood's design, created by Earle Sumner Draper for E. C. Griffith, pointed up just which aspects of Progressive planning Charlotte's elite found desirable. In the best Progressive tradition, Eastover's street layout consisted of a sedate web of gently curving, tree-lined avenues. Also in keeping with Progressive planning ideals, Eastover was a "restricted residential district" with racial covenants and minimum cost clauses that ensured a homogeneous grouping of expensive "dignified homes with spacious lawns."[55] Missing from the district was a central boulevard. Some Eastover streets were wider than others, but basically every street functioned as a side street, quiet and secluded. Missing also was a grand connection to the outside city. During lot sales, brick gateposts marked entrances on Providence Road at Cherokee Road and on Randolph Road at Colville Road, but the gates soon disappeared. Draper also drew a proposal for a greenway park that would link into a wider urban park system, but it remained undeveloped (later the site of the Mint Museum of Art).[56] What Eastover adopted from the gospel of professional planning, in sum, were its techniques of seclusion—the strategies that fostered homogeneous neighborhoods, self-contained and set apart from the city. Today few ordinary Charlotteans could find their way into this enclave. It is probably no coincidence that Eastover remains a highly prestigious district more than seventy years after its creation.

By the end of the 1920s, debates over government's role in the built environment seemed resolved. Protected from any serious blue-collar challenge, Charlotte's commercial-civic elite controlled the political arena, and they agreed on definite limits to municipal action. Charlotte possessed just the "kind of government desired by the business element," observed visiting economist Edgar Thompson in 1926.[57] "The social structure of the city is extremely conservative, with well-understood class distinctions," agreed political scientists Harold and Kathryn Stone a short time later. "There is a hesitancy on the part of government officials to offer social services which would benefit the lower classes, and a strong prejudice against raising the tax rate to provide services which are thought unessential."[58] In particular, Charlotte leaders agreed wholeheartedly that the city should stay far away from any effort to plan or guide urban development. Few would have guessed how dramatically that stance would change after 1930.

[While residential segregation] of course involved many ad hoc decisions by individuals and by city, county, state and federal governments . . . the clear fact however is that the displacement occurred with heavy federal financing and with active participation by local governments.—Judge James McMillan, *Swann v. Charlotte-Mecklenburg Board of Education,* 1969

BY THE END of the 1920s, Charlotteans had undergone a conceptual shift in their definition of a desirable urban landscape. Only a generation earlier, citizens of every kind had lived intermingled like salt-and-pepper on a grid of streets planned by the city fathers. Now Charlotteans resided in a patchwork pattern of self-contained neighborhoods, each distinct in its developer-devised street system and each largely homogeneous in its racial and economic makeup.

Over the next forty years the town would undergo further sorting. From the patchwork quilt of 1930—where, for example, neighborhoods as diverse as blue-collar Belmont, white-collar Elizabeth, and black Brooklyn all coexisted contiguously on the city's east side—Charlotte would push separation to an extreme, finally splitting the city into pie-shaped wedges defined by race and income. This transformation was perhaps less conceptually radical than the earlier switch from unsorted to sorted, but it was at least as dramatic in its effect on the landscape. Increasingly, wealthy whites lived—and shopped—in southeast Charlotte, while African Americans concentrated on the northwest side, and low- and moderate-income whites resided to the northeast and southwest. By the mid-1970s in Charlotte, historian William T. Moye observed, "a definite sectoral pattern emerged with the population highly segregated by race and class."[1] (See fig. 1.)

A casual observer might attribute this change to simple growth, abetted by increased automobile ownership and general American post–World War II prosperity, but the shift went deeper than mere enlargement of existing patterns. Westside areas that had once held white-collar white residents, such as Wesley Heights, now became exclusively black. Eastside black districts, including Brooklyn most notably, were emptied of African Americans. Downtown, traditionally the hub of all public building, began to lose out to the wealthy suburbs when city council made decisions on where to locate community facilities. The city was not just expanding, but reorganizing.

Of the factors propelling Charlotte's sectoral reorganization, the strongest may have been the actions of the federal government.[2] For most of American history, Washington had made little direct impact on city affairs; government remained largely in hometown hands, and in the Queen City that meant a "hands-off" attitude toward urban development. Starting with the New Deal of the 1930s, however, the federal government's role as a funder of projects began to grow. Much of that money was channeled through local government, pushing municipalities to become more and more active. New Deal construction grants, public housing and middle-class mortgage programs, highway aid, urban renewal, initiatives encouraging planning and zoning, and even tax breaks for shopping center construction all provided unprecedented power to reshape cities. A surprising number of the programs themselves explicitly promoted the ideal of racial and economic homogeneity. Others could be used to that end by local leaders who were so predisposed. In Charlotte, as in other Southern cities, the result was a notable sharpening of race and class segregation during the era of the "federal city."

A GOOD PLACE TO DO BUSINESS

Charlotte's economy continued to expand as the city moved into the mid-twentieth century. The diversified economic base forged at the turn of the century—resting on the three legs of manufacturing, wholesaling/transportation, and banking—gave the Queen City an adaptability that smoothed economic bumps. Manufacturing increased steadily, with the number of plants and the number of workers doubling between the late 1910s and the late 1940s. Textiles continued to be the largest manufacturing employer into the 1950s, with food processing a close second. Wholesaling and banking expanded even faster than manufacturing. By 1950 Charlotte ranked twenty-ninth among American cities in wholesale sales, despite being only sixty-ninth in population. Likewise the banks established by mill men and real estate developers grew wealthy handling the financial transactions of the piedmont, funneling the region's finances through the towers of South Tryon Street. A 1951 profile in *Business Week* approvingly dubbed Charlotte "a paper town—because most of its business is done on paper."[3]

The city was thus perfectly positioned as the United States entered the "information age" in the decades after World War II. Queen City banks expanded and merged until Charlotte became the financial center not just of the Carolinas but of the entire Southeastern United States. During the 1950s Charlotte institutions began appearing regularly on lists of the country's largest banks. By 1970 Charlotte-based North Carolina National Bank (the offspring of developer George Stephens's American Trust and the Holt textile family's Commercial National) ranked forty-seventh in the nation, and neighboring First Union ranked fifty-ninth. Wachovia and First Citizens, based elsewhere in the state but maintaining major operations on South Tryon Street, held similarly high positions.[4] At the end of the 1970s the Chamber of

Commerce would be able to boast that deposits held by banks in Charlotte exceeded those for any comparable area between Philadelphia and Dallas, surpassing even the flashier city of Atlanta.[5]

Charlotte's distribution economy also prospered in the decades following World War II. The city had developed as a truck terminal with North Carolina's Good Roads movement of the 1920s. Federal highways and the construction of Douglas Airport—begun with a New Deal grant in 1938 and enlarged by the Air Force during World War II—added valuable transportation connections. When the United States began its Interstate Highway program, Charlotte became an important crossroads on this network as well. Interstate 85 paralleled the old Southern Railway mainline connecting the city to Richmond and Atlanta. Interstate 77 realized a dream that dated back at least to the ill-fated Atlantic, Tennessee and Ohio Railway; the expressway at last gave Charlotte a swift route to the Midwest. Trucking companies thrived around the crossroads. By the late 1960s local boosters made the claim that only Chicago served as home base for more tractor-trailer rigs than Charlotte.[6]

The city's broad wholesaling strength, together with the diverse investments of the banks, meant that Charlotte barely felt the decline of the cotton manufacturing industry in the Carolinas after the Second World War. The Johnston textile chain sold off its mill housing to residents in the 1950s, and the firm's mighty Highland Park #3 mill closed in 1969.[7] When the town's last spinning mill fell silent in 1975, it merely occasioned nostalgic newspaper stories far from the front pages. Charlotte had long since ceased to see itself as a cotton town.[8] Civic leaders now spoke of the Queen City as a model example of the prosperity of America's southern Sunbelt.

Triumphant in the economic sphere, businessmen also dominated the town's political life. The system of at-large elections and voting restrictions created at the turn of the century continued to limit political participation well into the 1960s, ensuring that only well-financed candidates won office.[9] Civic leaders made no secret of business's influence at City Hall. "Scratch beneath the surface of any local government program in Charlotte or Mecklenburg these days and you're likely to find a Chamber of Commerce committee," wrote the *Charlotte Observer* approvingly in the 1950s.[10] "Charlotte is run, primarily and well, by its Chamber of Commerce," the paper reiterated a few years later. "We are pleased to acknowledge its bossism and wish it continued health."[11]

That uncontested business bossism would have considerable effect on Charlotte's built environment. More often than not, the businessmen who set government policy made their homes in the exclusive Eastover and Myers Park neighborhoods or nearby. As municipal leaders debated the disposition of the growing cornucopia of federal funds, they tended to direct the most desirable projects to the southeast side of town where they and their neighbors could best enjoy them. Less desirable things got pushed elsewhere. It could be a subtle process, as innocent as a councilman happening upon an auspicious site for a project on his daily drive to work. But the more that officeholders tended to come from only a single area, the more lopsided the city map became.

NEW DEAL CONSTRUCTION PROJECTS

When large-scale federal aid arrived with the New Deal of the 1930s, Charlotte got in line grudgingly. Washington had always played a role in urban development in America, but that role had been relatively modest: building post offices and military installations, dredging harbors, and aiding railroad construction. Then the United States plunged into the Great Depression, pushing President Franklin D. Roosevelt to launch the modern era of federal activism. A host of agencies sprang up to provide relief for unemployed workers and to search for ways to stimulate the stumbling economy. In most instances Washington set general program guidelines and provided money, then looked to localities to devise and administer specific projects.[12] In Charlotte the commercial-civic elite expressed considerable initial skepticism at the New Deal. The *Observer* raged against federal meddling and predicted that assistance would destroy initiative among the unemployed. Roosevelt "has on his side the mongrel groups of both races and classes who either have a personal grievance to gratify or social or economic goal to attain," the paper charged.[13] "We feel it is not too late, as some aver, for America to prove to the world that Capitalism can work."[14] Nonetheless, the newspaper urged the city to apply for aid. "People of this community," the editors temporized, "will be compelled to pay their proportionate part of the Federal debt that lies behind this lending-spending program whether they secure a portion of these funds or not."[15]

As programs got under way, civic leaders discovered that the money could do more than simply aid the unfortunate. Officials utilized New Deal dollars to reinforce the desirability of Charlotte's east side, particularly the southeast sector. The local allocations of FDR's Federal Emergency Relief Administration (FERA) (1933–35) and its sister program, the Civil Works Administration (CWA) (1933–34), demonstrated the tendency.[16] The programs provided money to create "make-work" projects for the unemployed. Among the top

TABLE 7. Largest New Deal FERA/CWA Projects in Mecklenburg, 1933–1935

Project Title	Budget	Sector Affected
Street construction, northeast section of Charlotte	$97,270	northeast
Privy construction, countywide	95,406	all
Street construction, southeast section of Charlotte	87,180	southeast
Administrative	65,335	all
Improvement to municipal stadium, Charlotte	64,888	southeast
Relief wood yards	48,979	all?
Reerection of old Mint Building, Eastover	46,725	southeast
Wilkerson Blvd. beautification	40,983	west
Street and sidewalk repair, Charlotte	38,540	all?

Source: *Emergency Relief in North Carolina*, pp. 498–500.

items on the FERA/CWA budget were privy construction and wood cutting for poor residents, and street and sidewalk repair in unspecified parts of the city. Most of the rest of the biggest outlays, however, specifically benefited eastern inhabitants. FERA/CWA laborers graded and paved streets in the city's northeast and southeast sectors, increasingly the favored areas of residence of the upper crust. Among the streets improved was Queens Road in Myers Park. Other FERA/CWA crews were put to work building public facilities in white-collar areas. In Elizabeth they constructed Municipal Stadium as part of an effort to spruce up whites-only Independence Park. In wealthy Eastover, FERA/CWA labor helped create the Mint Museum of Art. The historic U.S. Mint located downtown on Mint Street was about to be razed to allow expansion of the Post Office. New Deal workers took the old building apart brick by brick and moved it to Eastover.[17] The location, on a secluded lane amidst the neighborhood's fine houses, suited wealthy patrons but made access difficult for most citizens of the city. In all, of the projects that affected one particular sector, three of five aided southeast Charlotte.

Municipal Stadium and the Mint Museum of Art were not the only instances of civic leaders using New Deal dollars to situate important public institutions in Charlotte's southeast sector. After the FERA/CWA ended, President Roosevelt's Public Works Administration (PWA) took over the funding of local improvement projects.[18] In 1938, at the urging of a group of Charlotte physicians, the city applied for a PWA grant to upgrade hospital facilities.[19] The doctors wanted to remodel St. Peter's Hospital, the downtown facility that had functioned as the city's principal white health-care institution since the 1870s.

St. Peter's was owned by the Episcopal Church, however, and federal guidelines required that PWA funds could be used only for publicly owned facilities. The lure of the grant, nearly half a million dollars, quickly overcame qualms about the expansion of municipal government. The city took control of St. Peter's and in short order decided to replace the antiquated facility with a brand new building. Instead of the downtown site, officials chose a spot two miles from the center of the city. Memorial Hospital rose on land neatly located between Dilworth and Myers Park in southeast Charlotte.

HOLC REDLINING

At the same time that New Deal construction programs improved roads and created public facilities, the Home Owners' Loan Corporation (HOLC) reinforced Charlotte's emerging sector pattern in more subtle ways. Chartered by Congress to shore up America's faltering mortgage market, the HOLC undertook a massive effort to standardize credit analysis across the nation. It sent out appraisers to map urban neighborhoods according to credit risk. Such a body of information would allow investors to underwrite mortgages knowledgeably no matter how distant the city. While the maps helped accomplish that goal, they also contributed to sharpening patterns of spatial segregation.[20]

Appraisers arrived in Charlotte in 1937 to analyze the city according to HOLC guidelines. They explored the town, examined real estate records, and met with eleven leading developers and real estate bankers to ask about lending practices.[21] Based on the research, the HOLC produced a map of the city showing the creditworthiness of each area (see color fig. 3). Districts that they deemed the best credit risks received A or B ratings and were colored green or blue on the map. Less desirable areas got a C or D and appeared in yellow or red. The draft map was then "checked with competent local real estate brokers and mortgage lenders" and sent to Washington, where copies were printed for circulation.[22] The finished maps were mailed to banks and real estate appraisers nationwide, with the strict proviso that they be used only by finance professionals and not shown to the general public.

The HOLC rating system showed at least two significant biases: against older neighborhoods and against neighborhoods with diverse or "undesirable" ethnic groups. To win the top A rating, areas had to be current "hotspots . . . not yet fully built up," explained the report that accompanied the map. To qualify for a B rating, areas had to possess similar desirability but be more completely developed. "They are like a 1935 automobile—still good but not what people are buying today who can afford a new one." More importantly, the system explicitly rewarded segregation. The best districts, the report stated flatly, "are homogeneous." The criteria for C and D ratings drove home both points:

- C areas are characterized by age, obsolescence, and change of style; expiring restrictions or lack of them; infiltration of lower-grade population . . . ; "Jerry" built areas are included as well as neighborhoods lacking homogeneity. . . .
- D areas represent those neighborhoods in which the things that are now taking place in the C neighborhoods, have already happened. They are characterized by detrimental influences in a pronounced degree; undesirable population or an infiltration of it.[23]

In practice only well-to-do suburbs got the highest grades. In Charlotte just four areas won the coveted A rating: Myers Park, Eastover, and the Olmsted portion of Dilworth, all in the southeast sector, and a small tract adjoining the Charlotte Country Club to the northeast. More areas received the B rank, all of them middle-income white neighborhoods. Most lay on the east side: Crescent Heights, parts of Dilworth and Elizabeth, Chantilly, and much of Plaza-Midwood. One westside area also won a B: Wesley Heights, located between West Trade and West Morehead Streets. Its presence was a reminder of the older patchwork pattern; prosperous whites had not always shunned the west side. But the future was against Wesley Heights, the report suggested: "The present major development is toward the southeast."[24]

In contrast to the greens and blues of Charlotte's high-income areas, working-class and African American districts were awash with yellow and red. In Northern cities the HOLC stricture against "undesirable population" often meant Jews and immigrants; in the South it referred to low-income whites and all African Americans. Charlotte's blue-collar white neighborhoods garnered Cs and sometimes Ds. Districts with black residents received nothing higher than D. The HOLC evaluators considered such "lower grade" groups to be automatic bad credit risks. Thus the Wilmoore neighborhood, a well-maintained white suburb of one-family and two-family homes occupied by some upper blue-collar as well as lower white-collar residents, merited a C. Blacks got Ds regardless of income level. The appraisers acknowledged that African Americans owned quite handsome residences in some areas, particularly along Beatties Ford Road near Johnson C. Smith University, but emphasized that no exceptions to the racial D ranking would be made.[25]

The map gave low grades as well to districts of mixed land use. Fourth

Ward, even with its new apartments, received a C. So did the Elizabeth Avenue section of Elizabeth, which had some neighborhood shops among its still-desirable houses. North Charlotte, with its mix of single-family houses, rented mill cottages, and the shops along Thirty-Sixth Street, rated a D. In the eyes of the federal appraisers and their local consultants, single-family houses should not coexist with apartments or corner grocery stores.

Despite HOLC disclaimers that some good risks could be found in all areas, a poll of banks nationwide at the end of the 1930s confirmed that many lenders now offered home loans in A and B areas only.[26] The HOLC's work served to solidify practices that had previously only existed informally. As long as bankers and brokers calculated creditworthiness according to their own perceptions, there was considerable flexibility and a likelihood that one person's bad risk might be another's acceptable investment. The HOLC wiped out that fuzziness by getting Charlotte's leading real estate agents to compare notes, and then publishing the results. The handsomely printed map with its sharp-edged boundaries made the practice of deciding credit risk on the basis of neighborhood seem objective and put the weight of the U.S. government behind it. Blacks, upwardly mobile whites, and people wishing to put down roots in established neighborhoods found it increasingly difficult to borrow money.

Evidence in Charlotte suggests that the HOLC survey influenced investment practices for decades. The map froze patterns of the mid-1930s and objectified borderlines between areas, with sometimes odd effects. Dilworth proved a striking example. The survey sliced the suburb into three areas: an A section along recently developed Dilworth Road, a larger B section nearby, and a C section along increasingly commercial South Boulevard. The boundaries, somewhat haphazardly delineated, became a self-fulfilling prophecy over the years. Dilworth Road East in the A section, for instance, remained a very desirable middle-class area into the 1970s. Kingston Avenue two blocks away in the B section, just a bit more built-up in 1937, became a mix of rental and owner-occupied dwellings during the same period. Park Avenue, one block parallel to Kingston and lined with exactly the same kind of houses, happened to fall within the C section on the HOLC map. It became entirely rental and was allowed to run down, and many of its houses were demolished by the 1970s.

The 1937 survey not only encouraged disinvestment in existing low-income, mixed-use and black areas, it also shaped development decisions in new parts of town. Real estate brokers realized that in order to stand the best chance of finding investors, projects needed to be homogeneous and as far as possible from "lower grade populations." No longer could a prudent developer take a chance on building an upper-income subdivision near a lower-income or black neighborhood, where appraisers might consider it threatened by "infiltration." The smart strategy would be to cluster all projects aimed at a particular income level in one sector of the city.

FEDERAL AID TO HOMEBUYERS

While the HOLC encouraged sector development by whispering in the ears of lenders, another New Deal program shaped suburbanization even more directly. In 1934 President Roosevelt created the Federal Housing Administration (FHA) as a companion to the HOLC.[27] To cut unemployment in the construction industry and at the same time stimulate the home finance market, the FHA set up an ambitious program of mortgage insurance. It used federal money to insure bankers against the possibility of default by borrowers. By thus cutting risk of losses, the program encouraged banks to offer long-term mortgages, an important innovation. The old system of high downpayments and short-term loans gave way to today's familiar twenty- or thirty-year loans with small downpayments. FHA mortgage aid, scholars agree, played a major role in making the United States a suburban nation. The FHA subsidies, supplemented after 1944 by a similar effort administered by the Veterans Administration (VA), put home ownership within reach of millions of moderate-income Americans.[28] FHA and VA loans accounted for "nearly a quarter of the new housing units during the period of 1946 through 1967" constructed in the United States.[29] Charlotte alone had 15,000 VA mortgages by 1962.[30] The influence of the programs extended even beyond those impressive numbers. In order not to exclude any potential sales, developers eagerly followed federal guidelines for all their houses.

The FHA, like the HOLC, strongly encouraged homogeneous suburbs. Its *Underwriting Manual* spelled out two key requirements for approval of FHA financing: "economic stability" and "freedom from adverse influences." In practice this meant an absence of nonresidential land uses, and it meant a strict separation by race and income level. "Areas surrounding a location are investigated to determine whether incompatible racial and social groups are present, for the purpose of making a prediction regarding the probability of the location being invaded by such groups," advised the *Manual*. Within neighborhoods, the agency urged the use of deed restrictions and exclusionary zoning. "If a neighborhood is to retain stability," the *Underwriting Manual* stated emphatically, "it is necessary that properties shall continue to be occupied by the same social and racial classes."[31]

The FHA emphasis on homogeneity had numerous effects on the design and development of American suburbs. To ensure separation, the agency encouraged winding street patterns that limited outside access. Most avenues in a subdivision should not "carry through or be connected to existing streets," FHA guidelines recommended. "The minor residential streets should follow the topography closely . . . with the result that an attractive unforced curvilinear layout is secured," promoting the all-important "privacy of the residential area."[32] In the eyes of FHA officials, homogeneity could be best guaranteed through the creation of large subdivisions developed completely under the control of a single company. Previously a neighborhood typically had been the product of many small entrepreneurs, from the real estate agent who laid out the streets to the numerous carpenter-speculators who erected individual dwellings. In contrast the FHA explicitly favored developers who operated on a grand scale. The ideal developer would do everything from buying the raw farmland to constructing and selling the houses. "The Authority," officials stated, "seeks especially to encourage that type of operative builder who, preferably, assumes responsibility for the product from the plotting and the development of the land to the disposal of completed dwelling units."[33]

In Charlotte a new generation of large-scale operative builders rose to prosperity in the FHA environment. C. D. Spangler Sr. was one, a graduate of a local business school who got his start as executive secretary to pioneer suburban developer Edward Dilworth Latta, then went out on his own in the late 1930s.[34] Lex Marsh Jr. established Marsh Realty at the same time and went on to create the Charlotte Association of Homebuilders to lobby the FHA and other government agencies on behalf of suburban developers.[35] John Crosland entered the business in 1937 bringing a background that perfectly illustrated the mix of financial and management skills required for an operative builder. Educated at the University of North Carolina, Crosland worked for the real estate loan office of the American Trust bank and managed a local lumberyard before trying homebuilding.[36] Charles Ervin was the only one of the new big developers with actual hands-on construction skills. He practiced bricklaying in the navy, then went to Duke University under an officer training program. After World War II he came to Charlotte to run a pair of grocery stores with his brother, and he put his bricklaying skills to use erecting a house for himself. Before the house was finished, an eager veteran offered a price

Ervin could not refuse. With that lesson in the strength of postwar demand, Ervin launched his own homebuilding company.[37]

Charles Ervin and his competitors built houses not one at a time but a neighborhood at a time. Typically they developed subdivisions of 150 to 250 lots each, laying out curving, self-contained street systems and erecting most or all of the residences. Some dwellings went up "on spec" while others were "custom built" to the tastes of particular buyers. Whether spec or custom, the houses usually represented variations on a few stock plans carefully designed for cost-saving construction. In each subdivision, dwellings were built to sell within a tightly determined price bracket. One Ervin development in the early 1950s, to cite an extreme example of this homogeneity, advertised homes "in a range from $10,300 to $10,500."[38]

In short order a wide band of new houses encircled Charlotte. Burgeoning suburbs rapidly tripled the city's built-up area, from barely twenty square miles at the start of the depression to more than sixty-five square miles by the 1960s.[39] John Crosland alone erected some 6,500 dwellings in more than a dozen major subdivisions during his career.[40] Charles Ervin boasted more than 10,000 houses. During the early 1960s the Ervin Company—with subsidiaries handling everything from land acquisition to interior decorating—ranked as the seventh-largest homebuilding firm in the United States.[41]

The cost and character of subdivisions followed a distinct sectoral pattern. The southeast, and to a lesser extent the northeast near the Charlotte Country Club, were the places for developments with big houses on generous lots. Buyers with smaller incomes settled in subdivisions in the east and southwest. African Americans were directed toward the northwest. It got to the point that a prospective buyer could consult his or her pocketbook, then pick the appropriate radial thoroughfare leading out of town. The buyer was bound to find affluent suburbs off Randolph Road or Providence Road, middling developments off Central Avenue or South Boulevard, humbler dwellings along West Morehead Street or Freedom Drive or Rozzells Ferry Road, and black areas on Beatties Ford Road.

A 1955 flyer advertising Charles Ervin's subdivisions showed the sectoral pattern in practice.[42] Descriptions emphasized the homogeneity of house prices within each development and assured readers that "the Ervin Company always plans its subdivisions according to the standards set by the FHA." The firm's Country Club Acres subdivision to the northeast and Providence Park to the southeast offered residences in the "$20,000 price bracket" aimed at high-income white businessmen and professionals. In the southwest a development on West Morehead Street called Westerly Hills targeted families of more middling incomes with houses at $11,000 to $14,500. Further west Ervin created Beechwood Acres, with $10,000 cottages for blue-collar buyers off Rozzells Ferry Road, "ideally located for those wishing a lower-priced home." To the northwest, off Beatties Ford Road along Oaklawn Avenue, was Oaklawn Park with $10,000–$12,000 houses "for the colored citizens of Charlotte."

The construction of new neighborhoods in northwest Charlotte for African Americans represented a concerted policy on the part of the city's white leaders, in association with the FHA. Unlike the urban North, where blacks often remained boxed into inner-city ghettos, real estate developers in Southern cities typically built houses for black buyers on the suburban fringe.[43] Historians are not certain about the explanation for the regional difference. Smaller Southern cities may have had more suburban land within easy reach, or perhaps the region's long-established black middle class was too tempting a market to ignore. The old nineteenth century pattern of African American clusters at the edges of Southern towns probably played a part as well, providing nuclei for twentieth century extensions. It seems certain, in any case, that federal financing and subdivision guidelines contributed to the new development. FHA/VA mortgages made it possible to build houses at prices that middle-class blacks could afford. And by offering opportunities in one specified sector, developers met FHA requirements to protect their subdivisions elsewhere from the threat of "invasion" by nonwhites.[44]

In Charlotte the timing of black suburbanization showed the influence of the new federal programs. "Far-sighted men" had identified the west side as the city's future Negro area as early as 1912, but twenty-five years passed without much action being taken.[45] Washington Heights, created in the 1910s, established a fashionable black outpost west of Johnson C. Smith University, but as late as the mid-1930s downtown's First Ward and Second Ward (Brooklyn) neighborhoods remained the center of black residence. That started to change in the late 1930s and 1940s as FHA and VA mortgages became available and developers began earnestly erecting westside dwellings for sale to blacks. Their efforts were aided in 1938 when officials announced construction of West Charlotte High School out Beatties Ford Road past the edge of existing black settlement, creating an additional magnet drawing ambitious African American families westward.[46]

The transformation was already evident by 1950. An FHA observer noted "the decided shift of Negroes away from the three older wards of the city. . . . Between 1940 and 1950, Wards 1, 2 and 3, which have long been areas of heavy Negro concentration, collectively lost population to the extent of 4032 persons," while wards to the west of downtown gained. The chief reason was the large amount "of newly-constructed housing for non-white occupancy to the northwest."[47] Additional FHA-assisted subdivisions during the 1950s reinforced the sectoral trend. Ervin's Oaklawn Park and C. D. Spangler's 1954 University Park a bit farther out Beatties Ford Road confirmed the northwest as the location for Charlotte's African American middle and upper class. "All houses," reminded a University Park ad, "have been approved for both FHA and VA financing."[48]

FEDERAL AID LAUNCHES PUBLIC HOUSING

At the same time that Washington's mortgage programs spurred construction of neighborhoods of new single-family houses, a much smaller effort aided low-income renters. Federal incentives introduced during the New Deal encouraged cities to create America's first "public housing." Like the FHA and VA, these efforts continued long after the 1930s. And as with the mortgage programs, local leaders made use of public housing as a tool to reinforce the sectoral growth of the city.[49]

In Charlotte elected officials had shown little interest prior to the New Deal in the housing conditions of the poor.[50] In 1916 V. S. Woodward, who headed Charlotte's private Associated Charities, had attempted to get the city to take action against slum owners. Speaking before a local women's club, he described more than fifty alleys and crowded courts with "not a bath room, a toilet, or even running water in any of them; not a vestige of paint on the exterior. . . . For years our society has had frequent calls to visit the families who have lived in these hovels." Such pockets of poverty were usually hidden away from main thoroughfares and thus out of the view of wealthy whites. Still, the effects reached far beyond the unfortunate occupants, he warned his white-collar listeners: "Can any of you state with any degree of certainty where the fly that dashed through your screendoor and lighted on the baby's oatmeal, had his previous meal?"[51] As a remedy the director proposed a most minimal government intervention: a comprehensive building code. Charlotte already had a rudimentary building ordinance, but it was written to protect property rather than people, requiring only fire-resistant construction. A better law would mandate indoor plumbing and regulate "lighting, ventilation, size and arrangement of rooms, percentage of lot covered by building, overcrowding, repairs, etc.," in order to ensure decent living quarters.

The director's modest proposal may have stirred the clubwomen but it made no impact at City Hall. The problem was that most inhabitants of the rundown housing were African Americans. And, as planner Earle Sumner Draper scribbled in a private note to John Nolen in 1916, "influential men responsible for disreputable negro sections."[52] In northern cities, political leaders courted the votes of slum residents by promising government action. In the South, where most poor African Americans had been stripped of the ballot by the literacy test and poll tax, there was little political incentive to address slum conditions. Until something happened to change the political calculus, Charlotte's influential men would see no need for government to take a hand in matters of housing.

That change came in the form of New Deal money. In the mid-1930s President Roosevelt's PWA funded a handful of pilot projects aimed at "slum clearance," razing dilapidated dwellings and erecting new public housing. The first and most highly publicized was in the South, an Atlanta effort known as Techwood Homes. The experiments' success led to the Wagner-Steagall Act of 1937, America's first federal housing law. It made available long-term loans for the construction of municipally owned low-income housing. To apply, a city had to set up a housing authority, which would construct the units and rent them to the working poor, whose rent money would in turn repay the loans.[53] The prospect of sizable construction projects funded at little cost to the local municipality sparked a sudden interest in public housing among urban leaders.

In Charlotte the local Business and Professional Women's Club took steps to see that the spark caught fire. Early in 1937 the organization brought Alonzo Moran, head of the Techwood Homes project, to Charlotte to meet with city leaders.[54] In addition the women persuaded the *Charlotte News* to conduct a graphic weeklong exposé of slum conditions. Front-page stories and photographs showed districts such as Blue Heaven, where "spider-legged houses teeter aside the creek, jampacked with negroes living four to ten persons in three rooms using—sometimes—outdoor toilets on the other side of the creek." As in 1916 the worst housing tended to be in black areas, but with white politicians in mind, the paper emphasized that there also existed "white slums . . . equally dangerous, equally disease-breeding, equally unlivable."[55]

The newspaper suggested two possible strategies to clean up the slums: institute a strong building code or apply for federal public housing money. The building code proposal dropped from debate almost instantly. It would impose rules on every owner of property and thus likely stir wide anger among Charlotte's white-collar voters. The public housing proposal sounded more attractive, since it asked no investments from property owners but instead promised an infusion of federal cash. Nonetheless it drew heated opposition from one powerful group: the real estate dealers who owned and managed Charlotte's existing rental stock. Government-owned apartments would take land off the local tax rolls, they complained, decreasing the city's tax base. And what was worse, "a great deal of property would lose value" if competition from new public housing threatened the profit margins on privately owned rental units.[56]

After considerable debate—much more strenuous than any generated by federal grants for the stadium, hospital, or art museum—the lure of federal dollars overcame all objections. City officials created the Charlotte Housing Authority and conducted a survey of existing conditions, which found some 4,500 residences—one-fifth of the city's dwellings—urgently in need of plumbing, heat, or other major improvements.[57] Study in hand, the authority applied for a $2.14 million Wagner-Steagall loan from Washington. On July 22, 1940, the first tenants took up residence at Fairview Homes, a 452-unit project for blacks, and on January 1, 1941, families began moving into Piedmont Courts, its 368-unit white counterpart.[58]

The Charlotte Housing Authority, under the direction of its wealthy white governing board, sited these developments and the ones that followed in accordance with the vision of the sorted-out city.[59] Piedmont Courts for whites went up in Belmont, the blue-collar neighborhood just northeast of downtown. Fairview Homes for blacks was constructed on the far northwest edge of the old black Greenville neighborhood, on Oaklawn Avenue between Beatties Ford Road and Statesville Avenue. The Fairview location was quite awkward for low-income residents, nearly two miles from the center of town and convenient to no places of employment. The chance to live in high-quality, affordable rental quarters, however, served as another means to attract African Americans away from downtown and into northwest Charlotte. Subsequent low-income housing reinforced the pattern. Charlotte built only two other publicly owned complexes before the late 1960s. Southside Homes for blacks opened in 1952 followed by Belvedere Homes for whites in 1953, both in the western part of the city.[60] At the same time developer C. D. Spangler, with assistance from the FHA, developed a large privately owned complex for black renters. Called Double Oaks, it occupied land next to Fairview Homes on the northwest side.[61]

Along with federal mortgage programs and public housing assistance, Washington's subsidy of highways and shopping centers helped to propel people toward the suburban periphery. Together, improved roads and new commercial developments in the 1950s and 1960s ended downtown's historic role as the coming-together place for all citizens. Instead of converging on one common meeting spot at the center of town, Charlotteans now visited separate shopping malls in each sector of the city.

Federal road aid first became available to America's cities in the late 1940s and 1950s. After a generation of funding highways only *between* cities, Washington began appropriating money for projects *within* urban areas with the Federal Highway Act of 1944. In 1956 allocations surged as the United States inaugurated the Interstate Highway program, one of the biggest public works efforts in human history. Washington now put up as much as 90 percent of the cost of road projects. For a mere 10 percent contribution, local officials discovered they "could reap the political benefits of more jobs, enhanced economic opportunities, and an expanding constituency."[62] Among the constituents most in favor of better highways were those individuals wealthy enough to invest in land at the edge of town. The only ones opposed were the few who might lose their homes during construction of a road.

Charlotte's commercial-civic elite moved quickly to take advantage of the new programs. In 1944 the city became one of the first urban areas in the nation to receive federal planning assistance.[63] Washington experts, in collaboration with state transportation planners and local elected officials, drew up a proposal for a grand new crosstown boulevard. The multilane highway would slice across the city from east to west, eliminating troublesome bottlenecks and creating a modern transportation showpiece. Best of all, Washington would put up nearly all of the $2 million cost. The local person most responsible for winning the crosstown boulevard project was Mayor Herbert Baxter. A lumber dealer, Myers Park resident, and president of the Myers Park Country Club, he possessed the contacts to line up support among Charlotte's civic leaders. Once the elite community was in agreement, Baxter broke the news to the general public. Charlotteans awoke on the morning of August 24, 1944, to headlines proclaiming, "Superhighway Endorsed: City Officials Give Assurance of Cooperation with State, Federal Groups."[64]

When residents saw the proposed route through the city's east side, protests erupted. From downtown the highway cut across the black Brooklyn and

FIG. 57. INDEPENDENCE BOULEVARD
Federally funded, Charlotte's Independence Boulevard sliced through center city and eastside neighborhoods in the late 1940s, carefully avoiding Myers Park. This early 1960s photograph suggests how the six-lane roadway transformed the once-residential Elizabeth neighborhood. Fourth Street crosses in the foreground, and Elizabeth Avenue crosses in the distance. (Courtesy of the Robinson-Spangler Carolina Room, Public Library of Charlotte and Mecklenburg County)

Cherry neighborhoods—a politically safe path, given the powerlessness of African American voters. From there, however, it swerved abruptly northeastward to miss Myers Park and surrounding upper-income neighborhoods. Instead, it ran across Elizabeth Avenue, through Independence Park, and northeastward out of the city via the middle-class Chantilly district. In much the same way that they had considered the original proposal, Mayor Baxter and his council okayed the route. "In those days it was customary for the city council to decide issues behind closed doors before publicly casting predetermined votes," writes Charlotte historian Dan Morrill. "They gathered on October 6, 1946, for an informal dinner meeting at the Myers Park Country Club, where Mayor Baxter was President. There they endorsed the . . . route through Chantilly."[65]

When Independence Boulevard, as the crosstown highway became known, opened in 1949, it kicked off a new era in Charlotte urban development. By later standards the road was considerably less than a superhighway; it met city avenues at grade, and portions of its narrow right-of-way even included on-street parking in the early years. Nonetheless, it marked the start of decades of federal road projects that would widen city thoroughfares and provide new connections to surrounding regions.[66] The climax of that trend came when Interstate 85 opened in 1962, followed by Interstate 77 in the 1970s.[67] The long gash that Independence Boulevard cut through Brooklyn exposed the squalor of the worst sections of that black neighborhood. The highway project alerted ordinary Charlotteans to the problems of slums, and at the same time it showed that Washington money could be used for demolition. In addition, Independence Boulevard helped open the city's suburban rim to development. When town fathers considered creation of a new municipal theater and coliseum in the mid-1950s, they looked not at downtown locations—where civic auditoriums had stood in the past—but at an eastside site out Independence Boulevard. Designed by pioneer modernist architect A. G. Odell, the 1955 Charlotte Coliseum boasted the world's largest columnless dome and became a suburban icon of Charlotte's post–World War II growth.

While federal highway aid as a spur to American suburbanization is generally acknowledged, Washington's role in the construction of suburban shopping centers is less well known. The notion of building a retail complex with parking at the door had occurred to American real estate developers almost as soon as cars began to be a factor in development. In the early 1920s promoter J. C. Nichols laid plans for Country Club Plaza in the midst of his residential subdivisions on the edge of Kansas City, often credited as the nation's first shopping center.[68] The idea spread slowly though; building an entire retail district from scratch tied up a great deal of capital, and renting stores offered a slow return compared with selling house lots. As late as 1946 there were only a handful of sizable shopping centers in the United States and none larger than 500,000 square feet.[69] After World War II, as Americans rushed to buy new suburban houses, shopping plazas began appearing in slightly greater numbers. The real boom, however, did not arrive until the late 1950s. Then, thanks to action by the federal government, shopping centers suddenly sprang up by the hundreds in America's towns and cities.

The Washington program that made the difference was an unexciting-sounding bit of tax law known as accelerated depreciation. Since the beginnings of the federal income tax in 1913, the government had recognized that buildings tend to deteriorate with the passage of time. The Internal Revenue Service had allowed businesses to deduct small amounts from their tax bills to reflect this slow depreciation of assets. The policy changed in 1954, however, as Congress cast about for ways to perk up a momentary slump in the national economy.[70] Hoping to spark construction investment, lawmakers passed a regulation entitling investors to take accelerated depreciation on new business buildings. Instead of a small deduction each year for decades, owners could write off most of the value of their structures in as little as seven years.

Accelerated depreciation transformed real estate development into a lucrative tax shelter. An investor making a profit from rental of a new building usually avoided all taxes on that income, since the "loss" from depreciation canceled it out. And if the depreciation exceeded profits from the building itself, the investor could use the excess to reduce other income taxes. Meanwhile, in the real world, real estate values were actually going up in America during the late 1950s and 1960s. Savvy investors discovered that they could build a structure, claim losses for several years while enjoying tax-free income from the property, then sell the project for more than they had originally invested.[71]

The tax break had an enormous impact on America's cities. Accelerated depreciation applied only to new construction, not to renovation of existing buildings.[72] Investors seeking the best return on their dollars looked away from traditional downtowns, where vacant land was scarce, and rushed to put their money into fresh suburban projects. Suddenly, all over the United States, shopping plazas sprouted like well-fertilized weeds. A study of the largest centers (over a half-million square feet) illustrated the transformation. As late as 1955 such projects were appearing at the rate of just three per year. The turning point came in 1956, following the tax change by two years, precisely the minimum time required to rush a building project from concept to completion. Twenty-five big shopping centers opened in 1956 alone, and thereafter new ones joined the roster at the rate of thirty per year through the 1960s.[73] Smaller centers proliferated even faster. By 1970 the United States had 14,271 shopping plazas of all shapes and sizes.[74]

Charlotte possessed no real suburban shopping centers before the start of accelerated depreciation. During the late 1920s and 1930s small clusters of shops had begun popping up on street corners in white-collar neighborhoods such as Elizabeth and Dilworth. Entrepreneurs would erect a store or two at a time, choosing locations on existing streetcar routes so customers could ride the trolley to shop. The first development to break those patterns appeared in 1928–29 on East Morehead Street near Myers Park. It featured a half-dozen stores created by a single developer, trimmed in the fashionable Tudor Revival architectural style. Catering to affluent Dilworth and Myers Park families, it stood far from trolley lines and instead offered parking for automobiles

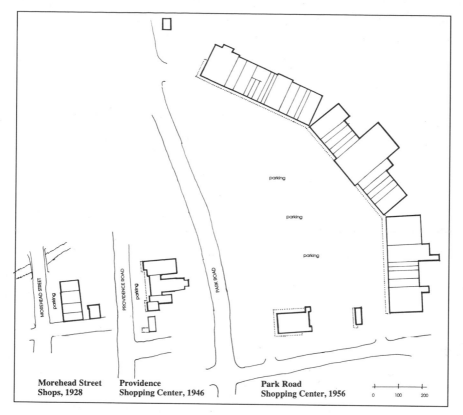

FIG. 58. FROM CONVENIENCE SHOPPING TO SHOPPING CENTER
Federal accelerated depreciation tax breaks instituted in 1954 ushered in the era of the large suburban shopping center. Previously, suburban shopping clusters had supplemented, rather than competed with, downtown. First of the new breed in Charlotte was the Park Road Shopping Center, 1956. (Drawing by author, reproduced with permission from the *American Historical Review*, October 1996)

at the door.[75] The next such project did not open until after World War II. In 1945 local developer Lloyd Goode announced construction of Providence Center, fronting Providence Road at the other edge of Myers Park. Anchored by a Colonial supermarket, Myers Park Pharmacy, and Manor movie theater, its half-dozen shops were intended to serve the adjacent neighborhood.[76] A handful of other such "neighborhood centers" followed, including Colony Center on Sardis Road south of Myers Park about 1950, and the Stanley Drugs center on Seventh Street in Elizabeth two years later.[77] The largest was Lex Marsh's Sedgefield Center, begun on South Boulevard near Marsh Road in 1950. It boasted a dozen shops plus dentists' and doctors' offices, providing conveniences for customers in the nearby Sedgefield and Starmount subdivisions.[78] As late as ten years after World War II, though, when it came time for serious shopping, most Charlotteans still traveled downtown.

That started to change when Park Road Shopping Center opened November 15, 1956.[79] Full-page newspaper ads trumpeted the arrival of Charlotte's first modern retail plaza, developed by local entrepreneur A. V. Blankenship on farmland just south of Dilworth. Thirty-five stores, arranged in a modernistic V-shaped row, looked out over an astounding 3,000 parking spaces. Two giant supermarkets anchored the main strip, one at each end, and the stores in between included a full-sized Woolworth's and Charlotte's first J. C. Penney Department Store. A separate freestanding building held a huge S&W Cafeteria—the company's first restaurant outside downtown—offering comfortable dining for families on an evening out. Steel canopies connected all the stores, protecting shoppers from the rain and complementing the understated International-style architecture. The new complex drew curious visitors from all over the city and surrounding countryside.

The gala opening of the Park Road Shopping Center turned out to be the first of many such events as developer after developer rushed to take advantage of accelerated depreciation. By 1961, barely five years later, the *Charlotte Observer* counted more than a dozen sizable shopping plazas sprinkled around the city.[80] "Shopping centers have popped up like wild onions," marveled a business reporter.[81] Charlottetown Mall on Independence Boulevard garnered the most attention. James Rouse, one of the nation's leading shopping center developers, leased the site of the old Thompson Orphanage between downtown and Myers Park and commissioned A. G. Odell to design a striking two-level complex. Completed in 1959, Charlottetown was the first enclosed mall in the Southeast and the fourth in the United States.[82] The climax of Charlotte shopping center construction came in 1970 when Southpark mall opened with 1 million square feet of new retail space. The site southeast of Myers Park had once been the farm of Cameron Morrison, famed as North Carolina's "Good Roads Governor" a generation earlier. Developers of the sprawling mall, significantly, were Charlotte's Belk and Ivey families. Despite owning downtown's largest department stores, the two retailers had decided in the early 1960s that tax incentives and shopping trends favored suburban real estate projects.[83] A spacious new Belk store and equally elegant Ivey's at Southpark supplanted the families' downtown stores as the flagships of the retail chains.

The proliferation of shopping centers added another dimension to Charlotte's sharpening sectoral pattern. Anyone with an automobile was of course free to shop anywhere, but residents tended to gravitate toward the retail centers in their sector of town. Southpark became the new "downtown" for the well-to-do residents of southeast Charlotte, a fact reflected in its mix of fine department stores, elegant jewelry shops, and fashionable clothing boutiques. Eastland Mall, a similarly large mall that opened in 1975 on Central Avenue on the northeast side of town, featured less-elaborate stores and tended to attract more middle-income shoppers. Meanwhile complexes such as Freedom Mall on the city's southwest edge aimed unmistakably at blue-collar customers.

PLANNING AND ZONING

Washington's widening array of urban programs worked a profound change in attitudes toward the proper role of local government in Charlotte. Well into the 1930s, Charlotte's commercial-civil elite had held to the tradition of minimalist government and, in particular, had adamantly opposed the notion of planning or zoning. The Chamber of Commerce had shot down John Nolen's 1917 effort to create a city plan, and in 1930 real estate developers had led the attack that torpedoed Herbert Swan's proposal for a zoning ordinance.[84] In the mid-1940s, however, the prospect of winning increased federal aid pushed business leaders to relinquish their long-cherished position.

Washington actions quietly began eroding local resistance during the late 1930s and early 1940s.[85] To get federal grants, civic leaders discovered they needed studies to prove that money was necessary, and plans to show how it would be spent. The chance to obtain Works Progress Administration dollars for public housing convinced the city to conduct its first survey of residential conditions in 1938. When urban highway grants became available a few years later, officials commissioned the town's first traffic study and a plan for thoroughfare improvements, "To Support Bid for US Funds," headlines explained.[86] America's entry into World War II brought a marked increase in federal activities. In Charlotte the need to work closely with federal agencies spurred election of an avowedly activist mayor. Herbert Baxter defeated a traditional minimalist-government candidate "on the promise that he would do everything possible to lead a progressive government at city hall and initiate measures [to] put Charlotte in the position at the end of the war to begin a program of improvement and expansion."[87] In office Mayor Baxter aggressively sought out new Washington programs and pushed Charlotte to do what was required to take advantage of them. When Congress rationed construction materials, Baxter commissioned a study to show that the Queen City deserved some of the scarce supplies.[88] When the War Mobilization and Reconversion Act of 1944 offered cash to help cities plan public works, Baxter won a grant to plan local sewer projects.[89] When it appeared that the federal government might fund other capital projects under the Lanham Act, Baxter arranged for studies documenting the city's needs for new parks and libraries.[90]

Gradually sentiment in Charlotte's business community began to grow in favor of a permanent municipal planning effort. The turning point came in 1944 when the Chamber of Commerce published *A Pattern for Charlotte*. The report looked toward the difficult transition from a wartime economy and urged the city to create an official planning commission. "We can hold our own . . . without assistance" from Washington, said the chamber, acknowledging the traditional position of business conservatives. But, the report declared, if "the Federal Government should appropriate funds for all and sundry projects, let us have plans for worthwhile projects ready."[91] On December 20, 1944, Mayor Baxter appointed the first Charlotte Planning Commission.[92]

Real estate boosters took the lead in setting the new commission's agenda. The reason for the developers' surprising turnabout could be found in the mortgage guidelines published by the FHA. FHA officials strongly encouraged planning as a means to promote "economic stability" and ensure "freedom from adverse influences" in federally assisted subdivisions.[93] The agency's *Circular No. 5: Subdivision Standards*, in particular, included "Zoning" and "Subdivision Regulations . . . enacted by the city, county or state" on its list of "Minimum Requirements."[94] With Myers Park real estate broker Frank Thies as chairman and banker-contractor Beaumert Whitton as vice-chairman, the Charlotte Planning Commission moved quickly to comply. In 1946 the commission approved a subdivision regulation law, which fulfilled federal guidelines by setting minimum street widths and lot sizes for new developments.[95] In 1947 the commission created Charlotte's first zoning ordinance.[96]

Zoning regulations added legal force to Charlotte's emerging sector pattern. Distinctions between the fashionable east side and the remainder of the city were sharply etched on the 1947 zoning map.[97] Rules provided for five levels of land use, ranging from "single family residence" at the top to a category tagged "industrial" at the bottom, which permitted any sort of construction. On the map the protective single-family designation went only to eastern neighborhoods, with the largest such zones covering parts of Myers Park and Dilworth and all of wealthy Eastover. Eastside suburbs not designated single family received the slightly less protective "residence 2" rating. In contrast, most of the west side was rated industrial, with only small patches of residence 2.

Black and blue-collar white neighborhoods near the center city received the harshest treatment under the 1947 zoning plan.[98] Working-class white dwellings in First Ward and adjoining Optimist Park were zoned industrial. So was all of the Brooklyn neighborhood with its black businesses and churches, the black portion of First Ward where the proud houses of Thad Tate and Bishop George Clinton stood, black Third Ward around Good Samaritan Hospital, and the old Greenville neighborhood near Fourth Ward. Downtown business leaders looked forward to the day when those areas would be cleared of houses and redeveloped. The newly appointed Zoning Board, made up of prosperous white executives from southeast Charlotte, chose zoning that encouraged the change.

To a much lesser degree, zoning also promoted change within white-collar residential districts. The trend toward neighborhood shopping, first seen in the 1920s, seemed to be gathering momentum with postwar projects such as the Providence Shopping Center. Fashionable single-family residences still predominated on streets such as Providence Road, Elizabeth Avenue, East Seventh Street, and Central Avenue. But real estate experts expected that to change. So the Planning Commission zoned those avenues "business" to permit commercial strip development.

Few people voiced objections in 1947, but over the long run such zoning policies would have far-reaching effects. The decision not to zone houses single-family tended to discourage families from purchasing. Instead it encouraged speculators to buy and hold properties, either renting out the dwellings or simply demolishing them, awaiting the day when the land would become ripe for business development. The presence of rundown rooming houses and vacant lots, in turn, tended to make adjoining areas less desirable for families. The process accelerated after 1962, when a revised ordinance sharply increased the amount of multifamily and nonresidential zoning in "outmoded" older neighborhoods. In time, struggles over the proper function of zoning—promotion of redevelopment versus protection of existing areas—would play a major part in the rise of neighborhood organizations in Charlotte.

SLUM CLEARANCE AND URBAN RENEWAL

While the new Charlotte Planning Commission moved swiftly to oversee suburban growth and institute zoning, aiding real estate developers by putting the city in compliance with FHA financing guidelines, it acted much less resolutely to improve conditions for the poor. In 1945 as the commission first convened, the notion of creating a strict building code came up again. Such an ordinance, which would require landlords to provide indoor plumbing, adequate windows for ventilation, and so on, had first been discussed by Charlotte clubwomen back in 1916 and had been formally proposed by the *Charlotte News* in the 1930s, to no avail. Now, however, the concept suddenly found a new champion: the Charlotte Real Estate Board. Mayor Baxter had announced he was considering another federal housing project for the city, and the Realtors—still staunchly opposed to public housing—seized upon the building code idea as an alternative. "These slum conditions were caused by a lack of planning in the past," the Realtors asserted, executing a blithe about-face from their position of the 1930s.[99] The group proposed a "standard house ordinance" mandating indoor toilets and sinks, electricity, minimum room sizes, and other essentials. Such a code, they promised, would do more to accomplish "slum clearance" than any federal public housing. The proposal passed directly into law, illustrating the political power of Charlotte's development industry. "City Council Adopts Realtors' Definition of Standard House," headlined the *Charlotte News* in the spring of 1945.[100] In gratitude Mayor Baxter politely dropped his public housing initiative. For all the Realtors' talk about remedying slum problems, however, the 1945 ordinance actually covered only new construction. The law thus helped assure "freedom from adverse influences" in outlying areas where builders sought FHA/VA mortgages, but it did nothing to disrupt business as usual in existing poor neighborhoods.

Not until 1948, spurred by a public health scare, did Charlotte finally extend the building code to all dwellings and hire a full-time enforcement officer.[101] Results were dramatic. Newspapers reported more than 2,000 dwellings brought up to standard during the first year.[102] The success drew nationwide attention. The National Association of Real Estate Boards, in the midst of a hard-fought campaign against public housing, seized on the Charlotte effort as a model of private initiative. The national board profiled the city's brand of slum clearance in a 1952 pamphlet, and the program in turn garnered praise in a scholarly study on trends in residential rehabilitation published in 1959.[103] By the time the book appeared, however, Charlotte real estate brokers and political leaders were no longer talking about slum clearance through code enforcement and local investment. Instead, their eyes glistened at the prospect of Washington-funded urban renewal.

From 1949 to 1974 the Federal Urban Renewal Administration offered a cash bonanza that encouraged cities to undertake redevelopment on an unheard-of scale.[104] Urban Renewal's original stated goal was to improve housing for low-income Americans. Launched under the Housing Act of 1949, the program proposed to tear down slums with government money, then sell the land to private developers at greatly reduced prices, enabling them to erect affordable new housing. City officials loved the concept, since local government put up less than a third of the cash. Real estate developers loved it, too, since they got development sites at far below market cost. Early model projects, such as Lake Meadows on the south side of Chicago, won national applause for replacing crumbling tenements with well-built, high-rise apartments available to low-income families and also to upper-income residents who might have otherwise forsaken the city. Over time, however, at the behest of urban leaders and the National Association of Real Estate Boards, Congress broadened Urban Renewal's focus significantly. In 1954 an amendment allowed 10 percent of allocations to be used for nonresidential purposes, a figure that was increased in 1959 and again in 1961.[105] Other changes permitted demolition of housing to provide public facilities such as convention centers and city offices. The definition of the slums to be demolished also loosened. Along with actual deteriorated housing, funds could be used to eliminate "blight," which was defined as inappropriate or incongruous land use.[106] Urban renewal became a powerful tool to clear land and convert it to whatever local politicians deemed a "better use."

As Charlotte leaders read each update of the urban renewal legislation, they recognized a potential windfall. On the heels of Congress's 1959 revisions, local officials began putting together a grant application for Charlotte. To head the project, they brought in Vernon Sawyer, who had helped administer earlier redevelopment efforts in Norfolk, Virginia. "Heart of Norfolk Blitzed in Urban Renewal," the *Charlotte News* headlined an enthusiastic profile of the new director. "This 250-year-old seaport has never been bombed by an intercontinental ballistic missile, although it sometimes seems a little that way."[107] Under Sawyer's leadership Charlotte used more than $40 million in federal money to flatten inner-city neighborhoods and replace them with glistening new developments.

Urban renewal efforts in Charlotte first targeted Brooklyn, the historic African American neighborhood just east of downtown. Back in 1912, "far-sighted men" had declared that "this section, because of its proximity to the center city, must sooner or later be utilized by the white population."[108] Federal money finally put that dream within reach. Between 1960 and 1967 Sawyer's Charlotte Redevelopment Authority razed Brooklyn in five stages.

Over the following decade the cleared land became the site of Charlotte's Government Plaza buildings, a showplace city park, widened thoroughfares connecting the downtown to the east side, plus a variety of private office and business ventures.

The Brooklyn project made no pretense at creating better quarters for residents. Not a single new housing unit went up to replace the 1,480 structures that fell to the bulldozer. Urban renewal demolition displaced 1,007 Brooklyn families.[109] Most moved to the western and northern sectors of the city. Belmont–Villa Heights, the white working-class district just north of downtown, abruptly became a black neighborhood in the mid-1960s. Wesley Heights on the west side and Wilmoore to the southwest experienced similar transformations.[110] Brooklyn's entrepreneurs had less luck at relocation. The old district's density and central location had provided a warm environment for small shops, both on the black main street along Second and Brevard and on street corners throughout the neighborhood. Urban renewal displaced 216 Brooklyn businesses. Many never reopened.[111]

With Brooklyn clearance under way, the Redevelopment Authority turned its attention to other areas of "inappropriate" land use. Additional urban renewal projects targeted Greenville and a large section of First Ward; like Brooklyn both were old African American neighborhoods, and both had been zoned industrial since 1947 to encourage redevelopment. The First Ward project did break one pattern set in Brooklyn: First Ward included construction of some public housing. In 1962 Urban Renewal Administration officials in Washington, embarrassed by the wholesale displacement going on in Brooklyn, threatened to end appropriations if the city did not erect some low-income housing.[112] In response the Charlotte Redevelopment Authority bulldozed the black residential core of First Ward and in 1967 erected Earle Village Homes on the site. Opponents pointed out that Earle Village actually contained fewer units than had been demolished in First Ward to create it and thus did little to solve the displacement problem. The Redevelopment Authority, one observer noted, "tore down an average of 1,100 black occupied units per year from 1965 to 1968 but erected only 425 new units during that time."[113]

While the Redevelopment Authority demolished vast areas of black homes and businesses, it took a much more tightly focused approach in the only two urban renewal projects that directly affected white districts. Officials excised a four-block pocket of blue-collar housing in Dilworth and replaced it with a senior citizens' complex during the early 1970s. At the same time they redeveloped a three-block section of downtown Charlotte. The site on East

Trade Street extended from Independence Square to North Brevard Street. Small storefronts there had served as the city's provision district in the early twentieth century; by the 1970s they held a mix of groceries, poolhalls, and eateries that catered largely to black and blue-collar white shoppers. With federal aid those enterprises gave way to a Charlotte Convention Center, a luxurious Radisson Hotel, and the skyscraper headquarters of NCNB bank.[114]

Private owners also caught the bulldozer fever of the urban renewal era. Banks and other investors took action to demolish low-income downtown housing they held outside the urban renewal zones. In 1966, for instance, financial institutions cleared eighty-six mill cottages in the Graham Street–Mint Street section of Third Ward; in 1969 a realty company razed a row of once-grand houses on Ninth and Tenth Streets in Fourth Ward; in 1972 a private owner demolished fourteen dwellings he held in First Ward.[115] Local tax laws contributed to the demolition drive. Property taxes in Charlotte, as in most American cities, were significantly lower on vacant land than on land with buildings. The tax savings from demolition often outweighed the income that could be gained from rental to a low-income family or small business. This was particularly true for commercial properties close to Independence Square, where owners could lease their empty lots for parking. By the late 1970s fewer residences or retail businesses remained within walking distance of the Square than had existed there at the turn of the century, when Charlotte was a small town of less than 20,000 residents.

QUESTIONING THE SORTED-OUT CITY

In 1971 Charlotte citizens found their community a focus of sudden national attention. Ruling on a lawsuit titled *Swann v. Charlotte-Mecklenburg Board of Education*, the U.S. Supreme Court set a landmark precedent for schools nationwide: students must be bused in order to achieve racial integration. The Swann case both summed up the results of decades of government-promoted segregation and also signaled the questions that were beginning to arise in Charlotte and in American society as a whole concerning the desirability of a sorted-out city.

The roots of the Swann case lay in the growth of the civil rights movement in Charlotte and the nation. Since the 1940s African Americans had been working steadily to change laws and practices that treated blacks unequally. In Charlotte black organizations took inspiration from World War II. "What are you doing on the homefront for our boys who are giving their all to preserve democracy?" asked the Charlotte National Association for the Advancement of Colored People (NAACP) in its first membership drives during the war.[116] Early victories included creation of a black city park in 1942 and campaigns to desegregate the municipal golf course and other city facilities during the 1950s.[117] Efforts stepped up in 1960 when students from Johnson C. Smith University held sit-ins at white lunch counters, refusing to leave until they were served. Meanwhile activists at the national level worked through the Supreme Court to outlaw Jim Crow regulations. Gradually they set precedents against spatial segregation in cases such as *Shelley v. Kramer*, which ended racial deed restrictions, and *Brown v. Board of Education*, which made separate schools illegal.[118] The insistent efforts of civil rights leaders forced Americans to look at their country with fresh eyes, to test the creed of democracy and equality against existing practices. Congress and the White House heeded the call. In 1965 they passed the Voting Rights Act, finally abolishing the system of poll taxes and tests that had barred many Southerners from the ballot box since the end of the 1890s.

The civil rights movement, and the Voting Rights Act in particular, meant that long-silent voices began to be heard in municipal politics in the South. In 1965 Frederick Douglass Alexander won election as the first black member of Charlotte's city council in the twentieth century. Alexander took care to maintain harmony with well-to-do whites; as long as the at-large electoral system remained in place, the city's southeast sector would dominate politics. But he openly questioned municipal actions that encouraged geographic division. Alexander called attention to the absurdities of segregation when he dismantled a fence dividing white Elmwood Cemetery from black Pinewood Cemetery; newspapers across the nation joined him in ridiculing a system that went to lengths to keep even the dead apart. Though his vote alone could not change policy, Alexander criticized urban renewal's relocation of African Americans to the northwest, an action "which unwisely cuts them off from the rest of the community," he warned. "We are building up a problem when we continue to segregate them off to one side of the community like we do now."[119]

In this atmosphere a local black student named Darius Swann, with support from the NAACP, challenged Charlotte's system of public school attendance. Technically the city-county school system had desegregated in the late 1950s in compliance with *Brown*. But in reality the sector arrangement of residential areas in Charlotte meant that as long as children went to school only within their own neighborhood, they would continue to attend class only with students of their own race. Great swaths of northwest Charlotte were 60 percent or more African American, while southern and eastern residential areas were 95 percent white. As late as 1963 only 42 of Charlotte-Mecklenburg's more than 18,000 black children attended a majority-white school.[120] As he constructed his case, Swann's attorney, a local African American lawyer named Julius Chambers, focused relentlessly on the role government had played in promoting residential segregation. Where government had helped create inequities, he argued, government had an obligation to find a remedy.

Chambers's strategy proved powerfully persuasive. James McMillan, the district court judge presiding in the case, was a prosperous white Charlottean who resided off The Plaza near the Charlotte Country Club. He first greeted Chambers's arguments with skepticism, but as evidence piled up, he shifted into agreement. "Local zoning ordinances starting in 1947," Judge McMillan wrote in his final ruling, had fostered a "pattern of low cost housing and industry to the west and high cost housing with some business and office developments to the east." Public housing placement and the industrial zoning of older black neighborhoods had pushed blacks toward the northwest, and pressure had increased with federal urban renewal. "Under the urban renewal program thousands of Negroes were moved out of their shotgun houses in the center of town and have relocated in the low rent areas to the west." Charlotte leaders, in sum, had consciously used their powers over the years to create a sectoral arrangement "where Negro residents have become concentrated almost entirely in one quadrant." While population movements "of course involved many ad hoc decisions by individuals and by city, county, state and federal governments . . . the clear fact however is that the displacement occurred with heavy federal financing and with active participation by local governments."[121] McMillan's 1969 ruling—affirmed by the U.S. Supreme Court in its landmark 1971 decision—held that busing was indeed needed to overcome the effects of government-promoted segregation.

The growing activism of civil rights groups during these years was paralleled by another grassroots organizational effort in Charlotte and other American cities: the neighborhood movement. In part the movement expressed widespread reaction against the heavy-handed spending of federal highway and urban renewal funds.[122] The closed-door decisions by Mayor Baxter concerning the route of Charlotte's Independence Boulevard, described earlier, were typical of municipal procedures all over the United States during the 1940s and 1950s. Political leaders and planners created projects with little thought to consulting ordinary citizens who would be affected. The resulting outcry led Washington to write a requirement for an initial public hearing into the

Urban Renewal Act of 1954. It quickly became clear that a single hearing was not enough. An amendment in 1962 mandated creation of a citizens' advisory council in each city. At first these often consisted of wealthy business leaders, but subsequent laws pushed officials to consult formally with the actual residents in each affected area, not only concerning urban renewal but also on other proposed federal projects.[123] Thrilled that authorities were at lasting listening, neighborhood groups began to organize everywhere in America in the late 1960s.

In addition to federal mandates for citizen participation, two other forces fed the neighborhood movement in Charlotte: enthusiasm for historic preservation and discontent with local zoning and road-building decisions. The late 1960s and 1970s witnessed a rising appreciation for older buildings throughout the United States. Young people, mostly from middle-income backgrounds, found fresh beauty in Victorian- and Bungalow-style houses, and they moved to rehabilitate residential districts that a previous generation had written off as hopelessly outmoded. In Charlotte the trend took hold in the original blocks of Dilworth in the late 1960s. It soon spread to Elizabeth, Plaza-Midwood, Myers Park, and downtown's Fourth Ward—all areas that had rapidly fallen from fashion as prestigious new suburbs opened farther out during the 1950s. When people rehabilitated homes in these areas, they found themselves at odds with the actions of the city's more conventionally minded leadership. Charlotte's zoning ordinance, the rehabilitators discovered, still offered the most protection to the newest suburbs in the southeast while marking older areas for redevelopment. Highway schemes reflected the same assumptions, routinely routing new thoroughfares through vintage neighborhoods.

Articulate citizens' groups coalesced around these issues in the early 1970s. Most often the groups arose in once-fashionable suburbs, now largely abandoned by the rich but still retaining the attractive dwellings and streetscapes of earlier days. The Elizabeth Community Association formed in 1970 to squelch a planned cloverleaf interchange that would have wiped out scores of houses at Hawthorne Lane and Independence Boulevard.[124] The Dilworth Community Association and Myers Park Homeowners Association both mobilized to seek protective residential rezoning in 1971.[125] About the same time a housewife restoring a Victorian manse on The Plaza organized neighbors to block a four-lane highway and then won restoration of residential zoning in much of the district, which the group named Plaza-Midwood.[126]

Struggles over development policies and civil rights issues during the 1960s and 1970s combined to feed a long-festering discontent with Charlotte's political structure. As neighborhood groups and rights advocates in growing numbers butted heads with city council, many Charlotteans began to openly question the wisdom of the at-large system of government. Was it good that elected officials came predominantly from a single sector of the city? Complained one county commissioner, "If the county is considered as a pie with Independence Square as the center, you could cut out one slice and find practically all the elected officials living there . . . all the school board members, all city councilmen except one, three of the [five] county commissioners, and all the members of the General Assembly delegation."[127] Such "concentration of governmental power in the southern part of Charlotte and Mecklenburg," he charged, was dangerously undemocratic.

Two series of events brought anger to a head. In the wake of Judge McMillan's 1969 busing decision, a school board led by members from southeast Charlotte proposed a transportation plan with an unmistakable geographic bias. "Those whites who would be bused into black areas of town generally came from working-class neighborhoods in the northern and western parts of the city," a journalist observed. "Students in the more affluent southeast quadrant of the county . . . would rarely be bused from their neighborhoods."[128] The affront sparked creation of the Westside Committee for Organization, made up of both working-class whites and blacks who came together to campaign for a more equitable plan. At the same time neighborhood groups on the east side of the city were losing patience over development struggles. Their breaking point came in 1974. A carefully argued rezoning effort initiated by the Myers Park Homeowners Association and supported by the city planning office was overturned by a city council that seemed more inclined to listen to development interests than to neighborhood residents. "Money Talked in Battle Over Rezoning," newspapers headlined.[129]

Disgruntled neighborhood groups from the east side and the west side now joined hands to bring about an overhaul of city election rules. Citizens went door-to-door to gather 5,000 signatures and force a referendum challenging the at-large method of election. In 1977 voters won a major modification of the system that had restricted political access in Charlotte since the days of disfranchisement.[130] Henceforth only four city council members would be elected at-large; the majority—seven—would be elected from individual districts.

The referendum opened a new chapter in the history of Charlotte, not only in government but also in the shaping of the built environment. The district system broke the grip that southeast suburbs had held on municipal decision making since the early twentieth century and that wealthy men had enjoyed since the earliest days of the city's history. In short order black and female residents from every corner of Charlotte became key players on city council, and in 1981, on the strength of the black-white neighborhood coalition, Harvey Gantt won election as the Queen City's first African American mayor.[131] With broader participation on city council came new faces on planning and zoning boards and other decision-making bodies. No longer would municipal actions automatically benefit one particular sector of the community.

The 1977 referendum also marked a less visible shift in urban thought. Increasingly, for many urban opinion makers, diversity was becoming the watchword of the modern city. The ideal of homogeneity, whether in government or land use, was no longer taken for granted as an automatic public good. Elected officials, zoning bodies, and even real estate developers now praised the notion of diversity rather than homogeneity. As the late 1970s gave way to the 1980s and 1990s, planners spoke of fostering mixed-use districts where housing and neighborhood shopping might coexist. Young families renovating old houses talked of the value of living with neighbors of different races and different income levels. Only a few decades earlier such ideas would have been deemed eccentric; now, to many Charlotte citizens, the goal of diversity seemed worth striving for.

AFTERWORD

Charlotte's experience demonstrates the ever-changing nature of the physical city. Notions of what constitutes desirable urban form are not timeless. Rather, they are the product of particular historical forces, which shift kaleidoscopically with the passing years. Separation by income, for instance, turns out to be neither an age-old human desire nor merely the product of impersonal economics and technology. Segregation by race, likewise, is not an age-old Southern constant, nor did it spring full-blown into its modern form upon the end of slavery.

As late as the 1870s Charlotte remained a city whose land use patterns more resembled a medieval trading town than a modern metropolis. Charlotteans knew about Northern urban fashions, as witnessed by the handsome Victorian architecture of the town's fine homes. But citizens held to old habits of intermingled salt-and-pepper land use long after class-segregated residential suburbs for white-collar workers and managers had become the fashion in more-industrialized cities. The lack of interest in separating land uses was particularly evident in the creation of Dilworth in 1891. The streetcar neighborhood was designed with elite housesites and also factories and lots for sale to less-prosperous whites and African Americans.

Two things acted together to shake this traditionalism. The construction of textile mills beginning in the 1880s brought large groups of factory workers to the city, men and women whose economic standing gave them an outlook on life that could often put them at odds with wealthy mill owners. By itself the task of finding accommodations for such large numbers of newcomers engendered a degree of separation, as indicated by the construction of mill villages adjoining Charlotte's second batch of mills in 1889. Then came the political challenge of Fusion in the mid-1890s. When millhands joined forces with small farmers and African American voters and mounted a substantial challenge to traditional elite rule, Charlotte's "better classes" began actively to move apart from the insolent "negroes and the lower class of whites."

Those at the top of the social pyramid now took steps to insulate themselves physically from the social and political confusion of this industrial society. Self-contained satellite cities such as North Charlotte came into being for blue-collar residents, with schools, churches, and stores as well as houses and workplaces. Black areas, likewise, became more sharply defined, and African American businesses, which had intermingled with white stores downtown, felt pressure to depart for a new black main street. White-collar neighborhoods came into being that were literally "exclusive," not only in subtleties such as complicated curving street systems but blatantly in the form of deed restrictions that forbade black residents and established minimum house costs to exclude blue-collar buyers.

Charlotte's experience during the crucial decades from the late 1870s through the 1920s provides a valuable comparison with the sorting-out witnessed two generations earlier starting during the 1810s–1830s in cities of the Northern United States. Foreign immigrants, whose arrival has been seen by scholars as one impetus for white-collar flight, played no role in Charlotte. This is true even if African Americans are considered as the South's immigrants; Charlotte's black percentage hit a high-water mark in 1880 and gradually decreased throughout the period described in this study. Likewise the presence of separate suburban governments is not a key factor in the sorting process, Charlotte's experience indicates. The city retained a single metropolitan government through the 1970s, due in large degree to the fact that white-collar suburbanites were able to hold tightly to political control.[1] Yet even without political barriers between areas, the city became increasingly segregated over time and experienced the same problems with disinvestment in poor neighborhoods and older commercial areas that are familiar to residents of more politically divided metropolitan areas.[2]

Charlotte's story also offers evidence that transportation does not automatically determine urban form. In the era of pedestrian travel, wealthy residents might have—by the logic of easy transportation—clustered close around Independence Square or even congregated on one "exclusive" side of town. Instead they lived the length of Trade and Tryon Streets and on several side streets, everywhere comfortably sharing blocks with fellow citizens of any station. This did not change with the arrival of new transportation technology. As a corollary to historian Henry Binford's finding that commuter neighborhoods developed outside Boston long before the streetcar era, this study suggests that Charlotte held to traditional land use customs even after the inauguration of trolley service. The workplaces and white and black residents of early Dilworth indicate that streetcars do not necessarily produce streetcar suburbs characterized by white-collar residential exclusivity.

The drive to separate groups by class and race, when it arose in Charlotte, came as a response to industrial change and the social tensions that change produced. The sorting-out of the city thus may be seen as a reaction to the wider reorganization of society brought on by the industrial revolution. Separation seemed the answer to the challenges of that particular tumultuous moment in history. But it turned out to be a strategy with consequences that lingered long after that historical moment.

Once in place, separation begat separation. People increasingly out of contact with their diverse urban neighbors came to take separation for granted as a natural law in human affairs. This tendency was accelerated after 1930 by actions of the federal government. Washington—acting on assumptions shared by many urbanites—underwrote suburban housing developments, shopping centers, urban renewal, and other programs designed to promote "homogeneous" and "appropriate" land use. Thanks to federal aid, local leaders could carry sorting-out to its logical extreme. The result was the creation of the late twentieth century's pronounced sector pattern of separation by color and income.

To what extent was Charlotte's sorting-out a "Southern" experience? Historians have debated the degree to which the South is a unique region versus one that merely lagged behind and eventually caught up with the North. Charlotte's experience suggests that similar processes indeed transformed the New South city much in the way that they had earlier reshaped Northern towns. In a sense Dixie communities did become more like Yankee ones after 1880. But the South's particular historical and racial environment affected the way similar processes worked themselves out over time, creating an urban form that remained identifiably Southern well into the last quarter of the twentieth century.

Sorting-out was not a matter of the South emulating Northern urban form; rather, it was a parallel response to the experiences of industrialization. When Dixie adopted the factory, it did not bargain for any accompanying social changes but they came anyway. Even amidst the strong parallels, race and historical context gave the sorting process a distinctly Southern flavor. The power that had so recently been enjoyed by the antebellum economic elite made the new challenges from below seem especially acute in the South. The presence of large numbers of African Americans provided Southern leaders a unique wedge, which they used skillfully to disfranchise a significant fraction of their opposition. The shift to at-large government completed this consolidation of political power during the 1900s. White-collar Charlotteans were hungrily grasping every tool that promised to reestablish the old relations of deference. Neighborhood planning, deed restrictions, and the latest in suburban architecture seemed to offer ways to keep the insolent strangers at bay. Just as vehemently, Charlotteans rejected such things as citywide park systems or comprehensive planning that sought to tie disparate social groups together. Scholars have noted similar patterns, particularly the fervor for at-large government and the reluctance to finance comprehensive plans, throughout the South during the early twentieth century.

Even after the 1920s, as nationwide incentives from the federal government became a leading influence on the built environment, Southern cities maintained a measure of distinctiveness. Many observers have pointed out that Southern Sunbelt cities seem to have embraced modern tendencies toward suburban sprawl to a greater extent that those of other regions. This tendency, it may be argued, springs from the events around the turn of the century. Thanks to the rules instituted to restrict political participation throughout the region, Southern white-collar civic leaders found themselves able to "speak with one voice" when applying for and spending federal aid. There were no countervailing voices—for instance, the big lower-class voting blocs that encouraged Chicago elected officials to at least make a show of improving slums and spreading the largess—to bring pressure against Dixie leaders. Southern elites had a relatively free rein to craft their cities in their own vision.

Changes in racial patterns confirmed that effectiveness. In 1940, rankings of America's most racially segregated cities showed roughly the same number of Northern and Southern cities among the twenty most-divided locales. By 1970, following three decades of federal aid, Southern segregation had worsened markedly. With a single exception every one of the nation's most severely segregated cities was now in Dixie. Charlotte had barely made the list in 1940; by 1970, under the direction of its Chamber of Commerce bosses, the Queen City had advanced to fifth place on the roster.

In the years since the mid-1970s the ideal of the sorted-out city has fallen from favor among public speakers concerned with urban form. This represents a dramatic turnabout in thinking. For much of the twentieth century, nearly all of the most socially concerned intellectuals in the United States viewed separation and homogeneity as best for the public good. From Progressive planners such as John Nolen to New Deal liberals at the HOLC and FHA, urban activists urged the sorting-out of cities by race and class. That conviction evaporated in the 1960s. Due perhaps in large part to the cultural concerns raised by the civil rights movement, Americans began to question the notion that people could be separate and yet equal.[3]

In Charlotte many of the urban initiatives of the late 1960s and 1970s reflected this new belief that diversity could be desirable. The young home-buyers who revitalized inner-city districts such as Fourth Ward, Dilworth, and Elizabeth eagerly moved onto streets with renters, blue-collar whites, and blacks as well as white-collar whites as neighbors. During the 1970s officials at the University of North Carolina launched University City, advertised as a mixed-use community intended to attract residents to the city's unfashionable northeast sector. On a more ephemeral but no less interesting note, a major Charlotte radio station won thousands of listeners in the early 1980s with its ongoing saga of "Peaches and Parker Myers" of Myers Park, a satire that poked

TABLE 8. Most Racially Segregated Cities in the United States, 1940 and 1970

	1940		1970	
Rank	City	Segregation Index	City	Segregation Index
1.	Norfolk, Va.	96.0	Shreveport, La.	97.4*
2.	Chicago, Ill.	95.0	Winston-Salem, N.C.	94.0*
3.	Roanoke, Va.	94.8	Augusta, Ga.	93.3*
4.	Atlantic City, N.J.	94.6	Montgomery, Ala.	93.2*
5.	Jacksonville, Fla.	94.3	Charlotte, N.C.	92.7*
			Dallas, Tex.	92.7*
6.	E. St. Louis, Ill.	93.8	Ft. Worth, Tex.	92.6*
7.	Greensboro, N.C.	93.1	Roanoke, Va.	91.8
			Memphis, Tenn.	91.8*
8.	Milwaukee, Wisc.	92.9	Atlanta, Ga.	91.5*
	Winston-Salem, N.C.	92.9	Birmingham, Ala.	91.5*
9.	Richmond, Va.	92.7	Greensboro, N.C.	91.4
10.	St. Louis, Mo.	92.6	Savannah, Ga.	91.2*
11.	Flint, Mich.	92.5	Mobile, Ala.	91.0*
12.	Cleveland, Ohio	92.0	Norfolk, Va.	90.8
	Wichita, Kans.	92.0	Richmond, Va.	90.8
13.	Dayton, Ohio	91.5	Tampa, Fla.	90.7*
	Evanston, Ill.	91.5		
14.	Toledo, Ohio	91.0	Macon, Ga.	90.2*
15.	Cincinnati, Ohio	90.6	Dayton, Ohio	90.1
16.	Indianapolis, Ind.	90.4	Houston, Tex.	90.0*
17.	Shreveport, La.	90.3	Chattanooga, Tenn.	89.9*
18.	Baltimore, Md.	90.1	Beaumont, Tex.	89.7*
	Charlotte, N.C.	90.1	Little Rock, Ark.	89.7*
19.	Detroit, Mich.	89.9	Knoxville, Tenn.	89.6*
	Canton, Ohio	89.9		
20.	Omaha, Nebr.	89.5	St. Louis, Mo.	89.3

* City was more segregated in 1970 than in 1940.
Source: Sorensen, Taeuber, and Hollingsworth, *Indexes of Racial Segregation for 109 Cities*, table 1.

fun at the insulated worldview fostered within the exclusive neighborhoods of southeast Charlotte.

Yet the legacy of a century of sorting-out remains. The desire for separation is now deeply ingrained. Ironically it is perhaps more ingrained in Sunbelt cities such as Charlotte, since booming post–World War II development means that little of the older neighborhood patterns survive as reassuring models. During the 1980s and 1990s Charlotte's central business district, for instance, has become noticeably less diverse as both department stores and stores serving blue-collar buyers have departed, leaving the area almost completely to white-collar offices and cultural facilities. At the same time, Charlotte's most vibrant locus of new development is now the area surrounding Southpark mall. With elite shops, offices, and white-collar housing, it has emerged as an Edge City—a virtual new town catering exclusively to the affluent.[4]

As Charlotteans—and city dwellers elsewhere across the county—look toward the twenty-first century, it is not at all clear which vision of the ideal city will triumph: separation or diversity. Will Charlotteans find ways to bridge the distances that have been created between black neighborhoods and white neighborhoods, between impoverished areas and wealthy suburbs? Will they find ways to overcome the distrust and the fear that distance can breed?

As Americans grapple with such issues, they can perhaps take heart from history. Separation by race and class has not been a constant in urban affairs, as Charlotte's story shows. It came as the product of particular concerns at particular times in the past. People created that separation. Their actions came at a moment, around the turn of the century, when new social forces unleashed by industrialization seemed to threaten familiar hierarchies. People reinforced that separation through much of the twentieth century, spurred on by a host of federal programs now largely abandoned. What people have created, they may choose to re-create.

INTRODUCTION

1. The study of the social forces underlying the "built environment" has emerged as a major interdisciplinary scholarly field in America during the last thirty-five years. Key works include sociologist Kevin Lynch's *Image of the City* (1960); planning critic Jane Jacobs's *Death and Life of Great American Cities* (1961); urban historian Sam Bass Warner Jr.'s *Streetcar Suburbs* (1962); anthropologist Amos Rapoport's *House Form and Culture* (1969); folklorist Henry Glassie's *Folk Housing in Middle Virginia* (1975); geographer James Vance's *This Scene of Man* (1977), revised in 1990 as *The Continuing City*; John Brinckerhoff Jackson's *Landscapes* (1970); and folklorists Dell Upton and John Vlach's *Common Places* (1986).

The present study also draws extensively on data assembled by specialists in the field of historic preservation. Since Congress funded the Historic Preservation Act of 1966, states and localities have systematically gathered information on America's built environment. Data are compiled in three forms: reports nominating structures and districts to the National Register of Historic Places, similar reports supporting local registers of historic sites, and comprehensive surveys cataloging all "architectural and historic resources" in a particular area. The reports and surveys include comprehensive photographic documentation, plus historic research including biographical information on owners and analyses of the sites' social and economic context. Charlotte has an excellent body of such studies compiled by the Charlotte Mecklenburg Historic Landmarks Commission and the North Carolina Division of Archives and History.

2. On Charlotte in the 1990s, see, for instance, profiles in the *New York Times*, August 24, 1991, and October 28, 1993. On the background of the city's recent economic growth, consult Clay, Orr, and Stuart, *North Carolina Urban Regions*; Clay and Stuart, *Charlotte*. In the summer of 1995 Charlotte-based NationsBank and First Union ranked as the fourth- and ninth-largest banks in the United States, making the city by far the largest banking center in the South (*Atlanta Constitution*, June 20, 1995). See also *New York Times*, July 18, 1993; Covington and Ellis, *Story of NationsBank*.

3. The first two book-length histories of Charlotte appeared during the initial New South boom: J. B. Alexander, *History of Mecklenburg County* (1902), and Tompkins, *History of Mecklenburg County* (1903). The next full-length treatment came in 1961: Blythe and Brockmann, *Hornets' Nest*. Poet Mary Norton Kratt prepared the most recent survey in 1980, *Charlotte: Spirit of the New South*, and updated it extensively in 1992.

4. For an urban geographer's description of Charlotte's sectoral pattern, read Gerald L. Ingalls, "Social and Economic Components of the Population," in Clay and Stuart, *Charlotte*, p. 26.

5. Radford, "Race, Residence, and Ideology"; Radford, "Testing the Model of the Preindustrial City"; Radford, "Social Structure and Urban Form." Similarly in Greensboro, North Carolina, see Kipp, "Urban Growth and Social Change," chap. 7, esp. p. 283; Marvin A. Brown, *Greensboro*, pp. 21, 41.

6. Doyle, *Nashville in the New South*, pp. 71, 120.

7. Silver, "Changing Face of Neighborhoods," pp. 93–126; Silver and Moeser, *Separate City*. Likewise for Miami, see Raymond A. Mohl, "The Twentieth Century City: Introduc-

tion," in Mohl, *Making of Urban America*, p. 197; Mohl, "Trouble in Paradise"; Mohl, "Making the Second Ghetto."

8. Park, Burgess, and McKenzie, *City*.

9. Hoyt, *Structure and Growth of Residential Neighborhoods*; Hoyt, *Where the Rich and the Poor People Live*.

10. Sjoberg, *Preindustrial City*, esp. pp. 97–100.

11. Paul Johnson, *Shopkeeper's Millennium*; Ryan, *Cradle of the Middle Class*; Binford, *First Suburbs*; Blackmar, "Rewalking the 'Walking City'"; Wilentz, *Chants Democratic*; Michael P. Conzen, "Morphology of Nineteenth Century Cities"; Michael P. Conzen, "Historical Geography," esp. pp. 89, 93, 102; Knox, *Urban Social Geography*, pp. 9–11, 24; Fishman, *Bourgeois Utopias*; Blumin, *Emergence of the Middle Class*, particularly p. 304; Blumin, "Black Coats to White Collars"; Blumin, "Hypothesis of Middle-Class Formation."

Perhaps the earliest scholar to recognize that shifts in American residential patterns were tied more to economic changes than to transportation innovations was—somewhat ironically—the pioneering urban historian Sam Bass Warner Jr. His initial 1962 book, *Streetcar Suburbs*, was taken by many readers as the confirmation of the Sjoberg thesis that elite residents had clustered downtown before the advent of horsecars and trolleys. But Warner called that idea into question with his next book, *Private City*, esp. pp. 6, 11–21. Land use had intermingled freely in the city in the revolutionary era, then had begun to sort out into distinct neighborhoods by class soon after 1800, well before any new transportation technology. In an accompanying 1968 *American Historical Review* article, Warner urged scholars to shift their attention from simple transportation change toward the "interaction of the events of industrialization" that "populated the city with a new set of social units: work groups" and propelled a new "residential segregation . . . by classes, ethnicity and race" (Warner, "If All the World Were Philadelphia," p. 43). More recently Warner has criticized writers who employ the "fiction . . . that technological change drives social change" (Warner, "Urban History," p. 76).

On nineteenth century sorting, see also Kostof, *City Assembled*, pp. 117–19; Stott, *Workers in the Metropolis*, esp. pp. 191–211; Cutler and Gillette, *Divided Metropolis*, pp. xiv–xv; Muller and Groves, "Emergence of Industrial Districts"; Henry Louis Taylor Jr., "Use of Maps in the Study of the Black Ghetto-Formation Process," esp. pp. 46–47; Taylor and Dula, "Black Residential Experience"; Kathleen N. Conzen, "Patterns of Residence in Early Milwaukee," in Schnore, *New Urban History*, pp. 145–83; Ward, "Place of Victorian Cities," particularly pp. 259, 377; Robert Lewis, "Segregated City."

Abroad, much work has been done on the sorting-out of English cities. See Pritchard, *Housing and the Spatial Structure of the City*, esp. pp. 186–87; Warnes, "Early Separation of Homes from Workplaces," esp. pp. 106–33; Girouard, *English Town*, pp. 238, 284; Vance, "Housing the Worker."

12. On the link between the growth of large-scale economic enterprises and social reorganization, see E. P. Thompson's seminal *Making of the English Working Class*. Also see Gutman, *Work, Culture, and Society*; Gary Nash, "The Social Evolution of Preindustrial American Cities, 1700–1820," in Mohl, *Making of Urban America*, esp. p. 35; Wallace, *Rockdale*; Prude, *Coming of the Industrial Order*; Levine, *Highbrow/Lowbrow*; Katz, *People of Hamilton*; Zunz, *Changing Face of Inequality*; Sugrue, "Structures of Urban Poverty."

13. On industrialization and urbanization in the New South era, see, for instance, Woodward, *Origins of the New South*; Tindall, *Emergence of the New South*; Gaston, *New South Creed*; Goldfield, *Cotton Fields and Skyscrapers*; Rabinowitz, *First New South*;

Ayers, *Promise of the New South*; Grantham, *South in Modern America*; Boles, *South through Time*.

14. The notion that existing Southern habits and desires decisively shaped the adoption of new ideas is bolstered by the work of anthropologists. Theorists once assumed that mainstream culture automatically obliterated local customs whenever the two came into contact. Instead, anthropological observers now agree that people tend to adopt only those portions of a new culture that seem useful to them. Other aspects may be twisted to fit local ideas or ignored altogether. On this process of "bricolage," see Levi-Strauss, *Savage Mind*, pp. 16–33; Frederick Barth, *Ethnic Groups*; Stephen Stern, "Ethnic Folklore and the Folklore of Ethnicity."

CHAPTER 1

1. Blythe and Brockmann, *Hornets' Nest*, pp. 16–18; Romine, *Mecklenburg*; Tompkins, *History of Mecklenburg County*, 1:1–34.

Initial settler Thomas Polk and many who followed during the 1750s and 1760s started their journey in southern Pennsylvania and northern Maryland. They were Scotch-Irish immigrants who had arrived in America through the port of Philadelphia, then made their way westward and southward in search of good farmland. They came down the Philadelphia Wagon Road, the colonies' greatest highway. It stretched from Pennsylvania through the Shenandoah Valley of Virginia, then dropped southward into the Carolina backcountry, where it joined the Great Trading Path. The place they chose to stop looked much like the place they had left, with rolling hills and small streams. Once settled in Mecklenburg, the newcomers set about re-creating familiar patterns. Presbyterian churches, the Scotch-Irish denomination, soon dotted the countryside. Today the county's oldest surviving dwelling is the 1774 two-story stone residence of wealthy farmer Hezekiah Alexander. It looks just like houses in Cecil County, Maryland, where Alexander and several other founding families, including the Polks, grew up. See *Charlotte Observer*, August 6, 1899, May 28, 1905; Blythe and Brockmann, *Hornets' Nest*, pp. 17–21; Parke Rouse Jr., *Great Wagon Road*, esp. p. ix. On early Mecklenburg architecture, see Boyte, *Houses of Charlotte and Mecklenburg County*.

2. On the Catawba Indians and their trade routes, see Merrell, *Indians' New World*; Douglas Summers Brown, *Catawba Indians*, esp. pp. 69–70, 102–3; Clay, Orr, and Stuart, *North Carolina Atlas*, pp. 15, 18.

3. Kratt, *Charlotte*, 2nd ed., pp. 17–18; Blythe and Brockmann, *Hornets' Nest*, pp. 21–24; Romine, *Mecklenburg*; Tompkins, *History of Mecklenburg County*, 1:28–34. As created in 1762, Mecklenburg was much larger than today, including all of Tryon and Cabarrus Counties and half of Union County. Tryon split off in 1768, Cabarrus was created in 1792, and Union formed in 1842. See Corbett, *Formation of the North Carolina Counties*, pp. 147–48.

4. Lt. Col. Banastre Tarleton, quoted in Foote, *Sketches of North Carolina*, p. 505.

5. Cornwallis captured Charlotte in 1780. See Kratt, *Charlotte*, 2nd ed., pp. 30–32; Blackwelder, *Old Charlotte and Mecklenburg Today*, pp. 32–33; Harkey, *More Tales from the Hornet's Nest*, pp. 9–19. On the wider context of Charlotte's role in Revolutionary fighting, see Morrill, *Southern Campaigns of the American Revolution*, esp. pp. 98–123, 208–9.

6. On the resolves and the declaration, see Kratt, *Charlotte*, 2nd ed., pp. 24–29; Blythe and Brockmann, *Hornets' Nest*, pp. 31–62; Lefler and Newsome, *North Carolina*, p. 205. The existence of the Mecklenburg declaration quickly became a point of pride in the

county. Today most historians regard the "Mec Dec" as a figment of patriotic imaginations. The argument seems moot, since the document had no impact on the rebellion.

7. Lt. Col. Banastre Tarleton, quoted in Kratt, *Charlotte*, 1st ed., p. 35.

8. Quoted in ibid., pp. 32–35.

9. Blythe and Brockmann, *Hornets' Nest*, p. 104; Mary Frances Barnes, "Eureka! Gold!," in Reynolds, *Charlotte Remembers*, p. 71; Clayton, *Close to the Land*, pp. 82–83. The Reed Gold Mine, site of that first discovery, is today a North Carolina State Historic Site.

10. Blythe and Brockmann, *Hornets' Nest*, p. 303; J. B. Alexander, *History of Mecklenburg County*, p. 119.

11. Jones, "Sketch of Charlotte," pp. 138–39; "Report to the Charlotte Mecklenburg Historical Properties Commission from the Mint Museum of Art." The mint was disassembled in 1933 and rebuilt in Charlotte's Eastover neighborhood as the Mint Museum of Art. See also Mary Frances Barnes, "Eureka! Gold!," in Reynolds, *Charlotte Remembers*; Kratt, *Charlotte*, 2nd ed., pp. 54–61; *Charlotte Journal*, March 7, 1845. Interestingly, the village of Dahlonega, Georgia, located farther down the same gold seam, experienced a similar strike and won a U.S. Mint that actually turned out more coins than Charlotte's. Dahlonega, though, remains a small town to this day.

12. According to Tompkins, *History of Mecklenburg County*, 1:94–96, "In 1802, the Legislature of North Carolina bought the patent right for this State, agreeing to pay Whitney for it by a special tax of two shillings and six pence on each saw used in a gin. . . . In . . . 1802, . . . Mecklenburg led all the other counties in the amount of this tax. . . . In 1804 Mecklenburg paid 212 pounds, and [adjacent] Lincoln county was second in the State with fifty-six pounds. In 1805, the tax amounted to 213 pounds, and Mecklenburg continued at the head of the list."

13. U.S. Bureau of the Census, *Third Census*, margin note at the end of the manuscript roll for Mecklenburg County.

14. *Charlotte Journal*, March 21, 1845. Such a trip was remembered in the *Charlotte Observer*, August 13, 1905.

15. My thinking on "structure of opportunity" owes a debt to Carlton, "Piedmont and Waccamaw Regions."

16. For an elegant, graphic portrait of the distribution of plantations and slaves in the South, see Hilliard, *Atlas of Antebellum Southern Agriculture*, pp. 36–38.

17. U.S. Bureau of the Census, *Third Census*, margin note at the end of the manuscript roll for Mecklenburg County. Tompkins's 1903 county history noted that liquor was omnipresent in early Mecklenburg. "It was much more convenient to market the surplus products [corn, rye, and fruit] in liquid form than in bulk, and the returns were larger and surer" (Tompkins, *History of Mecklenburg County*, 2:90). On the sale of piedmont North Carolina "spirits" in Charleston in this period, see Tullos, *Habits of Industry*, p. 56.

18. U.S. Bureau of the Census, *Sixth Census*. On crop diversity, see also J. B. Alexander, *Reminiscences of the Past Sixty Years*, pp. 174–75.

19. Data in this paragraph come from the U.S. Bureau of the Census, *Seventh Census*, "Statistics of North Carolina," pp. 210, 235–36. For descriptions of several of Mecklenburg's planter families, read Davidson, *Plantation World around Davidson*; Boyte, *Houses of Charlotte and Mecklenburg County*. On the deleterious effect of plantations on town growth elsewhere, see, for instance, Farmer, *In the Absence of Towns*.

20. Percentage estimates in this paragraph are based on published 1860 census data, plus a sample drawn from the 1850 manuscript census by Hoffman in her dissertation, "De-

velopment of Town and Country," pp. 6–47. On the social pyramid elsewhere in the Carolina backcountry, read Escott, *Many Excellent People*, pp. 12–18.

21. U.S. Bureau of the Census, *Sixth Census*. Black people comprised 39 percent of Mecklenburg population in 1850, 43 percent by 1860. See Greenwood, "Early History of Mecklenburg County," pp. 65–66.

22. On the family model of social relations in colonial America, a classic work is Demos, *Little Commonwealth*. Scholars sometimes describe the older personal, family-based, hierarchical social organization as "gemeinschaft," from the German word for "community-society." They contrast it with the more impersonal, individualistic, merit-oriented "gesellschaft" system, from the German term meaning "individual-society," which we live in today. See Tonnies, *Community and Society*. On deference, see Pocock, "Classical Theory of Deference"; Howard Newby, "Deferential Dialectic."

In the North, traditional deferential social relations disappeared by the mid-nineteenth century. In the South, they persisted much longer, until challenged by the economic changes of the post–Civil War era. See MacPherson, "Antebellum Southern Exceptionalism"; MacPherson, *Ordeal by Fire*, esp. pp. 5–37; Foner, *Reconstruction*; Foner, *Nothing but Freedom*; Harold Woodman, "Economic Reconstruction and the New South," in Boles and Nolen, *Interpreting Southern History*, pp. 254–307; Woodman, "Sequel to Slavery"; Ayers, "Toward a Synthesis of the New South"; Moore, Tripp, and Tyler, *Developing Dixie*. These authors build implicitly on the work of earlier historian David Potter, who identified a face-to-face "personalism" as a key antebellum Southern characteristic well before most American historians heard the terms "gemeinschaft" and "gesellschaft." "The culture of the folk survived in the South long after it succumbed to the onslaught of urban-industrial culture elsewhere. . . . Even in the most exploitative economic situations, this culture retained a personalism in the relations of man to man which the industrial culture lacks" (Potter, *South and Sectional Conflict*, pp. 15–16).

23. Sydnor, *American Revolution in the Making*, p. 108.

24. Free blacks had been able to vote in North Carolina but were stripped of the ballot in 1835. See Lefler and Newsome, *North Carolina*, p. 354.

25. In 1857 property qualifications were eliminated for statewide elections, though strenuous objections from the state's powerful eastern planters made it less than certain that the law would survive. See Escott, *Many Excellent People*, pp. 15–20; Lefler and Newsome, *North Carolina*, pp. 348, 377–79; J. B. Alexander, *Reminiscences of the Past Sixty Years*, p. 97.

26. Tompkins, *History of Mecklenburg County*, 1:91; Escott, *Many Excellent People*, pp. 15–20. For a portrait of some local squires, see Springs, *Squires of Springfield*.

27. J. B. Alexander, *History of Mecklenburg County*, p. 325. For descriptions of this mindset in the wider antebellum South, see Williamson, *Crucible of Race*, pp. 24–35; Tullos, *Habits of Industry*, pp. 82–83.

28. U.S. Bureau of the Census, *Sixteenth Census*, "North Carolina." This table conveniently lists "population of incorporated places of 10,000 or more from earliest census to 1940." Comparative data in this paragraph are drawn from this table and a similar one covering South Carolina.

29. Trelease, *North Carolina Railroad*; Lefler and Newsome, *North Carolina*, pp. 364–66; Cecil K. Brown, *State Movement in Railroad Development*.

30. *Charlotte Journal*, March 14, 1845. Biographical data are drawn from the 1850 manuscript census; O'Brien, "Power and Influence in Mecklenburg"; Hoffman, "Development of Town and Country," pp. 228–29; Tompkins, *History of Mecklenburg County*, vol. 2.

Though not on the original committee, wealthy South Carolina upcountry planter John Springs and his son Leroy, a Mecklenburg planter and merchant, became major players in the railroad effort. See Lacy K. Ford, *Origins of Southern Radicalism*, pp. 221–23; *Charlotte Observer*, December 12, 1943; Springs, *Squires of Springfield*; Springs family papers, Southern Historical Collection.

31. *Charlotte Journal*, March 28, 1845. For similar arguments, see ibid., October 23, 30, 1846, March 4, 1847.

32. This gives an interesting twist to a major debate among Southern historians. For years scholars have argued whether the post–Civil War South was shaped by planters or by "new men" who were more entrepreneurial, middle class, and town oriented. Historians have also asked why inland towns boomed after the war while older coastal communities languished.

Recently Gavin Wright has suggested that the economic changes wrought by the war itself changed planters' outlook. Before the war, lowcountry men of wealth had much of their investment in slaves, a very mobile asset. After the war the well-to-do lost their slaves but retained their real estate. In the process their mindset changed from that of "labor-lords" to "land-lords." They became very interested in projects that increased land value, particularly town building and railroad construction.

In the Carolinas, town growth rate rose sharply in the backcountry even before the Civil War. It is significant that the structure of opportunity in this area precluded large investments in slaves. The Mecklenburg evidence demonstrates that backcountry men of wealth were behaving like landlords in search of real estate profits well before the war.

The war subsequently mowed down heavily slave-oriented regions, forcing large planters to relearn the economic ropes. Men in the backcountry, however, were already skilled at making investments in railroads and towns. After 1865 they and their region stepped into the lead in the South.

See Gavin Wright, *Old South, New South*. The classic statement of the "new men" thesis is Woodward, *Origins of the New South*, esp. p. 20. The most vocal "old men" proponent in recent years is Genovese, *Political Economy of Slavery*. On the stagnation of ports and growth of inland towns, see, for instance, Doyle, *New Men, New Cities, New South*.

33. *Charlotte Journal*, October 23, 1846. For similar arguments, see ibid., March 21, 1845, March 4, 1847.

34. Ibid., March 21, 1845.

35. Ibid., June 10, 1847.

36. On the bidding war, see ibid., April 1, May 13, 20, June 10, 1847. The strategy worked so well that contributions from farm communities along the route actually exceeded those from Charlotte. See ibid., August 10, September 11, 1847. The total cost was $1.7 million, with $1.1 million from stock and $600,000 through loans and bond sales:

Charlotte, N.C.: $100,000 stock; $100,000 municipal subscription
York, S.C.: $24,000 stock (Springs, mostly)
Fairfield, S.C.: $209,000 stock
Chester, S.C.: $213,000 stock
Columbia, S.C.: $100,000 stock; $100,000 municipal subscription
Charleston, S.C.: $5,000 stock; $15,000 municipal subscription
S.C. state revolving fund: $272,000 loan.

See *Proceedings of the Fourth Annual Meeting of the Stockholders of the Charlotte and South Carolina Railroad, at Chesterville, November 19, 1851*. See also *Proceedings of the*

Stockholders of the Charlotte and South Carolina Railroad at Their Fifth Annual Meeting, pp. 4–5; Lacy K. Ford, *Origins of Southern Radicalism*, pp. 221–23. The contract for grading the line was let in May 1849. See Tompkins, *History of Mecklenburg County*, 1:125.

37. Tompkins, *History of Mecklenburg County*, 1:125–26; J. B. Alexander, *History of Mecklenburg County*, p. 325.

38. Robert Hall Morrison, quoted in Matthews, *History of Providence Presbyterian Church*, p. 105.

39. Though the line reached Charlotte in 1854, it was not fully complete until 1856. See Trelease, *North Carolina Railroad*; Blythe and Brockmann, *Hornets' Nest*, p. 260.

40. Blythe and Brockmann, *Hornets' Nest*, p. 261; Gilbert and Jefferys, *Crossties through Carolina*, p. 8; J. B. Alexander, *History of Mecklenburg County*, p. 147; *Charlotte Democrat*, May 21, 1896; Ashe, *Eminent and Representative Men*, p. 641; Ashe, *Biographical History of North Carolina*, 1:341–48.

41. Blythe and Brockmann, *Hornets' Nest*, pp. 261–62; Gilbert and Jefferys, *Crossties through Carolina*, p. 8.

42. Jones, "Sketch of Charlotte," pp. 139–41. Trading was also facilitated by the arrival of telegraph wires in 1853, which gave Charlotteans up-to-the-minute information about prices in all U.S. and international markets. See J. B. Alexander, *Reminiscences of the Past Sixty Years*, p. 337.

43. J. B. Alexander, *History of Mecklenburg County*, p. 119; Blythe and Brockmann, *Hornets' Nest*, p. 303. On a building from the 1850s boom that survived into the 1980s, see William Huffman, "Thomas Trotter Building," National Register Nomination.

44. Charlotte Chamber of Commerce, *1950 Census Data*. This pamphlet conveniently includes citywide and ward data back to 1850.

The 1850s boom helped spur Charlotte's division into wards. In 1851 officials split the city into two wards for election purposes. They redrew the lines in 1869 to create four wards. See Claiborne, *Jack Claiborne's Charlotte*, pp. 61–62. The creation of the wards also reflected Charlotte's 1852 switch from the old commissioner system to a city government elected directly by local voters. See Tompkins, *History of Mecklenburg County*, 1:119–20.

45. J. B. Alexander, *History of Mecklenburg County*, pp. 246–47.

46. *Charlotte Observer*, December 28, 1897; William Huffman, "The Charlotte Cotton Mill," Survey and Research Report. See also J. E. Oates obituary, *Charlotte Observer*, July 30, 1897.

47. This observation is recorded on an unnumbered page between pp. 132 and 133 in vol. 16 (Mecklenburg County), North Carolina, Dun Collection. On Williams, see J. B. Alexander, *History of Mecklenburg County*, pp. 378–79.

48. See n. 31 above.

49. Greenwood, *On the Home Front*; Clyde Osborne, "The War: Charlotte's Role," in Reynolds, *Charlotte Remembers*, p. 31; "Charlotte in the War between the States"; *Charlotte Observer*, June 30, 1948. Late in the war Charlotte's leading citizens sheltered the retreating Confederate president Jefferson Davis, who held one of his last cabinet meetings in the city. A marker placed by the North Carolina Division of Archives and History at 700 North Tryon Street reads, "Confederate Cabinet with President Davis held last full meetings April 22–26, 1865, in a house which was located here." The house is now gone. See Boyte, *Houses of Charlotte and Mecklenburg County*, p. 52.

50. Ed Smith, "Drama in April 1865," in Reynolds, *Charlotte Remembers*, p. 33; *Charlotte Observer*, August 6, 1933; Scharf, *History of the Confederate States Navy*, pp. 49–51, 373; Beers, *Confederacy*, pp. 244, 338, 375.

51. Quoted in Greenwood, *On the Home Front*, p. 1. One military unit from the city itself was the Charlotte Grays, whose officers were local storekeepers, including Elias B. Cohen and Thomas Trotter. A roster of the sixty-one-man company, which marched off to war in April 1861, may be found in the *Charlotte Chronicle,* June 10, 1891. For a first-person account of the war, read the 1862 diary of Mecklenburg County soldier W. E. Ardrey serialized in the *Charlotte Observer*, June 17, 24, July 15, 22, August 12, 1906.

52. On Confederate destruction of the Atlantic, Tennessee and Ohio line, see J. B. Alexander, *History of Mecklenburg County*, p. 301. An appeal for slave laborers, perhaps for this work, ran in the *Western Democrat*, July 5, 1864 (citation courtesy of Janette Greenwood). On General Sherman's damage to the Charlotte & South Carolina, consult *Charlotte Democrat*, May 21, 1896; Ashe, *Eminent and Representative Men*, p. 641; Ashe, *Biographical History of North Carolina*, 1:341–48.

53. Jones, "Sketch of Charlotte," p. 141.

54. Merrill et al., *American Cotton Handbook*, p. 50. In Charlotte, prices exceeded thirty cents a pound well into 1866. See *Western Democrat*, September 11, 18, 1866.

55. *Charlotte Observer*, September 13, 1903.

56. *Western Democrat*, June 4, 1867. See also *Charlotte Observer*, September 13, 1903; LeGette Blythe, "'Tis a Gude Place," in Reynolds, *Charlotte Remembers*, p. 13. New post–Civil War business buildings dominated the downtown by the time an illustrator recorded the city for *Harper's Weekly,* June 12, 1875. The article and its drawings are photographically reproduced in Kratt, *Charlotte*, 1st ed., p. 75.

57. *Branson's North Carolina Business Directory for 1869*, p. 98.

58. The architectural firm of Allen and Gregory was listed in ibid. Charlotte's postbellum banks were the First National Bank (1865); a branch bank of Brenizer, Kellog and Company of Greensboro (1867); Merchants and Farmers National Bank (1871); Farmers Savings Bank (1874); and Commercial National Bank (1874). The three nationally chartered institutions would grow as the city's main banking enterprises through the end of the century. See *Charlotte Observer*, July 17, 1904. This long article provides detailed data on sources of capital and names of bank founders and directors over the years 1865–1904. The initial postwar institution, the First National Bank, was set up by John Wilkes of the Mecklenburg Iron Works with partial funding from a group of Baltimore investors. Most of the rest of Charlotte's banking capital seems to have come from the Carolinas in these years. For instance, the Edwin M. Holt family of Alamance County, North Carolina's leading textile industrialists, picked Charlotte for their main banking venture. The 1904 *Observer* reporter wrote of the Commercial National Bank, "Mr. Edwin M. Holt . . . was the originator of the bank, but did not accept a directorship: he nevertheless 'pressed the button' up to the time of his death." On Commercial National Bank, see also *Charlotte Observer*, December 19, 1896.

59. The early presence of a cotton press in Charlotte tends to confirm one classic statement of the "central place" theory of urban location. German geographer August Losch based his theory on a study of city location in the cotton regions of the American Southwest, where "cotton growing determined for a long time the spatial organization of the economy. . . . The supply regions of the 15,000 cotton gins, which cleaned cotton and removed the seeds, were superimposed on the producing areas of the individual plantations; above these came the wider-meshed network of presses; above these again, the 500 oil mills; then the transport points; the collecting depots where the cotton is sorted and stored; and, at the top, the two principal export points with their enormous supply regions" (Losch, *Economics of Location*, pp. 11, 215–19). Losch's figures were actually drawn from

Moulton, *Cotton Production and Distribution in the Gulf Southwest*. Recently Losch's analysis has been extended to Georgia by Weiher, "Cotton Industry and Southern Urbanization." Losch's and Weiher's work is the basis for the discussion of cotton trade and Southern city growth in Goldfield, *Cotton Fields and Skyscrapers*, p. 88.

As accurate as Losch's statement seems about cotton processing and city size in the early twentieth century, Charlotte's experience indicates that those who interpret Losch as a chronological sequence of development may be historically inaccurate. Charlotte seems to have been a transport and collecting point for a wide region even before it got a cotton press. It definitely was already an important transport and collecting hub before the arrival of cotton oil mills in the 1880s—a technology pioneered by Charlotte entrepreneur D. A. Tompkins, as we will note in Chapter 2.

60. Jones, "Sketch of Charlotte," pp. 140–43. A good idea of the flow of the cotton trade can be gained from an 1885 description. "FIRST BALE—The first bale of new Cotton this season was received here Friday the 21st inst. It was raised near Cureton's Store, Lancaster County, S.C. W. J. Black and Son bought it at 10¾ cents per lb., and it was immediately shipped to the New York Cotton Exchange" (*Charlotte Home Democrat*, August 28, 1885).

61. Latham, *Cotton Movement and Fluctuations*, pp. 80–81; Jones, "Sketch of Charlotte," p. 139.

62. Blythe and Brockmann, *Hornets' Nest*, p. 261; Gilbert and Jefferys, *Crossties through Carolina*, p. 9.

63. Blythe and Brockmann, *Hornets' Nest*, p. 261; Gilbert and Jefferys, *Crossties through Carolina*, p. 9. Mecklenburg County put up $300,000 in public funds toward the project. See Tompkins, *History of Mecklenburg County*, 1:152.

64. Doyle, *New Men, New Cities, New South*, pp. 33–34. On the importance of rail connections into the Midwest for other Southern cities, see Doyle, *Nashville in the New South*; Carl V. Harris, *Political Power in Birmingham*. In the mid-nineteenth century, cities with superb rail connections or rail-water connections grew with astounding speed. The premier example is Chicago, which mushroomed from 30,000 to 90,000 people between 1850 and 1860, the same decade in which Charlotte advanced from 1,000 to 2,200. See, for instance, Monkkonen, *America Becomes Urban*, pp. 79–81.

65. *Charlotte Observer*, September 13, 1903.

66. Charlotte Chamber of Commerce, *1950 Census Data*.

67. Tucker, *Zeb Vance*, pp. 429–30, 439, 455; Dowd, *Life of Vance*, pp. 102–18; J. B. Alexander, *History of Mecklenburg County*, pp. 209–20. Another Confederate notable who came to Charlotte after the war was Anna Morrison Jackson, widow of General "Stonewall" Jackson. A daughter of Davidson College head Robert Hall Morrison, she returned to Mecklenburg after her husband's death. Her residence on West Trade Street became a center of the town's cultural life and a "shrine toward which all Confederates journeyed" until her death in 1915 (Greenwood, *On the Home Front*, pp. 18–19). On other elite arrivals, see Tompkins, *History of Mecklenburg County*, 1:151–52.

68. P. 90k, vol. 16 (Mecklenburg County), North Carolina, Dun Collection.

69. J. B. Alexander, *History of Mecklenburg County*, p. 379. For a matter-of-fact account of a local Jewish wedding, see, for instance, *Charlotte Observer*, September 8, 1897. Even Thomas Dixon, author of *The Clansman* and *The Leopard's Spots* (the basis for the racist film *Birth of a Nation*), spoke approvingly of Wittkowsky & Baruch (successor firm to Wittkowsky & Rintels) and Charlotte's other Jews. See Dixon, *Southern Horizons*, p. 101.

70. Escott, *Many Excellent People*, pp. 85–170; Foner, *Reconstruction*; Foner, *Nothing but Freedom*; Clark and Kirwan, *South since Appomattox*, esp. pp. 26, 31.

71. J. B. Alexander, *Reminiscences of the Past Sixty Years*, p. 85. The terms "better classes," "best people," and "lower caste" are used by J. B. Alexander, *History of Mecklenburg County*, pp. 325, 362–63.

72. J. B. Alexander, *History of Mecklenburg County*, p. 361.

73. J. B. Alexander, *Reminiscences of the Past Sixty Years*, p. 156, also p. 368.

74. J. B. Alexander, *History of Mecklenburg County*, pp. 362–63.

75. Hoffman, "Development of Town and Country," p. 130; O'Brien, "Power and Influence in Mecklenburg," p. 138. Scholars see a similar continuity of leadership before and after the Civil War elsewhere in the North Carolina backcountry. On Greensboro and Guilford County, read O'Brien, *Legal Fraternity and the Making of a New South Community*. On Salisbury and Rowan County, see Beck, "Building the New South." Charlotte, interestingly, seems to have experienced little of the organized violence whereby the old elite regained power in some other parts of the Carolinas, though there was an active chapter of the Ku Klux Klan, led by prominent citizen Hamilton C. Jones. See Hamilton, *Reconstruction in North Carolina*, pp. 462, 465, 477–80; Greenwood, *Bittersweet Legacy*, chap. 2.

76. The list of officials is found in the Charlotte City Clerk's Office, "Historical Records" binder. On Johnston, see Ashe, *Eminent and Representative Men*, p. 641; Ashe, *Biographical History of North Carolina*, 1:341–48.

77. Hohenberg and Lees, *Making of Urban Europe*, pp. 32–34. Similarly, see Vance, *Continuing City*, esp. pp. 154–55.

78. Cotter, Roberts, and Parrington, *Buried Past*, pp. 86–96, 447–50; Warner, *Private City*, p. 15. The pattern of apprentices lodging in the master's household during this period is also described in Rochester, New York, by Paul Johnson, *Shopkeeper's Millennium*, pp. 38–48.

79. Blumin, *Emergence of the Middle Class*; Blumin, "Black Coats to White Collars"; Blumin, "Hypothesis of Middle-Class Formation"; Wilentz, *Chants Democratic*; Gary Nash, "The Social Evolution of Preindustrial American Cities, 1700–1820," in Mohl, *Making of Urban America*, esp. p. 35; Prude, *Coming of the Industrial Order*.

80. On temperance, see Gutman, *Work, Culture, and Society*; Tyrell, *Sobering Up*. On etiquette, please consult Levine, *Highbrow/Lowbrow*; Kasson, *Rudeness and Civility*. On revivals, read Paul Johnson, *Shopkeeper's Millennium*; Wallace, *Rockdale*. On schooling, see Tyack, *One Best System*; Boyer, *Urban Masses and Moral Order*. The new industrial organization also brought major changes in family life, as white-collar women increasingly became identified as homemakers and nurturers of the young, rather than as partners in the family enterprise. See Ryan, *Cradle of the Middle Class*. Ryan drew on the landmark research by Welter, "Cult of True Womanhood."

81. Paul Johnson, *Shopkeeper's Millennium*; Ryan, *Cradle of the Middle Class*; Blumin, "Black Coats to White Collars"; Blumin, "Hypothesis of Middle-Class Formation"; Blumin, *Emergence of the Middle Class*; Binford, *First Suburbs*; Blackmar, "Rewalking the 'Walking City'"; Wilentz, *Chants Democratic*; Michael P. Conzen, "Morphology of Nineteenth Century Cities"; Michael P. Conzen, "Historical Geography," esp. pp. 89, 93, 102; Knox, *Urban Social Geography*, pp. 9–11, 24; Fishman, *Bourgeois Utopias*.

82. A typescript of the charter is in the Charlotte City Clerk's Office, "Historical Records" binder. In actuality Charlotte's streets meet at just a few degrees off 90, making each block a subtle parallelogram rather than a true rectangle. The notion of leaving land to be used in common was a medieval custom brought from England to America, visible in the well-known town commons still seen in New England. On colonial town planning elsewhere in North Carolina, see Allcott, *Colonial Houses in North Carolina*, pp. 7–17. For

discussions of the grid plan in urban history, consult Reps, *Town Planning in Frontier America*; Vance, *Continuing City*; Edward T. Price, "The Central Courthouse Square in the American County Seat," in Upton and Vlach, *Common Places*, pp. 124–45.

83. Blythe and Brockmann, *Hornets' Nest*, pp. 172–73.

84. The 1815 city limits formed a large parallelogram, delineated by a dotted line labeled "original boundary" on the Beers map of 1877.

85. For a description of the first courthouse, read Blythe and Brockmann, *Hornets' Nest*, pp. 22, 167. A photo of a conjectural reconstruction of the building follows p. 176.

86. Jones, "Sketch of Charlotte."

87. Ibid. For a less detailed description of the town in 1825, see Tompkins, *History of Mecklenburg County*, 1:92–93. Recollections of Charlotte as it looked in the late 1830s were similar: "Only seven regular business houses in the town," plus three taverns, two churches, and one newspaper, according to the *Charlotte Chronicle*, September 23, 1887.

88. Jones, "Sketch of Charlotte." John Irwin was remembered as "a banker and merchant prince of Charlotte in the first half of the last century" in an article in the *Charlotte Observer*, July 31, 1906. As historian Lisa Tolbert has pointed out, it was no accident that people in this era referred to almost every building as a "house": courthouse, storehouse, farmhouse, and so on. See Tolbert, "Constructing Townscapes."

89. *Charlotte Observer*, December 12, 1943. Thanks to Pete Felkner for this citation.

90. Jones, "Sketch of Charlotte."

91. Quote from December 31, 1852, recorded in "Extract from Minutes of the Governing Bodies of the City of Charlotte, North Carolina, 1816–1900," in "Historical Records of the City of Charlotte, North Carolina," notebook in the office of the Charlotte City Clerk. On August 24, 1855, the commissioners "Resolved . . . that the platt of the Town of Charlotte, as made and presented by James Parks, surveyor, . . . is hereby adopted as the Platt of Said Town, with the width of streets and extension thereof as set out in Said Platt" (City Council Minutes, vol. 2 [January 17, 1852–April 20, 1863]).

92. Beers, *Map of Charlotte and Mecklenburg County*.

93. Jones, "Sketch of Charlotte," p. 34.

94. As early as 1869 the R. G. Dun credit investigator noted that Wittkowsky & Rintels "Keep a general store, the largest in town. . . . Do a jobbing and retail business. Buy mainly from Philadelphia and N.Y., ⅔ for cash" (p. 102t, vol. 16 [Mecklenburg County], North Carolina, Dun Collection; see also p. 102z18).

95. Figures in this paragraph are based on computer analysis of *Beasley and Emerson's Charlotte Directory*. The directory listed each head of household, gave his race, occupation and/or employer, and a rough street address of his residence ("Myers Street, bet 8th and 9th"). I entered this data into a computer, then sorted it by race, occupation, employer, and location.

96. U.S. Bureau of the Census, *Tenth Census*.

97. See nn. 92 and 95 above. For mapping purposes I divided heads of household into three groups. First were business owners. Second were white-collar workers who worked for someone else. Third were those people engaged in manual labor, excepting those few craftsmen listed as owning their own business. This scheme may slightly overstate the number of laborers, since some men listed as "carpenter," "mason," and such probably were contractors who owned their own business and had employees. This problem is likely balanced by the probability that the directory undercounted laborers; many of the listings that gave no occupation were probably transient laborers, and undoubtedly the most recent arrivals of this group were missed by the directory compilers.

98. The leading work on black neighborhoods in the South asserts that racial segregation happened quickly in the years immediately after the Civil War; see Rabinowitz, *Race Relations in the Urban South*, chap. 5. However, many close-grained studies now document persistence of intermingling at least into the 1880s. See George C. Wright, *Life behind a Veil*, chap. 4, esp. p. 103; Wintz, "Emergence of a Black Neighborhood"; Zane Miller, "Urban Blacks in the South, 1865–1920: An Analysis of Some Quantitative Data on Richmond, Savannah, New Orleans, Louisville, and Birmingham," in Schnore, *New Urban History*, pp. 184–204; McTigue, "Patterns of Residence"; Ambrose, "Redrawing the Color Line," p. 61; Porter, "Black Atlanta," chaps. 4, 5, and esp. 6.

99. For instance, Rabinowitz, *Race Relations in the Urban South*, pp. 97–98.

100. U.S. Bureau of the Census, *Ninth Census*, "Population by Race and Nativity."

101. Except along Trade and Tryon Streets, virtually all African Americans listed in the 1875–76 city directory can be matched with a streetfront house on the 1877 Beers map. For a discussion of African American alley housing, read Borchert, *Alley Life in Washington*.

102. These rim villages are clearly depicted, and in most cases named, on the first map to show detailed information about areas adjacent to the city; see Butler and Spratt, *Map of Charlotte Township*.

I have coined the "rim village" name, but the same pattern is described without a name in Rabinowitz, *Race Relations in the Urban South*, pp. 97–100; Wade, *Slavery in the Cities*, pp. 55–79, 275; Kellogg, "Negro Urban Clusters in the Post-Bellum South." In northern cities with sizable immigrant populations, similar clusters of immigrants appeared at mid-century on the urban periphery, according to Ward, *Cities and Immigrants*, pp. 105–13.

103. Residents in this area were listed as living at the south end of Mint Street. Blandville was not mentioned by name, but it was located at the south end of Mint.

104. Jones, "Sketch of Charlotte," pp. 140–41.

CHAPTER 2

1. On the New South movement, see Woodward, *Origins of the New South*; Tindall, *Emergence of the New South*; Gaston, *New South Creed*; Goldfield, *Cotton Fields and Skyscrapers*; Doyle, *New Men, New Cities, New South*; Rabinowitz, *First New South*; Ayers, *Promise of the New South*; Grantham, *South in Modern America*; Boles, *South through Time*. On the role of cotton manufacturing in the New South boom, see esp. Broadus Mitchell, *Rise of Cotton Mills in the South*; Hearnden, *Independence and Empire*; Hall et al., *Like a Family*; Tullos, *Habits of Industry*.

2. Quoted in MacPherson, "Antebellum Southern Exceptionalism," p. 233.

3. Brent Glass, *Textile Industry in North Carolina*, pp. 1–12; Richard W. Griffin, "North Carolina Cotton Manufacturers, 1808–1960," in Young, *Textile Leaders of the South*, p. 462. There is evidently some uncertainty as to the date of the Lincolnton mill. The year 1815 is given in Lefler and Newsome, *North Carolina*, pp. 396–97. The average North Carolina mill on the eve of the Civil War ran barely a thousand spindles, and only three outfits employed as many as 100 workers, according to Lefler and Newsome. "Not only was North Carolina a cotton textile pygmy alongside virtually every state of the Northeast [in 1860], but it was outclassed as well by such southern states as Virginia and Georgia" (Carlton, "Revolution from Above," p. 453). See also Griffin and Standard, "Cotton Textile Industry in Ante-Bellum North Carolina," pts. 1 and 2.

4. The quotes are from pp. 97 and 102a in vol. 16 (Mecklenburg County), North Carolina, Dun Collection. The Dun reports indicate that the factory resumed operation

fitfully after the Civil War, then shut its doors at the end of the 1860s. Despite its modest size, Neal's mill was well regarded in the antebellum backcountry. "Equipped with new and improved Northern machinery . . . it quickly acquired a reputation 'that made all its products sell easily.' . . . General Neal employed as agents two brothers, H. B. and L. L. Williams, who traveled over the State taking orders for the Catawba products" (Richard W. Griffin, "North Carolina Cotton Manufacturers, 1808–1960," in Young, *Textile Leaders of the South*, p. 468). See also Morrill, "Survey of Cotton Mills"; Dan L. Morrill, "The Neel House," Survey and Research Report. For local memories of the early mills, see *Charlotte Observer*, January 16, 1900.

5. *Charlotte Democrat*, January 16, 1880. It was standard practice for the technology-poor South to seek Northern technical assistance in building mills. See Beatty, "Lowells of the South"; Carlton, "Revolution from Above," pp. 460–61.

6. P. 102z, vol. 16 (Mecklenburg County), North Carolina, Dun Collection; *Charlotte Democrat*, November 14, 1879. R. M. Oates gained the appellation "Colonel" during a Civil War stint as quartermaster to a Confederate military unit. See R. M. Oates obituary, *Charlotte Observer*, December 28, 1897; J. E. Oates obituary, *Charlotte Observer*, July 30, 1897.

7. Pp. 86b and 102z, vol. 16 (Mecklenburg County), North Carolina, Dun Collection. Merchant Oates had some interesting connections with other Carolina textile men that may have influenced his willingness to finance Charlotte's first cotton factory. Oates's initial partner back in the 1850s had been Lewis Williams, who also served as salesman for pioneer Mecklenburg mill man William Neal (see n. 4 above). After the Civil War, when Oates went into partnership with his brothers, Lewis Williams became agent for E. M. Holt's considerable mercantile and real estate interests in Charlotte. Holt, of Alamance County, was North Carolina's leading textile manufacturer in the period, known for his innovations in weaving and dyeing. See p. 102s, vol. 16 (Mecklenburg County), North Carolina, Dun Collection. "E. M. Holt of Alamance and several of his sons . . . have large investments in Charlotte in real estate and stocks" (*Charlotte Democrat*, January 16, 1880). See also Chapter 4 of the present study.

8. The contractor was Robert H. Morris; see *Charlotte Observer*, August 21, 1880. On construction, see also *Charlotte Democrat*, January 30, 1880; *Charlotte Observer*, February 5, May 27, 1880; William Huffman, "The Charlotte Cotton Mill," Survey and Research Report.

9. *Charlotte Democrat*, April 29, 1881.

10. For a survey of Charlotte's major businesses in these years, see special editions of the *Charlotte Chronicle*, September 27, 1887, and March 27, 1891. See also the annual reports of the North Carolina Bureau of Labor and Printing, beginning in 1886.

11. *Charlotte Chronicle*, September 4, 1887.

12. Ibid. *Charlotte Observer*, October 6, November 18, 1897. The 1880s also saw the growth of some nontextile manufacturing in the city, notably the Charlotte Furniture Factory, which in 1887 had "forty-two skilled mechanics in the shops, and [up?] to twenty children who are engaged in caning chairs."

13. Tullos, *Habits of Industry*, pp. 151–61; Clay, "Daniel Augustus Tompkins"; Winston, *Builder of the New South*; Dan L. Morrill, "Atherton Mill House," Survey and Research Report; Brent Glass, *Textile Industry in North Carolina*, pp. 32–42; Navin, *Whitin Machine Works*, pp. 217–21. Paul Gaston lists Tompkins, Henry Grady, *Manufacturers Record* founder R. H. Edmonds, Raleigh newspaperman Walter Hines Page, and Louisville editor Henry Watterson as "the principal spokesmen for the emerging New South movement"

(Gaston, *New South Creed*, pp. 48–52). See also Broadus Mitchell, *Rise of Cotton Mills in the South*, esp. pp. 109–10, 117. A biographical article on Tompkins, originally in the September 1899 issue of *Southern Farm Magazine*, may be found reprinted in the *Charlotte Observer*, October 20, 1899.

14. Quoted in *Charlotte Observer*, May 17, 1981.

15. Quoted in William Huffman, "Old Alpha Mill," Survey and Research Report. For an additional description of the scheme, see *Charlotte Chronicle*, December 20, 1887. Osborne was probably the son of lawyer J. A. Osborne, who had been the driving force behind construction of the Charlotte & South Carolina Railroad before the Civil War. Scott had come to Charlotte at the end of the Civil War as an agent for the North Carolina Rail Road, then had gone into business as a commission merchant in 1873. See p. 102z17, vol. 16 (Mecklenburg County), North Carolina, Dun Collection. Scott's obituary appeared in the *Charlotte Democrat*, April 15, 1897. On D. A. Tompkins's promotion of installment financing, read Brent Glass, *Textile Industry in North Carolina*, p. 37. For a general discussion of Southern mill financing, see Carlton and Coclanis, "Capital Mobilization and Southern Industry."

16. *Charlotte Democrat*, January 27, 1888; Morrill, "Survey of Cotton Mills." Brown had been a merchant in Charlotte since the 1850s. He was the son of wealthy P. M. Brown, who had been partner in William Neal's antebellum cotton mill. See p. 94, vol. 16 (Mecklenburg County), North Carolina, Dun Collection.

17. *Charlotte Democrat*, February 3, 1888; Morrill, "Survey of Cotton Mills." Cohen had been partner in the city's second-largest dry goods firm in 1875; he was a merchant during the 1850s railroad boom; see p. 89, vol. 16 (Mecklenburg County), North Carolina, Dun Collection. Another key promoter of the Victor Mill was banker J. H. McAden; see *Charlotte News*, June 27, 1900.

18. Wade Hampton Harris, *Sketches of Charlotte*. Charlotte's experience counters the notion that New South industrial development, and thus town growth, was stimulated by "mills usually financed and often controlled by northerners" (Howard Rabinowitz, "Southern Urban Development, 1860–1900," in Brownell and Goldfield, *City in Southern History*, p. 108).

19. *Charlotte Democrat*, January 9, 1880. The passage of the tax break was probably speeded by the fact that R. M. Oates had been an alderman for many years and D. W. Oates currently served on the board. The Board of Aldermen took away the break from the Oateses in 1884 when a furniture factory asked for a similar favor. See *Charlotte Observer*, December 10, 1884.

20. *Charlotte Observer*, April 3, May 27, 1880. The houses are gone now, but their number and location can be confirmed in the 1896 Sanborn Insurance Map. More housing was added in 1886, when "a solid block of brick tenement houses was built" (*Charlotte Chronicle*, March 27, 1887).

21. *Charlotte Observer*, December 28, 1897; Morrill, "Survey of Cotton Mills." For a sensitive history of Carolina textile labor, read Hall et al., *Like a Family*; Tullos, *Habits of Industry*.

22. North Carolina Bureau of Labor Statistics, *Fourth Annual Report*, p. 23.

23. Kulik, Parks, and Penn, *New England Mill Village*; Zimiles and Zimiles, *Early American Mills*; Richard Candee, "Early New England Mill Towns in the Piscataqua Valley," in Garner, *Company Town*, pp. 111–38; *Encyclopedia of Textiles*. Similarly, for Philadelphia, see Scranton, *Proprietary Capitalism*, pp. 200–207, 252; Scranton, *Figured Tapestry*.

24. In most established Carolina piedmont cities, urban cotton mill villages seem to have

first appeared during the 1890s–1900s. See Marvin A. Brown, *Greensboro*, pp. 52–59; Carlton, *Mill and Town in South Carolina*; Brent Glass, *Textile Industry in North Carolina*, pp. 40–43.

25. The mill village also fit handily into another Carolina tradition. "The whole matter of providing . . . habitations for cotton mill operatives in the South may be summarized in the statement that they are essentially a rural people." Mill villages, with their one-story houses and space for gardens, would "preserve the general conditions of rural life" (Tompkins, *Cotton Mill*, pp. 34–35, 117). For an analysis of the mill village phenomenon and its meanings for both owners and workers, see Hall et al., *Like a Family*, pp. 114–32.

26. *Charlotte Democrat*, August 4, November 13, 1887.

27. Warner, *Streetcar Suburbs*; Kenneth T. Jackson, *Crabgrass Frontier*; Glaab and Brown, *History of Urban America*, pp. 158–61.

28. Kenneth T. Jackson, *Crabgrass Frontier*, p. 11; also see pp. 310–11.

29. Fishman, *Bourgeois Utopias*, p. 6.

30. The first horsecar ran January 1, 1887. See *Charlotte Chronicle*, September 4, 1887; *Charlotte Home Democrat*, October 1, November 19, 1886; *Charlotte News*, April 1, 1928; Dan L. Morrill, "Myers Park Streetcar Waiting Stations," Survey and Research Report. For background on the line's Charlotte investors, read William Huffman, "Old Alpha Mill," Survey and Research Report.

31. *Charlotte Chronicle*, August 18, 1887.

32. Morrill, "Edward Dilworth Latta"; Morrill, "Dilworth"; Bradbury, *Dilworth*.

33. R. G. Dun commented on Latta, October 1876: "Succeed J. A. Young and Son, all from the house of Edwin Bates & Co., New York. Have the character of being steady and reliable will do a fair business." December 1877: "Are doing a large and active business. Pay promptly and have good credit." November 1878: "Now 'E. D. Latta,' the bro having died. The standing is not affected, as E. D. will receive Walter Latta's estate" (p. 107, vol. 16 [Mecklenburg County], North Carolina, Dun Collection).

34. *Charlotte Chronicle*, September 4, 1887; North Carolina Bureau of Labor Statistics, *Fourth Annual Report*, pp. 128–29; *Charlotte Home Democrat*, September 25, 1885. Latta sold his retail clothing store in 1886 to concentrate on manufacturing; see *Charlotte Home Democrat*, December 29, 1886.

35. City directories. For Bland's obituary, see *Charlotte Observer*, September 19, 1922. Springs and Brevard were partners in the Charlotte Water Works; see *Charlotte Chronicle*, February 23, 26, 1887. Springs was the scion of one of the county's wealthiest families—son of Leroy Springs, who had backed the city's first railroad a generation earlier. See Springs, *Squires of Springfield*, pp. 291–92.

Latta's well-connected partners smoothed the company's way in city politics. In fall 1890 the Board of Aldermen magnanimously voted to build a new iron bridge at Morehead Street to carry Latta's streetcars over a railroad track, and officials also allowed the trolley line to run through the grounds of the town's South Graded School. In coming months the city granted the Four Cs exclusive franchises to provide heating and cooking gas to city residents and awarded the company Charlotte's first electric streetlighting contract. Such sidelines were important cash generators for trolley companies nationwide in this era.

36. Modern recessed rail replaced awkward T-rail in the streets, and "the cars which have been ordered are nearly twice the length of those now in use, furnished and upholstered in a style not surpassed by those in any other Southern city" (*Charlotte News*, March 14, 1891). For a thumbnail sketch of Charlotte trolley history, consult Harkey, *More Tales from the Hornet's Nest*, pp. 66–71.

37. *Charlotte Chronicle*, March 21, 29, 1891; Morrill, "Edward Dilworth Latta"; Morrill, "Dilworth."

38. For the context of Latta's boosterism, read Gaston, *New South Creed*. Latta's Dilworth columns appeared in the *Charlotte Chronicle* and the *Charlotte News* beginning in March 1891. They sometimes overlapped, but at other times different material appeared in each paper. Some columns were also reprinted in other newspapers in the region; the "bugle note of advertisement shall have been sounded and heard far and near. . . . The 4 Cs has engaged a column space in dozens of the leading newspapers of the country, and from now until the sale Charlotte and her numerous attractions will be told to the world" (*Charlotte Chronicle*, April 30, 1891).

39. *Charlotte News*, April 24, March 14, 17, 1891, quoted in Morrill, "Dilworth," pp. 2–3.

40. *Charlotte Chronicle*, March 22, April 30, May 8, 1891.

41. *Charlotte Observer*, July 17, 1891, quoted in Morrill, "Dilworth," pp. 2–3.

42. *Charlotte News*, March 28, 1891, quoted in Morrill, "Dilworth," pp. 2–3.

43. *Charlotte Chronicle*, April 22, 1891.

44. Ibid.

45. *Charlotte News*, May 19, 1891.

46. *Charlotte Chronicle*, April 22, 1891. For more on Druid Hill Park, consult Greene, *Baltimore*, p. 98; Olson, *Baltimore*, pp. 148, 169–70. Baltimore would continue to fascinate Latta. In 1911 he would hire the Olmsted Brothers to extend Dilworth, based on the firm's design of the posh Roland Park district in Baltimore. See Chapter 6 of the present study.

47. Quoted in Morrill, "Dilworth," pp. 6–7. The building as completed in April 1892 was somewhat simpler than the newspaper description. The structure no longer stands. For more on pavilions in the park, see *Charlotte Chronicle*, March 26, 1891. On Norrman's career, see Withey and Withey, *Biographical Dictionary of American Architects*, p. 444.

48. Hanchett, "Before Olmsted." Joseph Forsyth Johnson's publications included *Natural Principle of Landscape Gardening, Residential Sites and Environments*, and "Laws of Developing Landscape." The *Charlotte Chronicle*, March 15, 1897, included a tantalizingly brief profile of Johnson and an illustration of a proposal he submitted for the design of the grounds of the World's Columbian Exposition in Chicago. On Johnson's important work in Atlanta's Inman Park neighborhood, see Rick Beard, "Hurt's Deserted Village: Atlanta's Inman Park, 1885–1911," in White and Kramer, *Olmsted South*, pp. 200–220; Atlanta Urban Design Commission, *Atlanta Historic Resources Workbook*, p. 177; Edge, *Joel Hurt and the Development of Atlanta*, pp. 105–7.

49. *Charlotte News*, April 24, 1891, quoted in Morrill, "Dilworth," p. 7.

50. Ibid. On naturalistic park planning, see, for instance, Schuyler, *New Urban Landscape*; Newton, *Design on the Land*.

51. *Charlotte News*, April 27, 1891, quoted in Morrill, "Edward Dilworth Latta," p. 299.

52. *Charlotte Chronicle*, May 19, 1891.

53. *Morning Star*, May 22, 1891, quoted in Morrill, "Edward Dilworth Latta," p. 297.

54. According to the *Charlotte Chronicle*, May 19, 1891, "At night after the pyrotechnic display a balloon will be launched, attached to which will be a LOT IN DILWORTH. The Fortunate Finder of this box will be the recipient of a title to the lot named." Three balloons were indeed launched, the second of which held the tin box. It went off out of sight beyond Biddleville. A lucky passerby named J. E. Brown found it the next day along Beatties Ford Road and took title to lot 2 in block 69 on Springdale Avenue in southern Dilworth; see *Charlotte News*, May 21, 1891.

55. *Charlotte Chronicle*, May 20, 1891.

56. *Charlotte News*, May 20, 1891.

57. *Atlanta Journal*, quoted in 4Cs Column, *Charlotte News*, March 19, 1891.

58. *Charlotte News*, May 22, 1891.

59. For a series of maps showing lot sales in each of the early years, see Morrill, "Dilworth," p. 11.

60. Schuyler, *New Urban Landscape*; Newton, *Design on the Land*; Hanchett, "Before Olmsted."

61. The Boulevard was a grand 100 feet wide, while side streets were 60 feet wide; see *Charlotte Chronicle*, May 20, 1891.

62. As printed in the *Charlotte Chronicle*, May 20, 1891, "No house on the boulevard shall be nearer than twenty-five feet of the sidewalk, and no house built on lots fronting on the boulevard shall cost less than $2000 when completed. The purchasers are therefore assured that no shanty will be put in front of their dwellings on their handsome thoroughfare. This requirement does not apply to any lots except those on the boulevard." Dilworth lots had 50-foot frontage and 150- to 200-foot depth, quite similar to the dimensions found in town; see Morrill, "Dilworth," p. 5.

63. 1905 Sanborn Insurance Map, sheet 29.

64. A remnant of this complex, owned by the Four Cs' successor Duke Power, still stood in 1995 at South Boulevard and Bland Street.

65. *Charlotte Chronicle*, May 8, 1891. It is, of course, possible that the Four Cs simply made mistakes when they welcomed blacks and put industry and the grand boulevard in such close proximity. It seems unlikely, however, that six such well-connected members of the elite in such a small town could radically misread the tastes of their fellow well-to-do citizens.

66. Morrill, "Dilworth," pp. 11–13; Dan L. Morrill, "Atherton Mill House," Survey and Research Report. A second purchase of Dilworth land in February 1893 provided space for twenty-one mill houses. The nationwide depression that began in May 1893 undoubtedly hurt Latta's efforts to sell Dilworth lots, but Tompkins's purchases came well before the depression started. For a map showing how part of Tompkins's purchase was developed, see Mecklenburg County Register of Deeds Office, map book 151, p. 331.

67. Morrill, "Dilworth," pp. 11–13. C. C. Hook was architect of the factory; see *Charlotte Observer*, December 9, 16, 1893. Latta expanded the factory by two-thirds in 1899; see *Charlotte Observer*, September 1, 1899.

68. Morrill, "Dilworth," pp. 11–13; *Charlotte Democrat*, March 13, 1896.

69. Quoted in Morrill, "Dilworth," pp. 11–13; Bradbury, *Dilworth*.

70. Quoted in Morrill, "Dilworth," pp. 11–13. This initiative predated the May 1893 national financial panic, indicating that the reasons behind Latta's decisions were local rather than national. On the history of house financing in America, see Gwendolyn Wright, *Building the Dream*, pp. 100, 199, 240–41.

71. Quoted in Morrill, "Dilworth," p. 16.

72. Dan L. Morrill, "Mallonee-Jones House," Survey and Research Report. For more on Hook, see Chapter 6 of the present book.

73. William Huffman, "Harrill-Porter House," Survey and Research Report.

74. *Charlotte Chronicle*, September 5, 1887.

CHAPTER 3

1. This chapter's interpretation of the Populist challenge in North Carolina draws on three path-breaking studies: Kousser, *Shaping of Southern Politics*; Carlton, *Mill and Town*

in *South Carolina*; and Escott, *Many Excellent People*. See also Eric Anderson, *Race and Politics in North Carolina*; Steelman, "Progressive Era in North Carolina"; Hahn, *Roots of Southern Populism*; Crow and Durden, *Maverick Republican*; Billings, *Planters and the Making of a "New South"*; Crow, Escott, and Flynn, *Race, Class, and Politics in Southern History*; Goodwyn, *Democratic Promise*; Woodward, *Strange Career of Jim Crow*; Woodward, *Origins of the New South*; Lefler and Newsome, *North Carolina*, pp. 540–62; Powell, *North Carolina through Four Centuries*, pp. 422–42; McMath, *American Populism*.

Populism in the South represented much the same sort of challenge by those at the bottom of society against the traditional elite that had rocked the industrializing North two generations earlier. See Wiebe, *Opening of American Society*; Dahl, *Who Governs?*; Monkkonen, *America Becomes Urban*, pp. 117–20, 232–34; Glaab and Brown, *History of Urban America*, pp. 91–96; Warner, "If All the World Were Philadelphia," p. 41. See also MacPherson, "Antebellum Southern Exceptionalism."

2. *Charlotte Chronicle*, September 5, 1887. The terms "better classes" and "lower caste" are those used by J. B. Alexander, *History of Mecklenburg County*, pp. 325, 362–63.

3. Hoffman, "Development of Town and Country," p. 149.

4. This portrait, based on census and deed records, is drawn from ibid., pp. 152–53.

5. For the significance of fence laws (also known as stock laws) in the late nineteenth century South, see especially Hahn, *Roots of Southern Populism*, pp. 239–68.

6. Hoffman, "Development of Town and Country," pp. 171–73; *Charlotte Observer*, February 5, 15, 1885, August 24, 1906; *Southern Home*, January 10, 1879; *Charlotte Democrat*, October 2, 24, 1879, March 11, June 28, 1881; *Charlotte Home Democrat*, September 4, 1885; Escott, *Many Excellent People*, pp. 188–91.

7. Hoffman, "Development of Town and Country," p. 144. The situation would continue to worsen. By 1900 over 50 percent of Mecklenburg farmers would be tenants. See Hall et al., *Like a Family*, p. 6.

8. Hoffman, "Development of Town and Country," pp. 212–13, 217–18. Charlotteans—most conspicuously William Johnston—also controlled the county's railroads, which farmers depended on to ship goods.

9. Ibid., p. 173; *Charlotte Home Democrat*, January 1, 1886. This was part of a larger regional pattern. Around the same time, across the state at Southern Pines, "gates were torn down, fences burned and other violent acts of resistance performed," recalled a writer in the *Charlotte Observer*, August 17, 1897.

10. Hoffman, "Development of Town and Country," pp. 149–50; Greenwood, "Race and the Middle Class," n. 7.

11. *Code of the City of Charlotte* (1887), p. 49, also pp. 12, 32; *Charlotte Observer*, July 18, 1897. On disputes concerning cotton weighing and grading, see also *Charlotte Democrat*, May 6, June 17, July 8, July 29, 1873; *Southern Home*, June 2, 9, 1873; Hoffman, "Development of Town and Country," pp. 214–16.

12. Hoffman, "Development of Town and Country," p. 161.

13. Ibid., pp. 162–70.

14. Powell, *North Carolina through Four Centuries*, pp. 423–27; McMath, *Populist Vanguard*.

15. *Charlotte Chronicle*, October 5, November 8, 1887; see also November 29, 1890, January 20, September 9, 1891.

16. Ibid., August 26, 1891. On another Alliance speaker, see the *Charlotte Observer*, December 8, 1893.

17. Hoffman, "Development of Town and Country," p. 197.

18. Ibid., p. 198. The establishments struck in 1874 were the Sample & Alexander shoe and boot works, Charlotte's second-largest employer with some thirty workmen, and the Schiff Brothers saddle and harness shop, also among the dozen biggest establishments in the city, with twelve hands. See Chapter 1.

The tensions between the "better sort" and the growing body of blue-collar wage earners could be seen even in the theater columns: "The mob cannot appreciate fine acting and the mob cannot be excluded from the theatre, but there were those in the Opera House which are supposed to be people of refinement who set the mob the bad example" (*Charlotte Observer*, December 22, 1874, quoted in Barber, "Historical Study of the Theatre in Charlotte," p. 24). Also see Grundy, "From *Il Trovatore* to the Crazy Mountaineers." On links between nineteenth century industrialization and the differentiation of "highbrow" versus "lowbrow" taste, see Kasson, *Rudeness and Civility*; Levine, *Highbrow/Lowbrow*.

19. Letter by Daniel N. Cashion, published in the North Carolina Bureau of Labor and Printing, *Thirteenth Annual Report*, p. 163.

20. *Charlotte Home Democrat*, April 1886. See also August 28, 1885, March 5, 1886; Fink, *Workingmen's Democracy*; Escott, *Many Excellent People*, pp. 237–40; McLauren, "Knights of Labor in North Carolina."

21. A Boston journalist visited the Charlotte area and reported on mill operatives' lives in 1897; see *Charlotte Observer*, September 28–29, 1897. The most useful volume on Southern textile mill life is Hall et al., *Like a Family*. See also Carlton, *Mill and Town in South Carolina*; Tullos, *Habits of Industry*; I. A. Newby, *Plain Folks in the New South*; Byerly, *Hard Times Cotton Mill Girls*; Janiewski, *Sisterhood Denied*; Marc S. Miller, *Working Lives*. For older interpretations, read Morland, *Millways of Kent*; Potwin, *Cotton Mill People*; Herring, *Welfare Work in Mill Villages*; Lois MacDonald, *Southern Mill Hills*.

22. North Carolina Bureau of Labor Statistics, *Fourth Annual Report*, pp. 22–25.

23. *Charlotte Observer*, August 1, 1897.

24. *Charlotte Democrat*, March 20, 1896. The Victor Mill, whose water pollution angered city residents, suspended operation frequently in the mid-1890s as it attempted to solve the problems. See *Charlotte Democrat*, October 15, 22, November 9, 12, 1896, June 27, 1897. Southern textile mills also typically laid off employees for a week or two each summer to repair machinery. On such breaks at the Ada and Victor mills, see *Charlotte Observer*, July 27, 30, 1897.

25. *Southern Home*, January 30, 1880; *Charlotte Home Democrat*, March 12, 1886; *Charlotte Democrat*, June 4, 1896. The most frequent target of comment were unemployed men; mill owners preferred whenever possible to hire women with slender, nimble fingers and experience with home spinning and weaving. The appearance of male "idlers" led to charges that "the father is responsible" for the practice of putting children to work, not the mill owners; see *Charlotte Democrat*, October 29, 1896.

26. My understanding of Charlotte's prohibition movement comes largely from Greenwood, "Race, Class, and Prohibition"; Greenwood, *Bittersweet Legacy*. On the link between industrialization and prohibition efforts elsewhere in the United States, see Gutman, *Work, Culture, and Society*; Paul Johnson, *Shopkeeper's Millennium*; Ryan, *Cradle of the Middle Class*, esp. pp. 132–42; Blumin, *Emergence of the Middle Class*; Wilentz, *Chants Democratic*.

27. *Southern Home*, January 9, 1880.

28. Quoted in Greenwood, "Race, Class, and Prohibition," pp. 11–12.

29. Quoted in ibid., p. 12.

30. Quoted in ibid., p. 13.

31. Quoted in ibid.

32. Ibid., p. 14. The ongoing interest of businessmen in temperance was confirmed in the title of a pamphlet published following prohibition's 1904 triumph in the city: *It Helps Business and Is a Blessing: What Leading Businessmen, Bankers, Farmers and Laborers Say About Prohibition in Charlotte, N.C.*

33. Katz, *Irony of Early School Reforms*; Tyack, *One Best System*; Troen, *Public and the Schools*; Cremin, *American Education*.

34. Standard North Carolina histories celebrate beginnings of public education before the Civil War, but in reality opportunities were extremely limited until late in the century. See recent work by Leloudis, *Schooling the New South*; Link, *Hard Country and a Lonely Place*; Plank, "Why Study the South?"

35. Tompkins, *History of Mecklenburg County*, 1:166–70. On "industrial education" and the need for advanced schooling to train cotton mill managers, see the *Charlotte Observer*, January 25, 1885, June 9, 1893; *Charlotte Chronicle*, December 10, 1890, January 29, May 9, 1891, January 31, 1900. Charlotte had briefly experimented with the graded school idea back in 1873 when a minister opened what was later hailed as "the first graded public school in North Carolina." But it won so little support that by 1875 not only had it closed, but all public schooling in the city ceased, not to resume until the 1880s. See Blythe and Brockmann, *Hornets' Nest*, pp. 218–22; Alexander Graham, "History of the Charlotte City Schools Prior to 1900," in Harding, "Charlotte City Schools." For an early brief history of Charlotte graded schools, see *Charlotte News*, May 3, 1900. On pre–Civil War schools in Mecklenburg County, see *Charlotte Observer*, December 13, 1896.

36. *Charlotte Democrat*, July 23, 1896.

37. Boyer, *Urban Masses and Moral Order*; Carlton, *Mill and Town in South Carolina*, pp. 91–98, 183.

38. Mrs. John VanLandingham, in the *Charlotte Democrat*, April 17, 1896; *Charlotte Democrat*, May 28, 1896. Methodists seem to have led the effort. Charlotte factory owners now began building schoolhouses with their own money near the mills. On the Atherton Mill school, see Morrill, "Dilworth," p. 15. On the Louise Mill school, see *Charlotte Observer*, November 10, 1897, September 26, 1899. On the Highland Park Mill school, see *Charlotte Observer*, August 1, 1898. On the Chadwick Mill school, see *Charlotte Observer*, May 1, 1906. On the Elizabeth Mill school, see *Charlotte Observer*, September 5, 1906.

39. *Charlotte Observer*, December 9, 1893, December 3, 1896; Greenwood, *Bittersweet Legacy*, p. 129. Along with more systematic poor relief, Charlotteans also began organizing support for children. In 1887 St. Peter's Episcopal Church founded the Thompson Orphanage, which over the next years erected and occupied a campus of red brick buildings east of town (St. Mary's Chapel survives today). See Blythe and Brockmann, *Hornets' Nest*, pp. 329–30. "The orphan's bale of cotton was sold at auction last Friday afternoon by Col. Akers. The price paid was eleven cents [a pound]. The money will go to the children of the Thompson Orphanage" (*Charlotte Democrat*, May 29, 1891).

40. *Charlotte Chronicle*, July 15, 1887. Similar worries lay behind the shift to professional fire departments during the early decades of industrialization in Northern cities. See Laurie, "Fire Companies and Gangs in Southwark in the 1840s."

41. *Charlotte Chronicle*, January 31, 1891.

42. Kousser, *Shaping of Southern Politics*; Eric Anderson, *Race and Politics in North Carolina*; Escott, *Many Excellent People*; Woodward, *Strange Career of Jim Crow*; Rabinowitz, *Race Relations in the Urban South*.

43. A list of these individuals and their occupations may be found in Greenwood, *Black Experience in Charlotte-Mecklenburg*, section 2, p. 16.

44. *Charlotte Chronicle*, September 5, 1887.

45. J. B. Alexander, *History of Mecklenburg County*, p. 325.

46. Greenwood, "Race, Class, and Prohibition," p. 10.

47. Ibid.

48. Ibid., p. 11.

49. Ibid., p. 26. A service at the church is described in the *Charlotte Observer*, September 7, 1903.

50. For a brief profile of Schenck, see Clarkson, *History of the Law Library Association*, p. 3. On Schenck's activities in behalf of public education, see Harding, "Charlotte City Schools," p. 4. On the sale of Schenck's real estate holdings following his death, see the *Charlotte Observer*, May 24, 1904.

51. Quoted in Greenwood, "Race, Class, and Prohibition," p. 29. Significantly Heriot Clarkson, Charlotte's staunchest prohibitionist, became a leader in the white supremacy campaign of the 1890s. Soon after disfranchisement North Carolina's Baptist *Biblical Recorder* crowed, "As long hoped, the first fruits of disfranchisement of the negroes bids fair to be progress in legislation prohibiting the saloon." In 1904 Charlotte voters approved a prohibition ordinance.

52. Hoffman, "Development of Town and Country," p. 198. Most Carolina cities experienced similarly sharp rises in black population during the two decades after the Civil War.

53. During the 1870s Charlotte's black population growth actually outpaced white population growth, 1,458 to 1,163. The black rate of increase slowed slightly compared with that of whites after 1880, but the influx continued to be substantial in real numbers: a 1,796-person rise in African American population during the 1880s and 2,017 during the 1890s. See U.S. census data.

54. The favored part of downtown for black shoppers was the north side of East Trade Street from Jordan's Corner to the railroad crossing. See *Charlotte Observer*, September 19, 1897. For similar comments about train waiting rooms (which remained unsegregated in the 1880s), see the *Charlotte Home Democrat*, December 17, 1886; *Charlotte Chronicle*, June 4, 1891.

55. *Charlotte Home Democrat*, March 12, 1886. See also *Charlotte Democrat*, February 4, 11, 1881; *Charlotte Home Democrat*, September 24, 1886.

56. Moore-Parker, *Biddle–Johnson C. Smith University Story*.

57. Walls, *African Methodist Episcopal Zion Church*.

58. Logan, *Negro in North Carolina*, p. 111.

59. Brief mentions scattered among Charlotte newspapers of the period suggest that Houser was an important entrepreneur, builder of Rutherford County's Henrietta Mills among other major projects, and a political activist who supported prohibition and later debated disfranchisement. See, for instance, *Charlotte Democrat*, April 25, May 6, 1881; *Charlotte Chronicle*, December 25, 1887; *Charlotte Observer*, July 1, 1899, January 10, 1900. See also Hanchett, "Sorting Out the New South City," p. 174; Greenwood, *Bittersweet Legacy*, pp. 103, 106, 138–40.

60. Burke, *Brooklyn Story*, p. 41.

61. For example, *Charlotte Democrat*, May 29, 1891. Even before formal announcement of the new national party, it was clear that Charlotte Democratic leaders felt trouble brewing locally. In March the editor of the Democratic *Charlotte Chronicle* urged readers not to consider creating a third party; see *Charlotte Chronicle*, March 17, 1891. In April

local Democrats abandoned the age-old practice of nomination by open convention and replaced it with a secret ballot primary, whose count could be more easily controlled by party captains; see *Charlotte Chronicle*, April 2, 1891. The Democratic primary system, which would be a hallmark of Southern politics in the twentieth century, was instituted across the South in this period of Populist challenge. See Woodward, *Strange Career of Jim Crow*, pp. 84–85.

62. Escott, *Many Excellent People*, pp. 247–52.

63. Crow and Durden, *Maverick Republican*, p. 50; Kousser, *Shaping of Southern Politics*, pp. 182–95; Escott, *Many Excellent People*, pp. 231, 247–50; *Charlotte Observer*, November 19, 1898.

64. *Charlotte Observer*, June 2, 1896.

65. North Carolina Bureau of Labor Statistics, *Tenth Annual Report*, pp. 38–39.

66. *Charlotte Observer*, October 8, 10, 1896. The Democrats published editorials that berated the Populists for "engendering class prejudices" and assured workers that in America "every man has an opportunity to rise" (*Charlotte Observer*, November 3, 1896).

67. *Charlotte Democrat*, May 14, 1896.

68. Escott, *Many Excellent People*, p. 252.

69. *Charlotte Observer*, November 4, 1896.

70. In this era of Democratic-controlled newspapers, editors felt no need to report and analyze party losses in public print. Precinct analysis of the 1896 debacle appeared only after the situation began to turn around in the 1898 election. See *Charlotte Observer*, November 10, 1898.

A further confirmation of millhands' distaste for the Democratic Party was the fact, recalled much later by newspaper reporter H. E. C. Bryant, that it proved virtually impossible to sell subscriptions to the pro-Democratic *Observer* in any of the city's mill villages during the period around 1900—even in the Atherton village owned by the paper's publisher, D. A. Tompkins. See *Charlotte Observer*, January 14, 1945. On the role of labor in Southern Populism generally, see McMath, *American Populism*, pp. 108–42.

71. *Charlotte Observer*, January 29, 1897.

72. The Fusion-controlled county commission and the Democratically controlled city Board of Aldermen proved unable to jointly appoint a cotton weigher, resulting in a bitter lawsuit. See *Charlotte Observer*, September 5, 7, October 2, 16, December 28, 1897.

73. *Charlotte Democrat*, April 3, 1896.

74. *Charlotte Observer*, February 28, 1897.

75. Ibid., April 1, 1897. The genesis of the North Carolina literacy proposal is an interesting question. Durden and Crow suggest, on the evidence of a November 1897 letter, that Charlottean Heriot Clarkson brought the idea to North Carolina, inspired by an exchange of letters with Mississippi governor Vardeman. Ashe's earlier speech would seem to indicate that Ashe, rather than Clarkson, deserves the dubious honor. See Crow and Durden, *Maverick Republican*, pp. 139–40. An article reprinted in the *Observer*, however, suggests an intriguing alternative that predated the Mississippi amendment. "Captain Ashe's plan for educating the voter into a reader . . . is Tom Dixon's plan. Years ago, when a senior at Wake Forest, he wrote a thesis to be submitted at Johns Hopkins, promulgating the plan" (*Gastonia Gazette*, quoted in the *Charlotte Observer*, August 15, 1897). Thomas Dixon of nearby Shelby, North Carolina, was a prominent Baptist minister who would soon win international fame as author of *The Leopard's Spots* and *The Clansman*, best-selling racist novels dramatized in D. W. Griffith's epic film *The Birth of a Nation*. For more on Dixon's 1882 Wake Forest essay, see James Zebulon Wright, "Thomas Dixon," esp. pp. 70–72, 88.

76. Woodward, *Strange Career of Jim Crow*, pp. 83–84.

77. *Charlotte Observer*, April 1, 1897. Two days later the *Observer* repeated its endorsement of Ashe's literacy amendment, this time as a favorable alternative to a compulsory education law. "We do not believe that North Carolina will ever have compulsory education. We do not believe it ought to have" (*Charlotte Observer*, April 9, 1897). On the evils of compulsory education, see also Methodist bishop J. C. Kilgo in the *Charlotte Observer*, August 24, 1897.

78. Article from *Charity and Children*, reprinted in the *Charlotte Observer*, September 3, 1897. African American enthusiasm for schooling was indeed strong. An 1887 count of school-aged children in Charlotte had found "that there are but thirty-six more white children of school age, than colored children, in the city. This is probably explained by the fact that large numbers of colored children come here from the county to secure the benefits of the free graded school" (*Charlotte Chronicle*, August 20, 1887). This phenomenon was widespread in the South; see James Anderson, *Education of Blacks in the South*.

79. *Charlotte Observer*, August 24, 1897; Richard L. Watson Jr., "Furnifold M. Simmons and the Politics of White Supremacy," in Crow, Escott, and Flynn, *Race, Class, and Politics in Southern History*, pp. 126–72. A letter writer to a Charlotte paper on December 19, 1898, claimed that local Democrats had launched the state's first "White Supremacy Club" several months earlier. See clipping in scrapbook PC 175.21, bylaws in scrapbook PC 175.27, Clarkson Collection.

80. *Charlotte Observer*, October 8, 10, November 28, 1896. Despite the club's title, patrician lawyer Heriot Clarkson acted as its leader. By 1897 most of the actions of the regular Democratic Party seem to have taken place under the auspices of the Workingmen's Democratic Club. For example, see *Charlotte Observer*, March 13, 1897.

81. The *Observer* took glee in egging on blacks who demanded more patronage positions, requests that were actually quite reasonable in light of the fact that African Americans got far fewer jobs than their support for the Republican Party should have entitled them to. See *Charlotte Observer*, July 18, 23, October 14, 17, November 13, December 3, 1897.

82. As reported in the *Charlotte Observer*, September 13, 1898:

> Mr. Aycock's reply [to the Populist platform of appointing Negroes to jury duty] was like an inspiration. He said something like this: "I wouldn't think of it! Why you white men of Cabarrus don't even wait for the law when negroes have dishonored your helpless, innocent women." It was like a thunderbolt. Before he finished his sentence, his audience knew that he was alluding to the recent lynching in the county of two negroes who had violated a young girl, while she stayed at home at church time with the younger children on Sunday, then brutally murdered her to cover up their deeds. The room went wild. Men rose unconsciously to their feet! The thunder of cheering rose and fell and rose again. It was several minutes before the demonstration subsided. It was a masterstroke. The smile of triumph vanished from Populist faces.

83. Ibid., October 18, 1898.
84. Ibid., October 26, 1898.
85. Ibid.
86. Ibid., November 10, 1898.
87. Lefler and Newsome, *North Carolina*, p. 558.
88. *Charlotte Observer*, November 9, 1898.
89. Quoted in Kousser, *Shaping of Southern Politics*, p. 190. Similarly: "I was one of the men who helped to pass the amendment, and our purpose was to allow every white man to

vote that we wanted to vote and to allow no man to vote that we didn't want" (Hon. R. B. Glenn, quoted in the *Charlotte News*, July 26, 1900).

90. Woodward, *Origins of the New South*, p. 334.

91. Powell, *North Carolina through Four Centuries*, p. 438. The actual language of the North Carolina grandfather clause read, "No male person who was on January 1, 1867, or at any time prior thereto, entitled to vote under the laws of any State in the United States wherein he then resided, and no lineal descendant of such a person, shall be denied the right to register and vote at any election in this State by reason of his failure to possess the educational qualifications herein prescribed: Provided he shall have registered in accordance with the terms of this section prior to December 1, 1908."

92. Quoted in the *Charlotte News*, July 13, 1900; also see October 3, 1899, July 16, 24, 1900. Similar sentiments were expressed by the city's Populist *People's Paper*, October 14, 1898.

93. *Washington Post*, March 6, 1899, clipping in scrapbook PC 175.21, Clarkson Collection.

94. *Charlotte Observer*, May 20, 1900; *Charlotte News*, May 31, July 4, 5, 1900.

95. *Charlotte News*, August 1, 1900. The poem had run earlier in the Raleigh *News and Observer*, writes Kousser, *Shaping of Southern Politics*, p. 189.

96. *Charlotte Observer*, June 6, 1900.

97. The election was moved up to August so that voters would not be swayed by national issues—and so that any intimidation of black voters would not be indictable under laws affecting federal elections. See *Charlotte News*, July 31, 1900. Description of the float appeared in a clipping in scrapbook PC 175.18, Clarkson Collection.

98. Quoted in Lefler and Newsome, *North Carolina*, p. 558.

CHAPTER 4

1. U.S. Bureau of the Census, *Tenth Census*.

2. Burke Davis, *Southern Railway*; Tullos, *Habits of Industry*, pp. 138–43; Lefler and Newsome, *North Carolina*, p. 517; Blythe and Brockmann, *Hornets' Nest*, pp. 260–61. The Southern Railway's antecedents are described in Klein, *Great Richmond Terminal*. On the battle between urban promoters and outside consolidators over railroads in the South, read Klein, *Unfinished Business*, pp. 31–67.

3. McGuire, "Seaboard Air Line"; Gilbert and Jefferys, *Crossties through Carolina*, p. 9; Lefler and Newsome, *North Carolina*, p. 517; Blythe and Brockmann, *Hornets' Nest*, pp. 261–62; Kathleen P. Southern, "Seaboard Air Line Railroad Station," National Register Nomination. In cities throughout the South, the need for railroad connections by multiple companies became a critical issue in this period. See Klein, *Unfinished Business*, pp. 31–67; Doyle, *Nashville in the New South*, esp. pp. 19–31; Chesson, *Richmond after the War*; James Michael Russell, *Atlanta*.

4. Blythe and Brockmann, *Hornets' Nest*, pp. 261–63; Gilbert and Jefferys, *Crossties through Carolina*, p. 9; Fetters and Swanson, *Piedmont and Northern*, esp. p. 15; William H. Huffman, "Piedmont & Northern Railway Station," Survey and Research Report. The Piedmont & Northern tracks remain in use in the 1990s, though the system was converted to diesel power in 1950 and is now part of the Seaboard system. On building the Norfolk & Southern, see Charlotte newspapers for January and February 1912, particularly *Charlotte Evening Chronicle*, January 16, 18, 1912.

5. North Carolina Bureau of Labor Statistics, *Tenth Annual Report*, pp. 56–57.

6. North Carolina Department of Labor and Printing, *Thirty-Fifth Annual Report*, pp. 34–35; Morrill, "Survey of Cotton Mills"; Brent Glass, *Textile Industry in North Carolina*, esp. p. 44.

7. Tompkins, *History of Mecklenburg County*, 1:183.

8. The quote is from *Miller's Official Charlotte, N.C., City Directory*, p. 8. From the 1910s on, Southern boosters were making claims that their region surpassed New England. The 1927 date is from Mitchell and Mitchell, *Industrial Revolution in the South*, p. 3. See also Broadus Mitchell, *Rise of Cotton Mills in the South*. Two recent histories of the Southern textile region are Hall et al., *Like a Family*, and Tullos, *Habits of Industry*.

9. *Charlotte Observer*, September 29, 1899.

10. Ibid., July 28, 1897; see also November 27, 1897. An August article noted that local mills were even buying cotton from New York City; see ibid., August 1, 1897. For a summary of local cotton trade during 1880–1897, consult ibid., September 29, 1897. The regional flow of Deep South cotton into the Carolinas was discussed in ibid., February 24, 1901.

11. Ibid., October 12, 28, November 6, 1897, January 5, 6, 1898. By 1899 Charlotte boasted two such warehouses. See ibid., September 27, 1899; *Charlotte News*, October 13, 1899; Wade Hampton Harris, *Sketches of Charlotte*, No. 3, p. 23. One local source claimed that the bonded warehouse idea originated in Charlotte. "It was here the first company was organized and the first warehouses erected" (*Charlotte News*, September 23, 1899). The roofless walls of the Charlotte Bonded Warehouse survived in the early 1990s, visible from the north side of the Brookshire Freeway.

12. *Charlotte Observer*, September 29, 1899. By 1930 Charlotte would be "a great purchasing market, one of the largest in the South," where "practically all of the established firms in America who deal in cotton, are represented . . . by either their own representatives or by brokers" (Charlotte Chamber of Commerce, *Charlotte, North Carolina*, unpaginated).

13. In the South before the 1900s each mill was usually chartered as a separate corporate entity. Interlocking directorates might create de facto chains, as with the mills controlled by the Holt family, but on paper each mill was distinct, with its own roster of local investors. In the early twentieth century, as the need for capital outstripped local resources, mills began to organize into groups better to garner outside investment. Chadwick-Hoskins, incorporated February 18, 1908, was among the first such enterprises, and it ranked as the state's largest textile firm for almost a decade. The Chadwick-Hoskins Company brought together Charlotte's old Alpha and Louise mills and the 1894 Dover Mill south of the city at Pineville, as well as the Chadwick and Hoskins factories. Major financial backing came from William F. Draper of Hopedale, Massachusetts, a U.S. ambassador whose father had invented the universally popular Draper Loom. William's son A. J. Draper relocated in Charlotte to oversee the family investments and quickly became involved in other major projects, including creation of the Myers Park neighborhood. On mill financing in the South, see Brengle, *Architectural Heritage of Gaston County*, pp. 15–16; Ragan, "Leading Textile Mills in Gaston County"; Carlton and Coclanis, "Capital Mobilization and Southern Industry." On creation of Chadwick-Hoskins, see Mecklenburg County Register of Deeds Office, records of corporations, bk. 2, p. 313; Edgar Thompson, *Agricultural Mecklenburg and Industrial Charlotte*, pp. 139–40; William Huffman, "Old Charlotte Supply Company Building," Survey and Research Report. On the Draper family, consult Feller, "Draper Loom in New England Textiles"; Garner, *Model Company Town*; Galenson, "Migration of the Cotton Textile Industry," esp. p. 42; *Who's Who in America, 1908–1909*, p. 531.

14. Tullos, *Habits of Industry*, pp. 161–64; Maynor, *Duke Power*, p. 32; Durden, *Dukes of Durham*. For an early account by W. S. Lee, see the *Charlotte News*, May 21, 1906. For the

national context of Duke's activities, consult Hirsh, *Technology and Transformation in the American Electric Utility Industry.*

15. *Charlotte Observer,* July 8, 1906. The story was reprinted from the *Chicago Record-Herald.* See also Brent Glass, *Textile Industry in North Carolina,* esp. pp. 36, 44.

16. "Cole Manufacturing Company," Survey and Research Report.

17. "Nature Made It: Snowdrift Hogless Cooking Fat. Its Purity and Wholesomeness Guaranteed by the Southern Cotton Oil Company," ran a typical ad in the August 8, 1906, *Charlotte Observer.* It was "hogless" because it was intended to replace that staple of the Southern kitchen, lard. A competitor was also manufactured in Charlotte: Sunlight brand shortening made by Swift & Co. at a large plant on North Brevard Street (demolished ca. 1990). See *Charlotte News,* March 13, 1907.

18. On Barnhardt Manufacturing, see Reynolds, *Charlotte Remembers,* p. 159; *Charlotte Observer,* June 8, 1975. On Atlantic Cotton Waste, see *Charlotte News,* May 17, 1906; Edgar Thompson, *Agricultural Mecklenburg and Industrial Charlotte,* p. 151. Another such concern was the Southern Cotton Oil Company, which "secured a contract from the War Department for 10,000 Purity Cotton Felt Mattresses. . . . All of the lint secured at the oil mills of the company, including about 40,000 bales yearly, is shipped to the textile plant here, where it is made into mattresses. The factory has an output of about 1,000 mattresses a week" (*Charlotte Observer,* August 26, 1906).

19. *Charlotte Observer,* September 10, 1926. On Lance and Ford, see Kratt, *Charlotte,* 1st ed., pp. 101, 198.

20. *Charlotte News,* June 26, 1903.

21. Hall et al., *Like a Family,* p. 6, also pp. 36–38.

22. Data in this paragraph are based on analysis of totals for categories published by the U.S. Census for 1910, 1920, and 1930.

23. *Charlotte Observer,* November 9, 1906.

24. Ibid., November 6, 1897.

25. Ibid., March 14, 1900.

26. Ibid., February 22, 1900.

27. *People's Paper,* March 30, 1900; *Charlotte News,* May 12, 1904.

28. *Charlotte Observer,* May 18, July 20, August 31, 1905.

29. Ibid., March 14, 1900.

30. *Charlotte News,* March 13, 1900.

31. Ibid., January 31, 1901.

32. *Charlotte Observer,* June 5, 1902.

33. J. B. Alexander, *History of Mecklenburg County,* p. 169; similarly pp. 155–56. On Wittkowsky, see *Charlotte News,* August 15, 1903. On agitation for reinstituting the property qualification to vote in North Carolina in this period, see Steelman, "Progressive Era in North Carolina," pp. 216–17.

34. *Charlotte Observer,* August 2, 1903; Grundy, " 'We Always Tried to Be Good People.' "

35. On urban public health concerns in the era of industrialization, see Doyle, *Nashville in the New South,* pp. 82–86; Olson, *Baltimore,* p. 130. In the Carolinas the issue often pitted "town people" against "mill people." See Carlton, *Mill and Town in South Carolina,* pp. 153–56; Hall et al., *Like a Family,* p. 120. On Southern public health efforts at the turn of the century, see Woodward, *Origins of the New South,* pp. 425–26.

36. *Charlotte Observer,* August 2, 1903.

37. Ibid.

38. *Charlotte News,* January 22, 25, 26, February 6, 13, 1900.

39. Ibid., February 20, 1900. Also *Charlotte Observer*, February 21, 1900.

40. *Charlotte News*, February 21, 1900. Also *Charlotte Observer*, February 22, 1900.

41. "The neglect of vaccination," said the North Carolina Board of Public Health, was largely attributable to "prejudice against it on the part of many people, chiefly of the more ignorant classes" (*Charlotte News*, February 6, 1900).

42. *Charlotte News*, February 23, 1900. Indeed, authorities in nearby Gastonia stated, "It is believed that compulsory vaccination will be especially necessary among the negroes and the mill operatives, where there seems most danger of contagion" (*Charlotte Observer*, February 25, 1900).

43. *Charlotte News*, February 24, 1900.

44. Ibid., February 21, 1900.

45. *Charlotte Observer*, August 2, 1903.

46. *Charlotte Democrat*, May 29, 1891; *Charlotte Chronicle*, May 26, 1891.

47. The 1896 plat map does not include month or day, but its placement in the book indicates that it was filed in April. See Mecklenburg County Register of Deeds Office, deed book 112, p. 8. Even before the plat was officially recorded, an 1892 map of Charlotte showed Belmont's square blocks at the northeast edge of the city. See Butler and Spratt, "Map of Charlotte Township."

48. All the land comprising Belmont and North Charlotte had been the plantation of William Phifer before the Civil War. The Phifer family seems to have actively encouraged urban development, starting in the 1850s when they welcomed railroads through the property. By 1892 Eleventh, Twelfth, and parts of Thirteenth, Fourteenth (now Belmont), and Fifteenth Streets had been added beyond Phifer Avenue. See Butler and Spratt, "Map of Charlotte Township"; J. B. Alexander, *History of Mecklenburg County*, pp. 169–70. On the existence of houses on Thirteenth through Eighteenth Streets, see the *Charlotte Observer*, June 11, 1903. In the 1940s this area would gain the name Optimist Park, in honor of a playground created near Brevard and Seventeenth Streets by the Optimist Club. See *Charlotte Observer*, October 19, 1944.

49. Interestingly, the creation of the Southern Railway's freight yard east of Brevard Street occurred after most of the industries were in place. The Southern had purchased land in the area in the 1890s when the newly formed company was considering sites for its major locomotive repair shop. The Southern's management eventually decided against Charlotte and instead created an entire new town at Spencer in Cabarrus County. See Dreyer, *Spencer Architectural and Historic Inventory*. In 1907 the Charlotte site became a 1,000-car marshaling yard. See *Charlotte News*, December 11, 1906; *Charlotte Observer*, July 25, September 4, November 21, 1906.

50. William Huffman, "Old Alpha Mill," Survey and Research Report. See also Chapter 2 of the present study.

51. See nn. 66, 67, 68 below.

52. The earliest indication of a compress on this site is Butler and Spratt, "Map of Charlotte Township." On cotton compressing in 1890s Charlotte, see *Charlotte Observer*, November 27, July 28, 1897. The Charlotte Cotton Compress burned in 1899 and was rebuilt almost immediately. See *Charlotte News*, July 3, 8, August 11, 17, 1899. For a report on a year's activities at the compress, see the *Charlotte News*, January 31, 1906. By 1926 the facility employed "sixty colored men" (Edgar Thompson, *Agricultural Mecklenburg and Industrial Charlotte*, p. 155). The compress building was demolished in 1993, but its steam boiler and other machinery were preserved and moved to Denton, North Carolina. See *Charlotte Observer*, September 8, 1993.

53. *Charlotte Observer*, November 19, 1896, June 1, September 25, 1897; Sanborn Insurance Maps of Charlotte, 1900, plate 22, and 1911, plate 76; Morrill, "Survey of Cotton Mills." Louise Chadwick owned New York City's Hotel Jefferson. See *Charlotte News*, January 31, 1901.

54. *Charlotte Observer*, September 23, 1897.

55. Ibid., November 6, 1897. Few details are known about the Louise Mill walkout, a situation that typifies the modern scholar's frustrations in chronicling the history of non-elites in this period. The only surviving newspaper of the day is the *Observer*, a booster-oriented organ of the Charlotte elite that had no interest in providing publicity to strikers. The newspaper gave barely one column inch to the strike, compared with nearly four inches devoted to mill owner H. S. Chadwick's birthday party in ibid., September 23, 1897.

56. *Charlotte News*, April 9, 13, 1900.

57. *Charlotte Observer*, March 13, 1900.

58. *Charlotte News*, February 25, 1901. Labor tensions evidently remained high at the Louise Mill. Three years later 160 of the plant's 169 operatives walked out when management demanded they work for free to make up time lost because of a machinery breakdown. See *Charlotte News*, May 12, 1904; *Charlotte Observer*, May 13, 1904.

59. The replatting of the former park land was recorded in the Mecklenburg County Register of Deeds Office, deed book 151, p. 43. Belmont's blue-collar image was confirmed in a 1906 profile of the city. "Dilworth, Elizabeth Heights, Piedmont Park, and Myers Park are especially attractive as residence localities," while "Belmont, Highland Park, Atherton and Chadwick, are among the . . . mill settlements" (Julia Alexander, *Charlotte in Picture and Prose*, unpaginated).

60. North of Parkwood Avenue lay Villa Heights, with Grace, Union, Barry, and Lola Streets; see Mecklenburg County Register of Deeds Office, deed book 146, p. 59. Villa Heights also included the 1800–1900 blocks of Harrill, Allen, Pegram, Umstead, and Parson Streets. For advertisements of Villa Heights lots, see, for instance, *Charlotte News*, April 30, May 18, 30, 1900.

The East End subdivision, platted in 1903 by planter William Phifer's descendant George Phifer, extended Belmont's Seigle, Harrill, Allen, and Pegram Streets north to an existing county road, renamed Parkwood Avenue. See Mecklenburg County Register of Deeds Office, deed book 173, pp. 582–83; *Charlotte Observer*, May 16, 1903. See also ad for East End in *Charlotte News*, May 21, 1906.

Next to East End appeared the narrow 1902 subdivision dubbed Sunnyside, which included parts of present-day Kennon, Umstead, and Parson Streets, plus the 1600–1700 block of Hawthorne Lane. See Mecklenburg County Register of Deeds Office, deed book 173, p. 377.

In 1910 the Phifer family laid out Belmont's last subdivision, Phifer Heights, including the 1800 blocks of Seigle and McDowell Streets north of Parkwood Avenue. The family named a spring in this tract after W. F. Phifer's stepdaughter Cordelia White; today the city's Cordelia Park occupies the site. See Mecklenburg County Register of Deeds Office, map book 230, p. 78.

61. Information on Charlotte trolley routes is based in part on Mecklenburg County Register of Deeds Office, deed book 325, p. 330. The sale of the Charlotte Electric Railway to the Southern Public Utilities Company set forth the trolley lines as they existed in 1914. Information courtesy of Gaston County rail historian Earl Long.

62. The presence of shopping in blue-collar areas, but not in white-collar neighborhoods, has been noted elsewhere. See Conzen and Conzen, "Geographical Structure in

Nineteenth Century Urban Retailing"; Michael P. Conzen, "Historical Geography," esp. p. 94; Stilgoe, *Borderland*, pp. 208–12. On activities at the Caldwell Street cluster, see the *Charlotte Observer*, August 27, 1906, January 12, 1907; Charlotte City Council Minutes, vol. 27, February 26, 1930. In blue-collar districts elsewhere in America, corner taverns were a common sight along with the groceries and general merchandise shops. This was not the case in Charlotte, where the sale of liquor was prohibited from 1904 into the 1940s.

63. There is an extensive literature on immigrant neighborhoods in the industrial North. My understanding draws particularly on Zunz, *Changing Face of Inequality*. See also Zane L. Miller, *Boss Cox's Cincinnati*, pp. 25–40; Ward, *Cities and Immigrants*; Bodnar, *Transplanted*; Woods and Kennedy, *Zone of Emergence*. In their 1915 study Woods and Kennedy saw blue-collar districts as a key stepping-stone in the process of Americanizing immigrants. Boston's foreigners came first to the crowded tenements of the center city, then as they (or their children) saved sufficient money, they moved out to semisuburban factory districts. The most successful would theoretically move on from this "Zone of Emergence" into homes in white-collar suburbs. Recently Olivier Zunz has elaborated on these notions in his study of Detroit. He finds that between 1880 and 1900, Detroit neighborhoods functioned as ethnic enclaves within which enterprising individuals could rise in economic stature. After 1900, however, these economically mixed "zones" gave way to single-class blue-collar and white-collar neighborhoods. Research on social mobility is outside the scope of my study, but it appears that Charlotte's Belmont functioned differently from Northern zones. Without the forces of ethnic solidarity, there was nothing to keep prospering individuals in the neighborhood. Belmont had no equivalent of Italian neighborhood bank president J. J. Castellini in Cincinnati's zone, or Polish brewery owner Tomasz Zoltowksi in Detroit's. Lacking immigrant solidarity, Charlotte whites evidently went straight to the sort of single-class neighborhoods that Zunz sees developing only later in Detroit.

64. Belmont–Villa Heights church buildings include the blond brick, Gothic-style Belmont Park United Methodist Church (now Northside Nazarene), erected at Pegram and Fifteenth Streets in 1909; the unusual Prairie-influenced Villa Heights Associated Reform Presbyterian Church (now Parkwood AME), completed in 1910; and the Neoclassical-style Allen Street Baptist Church (now St. Paul Baptist), which dates from around 1920. At least one church began as a "missionary" effort among the millhands: Christ the King Center at Caldwell and Seventeenth Streets, built by the Episcopal Church in 1920 to replace an earlier wooden structure that had served as the company chapel for the Gingham Mill. See *Charlotte Observer*, August 22, 1905.

Compared with white-collar neighborhoods, which had notable Episcopal and Presbyterian congregations, Charlotte's blue-collar districts had more congregations of Baptist, Methodist, and the new charismatic Pentecostal Holiness branches of Protestantism. On the Holiness movement, see *Charlotte News*, December 20, 28, 1906. On millhand religion, see Hall et al., *Like a Family*, pp. 175–79; Pope, *Millhands and Preachers*, esp. pp. 126–40; Tullos, *Habits of Industry*; I. A. Newby, *Plain Folks in the New South*.

65. Beatty, "Edwin Holt Family"; Andrews, *Mills and the Men*, pp. 67–68; Ashe, *Biographical History of North Carolina*, 7:186; Lefler and Newsome, *North Carolina*, p. 399.

Holt's Charlotte involvement evidently began with establishment of E. M. Holt and Company Commission Merchants in the late 1860s to take part in Charlotte's post–Civil War cotton trade (a notable testament to the economic health of the Queen City, since Charlotte was over a hundred miles from the family's base of operations at Alamance). See Beatty, "Edwin Holt Family," p. 526; Mecklenburg County Register of Deeds, deed book 5,

p. 729. In 1874 Edwin Holt helped found the Commercial National Bank of Charlotte. See *Charlotte Observer*, December 19, 1896, July 17, 1904. By 1880 the *Charlotte Democrat* noted that "E. M. Holt of Alamance and several of his sons . . . have large investments in Charlotte real estate and stocks" (*Charlotte Democrat*, January 16, 1880).

The Holts seem not to have taken a direct hand in their Mecklenburg holdings, preferring to tend their mills close to home and let a trusted local merchant or lawyer oversee the more general investments at distant Charlotte. One early overseer was Lewis Williams (sometime partner of Mecklenburg cotton man Robert Oates). See p. 102s, vol. 16 (Mecklenburg County), North Carolina, Dun Collection. By the 1890s the overseer was Jesse S. Spencer, who held the post of president at the family's Commercial National Bank.

66. William Holt started his career as manager of the pioneering Alamance mill in the 1860s and went on to found Glencoe Mills near Burlington and Wennonah Mills at Lexington. See Young, *Textile Leaders of the South*, pp. 100–103; Brent Glass, "Southern Mill Hills," pp. 138–39. On creation of the Gingham Mill in Charlotte, see *Charlotte Chronicle*, May 27, June 6, 14, 16, 1891; Mecklenburg County Register of Deeds Office, records of corporations, bk. A, p. 221, and bk. 1, p. 337; Morrill, "Survey of Cotton Mills."

67. A biography of Johnston may be found in Young, *Textile Leaders of the South*, pp. 108–9, 766. His obituary ran in the *Charlotte News*, July 5, 1941. See also Blythe and Brockmann, *Hornets' Nest*, pp. 420–21.

68. Highland Park Manufacturing Company memo with penciled date July 25, 1964, in the files of the Robinson-Spangler Carolina Room, Public Library of Charlotte and Mecklenburg County. The Anchor concern evidently took over the existing Virgin Mill, chartered in 1891. See Mecklenburg County Register of Deeds Office, records of corporations, bk. 1, p. 48, and bk. A, p. 215; deed book 121, p. 224. See also Blythe and Brockmann, *Hornets' Nest*, p. 422.

69. Graham Romeyn Taylor, *Satellite Cities*. See also Glaab and Brown, *History of Urban America*, pp. 273–75; Gordon, "Class Struggle and the Stages of American Urban Development," in Perry and Watkins, *Rise of Sunbelt Cities*, pp. 74–77; Cutler and Gillette, *Divided Metropolis*, esp. pp. xiv, 27–55, 85; Gwendolyn Wright, *Building the Dream*, pp. 180–90; Kenneth T. Jackson, *Crabgrass Frontier*, pp. 183–84; Richard Harris, "American Suburbs." For a historical overview of company towns, see Garner, *Model Company Town*; Garner, *Company Town*.

70. Graham Romeyn Taylor, *Satellite Cities*; Buder, *Pullman*; Stilgoe, *Borderland*, pp. 252–58. On West Nashville, see Doyle, *Nashville in the New South*, pp. 98–100. Atlanta's Cabbagetown district developed as a blue-collar neighborhood around this same time. See Grable, "Other Side of the Tracks."

71. North Carolina Department of Labor and Printing, *Annual Report, 1910*, p. 272; Hall et al., *Like a Family*, p. 107.

72. Highland Park bought its 102 acres for $15,000 from the Pegram-Wadsworth Company, which held the undeveloped portions of the old William Phifer estate (see n. 48 above). See Mecklenburg County Register of Deeds Office, deed book 178, p. 210.

73. *Fifth Annual Report, Superintendent, Charlotte Waterworks*, pp. 2, 7, 8, 18, 20; Mecklenburg County Register of Deeds Office, deed book 178, p. 253, and deed book 129, p. 616; Blythe and Brockmann, *Hornets' Nest*, p. 129; *Charlotte Observer*, December 11, 1903.

74. Cramer had come to Charlotte as representative of the Whitin Machinery Works, one of New England's most important textile machinery makers. See Navin, *Whitin Machine Works*. By the mid-1900s Cramer had his main office in a handsome new building overlooking the Charlotte city hall, one branch office in Atlanta, and another in the very

cradle of American textiles, Pawtucket, Rhode Island. For background on Cramer, see Young, *Textile Leaders of the South*, pp. 50–51, 744–45; *Charlotte News*, August 15, 1983; Andrews, *Mills and the Men*, pp. 27, 211–14; Blythe and Brockmann, *Hornets' Nest*, p. 276. Cramer's report, "Recent Developments in Air Conditioning," was noted in the *Charlotte Observer*, May 18, 1906. See also Wade Hampton Harris, *Sketches of Charlotte*, 8th ed., pp. 38–39, 46; Barbara Ford, *Keeping Things Cool*, p. 32.

75. *Charlotte Observer*, February 27, 1903. On construction of the mill and village, see ibid., May 20, June 4, 18, 1903; William Huffman, "Highland Park Manufacturing Company Mill No. 3," National Register Nomination.

76. Cramer devoted seventy-three pages to illustrations of the architecture and machinery of Highland Park #3 in Cramer, *Useful Information for Cotton Manufacturers*, 3:1227–1300. The plans showed the huge two-story spinning wing and the one-story weaving wing set at right angles, connected by a smaller machine room, picker room, slasher room, and warping room so that the whole formed an unbroken L. More than 200 large windows plus a raised "monitor" along the center of each roof flooded the interior with natural light. The building followed standard mill construction practices, as worked out a generation earlier at the behest of New England fire insurance companies: brick walls, heavy wooden floors, and thick wooden framing designed to merely char in the event of fire rather than melting and buckling like iron would.

77. Local newspapers erroneously claimed that Highland Park #3 was North Carolina's first electric-driven mill; see *Charlotte Observer*, February 27, 1903. In fact, at least two earlier mills had been retrofitted with electric motors: McAden Mills in Gaston County and the Fries Manufacturing Company along the Yadkin River. See Brengle, *Architectural Heritage of Gaston County*, p. 284; Lefler and Newsome, *North Carolina*, p. 509; Blythe, *Robert Lee Stowe*, pp. 133–36. The first mill built for electric operation in the South is acknowledged to be the Columbia Mill at Columbia, South Carolina, now renovated as the South Carolina State Museum. See Sidney B. Paine, "Electric Power as Applied to Textile Machinery," in Young, *Textile Leaders of the South*, pp. 684–86. On the advantages of electric power, see Hall et al., *Like a Family*, p. 48; Duboff, "Introduction of Electric Power in American Manufacturing."

78. Cramer, *Useful Information for Cotton Manufacturers*, 3:1272. In 1904 J. B. Duke's Catawba Power Company began offering electricity to customers in Charlotte. Catawba Power could supply current more cheaply than Highland Park could make it, and, coincidentally, Catawba needed a steam plant at Charlotte to provide back-up in case transmission lines failed. About 1905 the two companies worked a trade, and Highland Park hooked into the Catawba system. By 1907 Catawba Power was building a transmission line from North Charlotte to the mills in Concord. See *Charlotte Observer*, January 6, 1907. On the beginnings of textile electrification in Cabarrus County, see the *Charlotte Observer*, October 24, 1906.

79. *Charlotte Observer*, February 2, 1907. For a brief profile of the Highland Park company in the 1920s, see Edgar Thompson, *Agricultural Mecklenburg and Industrial Charlotte*, p. 147. On the famous Amoskeag complex, see Hareven and Langenbach, *Amoskeag*.

80. The Duke investor was James B. Duke's nephew B. Lawrence Duke, a wealthy Durham financier. See William Huffman, "Mecklenburg Mill," Survey and Research Report; Mecklenburg County Register of Deeds Office, records of corporations, bk. 1, p. 344; Durden, *Dukes of Durham*, p. 85.

81. Morrill, "Survey of Cotton Mills." Johnston became president of the Highland Park corporation in 1906. See *Charlotte News*, February 15, 1906; Mecklenburg County Register

of Deeds Office, records of corporations, bk. 2, p. 3; Highland Park Manufacturing Company memo in the Robinson-Spangler Carolina Room, Public Library of Charlotte and Mecklenburg County. Johnston did not formally incorporate his family-owned Johnston Mill until 1921. See Mecklenburg County Register of Deeds Office, records of corporations, bk. 7, p. 1.

82. Charlotte city directory, 1933. The plant was designed by prolific mill architect Richard C. Biberstein, a protégé of Stuart Cramer. See William Huffman, "Richard C. Biberstein House," Survey and Research Report; Biberstein, Bowles, Meecham and Reed job records in the collection of the Department of Archives and Special Collections at the University of North Carolina at Charlotte.

83. A. F. Sullivan Co., of Greenville, S.C., erected the 200' × 300' Grinnell plant at a cost of $65,000. See *Charlotte Observer*, March 2, 1907. Both Highland Park #3 and the Mecklenburg Mill used Grinnell systems. See Sanborn Insurance Map of Charlotte, 1911, plate 89, on microfilm in the Robinson-Spangler Carolina Room, Public Library of Charlotte and Mecklenburg County. On Grinnell/General Fire Extinguisher and its Charlotte chief E. C. Dwelle, see also *Charlotte News*, December 23, 1899; *Charlotte Observer*, March 30, 1901; Mecklenburg County Register of Deeds Office, records of corporations, bk. 1, p. 106.

84. Sanborn Insurance Map of Charlotte, 1911, plate 89. On creation of the company, see the *Charlotte Observer*, October 21, 1905. South Atlantic's building is now gone.

85. Initially eight rows of cottages lined Davidson, Yadkin, Alexander, Myers, and McDowell Streets and spilled onto Faison, Mallory, and Charles (for Charles Johnston) Streets. See Cramer, *Useful Information for Cotton Manufacturers*, 3:1227; *Charlotte Observer*, June 18, 1903. Also *Charlotte Observer*, November 16, 1906. The company added other houses from time to time, the last probably being the Bungalow-style, two-family cottages on Faison Street, which appear to date from the late 1910s or 1920s. See Richard L. Mattson, Suzanne S. Pickens, and Kary L. Schmidt, "North Charlotte Historic District," and William Huffman, "Highland Park Manufacturing Company Mill No. 3," National Register Nomination.

On the social meaning of mill village design, read Brent Glass, "Southern Mill Hills"; Brent Glass, *Textile Industry in North Carolina*; Bishir et al., *Architects and Builders in North Carolina*, pp. 252–55; Margaret Crawford, "Earle S. Draper and the Company Town in the American South," in Garner, *Company Town*, pp. 139–72. On company-owned housing outside the South, see, for example, Alanen, "Corporate Vernacular"; Lizabeth A. Cohen, "Embellishing a Life of Labor."

86. *Southern Textile Bulletin*, December 25, 1919, p. 203. This Charlotte-based magazine's annual "Health and Happiness" issues from the late 1910s and 1920s are a gold mine for researchers interested in mill life, though readers need to be aware that stories most decidedly were told from the owners' viewpoint.

87. *Charlotte Observer*, August 23, 1906; Mecklenburg County Register of Deeds Office, records of corporations, bk. 2, p. 43; map book 209, p. 460; map book 230, p. 14. In addition, North Charlotte Realty stockholders included Jesse Spencer's widow and a longtime Holt associate named J. E. Prior, of New York City (probably the same as J. E. Prower, a major stockholder in the Highland Park Company in 1906).

88. Cramer, *Useful Information for Cotton Manufacturers*, 3:1227; *Charlotte Observer*, June 18, 1903.

89. City directory data. On an early business in this vicinity, see the *Charlotte Observer*, August 4, 1904. On shopping districts in blue-collar areas—but not in white-collar neigh-

borhoods—see Conzen and Conzen, "Geographical Structure in Nineteenth Century Urban Retailing," pp. 45–66; Michael P. Conzen, "Historical Geography," esp. p. 94; Stilgoe, *Borderland*, pp. 208–12. Incidentally, the North Charlotte district included no taverns, a fixture of blue-collar neighborhoods elsewhere in America, because Charlotte went dry from 1904 into the 1940s.

90. *Charlotte Observer*, June 20, 1906.

91. William Huffman, "Hand Pharmacy," Survey and Research Report.

92. The park was on the site of the old Mecklenburg County poorhouse. See *Charlotte Observer*, August 23, 1906. The name Electric Park was recalled by Richard V. Suddreth, Roy Grant, and Polly Grant in an interview with Thomas W. Hanchett in Charlotte, April 7, 1991. It is also mentioned in a story on a proposed school (never built), in the *Charlotte Observer*, May 26, 1911. The name neatly symbolized the park's location at the end of the electric trolley line, and it was also fitting in light of the innovative use of electric power at the nearby Highland Park #3 mill. On a company-sponsored picnic at the park, see *Southern Textile Bulletin*, September 6, 1923, p. 18.

At the YMCA, North Charlotte's mill owners provided organized recreation, music lessons, homemaking classes, visits from nurses, and the like. Such "welfare work" was common throughout the Carolinas in the early twentieth century as textile leaders searched for ways to build worker loyalty and instill what they regarded as middle-class values. See Hall et al., *Like a Family*, pp. 131–39. On "Welfare Work in the Mills," see the *Charlotte Observer*, July 23, 1906. On the importance of YMCAs in "moral training" of workers elsewhere, read Boyer, *Urban Masses and Moral Order*.

The North Charlotte YMCA initially occupied the former poorhouse on Thirty-sixth Street. In 1951 the YMCA and the Spencer Memorial Methodist Church swapped sites, with the YMCA moving to the church's old spot next to Highland Park #3, and the church erecting a new sanctuary where Electric Park had once been. See *One Hundredth Anniversary*, p. 8.

93. Station No. 5 stands on Laurel Avenue and No. 6 on Tuckasegee Road, both dating from 1929. The jail at the North Charlotte station has since been converted to offices. See E. R. Blalock of the Central Services Office of the City of Charlotte, telephone interview with Thomas W. Hanchett, January 1985.

94. On the Chadwick Mill, see the *Charlotte Observer*, February 11, July 4, August 12, 1901. On the Hoskins factory, see William H. Huffman, "Hoskins Mill," National Register Nomination. On both mills, see also Morrill, "Survey of Cotton Mills"; Edgar Thompson, *Agricultural Mecklenburg and Industrial Charlotte*, pp. 135–40. On the auction of lots in adjoining Thomasboro, see the *Charlotte News*, November 3, 1919. Development of the Chadwick-Hoskins/Thomasboro neighborhood is covered in Hanchett, "Charlotte and Its Neighborhoods," chap. 14.

95. Hall et al., *Like a Family*, p. 146.

96. Ibid., pp. 187–95; *Charlotte News*, May 10, 1919. A smaller, earlier walkout was mentioned in the *Charlotte News*, October 23, 1906.

97. Hall et al., *Like a Family*, pp. 190–94, 355. In 1923 a young *Charlotte Observer* intern named Wilbur J. Cash reported on the meetings "held in the Union Hall over the Hand Drug Company" (*Charlotte Observer*, August 14, 15, 18, 22, 25, 1923). Cash later became famous for his book *Mind of the South*. See Morrison, W. J. *Cash*, p. 37; Claiborne, "*Charlotte Observer*," p. 172.

98. Hall et al., *Like a Family*, p. 180. See also pp. 225, 232–33.

99. Ibid., p. 222.

1. White, "Black Sides of Atlanta"; Porter, "Black Atlanta," chaps. 4, 5, and esp. 6; Wintz, "Emergence of a Black Neighborhood"; Radford, "Race, Residence, and Ideology"; Radford, "Social Geography of the Nineteenth Century U.S. City"; George C. Wright, *Life Behind a Veil*, chap. 4, esp. p. 103.

On black neighborhood patterns in the South, see also Rabinowitz, *Race Relations in the Urban South*, particularly chap. 5; Kellogg, "Negro Urban Clusters in the Post-Bellum South"; Kellogg, "Formation of Black Residential Areas in Lexington"; Groves and Muller, "Evolution of Black Residential Areas"; Sumka, "Racial Segregation in Small North Carolina Cities"; Earl Lewis, *In Their Own Interests*, esp. pp. 8–28; White and Crimmins, "Urban Structure, Atlanta"; Byrne and White, "Atlanta University's 'Northeast Lot'"; Borchert, *Alley Life in Washington*; McTigue, "Patterns of Residence"; Spain, "Race Relations and Residential Segregation in New Orleans"; Benjamin Walter, "Ethnicity and Residential Succession: Nashville, 1850 to 1920," in Blumenstein and Walter, *Growing Metropolis*, pp. 3–32; Blassingame, *Black New Orleans*; Blassingame, "Before the Ghetto"; Wheeler, "Together in Egypt," esp. pp. 119–20; Brown and Kimball, "Mapping the Terrain of Black Richmond."

Several scholars have pointed out that the Southern pattern of several black clusters is very different from the twentieth century Northern pattern of single ghetto. For example, see Charles S. Johnson, *Patterns of Negro Segregation*, pp. 8–12; Taeuber and Taeuber, *Negroes in Cities*; Woofter, *Negro Problem in Cities*. On Northern patterns, see Weaver, *Negro Ghetto*; Spear, *Black Chicago*; Oscar Handlin, *Boston's Immigrants*, pp. 96–97; Philpott, *Slum and the Ghetto*; Katzman, *Before the Ghetto*, pp. 67–80; Kusmer, *Ghetto Takes Shape*; Trotter, *Black Milwaukee*; Taylor and Dula, "Black Residential Experience"; Massey and Denton, *American Apartheid*.

2. White, "Black Sides of Atlanta," p. 212.

3. Cell, *Highest Stage of White Supremacy*; Woodward, *Strange Career of Jim Crow*; Williamson, *Origins of Segregation*; Williamson, *Crucible of Race*, esp. pp. 249–56. For an overview of scholarship on the rise of Jim Crow, read La Wanda Cox, "From Emancipation to Segregation: National Policy and Southern Blacks," in Boles and Nolen, *Interpreting Southern History*, pp. 199–253.

4. Roger L. Rice, "Residential Segregation by Law"; Silver, "Racial Origins of Zoning"; Woodward, *Strange Career of Jim Crow*, p. 100. Several cities found ways to pass racial zoning laws even after the Supreme Court ruled such ordinances illegal in 1917. See Preston, *Automobile Age Atlanta*. During 1913–15 North Carolina considered a bill (sponsored by Charles S. Aycock's son-in-law) that would have required separate black and white districts in rural areas. See Jeffrey J. Crow, "An Apartheid for the South: Clarence Poe's Crusade for Rural Segregation," in Crow, Escott, and Flynn, *Race, Class, and Politics in Southern History*, pp. 216–59; *Star of Zion*, February 25, 1915; Harlan, *Booker T. Washington: The Wizard of Tuskegee*, pp. 423–25.

5. Toll, *Blacking Up*, p. 28.

6. Scholars have long debated the degree to which racial segregation was a reality before the 1890s. See Thelen, Rabinowitz, and Woodward, "Perspectives." Today most historians agree that significant changes in race relations did indeed occur in the 1890s. See, for instance, Williamson, *Crucible of Race*, pp. 249–56, 318; Cell, *Highest Stage of White Supremacy*; Rabinowitz, *First New South*, p. 139; Gilmore, "Gender and Jim Crow," p. 263.

7. *Charlotte Observer*, October 15, 1893, also October 13, 17, 19; *Star of Zion*, October 26, 1893; Greenwood, *Bittersweet Legacy*, pp. 150–51.

8. *Star of Zion*, March 14, 1895.

9. On the *Plessy* decision and its repercussions, read Kluger, *Simple Justice*, pp. 71–83.

10. *Charlotte News*, February 12, 1906.

11. *Charlotte Observer*, July 21, 1899. The action recalled the famous words of a Charleston editor who ridiculed the early stirrings of Jim Crow by suggesting reductio ad absurdum that if things kept on, courts might one day have "Jim Crow Bibles to kiss." Before long, writes historian C. Vann Woodward, "all the improbable applications of the principle suggested by the editor in derision had been put into practice—down to and including the Jim Crow Bible" (Woodward, *Strange Career of Jim Crow*, pp. 67–69).

12. *Charlotte Observer*, May 2, 1903. Barred from participating in the Mecklenburg County Fair, blacks organized their own Piedmont Colored Industrial Fair in 1902, 1903, and 1904. See *Charlotte News*, November 3, 1903; Buggs, "Negro in Charlotte," pp. 9–10, 12–13.

13. On baseball, see, for instance, the *Charlotte Observer*, July 18, 1893. On camp meetings, see ibid., August 15, 1897.

14. Ibid., May 2, 1903. Also *Charlotte News*, May 2, 1903. Similar sentiments were also expressed in religion. Congregations had often divided by color right after the Civil War, but now the line separating black and white members of the same denomination deepened into an ugly gash. At the 1906 convention of the Episcopal Diocese for Charlotte and the surrounding region, a Salisbury minister stood up to propose "an amendment be made as shall limit the membership of the convention to white clergy and white delegates from white parishes and missions." Debate ensued, climaxed by a speaker who "charmed the convention" when he said, "turning his attention to the negro ministers listening so attentively . . . , 'Your race has produced no great warrior, never painted a picture or wrote a great book. It sat 4,000 years by the water and never made a sail. It trod the earth all these centuries, trampled gold and diamonds under its feet, and never learned its wealth. We can never grow in this state, and I ask passage of this resolution.'" As the discussion continued, a reporter noted, "one of the colored men wept" (*Charlotte Observer*, June 15, 1906; also May 19, 1905). For more on racial tensions in religion, see *Star of Zion*, February 21, 1895; Mathews, *Religion in the Old South*, pp. 221–36.

15. Kratt and Hanchett, *Legacy*, p. 22. Latta Park was replaced in 1910 as the city's leading pleasure ground by Lakewood Park, on a new trolley line west of town. African Americans were barred completely from Lakewood, though eventually the owners condescended to open the facility to blacks for one week after the regular season. See *Charlotte Evening Chronicle*, September 17, 1910; ad in *Star of Zion*, September 7, 1911.

16. *Charlotte Observer*, August 18, 1906. Similarly, during September 1905 the *Charlotte News* carried extensive coverage of lynchings in New Bern, North Carolina, and Abbeville, South Carolina. See *Charlotte News*, September 1, 20, 1905. The same month saw stories about a Rock Hill grocer who shot a black customer who tried to return some sugar he had purchased, and about a Wilmington lumberyard that replaced all its Negro workers with whites. See *Charlotte News*, September 22, 23, 1905.

When actual news ran thin, reporters delighted in concocting tales about foolish "darkeys" and "coons," often written in dialect. For instance, see "All Coons Look Alike," *Charlotte News*, July 10, 1900; also *Charlotte Observer*, September 28, 1906. The most prolific dialect writer was H. E. C. Bryant, for example, *Charlotte Observer*, May 10, 1903,

May 8, 1904. (For a profile of Bryant, see the *Charlotte Observer*, January 7, 1945.) Not all African Americans came in for equal scorn. Newspapers looked fondly at older blacks who still showed the deference learned in slavery. "The 'before de war' darkey was one of the most faithful of beings, and it is a pity that the younger generation have not inherited more of his virtues" (*Charlotte News*, August 31, 1900; also *Charlotte Observer*, August 16, 1901).

17. While admitting that "as a piece of art 'The Clansman' was extremely poor stuff," the *Observer* applauded the message conveyed in "the innate power of its situations and the bitter history it revives" (*Charlotte Observer*, March 14, 1907). Dixon, who grew up in nearby Shelby, first brought his road company to Charlotte with *The Clansman* in 1905. See *Charlotte Observer*, October 12, 14, 1905. In the audience was Boston planner John Nolen, who was horrified by the play and the reaction it garnered. His notes are in the John Nolen papers. The *Observer*'s support of Dixon dated back at least to 1902, when it serialized his novel *The Leopard's Spots*. See *Charlotte Observer*, February 22, 1902. On Roosevelt, see *Charlotte Observer*, September 4, 1904.

18. Following the Atlanta riot, Charlotte received a "notable influx of negroes" (*Charlotte Observer*, November 29, 1906). The riot evidently caused much apprehension on the part of white authorities throughout the South. The Charlotte Artillery assured citizens that it was heavily equipped "in case of riots," and Durham leaders talked of organizing a military company to guard their town. See *Charlotte Observer*, November 20, 1906; *Charlotte News*, November 22, 1906. Early in 1907 newspapers announced that artillery was being distributed "throughout the state for riot purposes" (*Charlotte Observer*, February 4, 1907). For background on the Atlanta riot, see Williamson, *Crucible of Race*, pp. 209–23; Harlan, *Booker T. Washington: The Wizard of Tuskegee*, pp. 299–304.

19. *Charlotte Observer*, September 27, 1906.

20. *Public Laws of North Carolina*, 1907, pp. 1238–39; Stephenson, *Race Distinctions in American Law*, p. 228. All over the South most streetcar systems did not institute Jim Crow laws until after 1900. See Meier and Rudwick, "Boycott Movement against Jim Crow Streetcars"; Graves, "Jim Crow in Arkansas."

21. *Star of Zion*, March 14, 1895.

22. Ibid., February 26, 1903. The AME Zion denomination's 1906 conference focused on disfranchisement and Jim Crow; leaders moved the meeting from Charlotte to New Jersey "as they feel they can discuss more freely the various phases of the race problem [t]here than in any Southern city" (*Charlotte Observer*, July 31, 1906).

23. *Charlotte News*, April 16, 1907. The *Charlotte Observer*, April 16, 1907, referred to the protester as Joe "Robertson." See Greenwood, *Bittersweet Legacy*, pp. 236–37. Actions such as Robinson's would become a quiet tradition among Southern blacks, according to recent research by Robin D. G. Kelley, *Race Rebels*.

Along with vocal protests, African Americans disgusted by the rise of Jim Crow also voted with their feet. During the late 1890s and 1900s the city experienced what one reporter called an "Ebony Exodus" as blacks left to find work farther north in mines, on railroad track gangs, and as domestics in Northern cities. See *Charlotte News*, October 10, 1899, April 2, 1900; *Charlotte Observer*, May 20, 22, June 23, July 19, 23, August 11, 19, October 12, 27, November 8, 12, 1903, May 5, 8, 1904.

24. Greenwood, *Bittersweet Legacy*; Greenwood, *Black Experience in Charlotte-Mecklenburg*, section 4; Buggs, "Negro in Charlotte." Tax lists giving black and white income and personal property appeared in the *Charlotte Observer*, September 6, 26, 1903. On Charlotte's population of skilled black artisans, see DuBois, *Negro Artisan*, pp. 135–36.

On Houser, see n. 59 in Chapter 3 above. On Wyche, see the *Charlotte Observer*, August

15, 1906; Greenwood, *Black Experience in Charlotte-Mecklenburg*, section 4, p. 31. On Sanders, see Moore-Parker, *Biddle–Johnson C. Smith University Story*, pp. 12–15, 40. Sanders's obituary appeared in the *Charlotte Observer*, March 7, 1907; see also memorial service, March 20. On Lomax, see *Charlotte Observer*, April 1, 1908; Walls, *African Methodist Episcopal Zion Church*. On Taylor, see Burke, *Brooklyn Story*, p. 33; *Charlotte Observer*, April 25, 28, May 30, 1898; *People's Paper*, June 3, 1898. Earlier, Colonel Taylor had been "chief marshall of the Colored State Fair" in Raleigh (*Charlotte Observer*, August 18, 1897). Generally on North Carolina's postbellum generation of African American strivers, see Logan, *Negro in North Carolina*.

25. Burke, *Brooklyn Story*, p. 41; Greenwood, *Black Experience in Charlotte-Mecklenburg*, section 4, pp. 2–4; Greenwood, *Bittersweet Legacy*; Kratt, *Charlotte*, 1st ed., pp. 72–73. Biographical sketches of Williams appeared in *Star of Zion*, March 3, 1898, September 20, 1917. His death was noted in *Charlotte Observer*, June 9, 14, 1924, and *Star of Zion*, June 19, 1924. Williams's wife was Jennie Coleman Williams, a "near relative of" Warren Coleman, proprietor of the famed black-owned cotton mill in Concord, North Carolina, 1897–1904. On Coleman, read J. K. Rouse, *Noble Experiment of Warren C. Coleman*.

26. Williams accepted his post March 1, 1898. He served as the U.S. top diplomat in Sierra Leone for seven years, stationed at the busy port of Freetown, providing assistance to American citizens in the region and especially to American business firms. Among his efforts "to improve our opportunities for trade extension in these colonies" was a report, "Opportunities for the Introduction and Sale of American Cotton Goods in West Africa." Williams took leaves to return home briefly in 1899, 1901, 1903, and 1905. Each trip cost nearly $500, which ate up much of the position's modest $1,500 annual salary. On the 1905 visit to Charlotte, Williams requested several extensions of his leave to recover from "African fever." Over a period of months Williams weighed his health problems and the State Department's unwillingness to increase his salary or transfer him to a better-paid post. He decided not to return to Sierra Leone and on April 12, 1906, resigned his position. See "Despatches from U.S. Consuls in Sierra Leone, 1858–1906," National Archives, Washington, D.C. See especially March 1, October 25, 1898, September 25, 1899, October 10, 1901, October 7, 26, 1905, April 12, August 10, 1906. Also see *Charlotte Observer*, August 3, 4, 1903.

27. J. T. Williams, letter to W. C. Smith, April 11, 1905, in the collection of Smith's daughter Rosa Smith of Charlotte. Quotation courtesy of Janette Thomas Greenwood.

28. This discussion is based on maps that I prepared of race and residence in First Ward for three sample years: 1876, 1889, and 1910. The 1876 information, as noted in Chapter 1, was drawn from Charlotte's first city directory. All directory entries were fed into a computer, then sorted by street address. The resulting list was plotted on a copy of the Beers map of 1876, the first map showing buildings in the city (color fig. 1). A similar procedure was followed for 1889, except that no building-by-building map was available. Data were plotted on a standard street map of the period. For 1910 the city directory included a street list with residents identified by race. This information was plotted on the 1911 Sanborn Insurance Map, which showed every structure in the ward (color fig. 2).

29. Radford, "Race, Residence, and Ideology."

30. This tends to disprove the conventional wisdom that once an area became black, it would be forsaken by whites. See, for instance, Rabinowitz, *Race Relations in the Urban South*, pp. 97–98.

31. John Michael Vlach, "The Shotgun House, an African Architectural Legacy," in Upton and Vlach, *Common Places*, pp. 68–78. No one has attempted to date the spread of the idea to North Carolina, but my estimate that it arrived around 1900 jibes with available

scattered evidence. See Bainbridge and Ohno, *Wilson Historic Buildings Inventory*, p. 183; Bishir, *North Carolina Architecture*, pp. 434–38. Interestingly, Tompkins included a shotgun among his designs for rental mill cottages in *Cotton Mill*, fig. 32. A rare example clearly based on Tompkins's book stood in the 1980s at 1216 Clement Avenue near Barnhardt Manufacturing off Central Avenue in the Plaza-Midwood neighborhood.

32. Mecklenburg County Register of Deeds Office, deed book 218, p. 166. City directories showed no houses in the block until 1902. On Hood, see city directories; also advertisement for J. G. Hood & Co. Department Stores, 8 & 10 East Trade Street, in the *Charlotte News*, September 1, 1905.

33. *Charlotte Observer*, January 30, 1907; Mecklenburg County Register of Deeds Office, deed book 218, p. 166.

34. City directory, 1902. On black occupations in Southern cities, see Rabinowitz, *Race Relations in the Urban South*, pp. 60–96; Earl Lewis, *In Their Own Interests*, pp. 12–15.

35. *Charlotte Observer*, November 12, 1923. Tate's obituary ran in the *Charlotte Observer*, March 30, 1951; Greenwood, *Black Experience in Charlotte-Mecklenburg*, section 4, pp. 8–10.

36. Quoted in the *Charlotte Observer*, July 22, 1982; Greenwood, *Black Experience in Charlotte-Mecklenburg*, section 4, pp. 11–17; Greenwood, *Bittersweet Legacy*, pp. 240–42; Walls, *African Methodist Episcopal Zion Church*; Mecklenburg County Register of Deeds Office, deed book 110, p. 575; also deed book 121, p. 594; deed book 127, p. 21; deed book 139, pp. 80, 374. Photographs of Bishop Clinton and Marie Clinton appeared in the *Star of Zion*, May 1, 1924. Pictures of the bishop and his house may be found in Watson, *Colored Charlotte*.

37. *Charlotte Observer*, August 27, 1906.

38. On Clinton Chapel and Charlotte's importance as an AME Zion center, see Greenwood, *Black Experience in Charlotte-Mecklenburg*, section 3, pp. 2, 30–31; Dillard, "Negro in the Political, Economic, and Social Development of Charlotte," p. 19; Mead, *Handbook of Denominations in the United States*, pp. 146–47. On First Baptist, see Greenwood, *Black Experience in Charlotte-Mecklenburg*, section 3, pp. 2, 30–31; Dillard, "Negro in the Political, Economic, and Social Development of Charlotte," pp. 18–19. On St. Michael's Church, see *Charlotte Observer*, November 22, 1908, September 2, 1934.

39. Chesnutt, *Charles Waddell Chesnutt*, pp. 8–15; *North Carolina Authors*, pp. 19–20. Chesnutt's papers at Fisk University include the diaries he kept as a young man in Charlotte, but they focus on his tribulations as a rural summer school teacher rather than on activities in the city. Chesnutt returned to the city for a visit in 1901, giving readings at Biddle and at Grace AME Zion Church. See *Charlotte Observer*, February 25, 1901; *Charlotte News*, February 25, 1901.

40. On the school's fifteenth anniversary, see *Charlotte Observer*, October 1, 1898; see also November 22, 1908, May 13, 1914, September 2, 1934.

41. *Charlotte Chronicle*, December 18, 1888; Buggs, "Negro in Charlotte," pp. 42–45. Local tradition holds that Good Samaritan was the first or only black hospital in the South when it opened, but such was not the case. Data assembled in 1929 by the American Medical Association, "Hospital Service in the United States," listed the Georgia Infirmary in Savannah (1832), the Freedman's Hospital in the District of Columbia (1865), and the North Carolina State Hospital at Goldsboro (1880) as earlier African American hospitals. Good Sam, added onto many times, remained Charlotte's black health-care facility until the desegregation era of the 1960s. During the 1970s and 1980s it was a nursing home, then it was demolished in 1990 to make way for Ericsson Stadium. See William Huffman,

"Good Samaritan Hospital," Survey and Research Report; Greenwood, *Bittersweet Legacy*, pp. 111–12; Glenton, *Story of a Hospital*, p. 18; *Charlotte News*, June 25, 1936; Protestant Episcopal Church in the U.S., *Church's Work among Negroes*. Generally on African American hospitals, see Rice and Jones, *Public Policy and the Black Hospital*.

42. This pattern of black businesses mingled among white ones downtown also held into the 1890s in Atlanta, Georgia, and Lexington, Kentucky. See Porter, "Black Atlanta," chap. 5; White, "Black Sides of Atlanta," p. 212; Kellogg, "Formation of Black Residential Areas in Lexington," pp. 49–51.

43. Directories varied in the completeness of black coverage. This description is based on the 1897 city directory. On African American shoppers "thick on East Trade Street," see *Charlotte Observer*, August 20, 1905.

44. Burke, *Brooklyn Story*, p. 34; *Star of Zion*, March 22, 1894.

45. The Logtown name was mentioned in a Second Ward deed in the Mecklenburg County Register of Deeds Office, deed book 151, p. 641. On the 1892 Butler and Spratt "Map of Charlotte Township," a Logtown Road led in from the country toward Second Ward. See also Moore-Parker, *Biddle–Johnson C. Smith University Story*, p. 5.

46. The school was established in 1882, and the building was constructed in 1886. See Harding, "Charlotte City Schools," pp. 10–13; Greenwood, *Black Experience in Charlotte-Mecklenburg*, section 3, page 31; Dillard, "Negro in the Political, Economic, and Social Development of Charlotte," pp. 29–31; Blythe and Brockmann, *Hornets' Nest*, p. 222. For a turn-of-the-century description, see *Charlotte Observer*, May 26, 1905. Pictures are in Burke, *Brooklyn Story*, pp. 1, 12.

47. *Charlotte Chronicle*, August 20, 1887; also *Charlotte Democrat*, February 18, 1887. A black Charlotte minister echoed this observation in the *Charlotte Observer*, April 3, 1907. The phenomenon is also noted in James Anderson, *Education of Blacks in the South*.

48. *Charlotte Observer*, September 24, 1904. On debate over creating the library, see ibid., May 13, 1901, May 10, 1904. A photo is in Ryckman, *Public Library of Charlotte and Mecklenburg County*, pp. 8, 19–20. Black brick contractor W. W. Smith built the structure; see *Charlotte Observer*, March 3, 1905. Carnegie, the era's richest man and the founder of the company that became United States Steel, is remembered today for the more than 1,400 public libraries he endowed between 1889 and 1919. See Cherry, "Carnegies Live"; Bobinski, *Carnegie Libraries*. Winston and Greensboro, North Carolina, followed Charlotte's lead and had white Carnegie libraries under construction by 1905. See *Charlotte News*, July 1, 1905. Durham's Sanford L. Warren Public Library is said to be North Carolina's second-oldest black public library, ca. 1916. See Roberts, Lea, and Leary, *Durham Architectural and Historic Inventory*, p. 127.

49. *Charlotte News*, September 13, 1905; Buggs, "Negro in Charlotte," pp. 39–40. Games between the Fats and the Leans were evidently a popular fund-raising practice in Charlotte's black community. On a game benefiting Good Samaritan Hospital, see *Charlotte Observer*, April 27, 1906.

50. The earliest references I have found to Second Ward as "Brooklyn" appeared in 1897. "Dr. Houser, colored, is building a $2000 residence in Brooklyn," the *Observer* noted in July, and in November the newspaper mentioned an accident that had befallen a workman who resided there. See *Charlotte Observer*, July 15, November 6, 1897. AME Zion leaders in Charlotte would have been especially cognizant of the New York borough debate, because the denomination's "mother church" was in Manhattan. Annexation of Brooklyn, New York, was discussed in the *Star of Zion*, March 8, 1894. Brooklyn finally became a New York City borough in 1898. See Kenneth T. Jackson, *Crabgrass Frontier*, pp. 142–43.

Interestingly, Wilmington, North Carolina, also had an African American district known as Brooklyn in the late 1890s. See Prather, *We Have Taken a City*, pp. 21–22. So did Raleigh, North Carolina (personal communication with Catherine W. Bishir, Survey Coordinator, North Carolina State Historic Preservation Office, 1993).

51. City law official E. M. Shannonhouse at a meeting of the Board of Aldermen, quoted in the *Charlotte Observer*, May 6, 1902.

52. Watson, *Colored Charlotte*, unpaginated; *Charlotte Observer*, February 11, 1906. The company flourished until the Great Depression. See Greenwood, *Black Experience in Charlotte-Mecklenburg*. An earlier Charlotte-based insurance company was the People's Benevolent and Relief Association, chartered 1897. It was said to be the "oldest colored organization of its kind in North Carolina" when it went bankrupt in 1906. The association's assets were purchased by Durham's black-owned North Carolina Mutual Life Insurance Company. See *Charlotte Observer*, November 17, 18, 21, 22, 1906; Buggs, "Negro in Charlotte," pp. 28–31; Dillard, "Negro in the Political, Economic, and Social Development of Charlotte," p. 1.

African American insurance companies also emerged in several other Southern cities during the late 1890s and early 1900s. See Weare, *Black Business in the New South*; Alexa Benson Henderson, *Atlanta Life Insurance Company*.

53. Cell, *Highest Stage of White Supremacy*, pp. 258, 272–75. W. E. B. DuBois first proposed the idea of a Negro Business League, which Booker T. Washington quickly made a reality. See Harlan, *Booker T. Washington: The Making of a Black Leader*, pp. 266–71; Harlan, *Booker T. Washington: The Wizard of Tuskegee*, esp. pp. 218–19, 229; Gavins, "Urbanization and Segregation."

On black main streets, see Porter, "Black Atlanta," chap. 5; White, "Black Sides of Atlanta," p. 212; Kellogg, "Formation of Black Residential Areas in Lexington," pp. 49–51; Carter, *Urban Negro in the South*. Such commercial centers are quite similar to the "surrogate downtowns" that geographers describe within ethnic enclaves. See Michael P. Conzen, "Historical Geography," p. 94.

54. The company bought the land in 1907; see Mecklenburg County Register of Deeds Office, deed book 228, p. 248. The directors announced that plans would soon be drawn for a three-story structure costing some $15,000, with commercial space on the ground floor and offices above. See *Charlotte Observer*, December 19, 1907. The building was completed in time to appear on the 1911 Sanborn Insurance Map.

55. The Afro-American Mutual Insurance building and AME Zion Publishing House are attributed to Smith on the basis of their stylistic similarity to the M.I.C. Building, which he is known to have designed. See Hanchett, "W. W. Smith." Smith's Rock Hill building for Afro-American Mutual still stands, though the Charlotte structure is gone. Both were pictured in Watson, *Colored Charlotte*. For more on Smith, see William Huffman, "Grace AME Zion Church," Survey and Research Report; *Tenth Anniversary*.

56. Burke, *Brooklyn Story*, p. 34. The Brooklyn business district showed up clearly on the 1929 Sanborn Insurance Maps of Charlotte. W. W. Smith's building for the AME Zion Publishing House was torn down in the 1960s; the institution occupies a modern building on almost the same site in the 1990s.

57. City directories. On the movie theater, see the *Charlotte News*, August 20, 1919.

58. Williams bought the tract while on leave from Africa in 1901 and platted it during his final leave in 1905. See Mecklenburg County Register of Deeds Office, deed book 151, p. 641; deed book 190, p. 431. It is possible that the name also carried a reference to the then-

fashionable Williamsburg suburb of New York's Brooklyn. See Kenneth T. Jackson, *Encyclopedia of New York City*, p. 1264.

59. Williams bought the Hotel Williams site in 1910 and 1911; see Mecklenburg County Register of Deeds Office, deed book 256, p. 386; deed book 263, p. 445; deed book 268, p. 474. By 1914 he was mentioned in Watson, *Colored Charlotte*, as proprietor of the hotel. J. T. Sanders ran the Sanders Hotel nearby on South Caldwell Street, and the Hotel Alexander for blacks later became a fixture on North Myers Street in First Ward.

60. Information from Charlotte city directories. Williams's one-time partner, J. T. Sanders, now controlled the drugstore.

61. The house was demolished in the early 1980s; see *Charlotte Observer*, June 13, 1980. Williams used leading white architect Louis Asbury for the renovation of his residence and for the design of the Hotel Williams. See entries for May 1, 1913, July 9, 1914, and October 13, 1923, in Asbury's job book, vols. 28–29, Asbury papers.

62. Quotation from interview with Aurelia Tate Henderson, in Greenwood, "Black Experience," section 4, p. 10; William Huffman et al., "Mecklenburg Investment Company Building," National Register Nomination.

63. For the early history of these rim villages, see Chapter 1. The settlements are shown on the 1892 Butler and Spratt, "Map of Charlotte Township." Greenville and Irwinville fell to the bulldozers of urban renewal in the late 1960s and early 1970s. Blandville met the same fate a decade or so later. Two Blandville shotgun houses were moved to the grounds of the Afro-American Cultural Center in First Ward. Cherry survived into the 1990s. Its history is explored in Hanchett, "Charlotte and Its Neighborhoods"; Hanchett, "Sorting Out the New South City," pp. 285–86.

64. On the early years of Biddle Institute, the best source is George, *100 Years*, pp. 3–5. See also Moore-Parker, *Biddle–Johnson C. Smith University Story*, pp. 3–5; Greenwood, *Bittersweet Legacy*; *Charlotte Observer*, February 26, 1901; Mecklenburg County Register of Deeds Office, deed book 9, p. 323.

65. Mecklenburg County Register of Deeds Office, deed book 7, p. 512.

66. George, *100 Years*; Moore-Parker, *Biddle–Johnson C. Smith University Story*; Greenwood, *Bittersweet Legacy*. For a recollection of Sanders and Davis, see interview with Rev. Hercules Wilson in Buggs, "Negro in Charlotte," p. 35.

67. Dan L. Morrill, "Biddle Hall" and "Carter Hall," Survey and Research Reports. See also Dan L. Morrill, "Teachers' House at Johnson C. Smith University," Survey and Research Report.

68. Butler and Spratt, "Map of Charlotte Township."

69. Moore-Parker, *Biddle–Johnson C. Smith University Story*; William Huffman, "Old Carnegie Library at Johnson C. Smith University," Survey and Research Report; *Charlotte Evening Chronicle*, October 29, 1910, April 12, 14, 1911; *Charlotte Observer*, November 16, 1911.

70. *Charlotte Observer*, April 25, 27, 1903, June 9, 1906.

71. Ibid., December 23, 1905.

72. Napoleon Brown, interview with Thomas W. Hanchett in Charlotte, February 1986. Into the 1990s Biddleville's closely spaced houses and narrow streets gave it a distinct "village" feeling. Resident Barzilla Thomas recalled that all the dwellings along Campus and Solomon Streets had been there since his youth before World War I (Barzilla Thomas, interview with Thomas W. Hanchett in Charlotte, July 1981).

73. Wesley Heights represented the first Charlotte work by developer E. C. Griffith, who

later created the posh Eastover neighborhood. See William Huffman, "The Cedars," Survey and Research Report; Mecklenburg County Register of Deeds Office, map book 332, pp. 254, 272; map book 3, p. 225; records of corporations, bk. 5, p. 43; records of corporations, bk. 6, p. 51; records of corporations, bk. 10, p. 133.

74. Mecklenburg County Register of Deeds Office, map book 3, pp. 34–35.

75. Ibid., deed book 101, p. 1. Alexander also played a leading role in the development of the white Elizabeth streetcar suburb across town. See Dorothy Frye, "W. L. Alexander House," Survey and Research Report.

76. On J. T. Sanders's purchase, see Mecklenburg County Register of Deeds Office, deed book 101, p. 165. Other early sales in Western Heights are recorded in deed book 91, pp. 426, 435, 449, 560, 563; deed book 92, pp. 102, 342, 375, 479, 485; deed book 93, p. 291; deed book 98, pp. 340, 469; deed book 101, p. 184; deed book 104, pp. 168, 232, 347, 434, 496; deed book 108, p. 593; deed book 110, pp. 67, 515; deed book 112, p. 150; deed book 123, p. 328; deed book 127, p. 458; deed book 134, p. 461; deed book 139, p. 387; deed book 140, p. 165; deed book 144, pp. 410, 428–30; deed book 170, p. 420.

77. Fields, *Lemon Swamp and Other Tales*, pp. 156–73. The first city directory to list Flint Street, 1918, showed the 100 block as white and the 200 block as black. Her house is no longer standing.

78. Many of these, along Frazier and Summit Avenues, were bulldozed in 1983 and replaced by public housing.

79. Watson, *Colored Charlotte*. A copy of the pamphlet is in the Special Collections Room of the library at Queens College. A brief story about the pamphlet appeared in the *Star of Zion*, January 7, 1915.

80. J. T. Sanders was a particularly energetic businessman and community leader. He owned one of the city's three black hotels, the Sanders Hotel on South Caldwell Street, and was a partner with J. T. Williams in the Queen City Drug Store. On Sanders's banking activities, see the *Charlotte Observer*, June 24, 1897. On his real estate dealings, see n. 76 above. He also practiced as a lawyer; see Clarkson, *History of the Law Library Association*, p. 3. In 1905 Sanders challenged Jim Crow politics and ran—unsuccessfully—for alderman from Second Ward; see *Charlotte Observer*, April 1, 1905. See also Greenwood, *Bittersweet Legacy*.

81. According to Spear, *Black Chicago*, p. 23n, "The Negro class structure . . . does not always correspond with the white class structure. The Negro upper class, for instance, includes professional people, whose white counterparts are usually considered middle class. At the same time, postal clerks, Pullman porters, waiters and other occupational groups that would belong in the upper lower class among whites have traditionally formed the core of the Negro middle class." See also Katzman, *Before the Ghetto*, esp. pp. 29–31, 135–74.

82. Watson, *Colored Charlotte*; Mecklenburg County Register of Deeds Office, map book 230, p. 228. For the project, Alexander formed a partnership called Freehold Realty with white partners John M. Scott and A. M. McDonald. See Mecklenburg County Register of Deeds Office, records of corporations, bk. 3, p. 468; records of corporations, bk. 6, p. 345. On subsequent development of the neighborhood, see Hanchett, "Sorting Out the New South City," p. 297.

Washington Heights may have been the first black streetcar suburb in the South. No other examples are known in North Carolina. Further afield, black developer Heman Perry created a black suburb for Atlanta in the 1920s. See White, "Black Sides of Atlanta," p. 219; Ambrose, "Redrawing the Color Line," pp. 81–82.

83. Mecklenburg County Register of Deeds Office, map book 230, p. 228. Many individ-

ual lot deeds mention that land is reserved for Lincoln Park. For instance, see Mecklenburg County Register of Deeds Office, deed book 358, p. 598. Today a church and apartments fill that hollow along Pitts Drive (originally Park Drive).

84. Watson, *Colored Charlotte*.

85. *Charlotte Chronicle*, September 23, 1912.

86. Information on early lot buyers is based on Mecklenburg County Register of Deeds Office, grantor records for Freehold Realty. Though Washington Heights streets were not listed in the city directory until much later, individual lot buyers sometimes did appear in the alphabetical section of the directory.

87. *Star of Zion*, June 8, 1916; Mecklenburg County Register of Deeds Office, deed book 312, p. 308.

88. Ads for Lethia Jones's salon may be found in Charlotte city directories. A profile of Jones appeared in the *Charlotte Observer*, March 15, 1945. Wanda Hendricks, a researcher for the Charlotte Mecklenburg Historic Properties Commission, interviewed Jones's niece Mabel Hunt in Charlotte, August 1984.

89. On Douglassville and Watson Park, see Watson, *Colored Charlotte*. H. L. McCrorey later took over Douglassville's development; today residents call it McCrorey Heights.

90. Though the story gives no attribution to the ideas, it seems likely that they were W. S. Alexander's. See *Charlotte Observer*, September 22, 1912. See also *Charlotte Chronicle*, September 23, 1912.

CHAPTER 6

1. *Charlotte Observer*, February 10, 1900; *Charlotte News*, August 10, 1900.

2. Kenneth T. Jackson, *Crabgrass Frontier*; Fishman, *Bourgeois Utopias*; Robert A. M. Stern, *Anglo-American Suburb*; Stilgoe, *Borderland*. On the suburban home, see David P. Handlin, *American Home*; Clark, *American Family Home*; Gowans, *Comfortable House*; Gwendolyn Wright, *Building the Dream*; Marsh, *Suburban Lives*. On early twentieth century suburban real estate development, see Worley, *J. C. Nichols*; Weiss, *Community Builders*; Bishir and Earley, *Early Twentieth-Century Suburbs*; Warner, *Streetcar Suburbs*.

3. *Charlotte Chronicle*, May 20, 1891; Mecklenburg County Register of Deeds Office, deed book 81, pp. 1, 55.

4. F. C. Abbott, *Fifty Years in Charlotte Real Estate*, pp. 17–18. For a picture, see *Charlotte Observer*, July 14, 1897. The school had met in temporary quarters during the 1896–97 school year. Elizabeth College was *not* a parent of today's Queens College. Queens grew out of an 1890s downtown institution called Presbyterian College. See McEwen, *Queens College Yesterday and Today*.

Women's colleges constituted a trend across the South in these years, reflecting the growth of a white-collar class that did not need to put daughters to work in the family craft shop or farm. See Horowitz, *Alma Mater*; Bledstein, *Culture of Professionalism*; Dean, "Learning to Be New Women."

5. Quotations from an advertisement, *Charlotte Observer*, August 4, 1906. See also "New Teachers at Elizabeth" in the same issue.

6. For more on the other Elizabeth subdivisions, read Hanchett, "Charlotte and Its Neighborhoods"; Hanchett, "Sorting Out the New South City," chap. 6.

7. William Huffman, "Walter Brem House," Survey and Research Report; Blythe and Brockmann, *Hornets' Nest*, pp. 305, 309. Charlotte National became part of Wachovia Bank in the 1950s.

8. Abbott arrived in Charlotte in 1897, having first come to North Carolina's mountains for his health. See *Charlotte Observer*, November 13, 1897. The *Observer* surely had Abbott in mind two years later when it noted the existence of a new profession in the city: "Modern industrial conditions have developed 'the promoter,'" one who "studies and proposes plans for profitable development" (*Charlotte Observer*, September 19, 1899). See Abbott's memoir, *Fifty Years in Charlotte Real Estate*; F. C. Abbott, *North Carolina's Finest Town*. A brief biographical sketch upon his election as head of the Charlotte Chamber of Commerce appeared in the *Charlotte News*, January 9, 1901.

9. *Charlotte Observer*, December 15, 1943; Kratt and Hanchett, *Legacy*, pp. 16–22. Among Stephens's earliest visits to Charlotte was one to give a talk on athletics at the YMCA. See *Charlotte Observer*, December 19, 1897. Off the field at Chapel Hill, Stephens had showed a similar leadership ability and affinity for new ideas. He won the presidency of the Athletic Association and the campus YMCA. As a part-time job, he worked for the state geologist on North Carolina's Good Roads campaign. Mecklenburg ranked among the leading counties in the campaign. See McKown, "Roads and Reform"; *Charlotte Democrat*, March 27, 1896.

10. Barrier, *On Carolina's Gridiron*, p. 55; *Collier's Weekly*, October 20, 1928. Thanks to Lew Powell and Mary Kratt for tracking down this story.

11. The Myers farmland is shown on Butler and Spratt, "Map of Charlotte Township." The tract was divided into 286 lots. See F. C. Abbott, *Fifty Years in Charlotte Real Estate*. Spratt's Piedmont Park design was described in the *Charlotte Observer*, July 8, 189; see also ad, October 12, 1899. It included present-day Sunnyside, Jackson, Piedmont, Prospect, and Beaumont Avenues. See Mecklenburg County Register of Deeds Office, deed book 146, p. 206. W. R. Myers obituary appeared in the *Charlotte Observer*, February 24, 1901.

12. A trolley eventually ran along Central Avenue. See *Charlotte Observer*, March 24, May 7, 10, 1901. Another was completed along Seventh Street in 1902. See ibid., March 8, 14, 1902.

13. Language was identical in the first two restricted deeds in Piedmont Park, March 6 and May 24, 1901. See Mecklenburg County Register of Deeds Office, deed book 150, p. 505; deed book 151, p. 457. Mecklenburg deeds are recorded in roughly chronological order, making it easy to page through the books until the first covenants appear. Prior to Piedmont Park, the only hint of restriction had been along the boulevard in Dilworth, which required 25-foot setbacks and a $1,250 minimum cost beginning about 1898 (Mecklenburg County Register of Deeds Office, deed book 129, p. 128). No other Dilworth lots carried any restrictions, and not even boulevard deeds mentioned race (for instance, Mecklenburg County Register of Deeds Office, deed book 129, p. 9). See also Chapter 2 above.

14. Greater Charlotte Club, *Queen Charlotte, the Hydro-Electric Center*.

15. Wiebe, *Search for Order*.

16. A comprehensive history of the use of deed restrictions in U.S. cities is greatly needed. The primary research that has been done so far is mostly by historians looking at single cities or by specialists in real estate law who have limited interest in how use of the tool changed over time. See Worley, *J. C. Nichols*, pp. 124–55; Weiss, *Community Builders*, pp. 68–72; Ebner, *Creating Chicago's North Shore*, pp. 67–68; Stach, "Deed Restrictions and Subdivision Development in Columbus"; Burgess, *Planning for the Private Interest*; Savage, *Architecture of the Private Streets of St. Louis*, pp. 6–8; Hunter, *Westmoreland and Portland Places*, pp. 21–22; Stilgoe, *Borderland*, pp. 223–24; Monchow, *Use of Deed Restrictions*. For a period argument in favor of restrictions, see Charlotte landscape architect Earle Sumner Draper, "Landscape Artist's Concept of Subdivisions." In 1948, in the landmark

case of *Shelley v. Kraemer*, the Supreme Court ruled that racial covenants were unenforceable. See Kluger, *Simple Justice*, pp. 118–20, 246–55; Vose, *Caucasians Only*. Today nonracial deed restrictions are still a fairly common tool for controlling land use in new upperincome subdivisions.

17. For instance, Mecklenburg County Register of Deeds Office, deed book 291, p. 530.

18. For instance, ibid., deed book 358, p. 599.

19. Naturalistic landscape architecture had originated in England, then came to the United States with the "rural cemetery" movement of the 1830s and 1840s. Olmsted subsequently introduced it to American urban park and neighborhood design. See Schuyler, *New Urban Landscape*; Cranz, *Politics of Park Design*; Schultz, *Constructing Urban Culture*, pp. 154–61; Roper, *FLO*; Zaitzevsky, *Frederick Law Olmsted and the Boston Park System*; Boyer, *Urban Masses and Moral Order*, pp. 54–64; Reps, *Making of Urban America*, pp. 339–48; Newton, *Design on the Land*; Archer, "Country and City in the American Romantic Suburb"; Hanchett, "Before Olmsted."

20. William Huffman, "Settler's Cemetery," Survey and Research Report.

21. Kratt and Hanchett, *Legacy*, p. 21.

22. Latta tried again and again to get the city to take over the various amenities he had installed in Dilworth. For instance, see Charlotte City Council Minutes, April 2, 1894.

23. *Charlotte Observer*, November 13, 1903; *Charlotte News*, February 2, March 8, 1904.

24. Mecklenburg County Register of Deeds Office, deed book 146, p. 206. This would eventually become an arm of Independence Park known as the Sunnyside Rose Garden. Independence Boulevard obliterated it in the 1940s.

25. Dan L. Morrill, "Independence Park," Survey and Research Report; Kratt and Hanchett, *Legacy*, pp. 21–22.

26. The name harked back to the Mecklenburg Declaration of Independence. See Dan L. Morrill, "Independence Park," Survey and Research Report; also, *Charlotte Observer*, August 5, 1904.

27. Hancock, "John Nolen and the American City Planning Movement"; Hancock, *John Nolen*; John Hancock, "John Nolen: The Background of a Pioneer Planner," in Krueckeberg, *American Planner*, pp. 37–57. Nolen's extensive papers form collection 2903 in the Department of Manuscripts and Archives at Cornell University. See Kratt and Hanchett, *Legacy*, pp. 23–30.

28. Buder, *Visionaries and Planners*; Girouard, *English Town*, pp. 308–9.

29. Kratt and Hanchett, *Legacy*, p. 24.

30. For instance, there seem to have been at least two sets of drawings for Settlers Cemetery, one published in the *Charlotte Observer*, May 7, 1906, and a more extensive one noted in Nolen's job book in June 1907. Other evidence of the piecemeal nature of Nolen's Park and Tree Commission work may be gleaned from the *Charlotte Observer*, March 29, 1907. Two years after Nolen was first engaged, it reported that a topographical map of the Independence Park land had just been sent north and Nolen was preparing a scheme for a drive through the property. No overall Independence Park plan survives among Nolen's papers at Cornell University.

31. Quoted in Kratt and Hanchett, *Legacy*, p. 28. The reprinted speeches are in scrapbooks in the Nolen papers. See, for instance, the *Charlotte Observer*, April 20, 1907. The *Observer* took a special interest in Nolen's work because its owner was D. A. Tompkins, Park and Tree Commission chairman.

32. Nolen job book, Nolen papers; Hanchett, "John Nolen and the Planning of Savannah's Daffin Park."

33. Nolen job book, Nolen papers; Hanchett, "John Nolen and the Planning of Savannah's Daffin Park"; Kratt and Hanchett, *Legacy*, pp. 25–26; *Charlotte Observer*, August 24, 25, 1905.

34. A private resort for wealthy business leaders and their families, Kanuga included a lodge and more than fifty cottages. See *Charlotte Evening Chronicle*, July 23, 1910; *Charlotte Observer*, December 15, 1943. Today Kanuga is a retreat operated by the Episcopal Church.

35. The absence of stores was a pattern in elite suburbs all over America. See Stilgoe, *Borderland*, pp. 208–12; Conzen and Conzen, "Geographical Structure in Nineteenth Century Urban Retailing"; Michael P. Conzen, "Historical Geography," esp. p. 94.

36. On St. Martin's Church, see *Charlotte Observer*, April 6, 1912; *St. Martin's Chapel*. On Hawthorne Lane Methodist, funded by developer B. D. Heath and department store owner J. B. Ivey, both of whom lived nearby in Piedmont Park, see *Charlotte Observer*, April 17, 1942. The desire of some white-collar congregations to distance themselves from blue-collar Charlotte was explicitly stated by Methodist minister Gilbert T. Rowe, *Charlotte Observer*, August 2, 1903.

37. Dorothy Frye, "Staten Mansion," Survey and Research Report; William Huffman, "William Henry Belk Mansion," Survey and Research Report. Information on other residents in this paragraph and the next is from city directories.

38. On the uses of architecture to create social distance, see Glassie, *Folk Housing in Middle Virginia*; Bronner, "Manner Books and Suburban Houses," p. 65; Rybczynski, *Home*, esp. p. 39; Williams, *Homeplace*, pp. 60, 93.

39. On the symbolism of the suburban lawn, see Kenneth T. Jackson, *Crabgrass Frontier*, pp. 54–61; Groth, "Lot, Yard, and Garden," pp. 29–35; Jenkins, *Lawn*. Southern commentators have sometimes pointed to the region's recent agrarian heritage as one reference point for suburban lawns. This may be the case, but front lawns had not always been a fixture of Southern towns. The houses built for wealthy Charlotteans in the early nineteenth century around Independence Square fronted directly on the street. The pattern can also be seen at Colonial Williamsburg.

40. Descriptions of this post-Victorian shift are in Gwendolyn Wright, *Moralism and the Model Home*; Hanchett, "Four Square House"; Gowans, *Comfortable House*; Bishir, *North Carolina Architecture*.

41. Nye, *Bill Nye*, pp. 321–23. Charlotte newspapers carried Nye's column from time to time and may have printed this one. See, for instance, the *Charlotte News*, February 6, 1904.

42. That first Colonial house for J. Frank Wilkes on Morehead Street no longer stands. See *Charlotte Observer*, September 19, 1894; Morrill and Little-Stokes, "Architectural Analysis." Hook's new distaste for Victorian extravagance was probably triggered partly by his visit to the 1893 World's Columbian Exposition in Chicago, where he admired both the neoclassical designs and the stripped-down modernism of architect Louis Sullivan. Hook described his trip in the *Charlotte Observer*, September 28, 1893. Hook's career is explored in depth in a thesis by Michelle Michael, "Rise of the Regional Architect."

43. *Charlotte Observer*, December 20, 1903; Bishir, *North Carolina Architecture*, pp. 418–25; Charlotte V. Brown, "The Day of the Great Cities: The Professionalization of Building, 1900–1945," in Bishir et al., *Architects and Builders in North Carolina*, pp. 298–302. Hook's belief in the deeper social significance of refined taste was quite similar to that of Rev. Gilbert T. Rowe, in Chapter 4 of the present book.

44. *Charlotte Observer*, September 19, 1899, April 4, 1902. Heath's house became a

church fellowship hall in 1937 and was subsequently demolished. A Salvation Army thrift store stood on its site in 1995. See *Charlotte News*, August 22, 1937.

45. Dorothy Frye, "Staten Mansion," Survey and Research Report; William Huffman, "William Henry Belk Mansion," Survey and Research Report.

46. The term "Rectilinear" was coined by Hasbrouk and Sprague, *Survey of Historic Architecture*, pp. 8–14, 16–19. For discussions of Rectilinear or Four Square architecture, see Hanchett, "Four Square House"; Bishir, *North Carolina Architecture*, p. 425; Gowans, *Comfortable House*, pp. 84–93; Poore and Labine, *Old House Journal Compendium*, pp. 13–14.

Charlotteans did not take up every popular post-Victorian style during the 1900s and 1910s. As in other matters, they picked and chose among the items on the national menu. In the Midwest, Chicago architect Frank Lloyd Wright introduced the Prairie style, which radically abandoned familiar house shapes and interior arrangements. To Charlotteans, as to many Southerners, the low-slung Prairie houses seemed too much of a break with custom. Not a single residential example of the style appeared in the city during the first two decades of the twentieth century.

47. *Charlotte News*, January 14, 1904; William H. Huffman and Thomas W. Hanchett, "Charles W. Parker House," Survey and Research Report.

48. Lancaster, *American Bungalow*; Lancaster, "American Bungalow"; King, *Bungalow*; King, "Bungalow"; Gwendolyn Wright, *Building the Dream*, pp. 158–76; Clark, *American Family Home*, pp. 171–92; Gowans, *Comfortable House*, pp. 74–83. Bungalows were extremely popular among North Carolinians. See Bishir, *North Carolina Architecture*, pp. 426–30. One of the state's earliest was for D. G. Maxwell, outside Charlotte, a house "built on the plan of a bungalow, with a veranda all around it. It will be rustic in design, the outer walls being finished in cedar slabs" (*Charlotte Observer*, February 20, 1901).

49. *Charlotte Observer*, May 28, 1911.

50. "Mr. Fred L. Bonfoey, a well-known architect in this city . . . has made a specialty of bungalows, and during the course of the past year has designed more than 50 of these homes, which have become so popular with residents of the Queen City" (ibid., May 26, 1911). Building permits for two of the houses in the row on East Eighth Street show Bonfoey as the architect; the others list no designer but are likely also by him.

51. Dorothy Frye, "Crowell-Kemp House," Survey and Research Report. On Hal Kemp, see the *Charlotte Observer*, March 1, 1932, April 12, 1933, December 22, 1940; Kinkle, *Complete Encyclopedia of Popular Music and Jazz*, entries 542, 1003, 1841.

52. For histories of subdivisions listed in this paragraph, read Hanchett, "Charlotte and Its Neighborhoods." A 1924 Chamber of Commerce brochure emphasized the existence of desirable suburbs at every point of the compass. See Wade Hampton Harris, *Charlotte*, p. 40; similarly, *Charlotte Observer*, February 10, 1900.

53. On Chatham Estates, read Hanchett, "Charlotte and Its Neighborhoods"; Hanchett, "Sorting Out the New South City."

54. Hanchett, "Charlotte and Its Neighborhoods"; Hanchett, "Sorting Out the New South City"; Bradbury, *Dilworth*.

55. Hanchett, "Before Olmsted"; White and Kramer, *Olmsted South*; Sanders, "Frederick Law Olmsted's Plan for Druid Hills"; Schalck, "Planning Roland Park."

56. Kenneth T. Jackson, *Crabgrass Frontier*, p. 341, also p. 76.

57. A list of dividends for various Charlotte businesses during 1906 showed W. S. Alexander's Southern Real Estate declaring a 50 percent return, compared with the First National Bank at 10 percent. See *Charlotte Observer*, January 11, 1907. The profitability, not

surprisingly, led to a boom in the number of real estate companies in the city. See ibid., February 6, 1907.

58. Hays, *Conservation and the Gospel of Efficiency*. On the growing romanticization of nature during the nineteenth and early twentieth centuries, see Schmitt, *Back to Nature*; Machor, *Pastoral Cities*; Burns, *Pastoral Inventions*; Stilgoe, *Borderland*; Reps, *Making of Urban America*, pp. 339–48; Archer, "Country and City in the American Romantic Suburb."

59. Mel Scott, *American City Planning*, pp. 47–109; Schuyler, *New Urban Landscape*; Peterson, "City Beautiful Movement." William H. Wilson, *City Beautiful Movement*, suggests that the Columbian Exposition was only one of the inspirations for the movement. An essay, "The City Beautiful," appeared in the *Charlotte News*, April 8, 1901.

60. There is abundant scholarly literature on the urban Progressives. For instance, see Schiesl, *Politics of Efficiency*; Stave, *Urban Bosses, Machines, and Progressive Reformers*; Hays, "Politics of Reform in Municipal Government."

61. Mel Scott, *American City Planning*, pp. 163–66; Glaab and Brown, *History of Urban America*, pp. 251–68.

62. Silver, "Changing Faces of Neighborhoods," p. 111. For background on this ideal in the social sciences, see Melvin, *Organic City*. One of the few dissents against the ideal of the homogeneous neighborhood in the first half of the twentieth century was Isaacs, "Neighborhood Unit as an Instrument for Segregation."

63. "Except for Lewis Mumford, Nolen also was perhaps the profession's most versatile and prolific writer, producing six books, more than one hundred major articles, reports, technical monographs, and many minor papers" (Hancock, *John Nolen*, pp. 16–17). See also Hancock, "John Nolen and the American City Planning Movement," esp. pp. 41–42; John Hancock, "John Nolen: The Background of a Pioneer Planner," in Krueckeberg, *American Planner*, pp. 37–57.

64. Nolen, *Replanning Small Cities*, p. 146. See also Nolen, *City Planning*, pp. 37, 76–85; Nolen, *New Ideals in the Planning of Cities, Towns, and Villages*, pp. 96–100.

65. Nolen, *Replanning Small Cities*, pp. 94–95.

66. Ibid., p. 10.

67. John Nolen, "Neponset Garden Village, East Walpole, Mass.: General Plan and Recommendations," 1913, bound typescript in Nolen papers; Engst and Hickerson, *Urban America*, pp. 8–9, 43. See also Nolen's 1916 Kistler Industrial Village in Nolen, *New Towns for Old*, pp. 66–74.

68. Nolen, *New Towns for Old*, pp. 62–64; Wolfe, *Kingsport, Tennessee*, p. 51; Nolen, *Comprehensive City Plan*, p. 65.

69. Nolen, *New Towns for Old*, p. 110.

70. Ibid.

71. Nolen, *Replanning Small Cities*, p. 2. See also Olmsted and Nolen, "Public Open Space in American Towns and Cities."

72. Nolen, *Replanning Small Cities*, p. 156.

73. Hanchett, "Sorting Out the New South City," chap. 7.

74. Ibid.

75. The following discussion of Myers Park draws on Kratt and Hanchett, *Legacy*; Thomas W. Hanchett, "Myers Park Historic District," National Register Nomination; Hanchett, "Charlotte and Its Neighborhoods," chaps. 2 and 8. Stephens, Draper, and Wood formed the original Stephens Company. Lee and a man named John M. Miller Jr.,

about whom little is known, joined a few months later. See Mecklenburg County Register of Deeds Office, records of corporations, bk. 3, pp. 215, 333; see also bk. 4, p. 407; bk. 7, p. 310; bk. 10, p. 152; bk. 12, p. 495; bk. 18, p. 591.

76. "For Rent: Nice five acre Suburban Home with new six-room cottage. Large porches. Good well of water and barn. On Providence Road at Myers Park" (*Charlotte News*, June 11, 1904). W. R. Myers sometimes also referred to this cluster of suburban homesites as Central Park. See *Charlotte Observer*, June 13, 1904; see also April 9, 15, 1905, August 15, 1906.

77. Claiborne, "*Charlotte Observer*," pp. 140–67.

78. *Manufacturers Record*, November 3, 1921.

79. Nolen, *Replanning Small Cities*; James Arthur Glass, "John Nolen and the Planning of New Towns"; Thomas W. Henderson, *John Nolen's City Planning Work in the South*.

80. Nolen plan book, Nolen papers; Hancock, *John Nolen*; Robert A. M. Stern, *Anglo-American Suburb*, p. 63.

81. Hancock, *John Nolen*, p. 16.

82. *New York Times*, February 19, 1937. Evidence suggests that Nolen was America's second most prolific planner during the 1910s and 1920s, surpassed only by Harland Bartholomew. See Norman J. Johnston, "Harland Bartholomew: Precedent for the Profession," in Krueckeberg, *American Planner*, pp. 283–84.

83. Nolen, *New Towns for Old*, p. 100.

84. Worley, *J. C. Nichols*, esp. p. 78.

85. Nolen, *New Towns for Old*, p. 103.

86. Ibid., p. 101.

87. Ibid., p. 103.

88. *Charlotte Observer*, August 29, 1912, quoted in Dan L. Morrill, "Myers Park Streetcar Waiting Stations," Survey and Research Report. There are indications that smaller gates were planned, and possibly built, where Arsdley Road and Colonial Avenue meet Providence Road. See *Charlotte Observer*, October 10, 1912; *Manufacturers Record*, July 4, 1912; Frank Thies Jr., interview with Thomas W. Hanchett in Charlotte, May 1984.

89. Zunz, *Changing Face of Inequality*; Ebner, *Creating Chicago's North Shore*.

90. McEwen, *Queens College Yesterday and Today*; *Charlotte Observer*, December 5, 1943.

91. "Revised Sketch of Stores Group," March 1912, in map case in Nolen papers. A similar row built in Roland Park in 1896 is sometimes credited as America's first suburban shopping center. Other scholars, including historian Kenneth Jackson, point to projects begun in the 1910s in Kansas City's Country Club District. Interestingly, it was John Nolen who planned the Country Club District's first major such facility, Brookside Shops (later known as Colonial Shops), in 1915. See Worley, *J. C. Nichols*, pp. 33, 236–41; Kenneth T. Jackson, *Crabgrass Frontier*, p. 258. Myers Park's limited retail facilities in its early years were part of a nationwide custom in elite suburbs. See Conzen and Conzen, "Geographical Structure in Nineteenth Century Urban Retailing"; Michael P. Conzen, "Historical Geography," esp. p. 94; Stilgoe, *Borderland*, pp. 208–12.

92. Constructed in 1917, the Community Store was a small, two-story structure set back from the street and designed to "look more like a residence than a store" (*Charlotte News*, May 4, 1917). Later, in the 1920s, Earle Sumner Draper designed a small strip of shops on Morehead Street, just outside Myers Park. Much altered during succeeding decades, it was replaced by a new shopping strip in the 1980s. See Kratt and Hanchett, *Legacy*, pp. 58–59,

142. Ironically, the intersection of Queens and Providence eventually became the neighborhood's main commercial district, with a gaggle of stores opposite the Presbyterian and Methodist churches, much less graceful than Nolen's 1911 proposal.

93. Earle Sumner Draper, interview with Earle Sumner Draper Jr. on behalf of the Myers Park Homeowners Association, at Vero Beach, Florida, June 1971, transcript and tapes in Draper interviews. The playlot was shown on the 1911 map of Myers Park printed in Nolen, *New Towns for Old*, p. 102. Residents remember that the playground remained in use until the first generation of Myers Park youngsters grew up; then it was closed, and the land was split up among adjoining property owners.

94. See Myers Park, vertical file in the Robinson-Spangler Carolina Room, Public Library of Charlotte and Mecklenburg County; also see present-day property tax records.

95. Hope that the greenways would be built remained alive as late as 1921, when Draper wrote, "Natural features such as ravines and borders of streams are reserved as parkways and planted for future development as part of the park system of Charlotte" (*Manufacturers Record*, November 3, 1921).

96. Virtually all of the Myers Park drawings survive in the Nolen papers.

97. Earle Sumner Draper, interview with Earle Sumner Draper Jr. on behalf of the Myers Park Homeowners Association, at Vero Beach, Florida, June 1971, transcript and tapes in Draper interviews.

98. On Draper's important planning career, see Thomas W. Hanchett, "Earle Sumner Draper: City Planner of the New South," in Bishir and Earley, *Early Twentieth-Century Suburbs*, pp. 78–79; Kratt and Hanchett, *Legacy*; Newton, *Design on the Land*, pp. 487–89, 500–502; *Who's Who in America* (1930), p. 712; Kay Haire Huggins, "Town Planning in the New South"; Kay Haire Huggins, "Town Planning in North Carolina," p. 19.

On Draper's mill village designs, see Margaret Crawford, "Earle S. Draper and the Company Town in the American South," in Garner, *Company Town*, pp. 139–72; Brent Glass, "Southern Mill Hills." When Harvard planning expert Arthur Comey toured American new towns for a government report in 1939, he singled out Draper's work for highest praise. See Comey and Wehrly, "Planned Communities," esp. p. 24.

Draper's work for the Tennessee Valley Authority is discussed in Garner, *Model Company Town*, pp. 48–49; Creese, *TVA's Public Planning*. On Draper's TVA and Federal Housing Administration careers, see Mel Scott, *American City Planning*, pp. 312–15, 338, 353–54, 381.

Draper's papers are scattered and no complete list is known to exist of his work. Small Draper collections are in the archives of Duke University and Cornell University. John Nolen's personal collection of newspaper and magazine clippings, now at the University of North Carolina, Chapel Hill, includes a helpful file on Draper. In Charlotte the Myers Park Homeowners Association, Earle Sumner Draper Jr., and Harold Bursley Jr. (son of the man who took over Draper's practice in the 1930s) have modest collections of Draper material.

99. Earle Sumner Draper, interview with Earle Sumner Draper Jr., at Vero Beach, Florida, June 1971, transcript and tapes in Draper interviews; Earle Sumner Draper, interview with Thomas W. Hanchett at Vero Beach, Florida, August 1982. Nationally, a "planting craze . . . swept the borderlands after 1910, . . . a defense against mass society" (Stilgoe, *Borderland*, pp. 199, 206). In 1915 Draper also worked one day per week supervising construction of Nolen's industrial new town of Kingsport, Tennessee. See Wolfe, *Kingsport, Tennessee*, pp. 38–56.

100. *The Garden Magazine*, November 1919; *Manufacturers Record*, November 3, 1921;

Hagler and Nolen, "Town Planning Actualities"; Nolen, *New Towns for Old*, pp. 104–5; "Tree Cost Sheet," box 23, Nolen papers; Earle Sumner Draper, interview with Earle Sumner Draper Jr., at Vero Beach, Florida, June 1971, transcript and tapes in Draper interviews.

101. The 1912 Wade house was demolished to make way for a fancier dwelling in the 1920s. See William Huffman, "H. M. Wade House," "John Jamison House," and "Charles Moody House," Survey and Research Reports.

Construction dates for all houses in Myers Park were determined through the use of Charlotte water permit records (for houses built before the mid-1920s) and city directories (for houses from the mid-1920s onward). Dates are accurate to within two years.

102. Dan L. Morrill, "Lynnwood, the James B. Duke Mansion," Survey and Research Report.

103. Maynor, *Duke Power*; Tullos, *Habits of Industry*, pp. 161–71.

104. Charlotte Chamber of Commerce, *Charlotte, North Carolina*. On the national context of the shift from Bungalow to Colonial and Tudor styles in the 1920s, see Gowans, *Comfortable House*. See also George E. Thomas, "Architectural Patronage and Social Stratification in Philadelphia between 1840 and 1920," in Cutler and Gillette, *Divided Metropolis*, pp. 85–123.

105. Elsewhere in Charlotte, Keen did the Charles Lambeth House on Hermitage Road in Myers Park and the Charlotte Country Club in Plaza Midwood. Keen's work in Charlotte, Winston-Salem, and the golf resort of Pinehurst offers an indication of the degree to which North Carolina's business leaders were becoming an interlocking elite by the 1910s. See Davyd Foard Hood, "Winston Salem's Suburbs: West End to Reynolda Park," in Bishir and Earley, *Early Twentieth-Century Suburbs*, pp. 64–67; Bishir, *North Carolina Architecture*, pp. 446, 491.

106. Bishir, *North Carolina Architecture*, pp. 439–40.

107. At his peak Draper employed twenty to thirty assistants in Charlotte, with branch offices in Atlanta, Washington, D.C., and New York City. Among Draper's 100 elite neighborhoods are Forest Hills in Durham, Eastover in Charlotte, Hayes Barton in Raleigh, Emorywood in High Point, and Mayview Manor in Blowing Rock, plus Farmington at Charlottesville, Virginia, and Sequoia Hills at Knoxville, Tennessee. Through contacts made in Myers Park with the piedmont's textile men, Draper was also able to win commissions to plan nearly 150 mill villages, including the new towns of Spindale, North Carolina, and Chicopee, Georgia. In 1933 Draper left Charlotte to be chief planner with the Tennessee Valley Authority and later became a top official at the new Federal Housing Administration. See n. 98 above.

CHAPTER 7

1. Scholars attribute the nineteenth century rise of the downtown to changes wrought by industrialization, and they note a trend toward greater clustering of functions within the downtown as the century progressed. See Ward, "Industrial Revolution and the Emergence of Boston's Central Business District"; Martyn J. Bowden, "Growth of the Central Districts in Large Cities," in Schnore, *New Urban History*, pp. 75–109; Vance, "Emerging Patterns of Commercial Structure in American Cities"; Conzen and Conzen, "Geographical Structure in Nineteenth Century Urban Retailing"; John M. Marshall, "Residential Expansion and Central-City Change," in Blumenstein and Walter, *Growing Metropolis*, pp. 33–64; Goldfield and Brownell, *Urban America*, pp. 113–18.

2. *Charlotte Observer*, August 5, 1897.

3. Wade Hampton Harris, *Charlotte*, p. 26.

4. On the Kress chain, see Thomas, "Five and Dime Design." On the manager of that first Charlotte Kress Store, who went on to cofound the Iveys Department Store chain, see "David Ovens." Charlotte dime stores moved frequently, competing to create larger and finer buildings. The best-remembered Kress stood in the first block of South Tryon from the 1930s until it was demolished to make way for NCNB tower in the 1970s. The longest-lived Woolworth was a 1939 Art Deco structure a block away on North Tryon, which fell about 1990 to make way for another NCNB (NationsBank) tower.

5. By 1929 regional and national chain stores accounted for 37.83 percent of retail sales in Charlotte. See Edna May Douglas, "Analysis of the Retail Trading Area of Charlotte," pp. 147–59, 212. The rise of chain stores was a nationwide phenomenon during the 1910s and 1920s. See Atherton, *Main Street on the Middle Border*, pp. 240–41; Pusateri, *History of American Business*, pp. 277–80.

6. On Colonel Peters's nickelodeons, see *Charlotte Observer*, February 13, 1907. On the Carolina's opening, see ibid., March 6, 1927; Dan L. Morrill, "Old Carolina Theater," Survey and Research Report. Charlotte had no "theater district." Movie houses were scattered along the most desirable shopping streets. Other chain-owned theaters included the Imperial on South Tryon, the Alhambra on North Tryon, and the Charlotte on West Trade.

7. *Charlotte Observer*, June 1, 1904. Barringer had brought the very first auto to Charlotte "two years ago," according to the *Charlotte Observer*, May 8, 1903. In 1903 he announced he was "distributing agent" for Oldsmobiles. See ibid., July 8, 1903; Kratt, *Charlotte*, 1st ed., pp. 99–101; Blythe and Brockmann, *Hornets' Nest*, pp. 301–2, 372–73; *Charlotte: The Center*, January 1921, p. 7; *Charlotte Observer*, March 10, 1968.

8. Ford operated a parts distribution center in the city starting about 1915, then in 1924 built a full-fledged assembly plant out on Statesville Road: "Biggest Ford Plant in South to be Located at Charlotte" and employ 600 to 800 workers (*Charlotte Observer*, November 11, 1923; see also Wade Hampton Harris, *Charlotte*, pp. 17–18). Henry Ford's scheme to decentralize assembly proved short lived. The Charlotte plant manufactured Model Ts and Model As but then was shut down along with most of Ford's other regional assembly plants about 1932. The sprawling facility on Statesville Road was used during World War II as a Quartermaster Depot for the U.S. Army and remains in good condition today. See Kratt, *Charlotte*, 1st ed., p. 101; Blythe and Brockmann, *Hornets' Nest*, p. 301; Edgar Thompson, *Agricultural Mecklenburg and Industrial Charlotte*, pp. 145–46.

"Charlotte is one of the South's great automotive trade centers. . . . [In the] City of Charlotte . . . the number of persons whose livelihood is directly or indirectly gained from Carolinas automobile trade . . . is placed by the Automotive Merchants Association at 10,000 persons, or one in each eight of the city's population of 80,000 persons." All told, the association estimated, "the volume of this trade [is] annually approximating $100,000,000 [retail as well as wholesale] and dominating other lines of trade here" (*Charlotte News*, April 1, 1928). Charlotte's importance may have been established as early as the late 1910s, when a regional manager of the Willys-Overland car company was quoted as saying, "Charlotte is the second-largest automobile and accessories center in the South" (*Charlotte Observer*, January 25, 1919). See also Wade Hampton Harris, *Charlotte*, pp. 22–23; Edna May Douglas, "Analysis of the Retail Trading Area of Charlotte," pp. 126–27.

Charlotte's main rival as an auto distribution center for Dixie was Atlanta. Preston, *Automobile Age Atlanta*, gives the erroneous impression that Atlanta was the sole auto distribution center of the Southeast and thus probably overestimates the industry's impact on the emergence of Atlanta as the Southeast's preeminent urban place.

9. The Nabisco building stood in First Ward. On Nabisco history, see Pusateri, *History of American Business*, p. 283.

10. "A coffee-roasting establishment has been located at the corner of College and 4th streets. The firm is composed of Messers. John A. Bell, P. L. Lance and S. H. Van Emery" (*Charlotte Observer*, December 3, 1906). By the 1920s Lance had its own large building on Dilworth's South Boulevard. A description of Lance traveling salesmen appeared in the *Charlotte Observer*, July 11, 1926.

11. On construction of the A&P warehouse on Cedar Street near Hill Street, see *Charlotte Observer*, July 18, 1926. The building still stood in the early 1990s.

12. Holt, *Charlotte Country Music Story*; Ringer, *Bossmen*, pp. 29–32; Rust, *Victor Master Book*, pp. 146–48, 406–8, 571, 583–85, 599–604; Grundy, " 'We Always Tried to Be Good People.' "

13. Merchants and Farmers Bank left the provision district and took up the ground floor of the Johnston Building. See *Charlotte Observer*, January 20, 1924, May 6, 1978; Wade Hampton Harris, *Charlotte*, p. 20.

14. On American Trust, see Blythe and Brockmann, *Hornets' Nest*, pp. 303–9. On the roots of Commercial National, see n. 65 in Chapter 4 above. Construction of the 1911 Commercial National skyscraper followed an announcement that the bank, already the "largest in the Carolinas," was increasing its capital stock. See *Charlotte Observer*, January 2, 1907; for an architect's rendering, see April 14, 1911.

15. Reynolds, *Charlotte Remembers*, p. 153; Blythe and Brockmann, *Hornets' Nest*, pp. 303–10; Marsh and Marsh, *Charlotte*, p. 157. An extensive article on Charlotte's banks at the start of the century appeared in the *Charlotte Observer*, July 17, 1904. Charlotte's financial growth had a precedent. In Boston the burgeoning New England textile industry had triggered a similar banking boom in the early nineteenth century. See Ward, "Industrial Revolution and the Emergence of Boston's Central Business District."

16. Quotation from *Charlotte Branch, Federal Reserve Bank of Richmond*. See also "Carolinas Industrial Edition," *Charlotte Observer*, March 2, 1928; Blythe and Brockmann, *Hornets' Nest*, p. 308; *Business: North Carolina*, July 1983, pp. 35–38. For a map of the territory served from Charlotte, see *Digest of the Rulings of the Federal Reserve Board*, p. 642. The Charlotte branch was part of the Federal Reserve Bank of Richmond. See Coit, *Federal Reserve Bank of Richmond*, pp. 43–44. As early as 1899 local newspapers boasted that "Charlotte has more national banking capital than any one of the four largest and most prosperous Southern cities . . . Charleston, Mobile, Birmingham and Montgomery" (*Charlotte Observer*, September 29, 1899). For glimpses of banking activity in the city and at the long effort to get the Reserve branch, see, for instance, *Charlotte Observer*, November 24, 1915, January 1, 1920. On the impact of the branch, see Charlotte Chamber of Commerce, *Charlotte, North Carolina*. A table comparing banking activity in Charlotte with that in other U.S. cities, 1919–41, may be found in Federal Reserve, *Banking and Monetary Statistics*, pp. 240–41.

17. All three were designed by Charlotte's prolific church architect J. M. McMichael. On Tabernacle ARP, see *Charlotte Observer*, November 26, 1906; *Charlotte Evening Chronicle*, February 16, 23, 1911. On McMichael's Byzantine design for First Baptist (now Spirit Square Arts Center), read the *Charlotte Observer*, March 12, 1907. On the First ARP design, see *Charlotte Observer*, November 23, 1910; William Huffman, "Former First A.R.P. Church," Survey and Research Report. The final major downtown church of the era was First United Methodist on North Tryon. Its construction, on the former site of the Oates estate, was announced in the *Charlotte Observer*, July 30, 1926.

18. The name was changed at the suggestion of wealthy cotton broker John VanLandingham. See Charlotte City Council Minutes, October 10, 1895.

19. Gwendolyn Wright, *Building the Dream*, pp. 135–51; Gunther Barth, *City People*, pp. 28–57; Cromley, *Alone Together*.

20. *Charlotte Observer*, February 10, 1900.

21. Ibid., May 5, December 27, 1903. The Graham Apartments stood until the end of the 1970s, when they were replaced by the Discovery Place science museum. The Graham was actually the city's second such project, following the 1901 Ryder flats on Morehead Street, about which little is known. Third was "the nine city homes [townhouses] of Mr. W. F. Dowd, at the corner of Morehead Street and the Boulevard," reported under construction in June 1904. These were joined later that year by a fourth project, on North College at East Eighth, with five brick, two-story, six-room units renting at $25 per month. See ibid., June 17, 1904. On the "city-house" concept, see letter by architect C. C. Hook in ibid., May 20, 1904; also, March 24, 1901.

22. A loving description of the Blandwood Apartments, erected at 911 South Tryon near Morehead about 1914 and demolished in 1960, appeared in ibid., February 7, 1960. On construction of apartments on South Tryon at Morehead, see ibid., February 23, 1907. On apartments on North Tryon at Tenth Street, commissioned by Mrs. Latta C. Johnson to replace the carriage house of her family's mansion, see *Charlotte News*, May 7, 1917. All three buildings are now gone, but a large complex from the period, originally known as the Guthery Apartments and today called Tryon House, still stands on the east side of North Tryon between Eighth and Ninth Streets. By 1924 Charlotte boasted "ten apartment houses of the larger class and sixty-four of smaller proportions. The conveniences include elevator service, steam heat and approved sanitary devices" (Wade Hampton Harris, *Charlotte*, p. 41).

23. *Charlotte Observer*, April 2, 1927; *Charlotte News*, April 19, 1927. Another landmark apartment complex from the period in Fourth Ward is the Poplar. In 1929 optimistic New York City investors erected the grand multifamily tower well off Tryon Street at Tenth and Poplar Streets, designed in a stately Olde English style. It attracted prosperous tenants but remained an outpost in a declining neighborhood until Fourth Ward was rediscovered by young urban professionals in the late 1970s. See William Huffman, "Poplar Apartments," Survey and Research Report.

24. *Charlotte Observer*, July 28, 1899.

25. The Piedmont & Northern terminal closed in 1957. See *Charlotte Observer*, April 8, 1957; Fetters and Swanson, *Piedmont and Northern*.

26. *Charlotte Observer*, January 16, 1907.

27. See "Foreigners of Charlotte," ibid., July 23, 1906. Also, on a fruit stand run by a Greek named George Kiraka, see ibid., July 22, 1906.

28. Howell's Arcade burrowed northward into the middle of the block. It was built on the site of the failed Howell Cotton factory in 1911, just as Jim Crow pressure was rising. The double row of tiny storefronts initially held pawnshops and cheap clothing stores operated by whites and aimed at the farmers and laborers who frequented the provision district. Initial tenants included Silverstein Brothers Clothing and a loan outfit called the Charlotte Advance Company, both white-owned. But too few white businesses signed leases, and by 1914 the arcade developers shifted to leasing to black entrepreneurs grateful for any downtown location. By the late 1920s Howell's Arcade held a dozen African American enterprises ranging from Johnson-Moore Tailors to the "eating house" of Mary Galliard. Information from city directories and Sanborn Insurance maps; *Charlotte Observer*, September 21, 1944.

29. *Charlotte Observer*, February 13, 1907.

30. Officials attempted to end the curb market in 1926 by creating an official City Market near the new City Hall. See ibid., August 11, 1926. For a description of farmers selling watermelons along downtown streets, see ibid., August 15, 1897.

31. Covington, *Belk*; Blythe, *William Henry Belk*; William Huffman, "Belk Department Store," Survey and Research Report; *Charlotte Observer*, September 28, 1898. One major expansion came in 1927; see *Charlotte News*, May 1, 1927. Another took place ten years later; see *Charlotte News*, August 22, 1937. Belk eventually took over the Efird Department Store on North Tryon and combined the two facilities. The whole complex fell in the late 1980s to make way for the present NationsBank tower. On the class implications of the department store, see Lawrence, "Geographical Space, Social Space, and the Realm of the Department Store."

32. For the national context of department store growth, see Gunther Barth, *City People*, pp. 110–47. On the rise of department stores in Charlotte, see Edna May Douglas, "Analysis of the Retail Trading Area of Charlotte," pp. 71–72; Reynolds, *Charlotte Remembers*, pp. 151–52. On the 1924 Gothic-style Ivey's building, designed by Charlotte architect William Peeps, consult "Ivey Department Store," Survey and Research Report. On the 1923 Efird building, see William Huffman, "Belk Department Store," Survey and Research Report. On construction of Efird's and Ivey's, see *Charlotte Observer*, August 12, 1923.

33. Significantly, North Tryon was the only one of Charlotte's four main downtown streets that did not have a men's hat store. Note the Central Hat Shop on East Trade, National Hat Store on West Trade, and Piedmont Hat Shop on South Tryon.

34. William Huffman, "C. C. Coddington Building," Survey and Research Report; *Charlotte Observer*, March 13, 1927. Other automobile buildings in this era included the Oakland dealership at 507 South Tryon (see *Charlotte News*, April 14, 1917); Carolina Cadillac farther out South Tryon at Kathryn Street, designed by architect M. R. Marsh (see *Charlotte News*, May 29, 1926) (not to be confused with the later Thomas Cadillac showroom on North Church between Fifth and Sixth Streets); and Pettit Ford at Graham and Fourth Streets (initially intended as a Chrysler dealership) (see *Charlotte News*, April 1, 1928). In the 1920s Charlotte did not yet have an "automobile row." See Liebs, *Main Street to Miracle Mile*, pp. 77–93.

35. *Charlotte Chronicle*, December 7, 1887.

36. "Former Hovis Mortuary," Survey and Research Report. The business ended in 1965. See *Charlotte Observer*, November 5, 1965.

37. For a photo and history of St. Peter's Hospital, see *Charlotte News*, June 20, 1903. On enlargement of the building, see *Charlotte Observer*, June 19, 1898.

38. Blythe and Brockmann, *Hornets' Nest*, pp. 315–18; Wade Hampton Harris, *Charlotte*, p. 44. The Charlotte Sanitorium closed when Charlotte Memorial was built. See *Charlotte Observer*, September 13, 1944.

39. *Charlotte Observer*, July 21, 1906, April 12, 1907; *Charlotte News*, December 26, 1906; Dan L. Morrill, "North Carolina Medical College Building," Survey and Research Report; Lafferty, *North Carolina Medical College*.

40. "Professional Building," Survey and Research Report; Wade Hampton Harris, *Charlotte*, pp. 43–44; *Charlotte Observer*, August 12, 1923. The building was replaced by the TransAmerica Building in the mid-1990s.

41. *Charlotte News*, January 4, 1920. On the development of distribution centers, see Vance, *Merchant's World*.

42. Most of the offices had storage and shipping areas, plus a screening room where

exhibitors previewed films. See *Charlotte News*, March 2, 1983; *Charlotte Observer*, February 28, 1950. On the opening of the Paramount office at Church and Fourth Streets, see *Charlotte Observer*, November 4, 1923. Theatrical equipment suppliers also clustered around film row, such as Southern Theater Equipment in the 200 block of West Fourth Street. See *Charlotte Observer*, July 15, 1926.

43. Wade Hampton Harris, *Charlotte*, p. 3. Also Works Progress Administration, *Charlotte*, p. 36.

44. Robert Tompkins and Mary Alice Hinson, "Latta Arcade," National Register Nomination. Brevard Court, "an arcade without a roof," was named "in honor of Dr. R. L. Brevard who owned the site." As early as 1924 it was already functioning as "a kind of local cotton exchange" and was "largely inhabited by cotton brokers" (Wade Hampton Harris, *Charlotte*, pp. 19–20). A description of cotton trade in Charlotte may be found in Charlotte Chamber of Commerce, *Charlotte, North Carolina*.

45. Wade Hampton Harris, *Charlotte*, p. 20. See also Bishir, *North Carolina Architecture*, pp. 401–2.

46. *Charlotte Observer*, September 26, 1897; Clarkson, *History of the Law Library Association*.

47. A drawing and extensive description of Latta's never-built skyscraper appeared in the *Charlotte Observer*, July 23, 1899; see also July 12, 18, 1899. "Hayden, Wheeler & Schwend are the architects of the 4Cs building, Trinity Church, Elks temple and Mrs. Springs building" (Wade Hampton Harris, *Sketches of Charlotte, No. 3*, p. 25). The skyscraper's design was likely inspired by New York City's well-known Equitable Building.

48. *Charlotte Observer*, March 26, 1902. A photo of Abbott's Trust Building, which burned in the 1920s and was replaced by the Johnston Building, appears in Blythe and Brockmann, *Hornets' Nest*, pp. 288–89.

49. Dan L. Morrill, "The Independence Building," Survey and Research Report. For an architect's rendering, see *Charlotte Observer*, April 24, 1907. On the career of Milburn, based in Charlotte and later in Washington, D.C., see *Charlotte Observer*, November 13, 1897; Wodehouse, "Frank Pierce Milburn."

On the development of the American skyscraper, see Condit, *Rise of the Skyscraper*; Fitch, *American Building*; L. R. Ford, "Individual Decisions in the Creation of the American Downtown"; Huxtable, *Tall Building Artistically Reconsidered*; Domosh, "Imagining New York's First Skyscrapers."

50. An architect's rendering of the Commercial National tower appeared in the *Charlotte Observer*, April 14, 1911.

51. "The pinnacle of the First National Bank building is the highest point on any structure in the two Carolinas. . . . [No] other city in the Carolinas has a skyscraper with 20 stories" (*Charlotte Observer*, July 22, 1926; see also Marsh and Marsh, *Charlotte*, p. 102). For the national context of Charlotte's bank architecture, consult Nisbet, Wagg, and Tucker, *Money Matters*; Deborah C. Andrews, "Bank Buildings in Nineteenth Century Philadelphia," in Cutler and Gillette, *Divided Metropolis*, pp. 57–84.

52. Dan L. Morrill, "Masonic Temple," Survey and Research Report. On the history of Masonic and related organizations in Charlotte, see *Charlotte Observer*, January 16, 1945.

53. A special section on the opening of the Wilder Building appeared in the *Charlotte Observer*, June 13, 1926. The building was named for a Mrs. Wilder who had lived in a house on the site. To get her to sell, the skyscraper's developers built a penthouse for her atop the new tower. See *Charlotte Observer*, September 17, 1926.

54. On the Builders Building, see *Charlotte News*, June 27, 1926; *Charlotte Observer*, July

24, September 8, 1926. The Builders Building's arcade was razed in 1985 but the tower was renovated as the Peace Building. On the Law Building, see Clarkson, *History of the Law Library Association*; "Law Building," Survey and Research Report. The Law Building fell to make way for an expanded jail in the 1990s.

55. City directory data. For the Hotel Charlotte, New York City architect William Stoddard created a ten-story Neoclassical structure frosted in terra-cotta. The building fronted on West Trade, but its long facade faced westward so as to catch the eyes of travelers on the Southern Railway mainline three blocks away. See *Charlotte Observer*, August 12, 1923; Edward S. Perzel, "Hotel Charlotte," National Register Nomination. The building was demolished in the 1980s.

56. Charlotte Chamber of Commerce, *Story of Charlotte, Illustrated*.

57. For instance, Charlotte Chamber of Commerce, "*In the Heart of the Piedmont*," p. 7. On financial institutions' particular concern with image, see, for instance, Deborah C. Andrews, "Bank Buildings in Nineteenth Century Philadelphia," in Cutler and Gillette, *Divided Metropolis*, p. 67. On the importance of downtown as symbol, a theatrical stage-set embodying white-collar ideals, see Warner, *Private City*, pp. 187–88.

58. Cash, *Mind of the South*, p. 224. Well-dressed readers will notice that I am a bit sloppy in my comparison: a tuxedo is for evening wear, while a morning coat is for mornings.

59. Kratt, *Charlotte*, 1st ed., p. 99; *Charlotte Observer*, December 5, 1906; *Charlotte Chronicle*, February 5, 1912; *Charlotte News*, April 3, 1927. Auto ownership jumped to 22,159 by 1925.

60. *Charlotte News*, May 25, 1926. Historians have tended to assume that the automobile created the move of businesses to the suburbs; for instance, see Preston, *Automobile Age Atlanta*. But Charlotte data show that the move was clearly under way even in the 1900s, when only a few wealthy hobbyists owned motorcars.

61. On Dilworth's 1903 Holy Comforter Episcopal Church and 1909 Chalmers Memorial ARP Church, see Morrill and Little-Stokes, "Architectural Analysis," pp. 33, 55–56. On Elizabeth's churches, see n. 36 in Chapter 6 above.

62. Strong, *History of Mecklenburg County Medicine*, pp. 96–98. For a photo history of the institution, see the booklet *Seventy-fifth Anniversary, Mercy Hospital*.

63. Strong, *History of Mecklenburg County Medicine*, pp. 92–94.

64. On the early lack of retailing in elite suburbs, see Conzen and Conzen, "Geographical Structure in Nineteenth Century Urban Retailing"; Michael P. Conzen, "Historical Geography," esp. p. 94; Stilgoe, *Borderland*, pp. 208–12.

65. The Memphis-based Piggly-Wiggly chain, begun in 1916, pioneered the self-service grocery concept. See Liebs, *Main Street to Miracle Mile*, pp. 119–20; Pusateri, *History of American Business*, p. 278. Chain groceries grew rapidly in Charlotte; see *Charlotte News*, April 24, 1927. As in many localities, local grocers attempted to organize and halt the influx of chains. See *Charlotte Observer*, July 31, 1926.

66. *Charlotte News*, November 21, 23, 1906; *Charlotte Observer*, December 10, 1906.

67. Harding, "Charlotte City Schools," pp. 23, 34.

68. The institution that became Central High actually held its first classes in the 1920 Alexander Graham School building. As soon as the Central High building on Elizabeth Avenue was ready for occupancy, Alexander Graham became the city's first junior high school. See Edgar Thompson, *Agricultural Mecklenburg and Industrial Charlotte*, pp. 99–115; Harding, "History of Charlotte Schools," pp. 64–67; *Courses of Study*, pp. 51–52, 103–7. On completion of Second Ward High, see *Charlotte Observer*, August 17, 1923. Around

1904 a private Piedmont Industrial School had briefly operated near the Hoskins Mill, evidently offering a curriculum similar to what Tech High would eventually teach. See *Charlotte Observer*, May 22, 1904.

CHAPTER 8

1. Charlotte's experience is similar to the growth of the "Service City" that occurred in Northern cities during the early and mid-nineteenth century, just as that region was industrializing. See Monkkonen, *America Becomes Urban*. On the rapid growth of urban services elsewhere in the New South around 1900, see Kipp, "Urban Growth and Social Change," pp. 353, 368–94.

2. *Charlotte Chronicle*, July 15, 1887.

3. Tompkins, *History of Mecklenburg County*, 1:176. Compare with Monkkonen, *America Becomes Urban*, pp. 138–44. "A long-felt need was supplied in Charlotte yesterday when signs were put up on the streetcorners, giving news of the streets. . . . They are substantial metal signs with enameled lettering" (*Charlotte Observer*, November 20, 26, 1903).

4. Charlotte's municipal water department began operation in 1899. See *Fifth Annual Report*, pp. 15–19. On fish in the water pipes, see *Charlotte Observer*, January 3, 1885. On the early history of the waterworks, see *Charlotte Observer*, December 15, 1896; W. W. Franklin, "Water and Sewerage Facilities"; "Some High Spots in the History of Charlotte's Public Water Supply"; *Charlotte Observer*, September 5, 1987.

5. Tompkins, *History of Mecklenburg County*, 1:158; *Charlotte Democrat*, May 6, 1897; Charlotte City Council minutes, April 25, 1899.

6. Tompkins, *History of Mecklenburg County*, 1:158.

7. Blythe and Brockmann, *Hornets' Nest*, p. 177.

8. Charlotte's succession of city halls is pictured in Blythe and Brockmann, *Hornets' Nest*.

9. Dan L. Morrill, "Charlotte City Hall," Survey and Research Report. A description of the civic plaza, "parklike in trees [and] shrubbery," appeared in Wade Hampton Harris, *Charlotte*, p. 16.

10. Monkkonen, *America Becomes Urban*; Teaford, *Unheralded Triumph*; Schiesl, *Politics of Efficiency*; Wiebe, *Search for Order*; Zane L. Miller, *Boss Cox's Cincinnati*; Hays, "Politics of Reform in Municipal Government."

11. Goldfield, *Cotton Fields and Skyscrapers*, p. 101; Tindall, *Emergence of the New South*, p. 219; Luebke, *Tarheel Politics*, p. 35. Dewey Grantham agrees as well, though he credits Southern Progressives with a bit more interest in social reform. See Grantham, *Southern Progressivism*, pp. xvii–xviii, 417–18.

12. Goldfield, *Cotton Fields and Skyscrapers*, p. 101. For background on the commission plan, see Schiesl, *Politics of Efficiency*, pp. 135–40. The South's enthusiastic embrace of structural reform is particularly interesting in light of the fact that political machines and bosses were rare in Dixie. See Monkkonen, *America Becomes Urban*, pp. 120–21.

13. Kousser, *Shaping of Southern Politics*. A Charlotte editorialist noted the drop in turnout across the South following disfranchisement. See *Charlotte Observer*, May 12, 1901. In Greensboro, North Carolina, "local office holding became far more exclusive and elitist" during the decade after 1900. "Now fully 81.2 percent of the councilmen were members of the high white-collar stratum," compared with 50 percent during the decade 1880–1889 (Kipp, "Urban Growth and Social Change," pp. 341–43).

14. Brownell, *Urban Ethos in the South*; Blaine Brownell, "Urban South Comes of Age, 1900–1940," in Brownell and Goldfield, *City in Southern History*, pp. 15–153. Similarly on North Carolina in the 1940s, see Key, *Southern Politics in State and Nation*, p. 211.

15. On the importance of the structure of political discourse in determining government policies, particularly expenditures, see Terence J. MacDonald, *Parameters of Urban Fiscal Policy*.

16. On the desire for leaders who are "citizens of substantial experience in handling business [and] Upon whom is the stamp of character," see, for instance, *Charlotte News*, May 2, 1917. On the promise that "the commission charter would forever take the city government out of the grip of the professional politicians," read, for example, ibid., May 5, 1917. On Charlotte's commission government, see Edgar Thompson, *Agricultural Mecklenburg and Industrial Charlotte*, pp. 269–73.

17. *Charlotte News*, April 21, 1917.

18. Ibid., April 24, 1917. Interpolation from 1910 and 1920 census figures puts Charlotte's population at 42,641 in 1917. By comparison, turnout for the 1897 mayoral election (the last local election before disenfranchisement efforts began) had been higher, 3,071 voters, even though Charlotte then had barely 18,000 citizens. See Charlotte City Council Minutes, May 3, 1897.

19. Precinct (that is, ward) totals appeared in the *Charlotte News*, April 24, 1917. On the first commission, see ibid., May 9, 1917.

20. Akers, "Finances of the City of Charlotte," pp. 8–11.

21. Stone, Price, and Stone, *City Manager Government in Charlotte*, p. 57; also Edgar Thompson, *Agricultural Mecklenburg and Industrial Charlotte*, pp. 292–94.

22. Stone, Price, and Stone, *City Manager Government in Charlotte*, p. 58. This report, by the way, was not at all critical of the fact that the "better" citizens preferred the plan while ordinary voters opposed it.

23. Karr, "Brookline Rejects Annexation"; Teaford, *City and Suburb*; Kenneth T. Jackson, *Crabgrass Frontier*, p. 149. Significantly, cities in the South often continued to annex their suburbs as late as the post–World War II era, long after the process had virtually ceased in the North. See Carl Abbott, *New Urban America*, p. 55.

24. *Charlotte Observer*, January 14, 1885.

25. *Charlotte News*, May 1, 1906; *Charlotte Observer*, May 17, 1906. One plant that burned was Charlotte Pipe and Foundry, which subsequently left Dilworth. See *Charlotte News*, April 19, 1906; Beth Laney Smith, *Foundry*.

26. *Charlotte Observer*, February 7, May 3, 1906. For Dilworth discussions concerning ways to get fire protection, see *Charlotte News*, February 6, 1906; *Charlotte Observer*, February 6, May 16, June 7, 1906.

27. *Charlotte Observer*, February 7, 1906.

28. Ibid.

29. Ibid., February 15, 1906.

30. Ibid., February 4, 1907.

31. The Greater Charlotte Club was formed in October 1905. It replaced an older Board of Trade and Chamber of Commerce that dated to the nineteenth century. The Greater Charlotte Club in turn gave way to the present Chamber of Commerce in 1915. See Blythe and Brockmann, *Hornets' Nest*, p. 138.

32. *Charlotte Observer*, October 3, December 15, 1906.

33. A suggestion was floated and abandoned that Dilworth might come into the city as a borough, part of the municipal government in some respects yet independent in others, on

the model of the new boroughs of Brooklyn and Queens in New York City. See ibid., February 16, May 8, 1906.

34. The exact circumstances surrounding the shift were never reported; articles simply began talking more and more about extension. See *Charlotte News*, July 3, 5, 1906; *Charlotte Observer*, July 22, August 12, 1906. Such gaps in reporting were not unusual in the small city with its even smaller electorate. As one editor put it, "The *Observer* long ago ceased to vex its righteous soul about things that everybody knows are going to come to pass" (*Charlotte Observer*, November 9, 1906).

35. On real estate speculators, read the *Charlotte Observer*, October 3, December 15, 1906. The two-and-a-half-mile limit inspired newspaper editorials in Greensboro and Baltimore (probably instigated by well-connected opponents in Charlotte) ridiculing Charlotte as "The Rubber City," whose slogan should be "Watch Charlotte Stretch." Quoted in *Charlotte Observer*, December 4, 1906; *Charlotte News*, December 8, 1906. There was also some talk of extending the city limits all the way to the borders of Charlotte Township, but that was too far out for serious consideration. See *Charlotte Observer*, July 18, November 1, 1906.

36. *Charlotte News*, November 5, 27, 1906; *Charlotte Observer*, November 6, 25, 1906.

37. *Charlotte Observer*, October 2, November 25, 26, December 29, 1906, February 20, 1907. Clarkson's surviving letters and papers document his political connections and his leadership activities in the prohibition movement. See Clarkson collection, North Carolina State Archives; Clarkson papers, Southern Historical Collection; Johnnie Anderson, "Heriot Clarkson." Clarkson's interest in prohibition was summed up in the title of a pamphlet he first published in 1905: *It Helps Business and Is a Blessing: What Leading Businessmen, Bankers, Farmers, and Laborers Say About Prohibition in Charlotte, N.C.* See also Chapter 3 of the present book.

38. *Charlotte Observer*, December 29, 1906, February 19, 1907. Clarkson had developed excellent contacts as Democratic Party leader, state temperance leader, and member of the North Carolina House of Representatives, 1899–1901. See Powell, *Dictionary of North Carolina Biography*, pp. 382–83. Johnston's contacts were good, too, thanks to his partnership with the influential Holt family (see Chapter 4 of the present book).

39. Once again Charlotte newspapers carried no discussion of the alteration. A study of urban government in Birmingham, Alabama, found a similar pattern of power. Downtown businessmen controlled city politics and routinely outvoted the rich factory owners when interests diverged. The factory owners, however, proved savvy at using influence with state government to get their way on key issues. See Carl V. Harris, *Political Power in Birmingham*.

40. *Charlotte News*, January 4, 5, 6, 8, 1920; *Charlotte Observer*, January 3, 4, 5, 7, 1920.

41. *Charlotte Observer*, July 2, 1922; Kratt and Hanchett, *Legacy*, pp. 119–20. The area that incorporated did not include the portions of the neighborhood already within the city (the border cut across the suburb near the Duke mansion).

42. *Charlotte Observer*, April 15, 1927. At the last minute the *Charlotte News* gingerly raised similar questions in an editorial, May 2, 1927.

43. *Charlotte News*, May 4, 1927.

44. Mel Scott, *American City Planning*; Silver, "Urban Planning in the New South."

45. John Nolen to George Stephens, March 2, 1917. Stephens expressed similar sentiments: "I consider our most important work with the people in Myers Park to be that of leading them into wanting the things that you are able to plan for them" (George Stephens to John Nolen, April 6, 1916, folder 4, box 98, Nolen papers).

46. John Nolen, "Civic Survey, Charlotte North Carolina: Report to the Chamber of Commerce, 1917," box 23, Nolen papers. In a 1977 interview Earle Sumner Draper remembered drawing up the preliminary plan sketch. See *Charlotte Observer*, August 22, 1977. The sketch was based on an earlier student paper by a young member of Nolen's staff. See Alfred E. Muller, "City Plan for Charlotte, November 1913," box 23, Nolen papers. Nolen described the survey process in general in *New Ideals in the Planning of Cities, Towns, and Villages*, pp. 11–12, 31–39.

47. John Nolen to David Ovens, September 1, 1916; E. N. Ferris to John Nolen, January 1, 1917; John Nolen to E. N. Ferris, January 10, 1917; Thomas L. Black to John Nolen, August 10, 1917. Correspondence concerning the Charlotte city plan is in folders 4 and 5, box 98, Nolen papers.

48. In 1923 Charlotte lawyer Julia Alexander wrote Nolen asking for a copy of the civic survey, saying that the city had misplaced its copy. See Kratt and Hanchett, *Legacy*, p. 123. By the 1980s the survey was completely forgotten in Charlotte; the only extant copy was in the Nolen papers.

Charlotte's reluctance seems to have been part of a regional pattern. Southerners were markedly less enthusiastic about urban plans than were non-Southerners in this period, notes historian Blaine Brownell. Of 786 municipal planning commissions extant in 1930, only 71 were in Dixie. See Brownell, "Commercial-Civic Elite and City Planning," pp. 343–44. A good brief overview of Southern city planning history is Silver, "Urban Planning in the New South." See also F. Stuart Chapin Jr., "City Planning: Adjusting People and Place," in Vance and Demerath, *Urban South*, pp. 268–82; Brownell, *Urban Ethos in the South*, pp. 172–89; Koleen Alice Haire Huggins, "Evolution of City and Regional Planning"; Silver, *Twentieth Century Richmond*.

49. John Nolen to Clarence Kuester, March 1924, Nolen papers.

50. It was ironic that George Stephens's sometime partners F. C. Abbott and T. T. Allison led the attack, since Stephens had been planning's strongest champion in Charlotte. See *Charlotte News*, September 5, 1930. "Dealers in Real Estate believed they should have freedom to develop it as they liked, and the general public looked upon planning as a luxury that should not be purchased in hard times," concluded Stone, Price, and Stone, *City Manager Government in Charlotte*, p. 7; see also Koleen Alice Haire Huggins, "Evolution of City and Regional Planning." No copies of Swan's plan have been located.

51. Stephens departed "for reasons based on the welfare of my family in the matter of health" (*Charlotte Observer*, July 2, 1922). Cofounder A. J. Draper stayed on as Stephens Company vice-president until 1926. At that time S. D. Heath took over as president and A. J. Draper resigned, completing the shift from the original leadership. On the Asheville plan, see Nolen papers.

52. Draper remembers ceasing work for the company shortly after Stephens's departure, though he continued to do jobs for many Myers Park homeowners. See Earle Sumner Draper, telephone interview with Earle Sumner Draper Jr., November 1986. Civil engineers Blair & Drane had always produced the actual plat maps of Nolen and Draper streets, filed at the Mecklenburg County Register of Deeds Office. They stopped in 1926, and Smith took over with map book 332, p. 492. I surmise that this marked the effective end of Draper's influence over the design.

53. Kratt and Hanchett, *Legacy*; Thomas W. Hanchett, "Myers Park Historic District," National Register Nomination.

54. E. C. Griffith Co., "Subdivision Plat of Eastover"; Mecklenburg County Register of Deeds Office, deed book 614, p. 593; deed book 660, p. 25; Earle Sumner Draper, interview

with Thomas W. Hanchett at Vero Beach, Florida, August 1982. For more on Eastover, see Hanchett, "Charlotte and Its Neighborhoods," chap. 16.

55. E. C. Griffith Co., "Eastover, a Residential District Developed for the Discriminating Homebuilder" and "Eastover Restriction Agreement."

56. Eastover's efforts to repel outsiders continued into the 1980s. When the Mint Museum planned a major expansion in order to attract a wider range of visitors, neighborhood members demanded that a new entrance drive be created and a barrier be built so that museum visitors would not be able to get into the neighborhood. The demands were met.

57. Edgar Thompson, *Agricultural Mecklenburg and Industrial Charlotte*, p. 308.

58. Stone, Price, and Stone, *City Manager Government in Charlotte*, p. 55. Similarly, "officials of Charlotte seem to have taken the attitude that care of the poor was a private matter and not one that should concern municipal government" (Akers, "Finances of the City of Charlotte," pp. 55, 74).

CHAPTER 9

1. Moye, "Charlotte-Mecklenburg Consolidation." "Several Sunbelt cities—among them Houston, Dallas, and Charlotte—have developed growth patterns that are racially and economically segmented. That is, well-to-do whites cluster in one sector, poor whites in another, poor blacks in a third" (Gurney Breckenfield, "Refilling the Metropolitan Doughnut," in Perry and Watkins, *Rise of Sunbelt Cities*, p. 239). "In October 1974 the Council of Municipal Performance reported that six Southern cities—Shreveport, Winston-Salem, Charlotte, Augusta, Montgomery and Dallas, had the most racially segregated housing in the country" (Edward F. Haas, "The Southern Metropolis, 1940–1976," in Brownell and Goldfield, *City in Southern History*, p. 189). On the sectoral pattern in Western and Southern cities, see Carl Abbott, *New Urban America*, pp. 82–97.

The notion that cities should grow in a sectoral pattern was first promoted by geographer Homer Hoyt in the 1930s. See Hoyt, *Growth and Structure of Residential Neighborhoods*. Hoyt worked as a consultant to agencies such as the Federal Housing Administration and the National Association of Real Estate Board's Urban Land Institute, where he helped formulate policies to encourage sectoral development. See Weiss, *Community Builders*, p. 149.

2. Washington subsidies actively promoted "racial and economic homogeneity," helping make it "the most important characteristic" of post–World War II neighborhoods in America, writes Kenneth T. Jackson, *Crabgrass Frontier*, p. 241, also pp. 190–218, 225–27; Doyle, *Nashville since the 1920s*, p. 125; Goldsmith and Blakely, *Separate Societies*; Massey and Denton, *American Apartheid*; Raymond A. Mohl, "The Twentieth Century City: Introduction," in Mohl, *Making of Urban America*, p. 197; Mohl, "Trouble in Paradise"; Mohl, "Making the Second Ghetto"; Silver, "Changing Face of Neighborhoods"; Silver and Moeser, *Separate City*; Squires, "Community Reinvestment"; Goldfield, *Cotton Fields and Skyscrapers*, p. 168. For background on federal funding and American cities, see Gelfand, *Nation of Cities*.

3. "Charlotte: Unsouthern, Untypical."

4. *Moody's Bank and Finance Manual*, 1955, 1960, 1965, 1970. In 1962 alone, "Wachovia moved up one place to thirty-fifth in the nation. NC National became number 56, gaining three places. First Citizens moved up nine places to become number 120. First Union advanced 14 places to become 128th in the nation" (*Charlotte Observer*, February 3, 1965). North Carolina's relaxed banking laws, which encouraged early development of statewide

branch systems, may have aided this growth. See *New York Times*, August 24, 1991; Covington and Ellis, *Story of NationsBank*.

5. Charlotte Chamber of Commerce, *Research Report*.

6. Covington, "Truck Stop," in Charlotte Trucking, vertical file, Robinson-Spangler Carolina Room, Public Library of Charlotte and Mecklenburg County.

7. The Johnston family controlled virtually all of North Charlotte by this point. So many houses went on the market at once ca. 1953 that the company had a standard deed printed for use in all transactions. For instance, see Mecklenburg County Register of Deeds Office, deed book 1633, pp. 367, 411. On the Highland Park #3 closure, see *Charlotte News*, March 13, 1975.

8. The Johnston Mill in North Charlotte was the last one running. See *Charlotte News*, March 13, 1975, August 19, 1978; *Charlotte Observer*, March 14, 1975. Textile employment in Charlotte dropped from 7,409 in 1954 to 3,400 in 1972. See Moye, "Charlotte-Mecklenburg Consolidation," p. 22.

9. In 1935 rules were modified slightly to require that at least one council representative reside in each ward, though all elections continued to be at-large. In 1945 this innovation was abandoned, and council returned to a pure at-large system. Circumstances in both cases were mysterious. The 1935 change was the work of state representative James A. Bell, who quietly convinced fellow legislators in Raleigh to amend the Charlotte city charter. No hint of his motive appeared in Charlotte newspapers. Local officials expressed considerable consternation but went along with the rules. See Stone, Price, and Stone, *City Manager Government in Charlotte*, pp. 60–61. The 1945 change also occurred without explanation. Years later Councilman Fred Alexander (who became the city's first twentieth century black elected official in 1965) suggested that the 1945 change had been made to foil the candidacy of Bishop Dale, a black pastor who had built a wide following via appearances on WBT radio. See *Charlotte Observer*, October 16, 1976. On Bishop Dale, see *Charlotte Observer*, April 8, 1957; Kratt, *Charlotte*, 1st ed., p. 166.

10. *Charlotte Observer*, March 13, 1958. On the 1940s–1960s dominance of Charlotte government by business leaders, see also Daniels, *Tarheels*; Edwin Yoder, *Charlotte Observer*, December 13, 1961; Moye, "Charlotte-Mecklenburg Consolidation," p. 160.

11. *Charlotte Observer*, February 12, 1960. "From 1935 to 1975, every mayor of Charlotte was the president or owner of his own business, with the only exception being an attorney." Past Chamber presidents served as mayor throughout most of the 1960s and 1970s. See Leach, "Progress under Pressure," p. 11; Coffin, *Brookshire and Belk*.

12. Monkkonen, *America Becomes Urban*, p. 156; Glaab and Brown, *History of Urban America*, pp. 297–98; Miller and Melvin, *Urbanization of Modern America*, p. 161; Teaford, *Twentieth Century American City*, pp. 74–75. The South received some $2 billion in federal aid, mostly to cities, during the New Deal. See Goldfield, *Cotton Fields and Skyscrapers*, pp. 181–82. On the New Deal in the South, see Tindall, *Emergence of the New South*, pp. 473–97, 608; Schulman, *From Cotton Belt to Sunbelt*; Mohl, "Trouble in Paradise"; Doyle, *Nashville since the 1920s*, chap. 4; Douglas L. Smith, *New Deal in the Urban South*; Biles, "Urban South in the Great Depression." On the ability of established economic elites to shape the New Deal in North Carolina, see Badger, *North Carolina and the New Deal*; Abrams, *Conservative Constraints*.

13. *Charlotte Observer*, November 7, 1944. North Carolina business leaders and politicians generally gave the New Deal a lukewarm welcome. See Badger, *North Carolina and the New Deal*. This upper-class antipathy was particularly evident in Charlotte voting

returns. In 1944, for instance, only two city precincts failed to produce majorities for FDR. Both were in the elite Seventh Ward (Eastover/Myers Park). See *Charlotte Observer*, November 7, 1944.

14. *Charlotte Observer*, July 14, 1938.

15. Ibid.

16. *Emergency Relief in North Carolina*, pp. 79, 82, 205–6, 236–37, 254, 260. Charles Gilmore, who directed early New Deal relief in Charlotte, lived in the Eastover/Myers Park area at 1057 Providence Road. For background on the FERA/CWA nationally, consult Graham and Wander, *Franklin D. Roosevelt*, pp. 65–66, 132–33.

17. Kratt, *Charlotte*, 1st ed., pp. 135–36.

18. For a thumbnail sketch of the PWA, see Graham and Wander, *Franklin D. Roosevelt*, pp. 336–38.

19. The speed with which the project unfolded in the newspapers indicated the behind-the-scenes nature of city government. Saturday papers carried stories that a grant was being sought. See *Charlotte News*, July 9, 1938. Word came the following Wednesday that federal guidelines required the hospital to be city-owned and on city land. See ibid., July 13, 1938; *Charlotte Observer*, July 13, 1938. On Thursday, headlines reported that city council had voted unanimously to create a Charlotte hospital authority to take over St. Peter's (which already owned the Dilworth site) and apply for the grant. See *Charlotte Observer*, July 14, 1938. A week later council voted a special bond referendum to raise the local share of the project. See *Charlotte Observer*, July 21, 22, 1938; Blythe and Brockmann, *Hornets' Nest*, pp. 318–19.

20. Kenneth T. Jackson, *Crabgrass Frontier*, pp. 95–203. See also Squires, "Community Reinvestment," pp. 4–5. For a case study of HOLC credit-mapping in a Southern city, see Mohl, "Trouble in Paradise."

21. The real estate men involved were S. T. Henderson of Home Realty, H. Y. Dunaway of Carolina Realty, O. J. Thies of Thies Realty, R. E. Agnew of Agnew and Brown, J. H. Carson of Carson Realty, Lex Marsh Jr. of Marsh Realty, and Frank E. Harlan and Lee Kinney, who had been HOLC appraisers and were now out on their own as real estate brokers. The bankers were R. S. Smith of Independence Trust, E. J. Cafferty of Mechanics Perpetual Building and Loan, and E. Y. Keesler of Mutual Building and Loan, representing the city's three main real estate lenders. "These parties agreed on the various classifications" (Sam R. Cook, "Confidential Report on Charlotte North Carolina" [1937], in "Charlotte, N.C. #1" folder, box 12, Home Owners' Loan Corporation Survey Files).

22. "Residential Security Map," box 12, Home Owners' Loan Corporation Survey Files. A brief description of each map area by HOLC staffer C. W. Nixon may be found in the "Charlotte, N.C., Master File" folder, ibid.

23. "Explanation: Charlotte, North Carolina," in "Charlotte, N.C.—Security Map and Area Description #1" folder, box 12, Home Owners' Loan Corporation Survey Files.

24. Sam R. Cook, "Confidential Report on Charlotte North Carolina" [1937], p. 2, in "Charlotte, N.C. #1" folder, box 12, Home Owners' Loan Corporation Survey Files.

25. Ibid. On the same tendencies in Miami, see Mohl, "Trouble in Paradise."

26. Kenneth T. Jackson, *Crabgrass Frontier*, p. 203.

27. Ibid.; Gwendolyn Wright, *Building the Dream*, pp. 240–43; Hayes, *Federal Government and Urban Housing*, pp. 79–106.

28. One positive impact in Charlotte, as elsewhere, of federal mortgage programs was a marked increase in home ownership. In 1940 the U.S. Census showed 7,000 Charlotte homeowners, compared with 18,180 tenants. By 1970 Charlotte had 39,943 owner-occupied

housing units, versus just 37,049 rental. See U.S. Bureau of the Census, *Sixteenth Census*, p. 226; U.S. Bureau of the Census, *1970 Census*. Nationally, see Tobey, Wetherell, and Brigham, "Moving Out and Settling In." On the VA program, see Wheaton, "Evolution of Federal Housing Programs," pp. 234–43, 375–82.

29. National Commission on Urban Problems, *Building the American City*, pp. 94–107; Wheaton, "Evolution of Federal Housing Programs," pp. 336–38.

30. *Charlotte Observer*, October 1, 1962.

31. FHA *Underwriters Manual*, quoted in Kenneth T. Jackson, *Crabgrass Frontier*, p. 208. See also Gwendolyn Wright, *Building the Dream*, pp. 247–48; Squires, "Community Reinvestment," pp. 4–6; Berry, *Open Housing Question* pp. 9–12. Also like the HOLC, the FHA favored new suburbs over existing neighborhoods. Over two-thirds of FHA loans went to new houses. See Kenneth T. Jackson, *Crabgrass Frontier*, pp. 206–7, 209–10. It became in many instances cheaper to buy a new home in the suburbs than to rent an existing dwelling in the city.

32. Federal Housing Administration, *Planning Neighborhoods for Small Houses*, pp. 17–15; Tunnard and Pushkarev, *Man-Made America*, p. 90; Kostof, *City Shaped*, pp. 80–82; Southworth and Ben-Joseph, "Street Standards and the Shaping of Suburbia."

33. Federal Housing Administration, *Circular No. 4*, p. 1; Weiss, *Community Builders*; Eichler, *Merchant Builders*; Mel Scott, *American City Planning*, pp. 455–58; Checkoway, "Large Builders, Federal Housing Programs, and Postwar Suburbanization."

34. Spangler came to Latta from schooling at Kings Business College in Charlotte. Among his first projects on his own was a group of tract houses along Romany Road and Park Avenue overlooking Latta Park. Later developments included Landsdowne and Shamrock Hills. See Mecklenburg County Register of Deeds Office, map index, and map book 3, p. 413.

35. Marsh was born in 1901 and first tasted the real estate game by going broke in the Florida land boom of the 1920s. He came to Charlotte and went broke again in real estate at the depths of the depression in 1932 before finally finding success in the FHA era. Projects included Sedgefield off South Boulevard and Barringer Woods. See Mecklenburg County Register of Deeds Office, map index; *Charlotte Observer*, January 24, 1971, November 16, 1989. On the homebuilders' association, see, for instance, ibid., March 11, 1945. Marsh personally spent considerable time in Washington during World War II lobbying for easing of building restrictions. See *Charlotte News*, September 12, 1945.

36. John Crosland was born in 1898 in Richmond County, North Carolina. His home-building company quickly became Charlotte's second biggest. By the time he turned the firm over to his son in 1973, his subdivisions included Beverly Woods, Club Colony, Plaza Hills, Morningside, Forest Park, Ashley Park, Spring Valley, Woodbridge, Laurel Woods, Foxcroft East, Coventry Woods, and Sardis Woods. See Mecklenburg County Register of Deeds Office, map index; *Charlotte News*, May 23, 24, June 14, 1977.

37. Ervin was a millionaire at age thirty-one, and by 1968 his company had built in the Charlotte area alone 10,000 single-family dwellings, 2,000 apartment units, and about 2 million square feet of retail, office, and warehouse space. See *Charlotte Observer*, April 14, 1957, May 1, 1960, August 24, 1962, March 10, 1968. Ervin suburbs ringed the city, including Raintree, Tanglewood, Idlewild, Derita Woods, Springfield, Montclaire, Starmount, and Westchester. See Mecklenburg County Register of Deeds Office, map index.

38. *Charlotte Observer*, October 23, 1955.

39. *Metrolina Atlas*. Density was about 4,240 persons per square mile in 1928; 3,096 in 1960. (It had been approximately 3,769 in 1885.)

40. *Charlotte News*, May 23, 24, June 14, 1977.

41. *Charlotte Observer*, May 1, 1960, March 10, 1968.

42. Ibid., October 23, 1955.

43. Taeuber and Taeuber, *Negroes in Cities*, p. 193; Wiese, "Driving a Thin Wedge of Opportunity"; Rabin, "Roots of Segregation"; Silver, "Changing Face of Neighborhoods."

44. In Memphis the strategy of providing black suburban opportunities in order to protect white areas in other parts of town was explicitly articulated during the 1950s by the Real Estate Board and Mayor Edmund Orgill. See Silver, "Changing Face of Neighborhoods," p. 117. Similarly in Atlanta, see Ambrose, "Redrawing the Color Line." See also Rabin, "Roots of Segregation." The mandate to protect other neighborhoods was more important than the direct FHA aid to blacks; African Americans received only 2 percent of all FHA-insured mortgages issued from the mid-1940s through the mid-1950s. See Squires, "Community Reinvestment," p. 6.

45. See Chapter 5 of the present study.

46. The school rose on farmland purchased from black leader Thad Tate. The facility later became Northwest Junior High when the city erected a new black West Charlotte High farther out Beatties Ford ca. 1960. See Harding, "Charlotte City Schools," p. 134.

47. Frank C. LeGost, "Analysis of the Housing Market of Charlotte, North Carolina, as of July 1, 1955," p. 3, mimeographed report in box 14, Records of the Federal Housing Administration.

48. In "Charlotte: A Good Place to Live, a Good Place to Do Business," supplement to the *Charlotte News*, 1954. For more on University Park, see the *Charlotte Observer*, February 7, 1960; Mecklenburg County Register of Deeds Office, map book 8, p. 449.

49. Silver, "Changing Face of Neighborhoods," pp. 102–6; Bayor, "Urban Renewal, Public Housing, and the Racial Shaping of Atlanta"; Goldfield and Brownell, *Urban America*, p. 352; Mohl, "Trouble in Paradise"; Doyle, *Nashville since the 1920s*, esp. p. 125.

50. Agitation to improve low-income housing had been growing in America's big cities since the late nineteenth century. By the 1910s many municipalities had introduced comprehensive building codes aimed at alleviating slum conditions. The inability of private initiatives and regulatory laws to remedy the situation, however, prompted calls for publicly owned housing, which finally became a reality with federal New Deal aid. See Gwendolyn Wright, *Building the Dream*, pp. 222–32; Glaab and Brown, *History of Urban America*, pp. 238–42; Fairbanks, *Making Better Citizens*.

51. V. S. Woodward, "Housing and Its Relation to Health in Our City," typescript in folder 5, box 98, Nolen papers. On history of the Charlotte Women's Club, founded ca. 1898, see the *Charlotte Observer*, November 15, 1903. Woodward's effort to involve Charlotte clubwomen was part of a wider trend toward "municipal housekeeping" during the Progressive era, as women sought to expand their sphere of influence from the home to the city. See Beard, *Women's Work in Municipalities*; Blain, *Clubwoman as Feminist*, pp. 73–119; Eugenie Ladner Birch, "From Civic Worker to City Planner: Women and Planning, 1890–1980," in Krueckeberg, *American Planner*, pp. 396–427. On such activities in the South, see Anne Firor Scott, *Southern Lady*, pp. 159–63.

52. Handwritten note on checklist titled "Civic Survey and City Plan, October 27, 1916," folder 4, box 98, Nolen papers.

53. Federal Works Agency, *First Annual Report*, pp. 159–89. On the PWA and Wagner-Steagall programs, see Gelfand, *Nation of Cities*, pp. 60–61, 11, 121; Gwendolyn Wright, *Building the Dream*, pp. 222–32. On Techwood, see Corley, "Atlanta's Techwood and University Homes Projects."

54. *Charlotte News*, March 11, 1937. For more on leadership by the women's club on the slum issue, see, for instance, the *Charlotte News*, July 8, 1937. The club's involvement was no accident. National public housing activists Helen Alfred and Catherine Bauer urged women's organizations across the country to help secure passage and implementation of the Wagner-Steagall Act. See Birch, "Woman-Made America: The Case of Early Public Housing Policy," in Krueckeberg, *American Planner*, pp. 149–75.

55. *Charlotte News*, February 7–12, 1937; also February 14, March 11, June 10, August 22, 1937. The *News*, locked in a circulation battle with the larger *Charlotte Observer*, specialized in crusading stories to build circulation and reputation in this period, while the arch-conservative *Observer* "steered clear of sensitive issues," according to Claiborne, "*Charlotte Observer*," p. 199. The slum series was penned by Cameron Shipp, mentor of noted Southern social critic W. J. Cash. See Bruce Clayton, "The Proto-Dorian Convention: W. J. Cash and the Race Question," in Crow, Escott, and Flynn, *Race, Class, and Politics in Southern History*, pp. 276–82.

56. *Charlotte Observer*, July 18, 20, 1938; Charlotte City Council Minutes, March 27, 1940.

57. Charlotte City Council Minutes, September 23, November 30, 1938; *Charlotte Observer*, February 14, 1945. The number amounted to nearly one-fifth of the city's housing stock (25,402 units in 1940). See *Charlotte News*, February 9, 1945.

58. Charlotte Housing Authority, *Public Housing in Charlotte*; Charlotte City Council Minutes, November 30, 1938; Harold Dillehay to Charles R. Brockmann, March 4, 1959, in Housing Authority file, Robinson-Spangler Carolina Room, Public Library of Charlotte and Mecklenburg County. For photographs of Charlotte's public housing projects, 1940–1970, see *Charlotte Observer*, December 8, 1985.

59. Edwin L. Jones, Frank Dowd, Earle Gluck, James A. Stokes, and L. R. McEliece made up the Housing Authority board; all were residents of Myers Park and Dilworth in southeast Charlotte. See *Charlotte News*, December 18, 1938; Charlotte city directories.

60. Charlotte city directories; Leach, "Progress under Pressure," p. 208.

61. *Charlotte Observer*, September 28, 1948; Frank C. LeGost, "Analysis of the Housing Market of Charlotte, North Carolina, as of July 1, 1955," p. 3, mimeographed report in box 14, Records of the Federal Housing Administration. On FHA financing for low-income rental housing in this period, see J. Paul Mitchell, *Federal Housing Policy and Programs*, pp. 87–88, 95.

62. Goldfield and Brownell, *Urban America*, p. 356. Scattered municipalities may have used New Deal money for particular road projects, but the 1944 act represented the first specific allocation to urban roads. See Federal Works Agency, *Sixth Annual Report*, p. 2. On the Highway Act of 1956 and the Interstate Highway program, see Gelfand, *Nation of Cities*, p. 183. For the history of federal highway funding, see Federal Works Agency, *First Annual Report*, pp. 93–130; Rose, *Interstate*.

63. Charlotte's crosstown boulevard project was announced that August, just weeks after the bill was signed. See *Charlotte Observer*, August 24, 1944. The city was one of fifty urban areas receiving planning aid during the legislation's initial two years. See Federal Works Agency, *Seventh Annual Report*, p. 66.

64. *Charlotte Observer*, August 24, 1944.

65. A series of public hearings after the fact brought forth other route proposals, but in the end the Chantilly decision stood. Some citizens charged that the path had been chosen in part to benefit former mayor Ben Douglas, whose family owned land where the boulevard crossed Elizabeth Avenue. See Morrill, "Road That Split Charlotte." On the naming of Independence Boulevard, see Charlotte City Council Minutes, May 4, 1949.

66. To court further federal aid, state and municipal officials conducted the first study of traffic flows within the city. See *Charlotte News*, February 6, 1945. At the same time, the Mecklenburg County Commission "approved a state highway plan for building secondary roads in Mecklenburg after the War," with the promise that the state and the federal government would provide substantial aid. See *Charlotte Observer*, February 6, 1945. And in 1946 municipal officials hired engineer James Marshall to draw up proposals for a system of improved local thoroughfares. See *Charlotte Observer*, February 26, 1946. Marshall subsequently played a major role in transportation planning and urban renewal in the city, and today Marshall Park downtown is named in his honor. See Claiborne, *Jack Claiborne's Charlotte*, pp. 7–8.

67. On Charlotte civic leaders' efforts to attract the interstate highways, see Moye, "Charlotte-Mecklenburg Consolidation," p. 42. On the opening of I-85 from Gastonia to Charlotte, see *Charlotte Observer*, August 21, 22, 1962. Like Independence Boulevard, the interstates avoided Charlotte's southeast sector. Route 177/277 in particular served as a valuable tool to continue the demolition of older neighborhoods close to the center city. Portions of Brooklyn, Greenville, and First Ward fell in the expressway's path.

68. Kenneth T. Jackson, *Crabgrass Frontier*, p. 258; Worley, *J. C. Nichols*. On the history of shopping centers, see also Longstreth, "Neighborhood Shopping Center"; Yehoshua S. Cohen, *Diffusion of an Innovation*; Liebs, *Main Street to Miracle Mile*, pp. 29–33; Hanchett, "U.S. Tax Policy and the Shopping Center Boom."

69. Kenneth T. Jackson, *Crabgrass Frontier*, p. 259; Yehoshua S. Cohen, *Diffusion of an Innovation*, pp. 36–37; Hanchett, "U.S. Tax Policy and the Shopping Center Boom."

70. Ture, *Accelerated Depreciation*. On depreciation prior to 1954, see Hogan, *Depreciation Policies and Resultant Problems*, pp. 2–15. Congress amended the code several times after 1954, most notably increasing incentives in 1981, then tightening them in 1986. See Hanchett, "U.S. Tax Policy and the Shopping Center Boom."

71. Ture, *Accelerated Depreciation*, pp. 53–54; Maisel, *Financing Real Estate*, p. 362; Gaylon E. Greer, *Real Estate Investment Decision*, pp. 83–84.

72. Ture, *Accelerated Depreciation*, p. 10.

73. Hanchett, "U.S. Tax Policy and the Shopping Center Boom." See also Yehoshua S. Cohen, *Diffusion of an Innovation*, pp. 36–37; Hoyt, "Status of Shopping Centers in the United States."

74. *Directory of Shopping Centers in the United States and Canada* (1970).

75. Charlotte city directories; Kratt and Hanchett, *Legacy*, p. 142. In 1911 John Nolen had sketched a small shopping center for Myers Park at Providence and Queens Roads, but it was never built. See Chapter 6.

76. Providence Center, designed by architect Charles Connelly, opened in January 1947 with a Colonial Stores supermarket, Providence Center Hardware, Huddleston's Florist, Manor Theatre, Union National Bank branch, U.S. Post Office branch, and Park Place Pharmacy. See *Charlotte Observer*, January 20, September 2, 1945, January 16, 1947. At the same time, Charlotte's center city merchants were complaining about lack of parking downtown. See *Charlotte News*, January 13–18, 1947.

77. *Charlotte News*, January 8, 1947; *Charlotte Observer*, February 28, 1950.

78. *Directory of Shopping Centers in the United States and Canada* (1965).

79. The Park Road Shopping Center had 350,000 square feet of retail space, compared with 50,000 in the earlier Sedgefield neighborhood center. See *Directory of Shopping Centers in the United States and Canada* (1959), pp. 161–66; Shopping Centers vertical file, Robinson-Spangler Carolina Room, Public Library of Charlotte and Mecklenburg

County; Mrs. A. V. Blankenship, interview with Thomas W. Hanchett in Charlotte, June 1982.

80. *Charlotte Observer*, April 23, 1961.

81. *Charlotte News*, November 11, 1959.

82. *Charlotte Observer*, October 26, 28, 1959; *Charlotte News*, October 27, 1959. On Charlottetown's subsequent history, read Lord, "Revitalization of Shopping Centers." See also Shopping Centers vertical file, Robinson-Spangler Carolina Room, Public Library of Charlotte and Mecklenburg County. The world's first enclosed mall was Southdale in Minneapolis, completed in the bumper year of 1956. See Liebs, *Main Street to Miracle Mile*, p. 31.

83. Belk's first shopping plaza store in North Carolina had opened in Greensboro's Friendly Center in 1957. By 1962 Belk and Ivey were already seeking land for what would become Southpark. See Covington, *Belk*, pp. 188, 200, 217–20.

84. *Charlotte News*, September 5, 1930. "Dealers in Real Estate believed they should have the freedom to develop it as they liked, and the general public looked upon planning as a luxury that should not be purchased in hard times" (Stone, Price, and Stone, *City Manager Government in Charlotte*). Though Charlotte's resistance was stronger than in some other Dixie cities, the South in general "contained relatively few city-planning committees" at the start of the 1930s, compared with other parts of the United States. See Brownell, "Commercial-Civic Elite and City Planning," p. 343. On Southern city planning, see also Silver, "Urban Planning in the New South"; Silver, *Twentieth Century Richmond*; Koleen Alice Haire Huggins, "Evolution of City and Regional Planning."

85. Hanchett, "Federal Government and the Rise of Municipal Planning." For background on American city planning trends, consult Mel Scott, *American City Planning*; Funigiello, *Challenge to Urban Liberalism*.

86. *Charlotte Observer*, February 26, 1946.

87. Ibid., May 7, 1944.

88. Ibid., April 21, June 1, July 27, 1944, March 17, August 5, 1945; Hanchett, "Federal Government and the Rise of Municipal Planning."

89. *Charlotte Observer*, June 20, 1947. On the War Mobilization and Reconversion Act, see Federal Works Agency, *Seventh Annual Report*, p. 1; Federal Works Agency, *Eighth Annual Report*, p. 4; Walker, *Planning Function in Urban Government*, p. 345.

90. *Charlotte Observer*, March 4, April 18, May 7, June 25, August 5, 1944. On Lanham Act grants for "community facilities," see Federal Works Agency, *Second Annual Report*, pp. 29–54; Funigiello, *Challenge to Urban Liberalism*, p. 45.

91. Roberts, *Pattern for Charlotte*. The first edition of the report appeared in April 1944. A revised and expanded edition came out later that year.

92. Charlotte City Council Minutes, December 20, 1944; *Charlotte Observer*, December 20, 21, 1944.

93. FHA evaluators would "insist upon the observance of rational principles of development in those areas in which insured mortgages are desired," emphasized the agency's *Circular No. 5*, pp. 3–4. In a speech to the National Association of Real Estate Boards, FHA official Seward Mott elaborated: "We found in small towns we were unable to insure loans because there was no zoning protection. . . . The best advice we can give these communities is that they organize and establish their own commission and thus gain control over the growth of the town, and get subdivision regulations. We will be glad to come down and tell you how to go about organizing a City Planning Commission" (quoted in Weiss, *Community Builders*, p. 150).

94. Federal Housing Administration, *Circular No. 5*, p. 8. See also Federal Housing Administration, *Planning Neighborhoods for Small Houses*.

95. Charlotte City Council Minutes, January 29, 1946. The subdivision ordinance had been specifically requested by the Charlotte Real Estate Board. See *Charlotte Observer*, February 4, 1945.

96. Charlotte City Council Minutes, January 14, 1947; *Charlotte Observer*, January 15, 1947. To administer the ordinance, the mayor appointed the Zoning Board of Adjustment, with Charlotte Real Estate Board president E. B. Dudley, architect Walter Hook, grocer W. P. Covington, office supply dealer William Shaw, and real estate broker Paul Guthery as chairman. See *Charlotte Observer*, February 5, 1947.

97. The zoning map first appeared in the *Charlotte News*, January 25, 1947; reprinted with full text of the ordinance February 5. An updated map appeared in the *Charlotte Observer*, May 5, 1949.

98. On similar tendencies elsewhere in the South, see Mohl, "Trouble in Paradise"; Silver, "Racial Origins of Zoning."

99. *Charlotte Observer*, February 4, 1945; Hanchett, "Federal Government and the Rise of Municipal Planning."

100. *Charlotte News*, March 1, 1945. For a sketchy history of building regulation in Charlotte prior to the 1940s, see Green, *Building Regulation and Inspection*.

101. Charlotte clubwomen led the campaign for comprehensive code enforcement: Business and Professional Women's Club, Charlotte Women's Club, Junior Women's Club, League of Women Voters, Charlotte Council of Parents and Teachers. See *Charlotte Observer*, August 19, December 30, 1948. As in 1937, their campaign included a photographic exposé of slum conditions. See *Charlotte News*, August 31–September 7, 1945. On the Real Estate Board's antipathy toward code enforcement, see, for instance, *Charlotte Observer*, October 23, 1947, August 15, 1948. Though the clubwomen won enforcement of most of the code in 1948, the Realtors succeeded in having requirements for indoor bathtubs further deferred until June 30, 1951. See *Charlotte Observer*, August 19, 1948.

102. *Charlotte Observer*, August 10, 1949. Rents went up markedly to cover the improvements, doubling in some cases.

103. National Association of Real Estate Boards, *Primer of Rehabilitation*; William W. Nash, *Residential Rehabilitation*, pp. 86–96, 106.

104. Scott Greer, *Urban Renewal*; Hirsch, *Making of the Second Ghetto*; Teaford, *Rough Road to Renaissance*; Silver, *Twentieth Century Richmond*; Bayor, "Urban Renewal, Public Housing, and the Racial Shaping of Atlanta"; Gelfand, *Nation of Cities*; Carl Abbott, *New Urban America*, pp. 146–69.

105. Carl Abbott, *New Urban America*, p. 149.

106. Scott Greer, *Urban Renewal*, pp. 30–33.

107. *Charlotte News*, June 6, 1960.

108. *Charlotte Observer*, September 22, 1912.

109. Redevelopment Commission of Charlotte, *Statistical Summary of Urban Renewal Program*. On displacement, see, for instance, *Charlotte Observer*, January 20, 1960.

110. White real estate agents directed blacks to particular formerly all-white areas on the north and west sides, but not toward the southeast. Brookshire Realty, run by the mayor's brother, mailed letters evicting white tenants in Wesley Heights and Seversville, for example, as it sought to transform that area from all-white to all-black. See *Charlotte Observer*, November 2, 3, 5, 6, 1965. Similarly elsewhere, see Orser, *Blockbusting in Baltimore*; Hirsch, "Massive Resistance in the Urban North"; Sugrue, "Crabgrass-Roots Politics."

111. See, for instance, *Charlotte Observer*, April 15, 1965. Data on the number of businesses displaced are from Redevelopment Commission of Charlotte, *Statistical Summary of Urban Renewal Program*.

112. *Charlotte Observer*, October 9, 10, 11, 13, 14, 1962.

113. Goldfield, *Cotton Fields and Skyscrapers*, p. 168.

114. *Charlotte News*, October 22, 1977.

115. Ibid., March 4, 1966; *Charlotte Observer*, May 24, 1969, March 30, 1972.

116. Charlotte NAACP flyer (1945), quoted in Leach, "Progress under Pressure," p. 70. Charlotte funeral home director Kelly Alexander succeeded in establishing Charlotte's first branch of the NAACP in 1940 and played a leading role in civil rights efforts over the following decades.

117. Leach, "Progress under Pressure," pp. 70–79.

118. Vose, *Caucasians Only*; Kluger, *Simple Justice*.

119. Quoted in Leach, "Progress under Pressure," p. 214.

120. Davison M. Douglas, *Reading, Writing, and Race*, p. 81.

121. James McMillan, "Opinion and Order Regarding Desegregation of Schools of Charlotte and Mecklenburg County, NC," April 23, 1969, p. 9., in box 3, folder 11, Chambers papers.
McMillan's decision rested on devastating evidence presented by Chambers that showed that the city government had actively promoted residential segregation over the years. Assisting Chambers in compiling and presenting the data was Philadelphia-based urban planning consultant Yale Rabin, a frequent expert witness for the NAACP in these years. The Rabin and Chambers testimony is on file at the National Archives, Southeast Region repository. The *Swann* case is civil case #1974, filed in the year 1968. Material pertaining to residential segregation may be found in "Answers to Interrogatories," stamped March 6, 1969, and in "Record on Appeal, Volume VII, Transcript of Proceedings, March 10, 1969, Part II," esp. pp. 544–678.
While McMillan's main decision dealt largely with racial segregation, his subsequent rulings on specific plans focused on economic segregation as well, rejecting initial proposals that would have exempted southeast Charlotte from busing. On economic segregation and the busing controversy in Charlotte, see Gaillard, *Dream Long Deferred*, pp. 57, 62–63, 111, 115, 117, 119–20, 123, 129, 131; Davison M. Douglas, *Reading, Writing, and Race*, pp. 202–3, 217–21, 229–43. McMillan's obituary appeared in the *New York Times*, March 7, 1995.

122. John Emmeus Davis, *Contested Ground*, esp. pp. 144–46.

123. The best exploration of the federal policies concerning citizen participation is Connerly, "Federal Urban Policy and the Birth of Democratic Planning." For specific examples, see also Silver, "Changing Face of Neighborhoods," pp. 120–21; Lubove, *Twentieth Century Pittsburgh*, pp. 161–65, 176.

124. Don Carroll, telephone interview with Thomas W. Hanchett, February 1984; Pam Patterson, telephone interview with Thomas W. Hanchett, February 1984. Both were past presidents of the Elizabeth Community Association, and both subsequently won seats on city council. The growth of active neighborhood organizations in white areas followed the lead of earlier such organization in black areas. On black Grier Heights's Eastside Council on Civic Affairs, ca. 1965, see Leach, "Progress under Pressure," p. 198.

125. Morrill and Little-Stokes, "Architectural Analysis"; William B. A. Culp of the Dilworth Community Association, telephone interview with Thomas W. Hanchett, February 1986; Bill Hodges of the Myers Park Homeowners Association, telephone interview with Thomas W. Hanchett, May 1983.

126. Dave Howard of the Charlotte City Planning Commission, telephone interview with Thomas W. Hanchett, December 1983; Francis Gay of the Plaza-Midwood Neighborhood Association, telephone interviews with Thomas W. Hanchett, December 1982, December 1983; Mary Anne Hammond of the Plaza-Midwood Neighborhood Association, telephone interviews with Thomas W. Hanchett, December 1983, July 1984.

127. *Charlotte Observer*, February 1, 1963. The speaker was commissioner Craig Lawing from northern Mecklenburg, an early proponent of district elections.

128. Gaillard, *Dream Long Deferred*, pp. 111, 155–57. See also Davison M. Douglas, *Reading, Writing, and Race*, chap. 9.

129. *Charlotte Observer*, March 24, 1974.

130. Moye, "Charlotte-Mecklenburg Consolidation," pp. 249–57; Gaillard, *Dream Long Deferred*, pp. 156–58; Coffin, *Brookshire and Belk*.

131. Gantt, not coincidentally, lived in the Fourth Ward historic district. On his election, see Edds, *Free at Last*, pp. 191–211; Davidson and Grofman, *Quiet Revolution in the South*.

AFTERWORD

1. Since the 1970s, well-to-do suburban areas around Charlotte have begun to resist annexation, including Matthews and Indian Trail in southeastern Mecklenburg County, as well as new communities created nearby in Union County, North Carolina, and York County, South Carolina.

2. Scholars stressing the importance of separate suburban governments include Rusk, *Cities without Suburbs*; Keating, *Building Chicago*; Teaford, *City and Suburb*. Significantly, cities in the South often continued to annex their suburbs as late as the post–World War II era, long after the process had virtually ceased in the North. See Carl Abbott, *New Urban America*, p. 55. It may well be, of course, that inequalities would have been even more severe if Charlotte had not had a single unified government.

3. The hottest development trend in the 1990s was the "urban village" concept. Developers and designers proposed new large-scale "villages" with centrally located shopping districts and a mix of housing types, intended to replicate small-town patterns from the era before sorting. In many cases such projects even gave up the notion of curving streets, returning to the old-fashioned grid in a symbolic refutation of the ideals of residential-only single-class planning. See Langdon, *Better Place to Live*.

4. Garreau, *Edge City*; Sharpe and Wallock, "Bold New City or Built-up 'Burb?'"; Fishman, *Bourgeois Utopias*, chap. 7.

BIBLIOGRAPHY

MANUSCRIPT COLLECTIONS

Baker Library, Graduate School of Business, Harvard University, Cambridge, Mass.
    R. G. Dun collection
Carolina Room, Greensboro Public Library, Greensboro, N.C.
Carolina Room, Hickory Public Library, Hickory, N.C.
Department of Manuscripts and Archives, Cornell University, Ithaca, N.Y.
    Earle Sumner Draper papers
    John Nolen papers
Department of Special Collections, Atkins Library, University of North Carolina,
    Charlotte
    Kelly Alexander papers
    Herbert H. Baxter papers
    Martin Boyer papers
    Julius Chambers papers
    Earle Sumner Draper interviews
    Plaza Midwood neighborhood collection
    VanLandingham family papers
Duke University, Durham, N.C.
    Earle Sumner Draper papers
Fisk University, Nashville, Tenn.
    Charles Chesnutt diaries
Library of Congress, Washington, D.C.
    Olmsted Associates collection
National Archives, Southeast Region, East Point, Ga.
    Swann v. Mecklenburg, 1968 civil case #1974.
National Archives, Washington, D.C.
    Despatches from U.S. Consuls in Sierra Leone, 1858–1906 (microfilm)
    Home Owners' Loan Corporation Survey Files (record group 195)
    Records of the Federal Housing Administration, Research and Statistics Division
        (record group 31)
North Carolina State Archives, Raleigh
    Heriot Clarkson collection
    Division of Negro Instruction collection
Planning Library, University of North Carolina, Chapel Hill
    John Nolen's personal collection of newspaper and magazine clippings
Robinson-Spangler Carolina Room, Public Library of Charlotte and Mecklenburg
    County, Charlotte, N.C.
Southern Historical Collection, Wilson Library, University of North Carolina,
    Chapel Hill
    Louis Asbury papers
    Heriot Clarkson papers
    Charles B. Jonas papers

Southern Oral History collection
Springs family papers
Special Collections Room, Johnson C. Smith University, Charlotte, N.C.
Special Collections Room, Queens College, Charlotte, N.C.

NATIONAL AND LOCAL LANDMARKS REPORTS (UNPUBLISHED)

Survey and Planning Branch, North Carolina State Historic Preservation Office,
Raleigh
  Cross, Jerry. "Washington Street Historic District, High Point." 1982.
  National Register Nominations
    Addison Apartments
    East Raleigh–South Park Historic District
    East Wilson Historic District
    Highland Park Manufacturing Company Mill No. 3
    Hoskins Mill
    Hotel Charlotte
    Latta Arcade
    Mecklenburg Investment Company Building
    Myers Park Historic District
    North Charlotte Historic District
    Seaboard Air Line Railroad Station
    Thomas Trotter Building
    Victoria
Charlotte Mecklenburg Historic Landmarks Commission, Charlotte
  Hanchett, Thomas W. "Charlotte and Its Neighborhoods: The Growth of a New
    South City." 1986.
  Morrill, Dan L. "Dilworth: Charlotte's Initial Streetcar Suburb." In "Architectural
    Analysis: Dilworth, Charlotte's Initial Streetcar Suburb," by Dan L. Morrill and
    Ruth Little-Stokes. Charlotte: Dilworth Community Association, 1978.
  ———. "A Survey of Cotton Mills in Charlotte, North Carolina." 1981.
  Morrill, Dan L., and Ruth Little-Stokes. "Architectural Analysis: Dilworth,
    Charlotte's Initial Streetcar Suburb." Charlotte: Dilworth Community
    Association, 1978.
  Morrill, Dan L., and Nancy Thomas. "New South Neighborhoods Brochure
    Series." 1981.
  "Report to the Charlotte Mecklenburg Historical Properties Commission from the
    Mint Museum of Art." 1975.
  Survey and Research Reports
    Walter L. Alexander House
    Atherton Mill House
    Belk Department Store
    Richard C. Biberstein House
    Biddle Hall
    Blair Building
    Walter Brem House
    Carter Hall

The Cedars
Charlotte City Hall
Charlotte Cotton Mill
Charlotte Supply Company
C. C. Coddington Building
Cole Manufacturing Company
Crowell-Kemp House
George E. Davis House
Excelsior Club
First ARP Church
Former Hovis Mortuary
Gautier-Gilchrist House
Good Samaritan Hospital
Grace AME Zion Church
Hand Pharmacy
Harrill-Porter House
F. O. Hawley Jr. Mansion
Independence Building
Independence Park
Ivey Department Store
John Jamison House
Law Building
Lynnwood (James B. Duke Mansion)
Mallonee-Jones House
Masonic Temple
Mecklenburg County Courthouse
Mecklenburg Mill
Charles Moody House
Myers Park Streetcar Waiting Stations
Neel House
Jake Newell House
North Carolina Medical College Building
Old Alpha Mill
Old Carnegie Library at Johnson C. Smith University
Old Carolina Theater
Charles W. Parker House
Piedmont & Northern Railway Station
Poplar Apartments
Professional Building
Randolph Scott House
St. Peter's Episcopal Church
Settler's Cemetery
Staten Mansion
Teachers' House at Johnson C. Smith University
VanLandingham Estate
Villalonga-Alexander House
H. M. Wade House

Charlotte City Clerk's Office. "Historical Records" binder.

Charlotte City Council Minutes.

Charlotte Housing Authority. *Public Housing in Charlotte: Better Homes for Better Citizens and a Better City: Report of the Housing Authority of the City of Charlotte.* Charlotte: Charlotte Housing Authority, [1944].

Charlotte Water Department. Water Permit records.

Code of the City of Charlotte. Charlotte: Hirst Printing Company, 1887.

Code of the City of Charlotte. Charlotte: Washburn Press, 1915.

Courses of Study, Junior and Senior High Schools. Charlotte: Charlotte City Schools, 1925–1926.

Digest of the Rulings of the Federal Reserve Board (1914–1927, Inclusive) Washington, D.C.: Government Printing Office, 1928.

Emergency Relief in North Carolina: A Record of the Development and the Activities of the North Carolina Emergency Relief Administration, 1932–1935. Raleigh: NCERA, 1936.

Federal Housing Administration. *Circular No. 4: Operative Builders.* FHA form 241. Washington, D.C.: Government Printing Office, 1937.

———. *Circular No. 5: Subdivision Standards for the Insurance of Mortgages on Properties Located in Undeveloped Subdivisions.* FHA form 2059. Washington, D.C.: Government Printing Office, 1938.

———. *Planning Neighborhoods for Small Houses.* Technical Bulletin Number Five. Washington, D.C.: Government Printing Office, 1936.

Federal Reserve. *Banking and Monetary Statistics.* Washington, D.C.: Board of Governors of the Federal Reserve System, 1941.

Federal Works Agency. *Eighth Annual Report: Federal Works Agency, 1947.* Washington, D.C.: Government Printing Office, 1947.

———. *First Annual Report: Federal Works Agency, 1940.* Washington, D.C.: Government Printing Office, 1940.

———. *Second Annual Report: Federal Works Agency, 1941.* Washington, D.C.: Government Printing Office, 1941.

———. *Seventh Annual Report: Federal Works Agency, 1946.* Washington, D.C.: Government Printing Office, 1946.

———. *Sixth Annual Report: Federal Works Agency, 1945.* Washington, D.C.: Government Printing Office, 1945.

Fifth Annual Report: Superintendent, Charlotte Waterworks, Charlotte, North Carolina. Charlotte, 1904.

Mecklenburg County Register of Deeds Office. Subdivision map index, map books, deed books, grantor/grantee indexes, records of corporations.

National Commission on Urban Problems. *Building the American City.* Washington, D.C.: Government Printing Office, 1969.

National Housing Agency. *Fourth Annual Report of the National Housing Agency: January 1 to December 31, 1945.* Washington, D.C.: Government Printing Office, 1946.

———. *Third Annual Report of the National Housing Agency: January 1 to December 31, 1944.* Washington, D.C.: Government Printing Office, 1945.

North Carolina Bureau of Labor and Printing. *Thirteenth Annual Report, 1899.*
    Raleigh: Edwards and Broughton and E. M. Ezzell, 1900.
North Carolina Bureau of Labor Statistics. *Fourth Annual Report of the Bureau of*
    Labor Statistics of the State of North Carolina for the Year 1890. Raleigh: Josephus
    Daniels, 1890.
——. *Tenth Annual Report, 1896.* Winston, N.C.: M. I. & J. C. Stewart, 1897.
North Carolina Department of Labor and Printing. *Annual Report, 1910.* Raleigh:
    Edwards and Broughton, 1910.
——. *Thirty-Fifth Annual Report, 1925–26.* Raleigh: Mitchell Printing Co., 1926.
Public Laws of North Carolina.
Redevelopment Commission of Charlotte. *Statistical Summary of Urban Renewal*
    Program, October 1972. Charlotte: Redevelopment Commission of Charlotte, 1972.
Sanborn Insurance Maps of Charlotte, 1886, 1900, 1905, 1911, 1929.
"Some High Spots in the History of Charlotte's Public Water Supply." Undated,
    unpublished manuscript in the files of the Charlotte Water Works.
United States Code: Congressional and Administrative News. 83rd Congress, Second
    Session. Vol. 3. St. Paul, Minn.: West Publishing, 1954.
U.S. Bureau of the Census. *1970 Census of Population and Housing.* Washington,
    D.C.: Government Printing Office, 1972. Table H1.
——. *Eighth Census: 1870.* "Populations of Civil Divisions Less than Counties."
    Table 3, p. 224.
——. *Ninth Census: 1880.* "Population by Race and Nativity." Table 6, p. 422.
——. *Ninth Census: 1880: Manufactures.* Vol. 2, table 4.
——. "Percentage of Total Area Planted in Cotton." 1880.
——. *Seventh Census: 1860.* "State of North Carolina: Population of Cities, Towns &
    c." Table 3, p. 339.
——. *Seventh Census: 1860.* "Statistics of North Carolina." Pp. 210, 235–36.
——. *Sixteenth Census: 1940.* "North Carolina." Number of Inhabitants, table 2.
——. *Sixteenth Census: 1940.* "Population and Housing: Families, General
    Characteristics." P. 226.
——. *Sixth Census: 1850.* "Statistics of North Carolina." Table xi.
——. *Tenth Census: 1880: Manufactures.* Vol. 2, table 4.
——. *Third Census: 1810.* Manuscript roll for Mecklenburg County.
U.S. Department of Agriculture. *Atlas of American Agriculture.* Washington, D.C.:
    Government Printing Office, 1918.

BOOKS AND ARTICLES

Abbott, Carl. *The New Urban America: Growth and Politics in Sunbelt Cities.* Rev.
    ed. Chapel Hill: University of North Carolina Press, 1987.
Abbott, F. C. *Fifty Years in Charlotte Real Estate, 1897–1947.* Charlotte: Privately
    published, 1947.
——. *North Carolina's Finest Town, the City of Charlotte, and What Some of Its*
    Newer Citizens Have to Say about It. Charlotte: Privately published, 1899.
Abrams, Douglas Carl. *Conservative Constraints: North Carolina and the New Deal.*
    Jackson: University of Mississippi Press, 1992.
Alanen, Arnold R. "Corporate Vernacular: Communities and Housing in Michigan's

Copper Country." In *Perspectives in Vernacular Architecture II*, edited by Camile Wells. Columbia: University of Missouri Press, 1986.

Alexander, J. B. *The History of Mecklenburg County from 1740 to 1900*. Charlotte: Observer Printing House, 1902.

——. *Reminiscences of the Past Sixty Years*. Charlotte: Ray Printing Co., 1908.

Alexander, Julia. *Charlotte in Picture and Prose*. Charlotte: Julia Alexander, 1906.

Allcott, John V. *Colonial Houses in North Carolina*. Raleigh: Carolina Charter Tercentenary Commission, 1963.

American Medical Association. "Hospital Service in the United States." *Journal of the American Medical Association* 92, no. 13 (March 30, 1929): 1043–1118.

Anderson, Eric. *Race and Politics in North Carolina, 1876–1902: The Black Second*. Baton Rouge: Louisiana State University Press, 1981.

Anderson, James. *The Education of Blacks in the South, 1860–1935*. Chapel Hill: University of North Carolina Press, 1988.

Andrews, Mildred Gwin. *The Mills and the Men: A History of the Southern Textile Industry*. Macon, Ga.: Mercer University Press, 1987.

Archer, John. "Country and City in the American Romantic Suburb." *Journal of the Society of Architectural Historians* 42, no. 2 (May 1983): 139–56.

Ashe, Samuel A. *Eminent and Representative Men of the Carolinas*. Vol. 2. Madison, Wisc.: Bryant and Fuller, [1892].

——, ed. *Biographical History of North Carolina, from Colonial Times to the Present*. 8 Vols. Greensboro, N.C.: Van Noppen, 1905–17.

Atherton, Lewis. *Main Street on the Middle Border*. New York: Quadrangle Books, 1954.

Atlanta Urban Design Commission. *Atlanta Historic Resources Workbook*. Atlanta: Atlanta Urban Design Commission, 1981.

Ayers, Edward L. *The Promise of the New South: Life after Reconstruction*. New York: Oxford University Press, 1992.

Badger, Anthony J. *North Carolina and the New Deal*. Raleigh: N.C. Department of Cultural Resources, 1981.

Bainbridge, Robert, and Kate Ohno. *Wilson Historic Buildings Inventory, Wilson, North Carolina*. Wilson, N.C.: City of Wilson and the N.C. Department of Cultural Resources, 1980.

Barney, William L. *Passage of the Republic: An Interdisciplinary History of Nineteenth Century America*. Lexington, Mass.: D. C. Heath, 1987.

——. "Patterns of Crisis: Alabama White Families and Social Change, 1850–1870." *Sociology and Social Research* 63, no. 3 (April 1979): 524–43.

Barrier, Smith. *On Carolina's Gridiron, 1888–1936*. Durham, N.C.: Seeman Printery, 1937.

Barth, Frederick. *Ethnic Groups: The Social Organization of Cultural Differences*. Boston: Little, Brown, 1969.

Barth, Gunther. *City People: The Rise of Modern City Culture in Nineteenth Century America*. New York: Oxford University Press, 1980.

Bass, Jack, and Walter DeVries, *The Transformation of Southern Politics: Social Change and Political Consequence since 1945*. New York: Basic Books, 1976.

Bayor, Ron. "Urban Renewal, Public Housing, and the Racial Shaping of Atlanta." *Journal of Policy History* 1, no. 4 (1989): 419–39.

Beard, Mary. *Women's Work in Municipalities*. New York: Appleton, 1916.

Beasley and Emerson's Charlotte Directory for 1875–76.

Beatty, Bess. "The Edwin Holt Family: Nineteenth Century Capitalists in North Carolina." *North Carolina Historical Review* 63 (October 1986): 511–35.

———. "Lowells of the South: Northern Influences on the Nineteenth Century North Carolina Textile Industry." *Journal of Southern History* 53, no. 1 (February 1987): 36–62.

Beck, John J. "Building the New South: A Revolution from Above in a Piedmont County." *Journal of Southern History* 53, no. 3 (August 1987): 441–70.

Beers, Henry Putney. *The Confederacy: A Guide to the Archives of the Government of the Confederate States of America*. Washington, D.C.: National Archives and Records Administration, 1986.

Bender, Thomas. *Community and Social Change in America*. New Brunswick, N.J.: Rutgers University Press, 1978.

Berry, Brian J. L. *The Open Housing Question: Race and Housing in Chicago, 1966–1976*. Cambridge, Mass.: Ballinger, 1979.

Beveridge, Charles E., and Carolyn F. Hoffman, comps. *Masterlist of the Design Projects of the Olmsted Firm*. Boston: National Association of Olmsted Parks, 1987.

Biles, Roger. "The Urban South in the Great Depression." *Journal of Southern History* 56, no. 1 (February 1990): 71–100.

Billings, Dwight, Jr. *Planters and the Making of a "New South": Class, Politics, and Development in North Carolina, 1865–1900*. Chapel Hill: University of North Carolina Press, 1981.

Binford, Henry. *The First Suburbs: Residential Communities on the Boston Periphery, 1815–1860*. Chicago: University of Chicago Press, 1985.

Bishir, Catherine W. *North Carolina Architecture*. Chapel Hill: University of North Carolina Press, 1990.

Bishir, Catherine W., Charlotte V. Brown, Carl R. Lounsbury, and Ernest H. Wood III. *Architects and Builders in North Carolina: A History of the Practice of Building*. Chapel Hill: University of North Carolina Press, 1990.

Bishir, Catherine W., and Lawrence Earley, eds. *Early Twentieth-Century Suburbs in North Carolina: Essays on History, Planning, and Architecture*. Raleigh: N.C. Department of Cultural Resources, 1985.

Blackmar, Elizabeth. *Manhattan for Rent, 1785–1850*. Ithaca, N.Y.: Cornell University Press, 1989.

———. "Rewalking the 'Walking City': Housing and Property Relations in New York City, 1770–1840." In *Material Life in America, 1600–1860*, edited by Robert St. George, pp. 371–84. Boston: Northeastern University Press, 1988.

Blackwelder, Ruth. *Old Charlotte and Mecklenburg Today*. Charlotte: Mecklenburg Historical Society, 1973.

Blain, Karen G. *The Clubwoman as Feminist: True Womanhood Redefined, 1868–1914*. New York: Holmes and Meier, 1980.

Blassingame, John. "Before the Ghetto: The Making of the Black Community in Savannah, Georgia, 1865–1880." *Journal of Social History* 6 (1973): 463–88.

———. *Black New Orleans, 1860–1880*. Chicago: University of Chicago Press, 1973.

Bledstein, Burton. *The Culture of Professionalism: The Middle Class and the Development of Higher Education in America*. New York: Norton, 1976.

Blumenstein, James, and Benjamin Walter, eds. *Growing Metropolis: Aspects of Development in Nashville*. Nashville: Vanderbilt University Press, 1975.

Blumin, Stuart M. "Black Coats to White Collars: Economic Exchange, Non-Manual Work, and the Social Structure of Industrializing America." In *Small Business in American Life*, edited by Stuart W. Bruchey, pp. 100–121. New York: Columbia University Press, 1980.

———. *The Emergence of the Middle Class: Social Experience in the American City, 1760–1900*. Cambridge: Cambridge University Press, 1989.

———. "The Hypothesis of Middle-Class Formation in Nineteenth Century America: A Critique and Some Proposals." *American Historical Review* 90 (April 1985): 299–338.

Blythe, LeGette. *Robert Lee Stowe, Pioneer in Textiles*. Belmont, N.C.: Heritage Printers, 1965.

———. *William Henry Belk: Merchant of the South*. Chapel Hill: University of North Carolina Press, 1950.

Blythe, LeGette, and Charles Brockmann. *Hornets' Nest: The Story of Charlotte and Mecklenburg County*. Charlotte: McNally of Charlotte, 1961.

Bobinski, George. *Carnegie Libraries*. Chicago: American Library Association, 1969.

Bodnar, John. *The Transplanted: A History of Immigrants in Urban America*. Bloomington: Indiana University Press, 1985.

Boles, John B. *The South through Time: A History of an American Region*. Englewood Cliffs, N.J.: Prentice-Hall, 1995.

Boles, John B., and Evelyn Thomas Nolen. *Interpreting Southern History: Historiographical Essays in Honor of Sanford W. Higginbotham*. Baton Rouge: Louisiana State University Press, 1987.

Borchert, James. *Alley Life in Washington: Family, Community, Religion, and Folklife in the City, 1850–1970*. Urbana: University of Illinois Press, 1980.

Boyer, Paul. *Urban Masses and Moral Order in America, 1820–1920*. Cambridge, Mass.: Harvard University Press, 1978.

Boyte, Harry C., Heather Booth, and Steve Max. *Citizen Action and the New American Populism*. Philadelphia: Temple University Press, 1986.

Boyte, Jack O. *Houses of Charlotte and Mecklenburg County*. Charlotte: Delmar Printing, 1992.

Bradbury, Tom. *Dilworth: The First 100 Years*. Charlotte: Dilworth Community Association, 1992.

Branson's North Carolina Business Directory for 1869. Raleigh: J. A. Jones, [1869].

Brengle, Kim Withers. *The Architectural Heritage of Gaston County, North Carolina*. Gastonia, N.C.: Gaston County, 1982.

Bronner, Simon. "Manner Books and Suburban Houses: The Structure of Traditional Aesthetics." *Winterthur Portfolio* 18, no. 1 (Spring 1983): 61–68.

Brown, Cecil K. *A State Movement in Railroad Development: The Story of North Carolina's First Effort to Establish an East-West Trunk Line Railroad*. Chapel Hill: University of North Carolina Press, 1928.

Brown, Douglas Summers. *The Catawba Indians: The People of the River*. Columbia: University of South Carolina Press, 1966.

Brown, Elsa Barkley, and Greg D. Kimball. "Mapping the Terrain of Black Richmond." *Journal of Urban History* 21, no. 3 (March 1995): 296–346.

Brown, Marvin A. *Greensboro: An Architectural Record*. Greensboro, N.C.: Preservation Greensboro, 1995.

Brownell, Blaine A. "The Commercial-Civic Elite and City Planning in Atlanta, Memphis, and New Orleans in the 1920s." *Journal of Southern History* 41, no. 3 (August 1975): 339–68.

——. *The Urban Ethos in the South, 1920–1930*. Baton Rouge: Louisiana State University Press, 1975.

Brownell, Blaine A., and David Goldfield, eds. *The City in Southern History: The Growth of Urban Civilization in the South*. Port Washington, N.Y.: Kennikat Press, 1977.

Buder, Stanley. *Pullman: An Experiment in Industrial Order and Community Planning, 1880–1930*. New York: Oxford University Press, 1967.

——. *Visionaries and Planners: The Garden City Movement and the Modern Community*. New York: Oxford University Press, 1990.

Burgess, Patricia. *Planning for the Private Interest: Land Use Controls and Residential Patterns in Columbus, Ohio, 1900–1970*. Columbus: Ohio State University Press, 1994.

Burke, DeGrandval. *The Brooklyn Story*. Charlotte: Afro-American Cultural Center, 1978.

Burns, Sarah. *Pastoral Inventions: Rural Life in Nineteenth Century American Art and Culture*. Philadelphia: Temple University Press, 1989.

Byerly, Victoria. *Hard Times Cotton Mill Girls: Personal Histories of Womanhood and Poverty in the South*. Ithaca, N.Y.: ILR Press, 1986.

Byrne, Ann D., and Dana F. White. "Atlanta University's 'Northeast Lot': Community Building for Black Atlanta's 'Talented Tenth.'" *Atlanta Historical Journal* 26, no. 2–3 (Summer–Fall 1982): 155–76.

Caldwell, A. B., ed. *History of the American Negro: North Carolina Edition*. Vol. 4. Atlanta: A. B. Caldwell, 1921.

Carlton, David. *Mill and Town in South Carolina, 1880–1920*. Baton Rouge: Louisiana State University Press, 1982.

——. "The Piedmont and Waccamaw Regions: An Economic Comparison." *South Carolina Historical Magazine* 88, no. 2 (1987): 81–100.

——. "The Revolution from Above: The National Market and the Beginnings of Industrialization in North Carolina." *Journal of American History* 77, no. 2 (September 1990): 445–75.

Carlton, David, and Peter Coclanis. "Capital Mobilization and Southern Industry: The Case of the Carolina Piedmont." *Journal of Economic History* 49 (March 1989): 73–94.

Carter, Wilmouth. *The Urban Negro in the South*. New York: Vantage, 1961.

Cash, W. J. *The Mind of the South*. New York: Vintage, 1941.

Cell, John W. *The Highest Stage of White Supremacy: The Origins of Segregation in South Africa and the American South*. Cambridge: Cambridge University Press, 1982.

Charlotte Branch, Federal Reserve Bank of Richmond: Fiftieth Anniversary, 1927–1977. [Richmond]: Federal Reserve Bank of Richmond, 1977.

Charlotte Chamber of Commerce. *1950 Census Data*. Charlotte: Chamber of Commerce, 1950.

——. *Charlotte, North Carolina: Diversified Industrial and Commercial Center.* Charlotte: Chamber of Commerce, 1930.

——. *"In the Heart of the Piedmont": Charlotte, North Carolina.* Charlotte: Observer Printing House, [ca. 1920].

——. *Research Report: The Charlotte Economy.* Charlotte: Greater Charlotte Chamber of Commerce, 1981.

——. *The Story of Charlotte, Illustrated.* Charlotte: Chamber of Commerce, 1915.

"Charlotte in the War between the States." *Confederate Veteran* 37, no. 5 (May 1929): 168–69.

"Charlotte: Unsouthern, Untypical." *Business Week*, August 11, 1951, pp. 70–84.

Checkoway, Barry. "Large Builders, Federal Housing Programs, and Postwar Suburbanization." *International Journal of Urban and Regional Research* 4, no. 1 (March 1980): 21–45.

Cherry, Susan Spaeth. "Carnegies Live." *American Libraries*, April 1981, pp. 184–88, 218.

Chesnutt, Helen M. *Charles Waddell Chesnutt: Pioneer of the Color Line.* Chapel Hill: University of North Carolina Press, 1952.

Chesson, Michael B. *Richmond after the War, 1865–1890.* Richmond: Virginia State Library, 1981.

Christaller, Walter. *Central Places in Southern Germany.* Englewood Cliffs, N.J.: Prentice-Hall, 1966.

Claiborne, Jack. *"The Charlotte Observer": Its Time and Place, 1869–1986.* Chapel Hill: University of North Carolina Press, 1986.

——. *Jack Claiborne's Charlotte.* Charlotte: Charlotte Publishing, 1974.

Clark, Clifford E., Jr. *The American Family Home, 1800–1960.* Chapel Hill: University of North Carolina Press, 1986.

Clark, Thomas D., and Albert D. Kirwan. *The South since Appomattox: A Century of Regional Change.* New York: Oxford University Press, 1967.

Clarkson, Heriot. *History of the Law Library Association of Charlotte.* Charlotte: Privately published, 1941.

[Clarkson, Heriot]. *It Helps Business and Is a Blessing: What Leading Businessmen, Bankers, Farmers, and Laborers Say about Prohibition in Charlotte, N.C.* 2nd ed. Charlotte: Executive Committee of Anti-Saloon League of Charlotte, 1908.

Clay, James W., and Alfred W. Stuart, eds. *Charlotte: Patterns and Trends of a Dynamic City.* Charlotte: Urban Institute of the University of North Carolina at Charlotte, 1987.

Clay, James W., Douglas M. Orr Jr., and Alfred W. Stuart, eds. *North Carolina Atlas: Portrait of a Changing Southern State.* Chapel Hill: University of North Carolina Press, 1975.

——. *North Carolina Urban Regions: An Economic Atlas.* Charlotte: Urban Institute of the University of North Carolina at Charlotte, 1983.

Clayton, Thomas H. *Close to the Land: The Way We Lived in North Carolina, 1820–1870.* Chapel Hill: University of North Carolina Press, 1983.

Cobb, James C. "Beyond Planters and Industrialists: A New Perspective on the New South." *Journal of Southern History* 54, no. 1 (February 1988): 45–68.

Cochrane, Thomas. *Frontiers of Change: Early Industrialization in America.* New York: Oxford University Press, 1981.

Coclanis, Peter. *The Shadow of the Dream: Economic Life and Death in the South Carolina Low Country, 1670–1920.* New York: Oxford University Press, 1989.

Coffin, Alex. *Brookshire and Belk: Businessmen in City Hall.* Charlotte: University of North Carolina at Charlotte, 1994.

Cohen, Lizabeth A. "Embellishing a Life of Labor: An Interpretation of the Material Culture of American Working-Class Homes, 1885–1915." In *Material Culture Studies in America*, edited by Thomas J. Schlereth, pp. 289–305. Nashville: AASLH, 1982.

Cohen, Yehoshua S. *Diffusion of an Innovation in an Urban System: The Spread of Planned Regional Shopping Centers in the United States, 1949–1968.* Research paper no. 140. Chicago: University of Chicago, Department of Geography, 1972.

Coit, Charles Guernsey. *The Federal Reserve Bank of Richmond.* New York: Columbia University Press, 1941.

Comey, Arthur C., and Max S. Wehrly. "Planned Communities." In *Urban Planning and Land Policies.* Vol. 2 of *The Supplementary Report of the Urbanism Committee to the National Resources Committee*, pp. 3–162. Washington, D.C.: Government Printing Office, 1939.

Condit, Carl. *The Rise of the Skyscraper.* Chicago: University of Chicago Press, 1952.

Connerly, Charles. "Federal Urban Policy and the Birth of Democratic Planning in Birmingham, Alabama, 1949–1974." In *Planning the Twentieth Century American City*, edited by Mary Corbin Sies and Christopher Silver, pp. 331–58. Baltimore: Johns Hopkins University Press, 1996.

Conzen, Kathleen N. *Immigrant Milwaukee, 1836–1860: Accommodation and Community in a Frontier City.* Cambridge, Mass.: Harvard University Press, 1976.

Conzen, Michael P. "Historical Geography: Changing Spatial Structure and Social Patterns of Western Cities." *Progress in Human Geography* 7, no. 1 (March 1983): 88–107.

———. "The Morphology of Nineteenth Century Cities in the United States." In *Urbanization in the Americas: The Background in Comparative Perspective*, edited by W. Borah, J. Hardoy, and Gilbert Stetler, pp. 119–42. Ottawa: National Museum of Man, 1980.

Conzen, Michael P., and Kathleen N. Conzen. "Geographical Structure in Nineteenth Century Urban Retailing: Milwaukee, 1836–1890." *Journal of Historical Geography* 5, no. 1 (1979): 45–66.

Corbett, David L. *The Formation of the North Carolina Counties, 1663–1943.* Raleigh: State Department of Archives and History, 1950.

Corley, Florence Fleming. "Atlanta's Techwood and University Homes Projects: The Nation's Laboratory for Public Housing." *Atlanta History* 31 (Winter 1987–88): 17–32.

Cotter, John L., Daniel G. Roberts, and Michael Parrington. *The Buried Past: An Archeological History of Philadelphia.* Philadelphia: University of Pennsylvania, 1993.

Covington, Howard E., Jr. *Belk: A Century of Retail Leadership.* Chapel Hill: University of North Carolina Press, 1988.

Covington, Howard E., Jr., and Marion A. Ellis. *The Story of NationsBank: Changing the Face of American Banking.* Chapel Hill: University of North Carolina Press, 1993.

Cramer, Stuart W. *Useful Information for Cotton Manufacturers*. 4 vols. [Charlotte]: Stuart Cramer, 1904–9.

Cranz, Galen. *The Politics of Park Design: A History of Urban Parks in America*. Cambridge, Mass.: MIT Press, 1982.

Creese, Walter L. TVA's *Public Planning: The Vision, the Reality*. Knoxville: University of Tennessee Press, 1990.

Cremin, Lawrence. *American Education: The National Experience, 1873–1876*. New York: Harper and Row, 1981.

Cromley, Elizabeth Collins. *Alone Together: A History of New York's Early Apartments*. Ithaca, N.Y.: Cornell University Press, 1990.

Crow, Jeffrey, and Robert Durden. *Maverick Republican: A Political Biography of Daniel L. Russell*. Baton Rouge: Louisiana University Press, 1976.

Crow, Jeffrey, Paul Escott, and Charles Flynn Jr. *Race, Class, and Politics in Southern History: Essays in Honor of Robert F. Durden*. Baton Rouge: Louisiana State University Press, 1989.

Crow, Jeffrey, and Flora Hatley, eds. *Black Americans in North Carolina and the South*. Chapel Hill: University of North Carolina Press, 1984.

Curry, Leonard P. *The Free Black in Urban America, 1800–1850: The Shadow of the Dream*. Chicago: University of Chicago Press, 1981.

——. "Urbanization and Urbanism in the Old South: A Comparative View." *Journal of Southern History* 40, no. 1 (February 1974): 43–60.

Cutler, William W., III, and Howard Gillette Jr., eds. *The Divided Metropolis: Social and Spatial Dimensions of Philadelphia, 1800–1975*. Westport, Conn.: Greenwood Press, 1980.

Dahl, Robert A. *Who Governs? Democracy and Power in an American City*. New Haven: Yale University Press, 1961.

Daniels, Jonathan. *Tarheels: A Portrait of North Carolina*. New York: Dodd, Mead, 1941.

"David Ovens: Man of the South for 1951." *Dixie Business* 24, no. 1 (Summer 1952): 10, 17.

Davidson, Chalmers G. *The Plantation World around Davidson*. Davidson, N.C.: Mecklenburg Historical Association, 1969.

Davidson, Chandler, and Bernard Grofman, eds. *Quiet Revolution in the South: The Impact of the Voting Rights Act, 1965–1990*. Princeton: Princeton University Press, 1994.

Davis, Burke. *The Southern Railway: Road of the Innovators*. Chapel Hill: University of North Carolina Press, 1985.

Davis, John Emmeus. *Contested Ground: Collective Action and the Urban Neighborhood*. Ithaca, N.Y.: Cornell University Press, 1990.

Davis, Stephen. "Empty Eyes, Marble Head: The Confederate Monument and the South." *Journal of Popular Culture* 16 (Winter 1982): 2–21.

Dean, Pamela. "Learning to Be New Women: Campus Culture at the North Carolina Normal and Industrial School." *North Carolina Historical Review* 68 (July 1991): 286–306.

Demos, John. *A Little Commonwealth: Family Life in Plymouth Colony*. New York: Oxford University Press, 1970.

Directory of Shopping Centers in the United States and Canada. Burlington, Iowa: National Research Bureau, 1965.

Directory of Shopping Centers in the United States and Canada. Burlington, Iowa: National Research Bureau, 1970.

Directory of Shopping Centers in the United States and Canada. Chicago: National Research Bureau, 1959.

Dixon, Thomas. *Southern Horizons: The Autobiography of Thomas Dixon*. Alexandria, Va.: IWV, 1984.

Domosh, Mona. "Imagining New York's First Skyscrapers, 1875–1910." *Journal of Historical Geography* 13, no. 3 (1987): 233–48.

Douglas, Davison M. *Reading, Writing, and Race: The Desegregation of the Charlotte Schools*. Chapel Hill: University of North Carolina Press, 1995.

Dowd, Clement. *Life of Vance*. Charlotte: Observer Printing House, 1897.

Doyle, Don H. *Nashville in the New South, 1880–1930*. Knoxville: University of Tennessee Press, 1985.

———. *Nashville since the 1920s*. Knoxville: University of Tennessee Press, 1985.

———. *New Men, New Cities, New South: Atlanta, Nashville, Charleston, Mobile, 1860–1910*. Chapel Hill: University of North Carolina Press, 1990.

Dozier, Richard K. *Places and Spaces: The Contributions, Aspirations, and Aesthetic Values of Afro-Americans as Reflected in Architecture*. Montgomery, Ala.: Montgomery Landmarks Foundation, 1982.

Draper, Earle Sumner. "A Landscape Artist's Concept of Subdivisions." *National Real Estate Journal*, January 11, 1926, pp. 32–35.

Dreyer, Martha A. *The Spencer Architectural and Historic Inventory*. Spencer, N.C.: Town of Spencer, 1984.

Duboff, R. B. "The Introduction of Electric Power in American Manufacturing." *Economic History Review* 20 (1967): 509–18.

DuBois, W. E. B., ed. *The Negro Artisan*. Atlanta: Atlanta University Press, 1902.

Durden, Robert F. *The Dukes of Durham, 1865–1929*. Durham, N.C.: Duke University Press, 1975.

Ebner, Michael. *Creating Chicago's North Shore: A Suburban History*. Chicago: University of Chicago Press, 1988.

Edds, Margaret. *Free at Last: What Really Happened When Civil Rights Came to Southern Politics*. Bethesda, Md.: Adler and Adler, 1987.

Edel, Matthew, Elliott Sclar, and Daniel Luria. *Shaky Palaces: Home Ownership and Social Mobility in Boston's Suburbanization*. New York: Columbia University Press, 1984.

Edge, Sara Simms. *Joel Hurt and the Development of Atlanta*. Atlanta: Atlanta Historical Society, 1955.

Eichler, Ned. *The Merchant Builders*. Cambridge, Mass.: MIT Press, 1982.

Encyclopedia of Textiles. 3rd ed. Englewood Cliffs, N.J.: Prentice-Hall, 1980.

Engst, Elaine D., and H. Thomas Hickerson. *Urban America: Documenting the Planners*. Ithaca, N.Y.: Cornell University Libraries, 1985.

Escott, Paul D. *Many Excellent People: Power and Privilege in North Carolina, 1850–1900*. Chapel Hill: University of North Carolina Press, 1985.

"Evolution of the Shopping Center." *The Community Builder's Handbook*. Washington, D.C.: Urban Land Institute, 1965.

Fairbanks, Robert B. *Making Better Citizens: Housing Reform and Community Development Strategy in Cincinnati, 1890–1960*. Urbana: University of Illinois Press, 1988.

Farmer, Charles J. *In the Absence of Towns: Settlement and Country Trade in Southside Virginia, 1730–1800*. Lanham, Md.: Rowman and Littlefield, 1993.

Feller, Irwin. "The Draper Loom in New England Textiles, 1894–1914: A Study of the Diffusion of an Innovation." *Journal of Economic History* 26 (September 1966): 320–47.

Fenn, Elizabeth A., and Peter H. Wood. *Natives and Newcomers: The Way We Lived in North Carolina before 1770*. Chapel Hill: University of North Carolina Press, 1983.

Fetters, Thomas T., and Peter Swanson Jr. *Piedmont and Northern: The Great Electric Interurban System of the South*. San Marino, Calif.: Golden West Books, 1974.

Fields, Mamie Garvin, with Karen Fields. *Lemon Swamp and Other Tales: A Carolina Memoir*. New York: Free Press, 1983.

Fink, Leon. *Workingmen's Democracy: The Knights of Labor and American Politics*. Urbana: University of Illinois Press, 1983.

Fishman, Robert. *Bourgeois Utopias: The Rise and Fall of Suburbia*. New York: Basic Books, 1987.

Fitch, James Marsten. *American Building: The Historical Forces That Shaped It*. 2nd ed. New York: Schocken Books, 1973.

Foner, Eric. *Nothing but Freedom: Emancipation and Its Legacy*. Baton Rouge: Louisiana State University Press, 1983.

——. *Reconstruction: America's Unfinished Revolution, 1863–1877*. New York: Harper and Row, 1988.

Foote, William. *Sketches of North Carolina*. New York: Robert Carter, 1846.

Ford, Barbara. *Keeping Things Cool: The Story of Refrigeration and Air Conditioning*. New York: Walker, 1986.

Ford, L. R. "Individual Decisions in the Creation of the American Downtown." *Geography* 58 (1973): 324–27.

Ford, Lacy K. *Origins of Southern Radicalism: The South Carolina Upcountry, 1800–1860*. New York: Oxford University Press, 1988.

Franklin, John Hope. *From Slavery to Freedom: A History of Negro Americans*. 3rd ed. New York: Vintage, 1969.

Franklin, W. W. "Water and Sewerage Facilities, City of Charlotte: Past, Present, and Future." *Journal of the North Carolina Section, American Water Works Association and North Carolina Sewerage and Industrial Wastes Association* 32, no. 1 (1956): 31–38.

Frisbie, W. Parker, and John D. Kassarda. "Spatial Processes." In *The Handbook of Sociology*, edited by Neil J. Smelzer, pp. 629–66. Newbury Park, Calif.: Sage, 1988.

Frisch, Michael. *Town into City: Springfield, Massachusetts, and the Meaning of Community, 1840–1860*. Cambridge, Mass.: Harvard University Press, 1972.

Funigiello, Philip J. *The Challenge to Urban Liberalism: Federal-City Relations during World War II*. Knoxville: University of Tennessee Press, 1978.

Gaillard, Frye. *The Dream Long Deferred*. Chapel Hill: University of North Carolina Press, 1988.

Garner, John S. *The Model Company Town: Urban Design through Private Enterprise in Nineteenth Century New England*. Amherst: University of Massachusetts Press, 1984.

——, ed. *The Company Town: Architecture and Society in the Early Industrial Age*. New York: Oxford University Press, 1992.

Garreau, Joel. *Edge City: Life on the New Frontier*. New York: Doubleday, 1991.

Gaston, Paul. *The New South Creed: A Study in Southern Mythmaking*. New York: Knopf, 1970.

Gavins, Raymond. "Urbanization and Segregation: Black Leadership Patterns in Richmond, Virginia, 1900–1920." *South Atlantic Quarterly* 79, no. 3 (Summer 1980): 257–73.

Geist, Johann Freidlich. *Arcades: The History of a Building Type*. Cambridge, Mass.: MIT Press, 1983.

Gelfand, Mark. *A Nation of Cities: The Federal Government and Urban America, 1933–1965*. New York: Oxford University Press, 1975.

Genovese, Eugene. *Fruits of Merchant Capital: Slavery and Bourgeois Property in the Rise and Expansion of Capitalism*. New York: Oxford University Press, 1983.

———. *The Political Economy of Slavery: Studies in the Economy and Society of the Slave South*. New York: Vintage, 1967.

George, Arthur A. *100 Years, 1867–1967: Salient Factors in the Growth and Development of Johnson C. Smith University*. Charlotte: JCSU, 1975.

Gilbert, John, and Grady Jefferys. *Crossties through Carolina*. Raleigh: Helios Press, 1969.

Gilmore, Glenda. "Gender and Jim Crow: Sarah Dudley Pettey's Vision of the New South." *North Carolina Historical Review* 68 (July 1991): 261–85.

Girouard, Mark. *The English Town: A History of Urban Life*. New Haven: Yale University Press, 1990.

Glaab, Charles N., and A. Theodore Brown. *A History of Urban America*. 3rd ed. New York: Macmillan, 1983.

Glass, Brent. "Southern Mill Hills: Design in a 'Public' Place." In *Carolina Dwelling: Towards Preservation of Place*, edited by Doug Swaim, pp. 138–49. Raleigh: North Carolina State University, 1978.

———. *The Textile Industry in North Carolina: A History*. Raleigh: North Carolina Division of Archives and History, 1992.

Glassie, Henry. *Folk Housing in Middle Virginia: A Structural Analysis of Historic Artifacts*. Knoxville: University of Tennessee Press, 1975.

Glenton, Mary V. *Story of a Hospital*. Hartford, Conn.: Church Missions, 1937.

Golden, Harry. *The Right Time: An Autobiography*. New York: Putnam, 1969.

Goldfield, David. *Cotton Fields and Skyscrapers: Southern City and Region, 1607–1980*. Baton Rouge: Louisiana State University Press, 1982.

———. *Urban Growth in the Age of Sectionalism: Virginia, 1847–1861*. Baton Rouge: Louisiana State University Press, 1977.

Goldfield, David, and Blaine A. Brownell. *Urban America: A History*. 2nd ed. Boston: Houghton Mifflin, 1990.

Goldin, Claudia. *Urban Slavery in the American South, 1820–1860*. Chicago: University of Chicago Press, 1978.

Goldsmith William W., and Edward Blakely. *Separate Societies: Poverty and Inequality in U.S. Cities*. Philadelphia: Temple University Press, 1992.

Goodwyn, Lawrence. *Democratic Promise: The Populist Moment in America*. New York: Oxford University Press, 1976.

Gowans, Allan. *The Comfortable House: North American Suburban Architecture, 1890–1930*. Cambridge, Mass.: MIT Press, 1986.

Grable, Stephen W. "The Other Side of the Tracks: Cabbagetown, a Working-Class

Neighborhood in Transition during the Early Twentieth Century." *Atlanta Historical Journal* 26, no. 2–3 (Summer–Fall 1982): 51–66.

Graham, Otis, Jr., and Meghan Robinson Wander, eds. *Franklin D. Roosevelt, His Life and Times: An Encyclopedic View*. Boston: G. K. Hall, 1985.

Grantham, Dewey. *Southern Progressivism: The Reconciliation of Progress and Tradition*. Knoxville: University of Tennessee Press, 1983.

——. *The South in Modern America: A Region at Odds*. New York: HarperCollins, 1994.

Graves, John William. "Jim Crow in Arkansas: A Reconsideration of Urban Race Relations in the Post-Reconstruction South." *Journal of Southern History* 55, no. 3 (August 1989): 421–48.

Greater Charlotte Club. *Queen Charlotte, the Hydro-Electric Center*. Charlotte: Greater Charlotte Club, 1913.

Green, Phillip J., Jr. *Building Regulation and Inspection in Charlotte and Mecklenburg County*. Chapel Hill: University of North Carolina Institute of Government, 1949.

Greene, Suzanne Ellery. *Baltimore: An Illustrated History*. Woodland Hill, Calif.: Windsor, 1980.

Greenwood, Janette Thomas. *Bittersweet Legacy: The Black and White "Better Classes" in Charlotte, 1850–1910*. Chapel Hill: University of North Carolina Press, 1994.

——. *On the Home Front: Charlotte during the Civil War*. Charlotte: History Department of the Mint Museum, 1982.

Greer, Gaylon E. *The Real Estate Investment Decision*. Lexington, Mass.: Lexington Books, 1979.

Greer, Scott. *Urban Renewal and American Cities: The Dilemma of Democratic Intervention*. Indianapolis: Bobbs-Merrill, 1965.

——, ed. *Ethnics, Machines, and the American Urban Future*. Cambridge, Mass.: Schenckman, 1981.

Griffin, Richard W., and Diffee W. Standard. "The Cotton Textile Industry in Ante-Bellum North Carolina." Pt. 1, "Origin and Growth to 1830." *North Carolina Historical Review* 34 (January 1957): 15–35.

——. "The Cotton Textile Industry in Ante-Bellum North Carolina." Pt. 2, "An Era of Boom and Consolidation, 1830–1860." *North Carolina Historical Review* 34 (April 1957): 131–64.

Groth, Paul. "Lot, Yard, and Garden: American Distinctions." *Landscape* 30, no. 3 (1990): pp. 29–35.

Groves, Paul A., and Edward K. Muller. "The Evolution of Black Residential Areas in Late Nineteenth Century Cities." *Journal of Historical Geography* 1, no. 2 (1975): 169–91.

Grundy, Pamela. "From *Il Trovatore* to the Crazy Mountaineers: The Rise and Fall of Elevated Culture on WBT-Charlotte, 1922–1930." *Southern Cultures* 1 (Fall 1994): 51–73.

——. " 'We Always Tried to Be Good People': Respectability, Crazy Water Crystals, and Hillbilly Music on the Air, 1933–1935." *Journal of American History* 81, no. 4 (March 1995): 1591–1620.

Gutman, Herbert. *Work, Culture, and Society in Industrializing America: Essays in American Working Class and Social History*. New York: Vintage, 1977.

Hagler, Guy, and John Nolen. "Town Planning Actualities: Some Recently Executed

Improvement Schemes in American Small Towns." *Review of Reviews* 62 (December 1920): 633–37.

Hahn, Steven. *The Roots of Southern Populism: Yeoman Farmers and the Transformation of the Georgia Upcountry, 1850–1890.* New York: Oxford University Press, 1983.

Hall, Jacquelyn Dowd, James Leloudis, Robert Korstad, Mary Murphy, Lu Ann Jones, and Christopher B. Daly. *Like a Family: The Making of a Southern Cotton Mill World.* Chapel Hill: University of North Carolina Press, 1987.

Hamilton, J. G. DeRoulhac. *Reconstruction in North Carolina.* Gloucester, Mass.: Peter Smith, 1964.

Hanchett, Thomas W. "Before Olmsted: The New South Career of Joseph Forsyth Johnson." *Atlanta History* 39 (Fall–Winter 1995): 12–27.

———. "The Federal Government and the Rise of Municipal Planning in the 1940s." *Journal of the American Planning Association* 60, no. 2 (Spring 1994): 197–208.

———. "John Nolen and the Planning of Savannah's Daffin Park, 1906–1909." *Georgia Historical Quarterly* 78, no. 4 (Winter 1994): 810–27.

———. "The Rosenwald Schools and Black Education in North Carolina." *North Carolina Historical Review* 65 (October 1988): 387–444.

———. "U.S. Tax Policy and the Shopping Center Boom of the 1950s and 1960s." *American Historical Review* 101 (October 1996): 1082–1110.

———. "W. W. Smith: Black 'Designer and Builder.'" *North Carolina Preservation* 67 (Spring 1987): 7–9.

Hancock, John L. *John Nolen: A Bibliographical Record of Achievement.* Ithaca, N.Y.: Cornell University, Program in Urban and Regional Studies, 1976.

Handlin, David P. *The American Home: Architecture and Society, 1815–1915.* Boston: Little, Brown, 1979.

Handlin, Oscar. *Boston's Immigrants, 1790–1880.* Rev. ed. New York: Atheneum, 1974.

Hareven, Tamara K., and Randolph Langenbach. *Amoskeag: Life and Work in an American Factory-City.* New York: Pantheon, 1978.

Harkey, W. Hugh, Jr. *Greetings from Charlotte: A Pictorial Postcard History of Charlotte.* Charlotte: Hornet's Nest Productions, 1992.

———. *More Tales from the Hornet's Nest.* Charlotte: Hornet's Nest Productions, 1992.

Harlan, Louis R. *Booker T. Washington: The Making of a Black Leader, 1865–1901.* New York: Oxford University Press, 1972.

———. *Booker T. Washington: The Wizard of Tuskegee, 1901–1915.* New York: Oxford University Press, 1983.

Harris, Carl V. *Political Power in Birmingham, 1871–1921.* Knoxville: University of Tennessee Press, 1977.

Harris, Richard. "American Suburbs: A Sketch of a New Interpretation." *Journal of Urban History* 15, no. 1 (November 1988): 98–103.

Harris, Wade Hampton. *Sketches of Charlotte.* Charlotte: Observer Printing House, 1889.

———. *Sketches of Charlotte, No. 3.* Charlotte: Wade H. Harris, 1899.

———. *Sketches of Charlotte.* 8th ed. Charlotte: Observer, 1909.

———, ed. *Charlotte.* Charlotte: City of Charlotte et al., 1924.

Hasbrouk, Wilbert R., and Paul E. Sprague. *A Survey of Historic Architecture in the Village of Oak Park, Illinois.* Oak Park, Ill.: Landmarks Commission of the Village of Oak Park, 1976.

Hayes, R. Allen. *The Federal Government and Urban Housing: Ideology and Change in Public Policy*. Albany, N.Y.: State University of New York Press, 1985.

Hays, Samuel P. *Conservation and the Gospel of Efficiency: The Progressive Conservation Movement, 1890–1920*. Cambridge, Mass.: Harvard University Press, 1959.

——. "The Politics of Reform in Municipal Government in the Progressive Era." *Pacific Northwest Quarterly* 55 (October 1964): 157–69.

Hearnden, Patrick. *Independence and Empire: The New South's Cotton Mill Campaign, 1865–1901*. DeKalb: Northern Illinois University Press, 1982.

Henderson, Alexa Benson. *Atlanta Life Insurance Company: Guardian of Black Economic Dignity*. Tuscaloosa: University of Alabama Press, 1990.

Henderson, Archibald. *Washington's Southern Tour, 1791*. Boston: Houghton Mifflin, 1923.

Henderson, Thomas W. *John Nolen's City Planning Work in the South*. Monticello, Ill.: Vance Bibliographies, 1987.

Herring, Harriet. *Welfare Work in Mill Villages: The Story of Extra-Mill Activities in North Carolina*. Chapel Hill: University of North Carolina Press, 1929.

Hilliard, Sam Bowers. *Atlas of Antebellum Southern Agriculture*. Baton Rouge: Louisiana University Press, 1984.

Hirsch, Arnold R. *The Making of the Second Ghetto: Race and Housing in Chicago, 1940–1960*. Cambridge: Cambridge University Press, 1983.

——. "Massive Resistance in the Urban North: Trumbull Park, Chicago, 1953–1966." *Journal of American History* 82, no. 2 (September 1995): 522–50.

Hirsh, Richard F. *Technology and Transformation in the American Electric Utility Industry*. New York: Cambridge University Press, 1989.

Hodge, David C. "Geography and the Political Economy of Urban Transportation." *Urban Geography* 11, no. 1 (1990): 87–100.

Hogan, William T. *Depreciation Policies and Resultant Problems*. Studies in Industrial Economics #8. New York: Fordham University Press, 1967.

Hohenberg, Paul, and Lynn Hollen Lees. *The Making of Urban Europe, 1000–1950*. Cambridge, Mass.: Harvard University Press, 1985.

Holt, George, ed. *The Charlotte Country Music Story*. Charlotte: Folklife Section of the North Carolina Arts Council, 1985.

Horowitz, Helen Lefkowitz. *Alma Mater: Design and Experience in Women's Colleges from Their Nineteenth Century Beginnings to the 1930s*. New York: Knopf, 1984.

Hoyt, Homer. "The Status of Shopping Centers in the United States." *Urban Land* 19, no. 5 (1960): 4–16.

——. *The Structure and Growth of Residential Neighborhoods in American Cities*. Washington, D.C.: Federal Housing Administration, 1939.

——. *Where the Rich and the Poor People Live: The Location of Residential Areas Occupied by the Highest and Lowest Income Families in American Cities*. Washington, D.C.: Urban Land Institute, 1966.

Huggins, Kay Haire. "Town Planning in North Carolina, 1704–1920." *North Carolina Architect* 20 (November/December 1973): 16–20.

Hunter, Julius K. *Westmoreland and Portland Places: The History and Architecture of America's Premier Private Streets, 1888–1988*. Columbia: University of Missouri Press, 1988.

Huxtable, Ada Louise. *The Tall Building Artistically Reconsidered: The Search for a Skyscraper Style*. New York: Pantheon, 1984.

Isaacs, Reginald. "The Neighborhood Unit as an Instrument for Segregation." *Journal of Housing* 5 (August 1948): 215–19.

Jackson, John Brinkerhoff. *Landscapes: Selected Writings of J. B. Jackson*. Amherst: University of Massachusetts Press, 1970.

Jackson, Kenneth T. *Crabgrass Frontier: The Suburbanization of the United States*. New York: Oxford University Press, 1985.

——, ed. *The Encyclopedia of New York City*. New Haven: Yale University Press, 1995.

Jacobs, Jane. *Cities and the Wealth of Nations: Principles of Economic Life*. New York: Vintage, 1985.

——. *The Death and Life of Great American Cities*. New York: Vintage, 1961.

Janiewski, Dolores. *Sisterhood Denied: Race, Gender, and Class in a New South Community*. Philadelphia: Temple University Press, 1985.

Jenkins, Virginia Scott. *The Lawn: A History of An American Obsession*. Washington, D.C.: Smithsonian Institution Press, 1994.

Johnson, Charles S. *Patterns of Negro Segregation*. New York: Harper and Brothers, 1943.

Johnson, Joseph Forsyth. "The Laws of Developing Landscape, Showing How to Make Thickets and Woodlands Reveal Their Natural Beauty." *Journal of the Royal Horticultural Society* 29 (1904–5): 595–624.

——. *The Natural Principle of Landscape Gardening: Or the Adornment of Land for Perpetual Beauty*. Belfast: Archer and Sons, 1874.

——. *Residential Sites and Environments, Their Conveniences, Gardens, Parks and Planting, etc.* New York: A. T. Delamare, 1898.

Johnson, Paul. *A Shopkeeper's Millennium: Society and Revivals in Rochester, New York, 1813–1837*. New York: Hill and Wang, 1978.

Jones, Charles R. "A Sketch of Charlotte." In *Beasley and Emerson's Charlotte Directory for 1875–76*, pp. 132–41. Charlotte: Beasley and Emerson, [1875].

Karr, Ronald Dale. "Brookline Rejects Annexation, 1873." In *Suburbia Re-examined*, edited by Barbara Kelly, pp. 103–10. Westport, Conn.: Greenwood Press, 1989.

Kasson, John. *Rudeness and Civility: Manners in Nineteenth Century Urban America*. New York: Hill and Wang, 1990.

Katz, Michael B. *The Irony of Early School Reform: Educational Innovation in Mid-Nineteenth Century Massachusetts*. Boston: Beacon, 1968.

——. *The People of Hamilton, Canada West: Family and Class in a Mid-Nineteenth Century City*. Cambridge, Mass.: Harvard University Press, 1975.

Katzman, David M. *Before the Ghetto: Black Detroit in the Nineteenth Century*. Urbana: University of Illinois Press, 1973.

Keating, Ann Durkin. *Building Chicago: Suburban Developers and the Creation of a Divided Metropolis*. Columbus: Ohio State University Press, 1988.

Kelley, Robin D. G. *Race Rebels: Culture, Politics, and the Black Working Class*. New York: Free Press, 1994.

Kellogg, John. "The Formation of Black Residential Areas in Lexington, Kentucky, 1865–1887." *Journal of Southern History* 48, no. 1 (February 1982): 21–52.

——. "Negro Urban Clusters in the Post-Bellum South." *Geographical Review* 47 (July 1977): 310–21.

Key, V. O. *Southern Politics in State and Nation*. New York: Knopf, 1949.

King, Anthony D. "The Bungalow: An Indian Contribution to the West." *History Today*, November 1982, pp. 38–44.

——. *The Bungalow: The Production of a Global Culture*. Boston: Routledge, 1984.

Kinkle, Roger D. *The Complete Encyclopedia of Popular Music and Jazz, 1900–1950*. New Rochelle, N.Y.: Arlington House, 1974.

Kipp, Samuel M., III. "Old Notables and Newcomers: The Economic and Political Elite of Greensboro, North Carolina, 1880–1920." *Journal of Southern History* 43, no. 3 (August 1977): 373–94.

Kirby, Jack Temple. *Rural Worlds Lost: The American South, 1920–1960*. Baton Rouge: Louisiana State University Press, 1987.

Klaus, Susan L. "Efficiency, Economy, Beauty: The City Planning Reports of Frederick Law Olmsted, Jr., 1905–1915." *Journal of the American Planning Association* 57, no. 4 (Autumn 1991): 456–70.

Klein, Maury. *The Great Richmond Terminal: A Study in Businessmen and Business Strategy*. Charlottesville: University Press of Virginia, 1970.

——. *Unfinished Business: The Railroad in American Life*. Hanover, N.H.: University Press of New England, 1994.

Kluger, Richard. *Simple Justice: The History of Brown v. Board of Education and Black America's Struggle for Equality*. New York: Vintage, 1975.

Knox, Paul. *Urban Social Geography: An Introduction*. 2nd ed. New York: John Wiley and Sons, 1987.

Kostof, Spiro. *The City Assembled: Elements of Urban Form through History*. London: Thames and Hudson, 1992.

——. *The City Shaped: Urban Patterns and Meanings through History*. London: Thames and Hudson, 1991.

Kousser, J. Morgan. *The Shaping of Southern Politics: Suffrage Restriction and the Establishment of the One-Party South, 1880–1910*. New Haven: Yale University Press, 1974.

Kratt, Mary Norton. *Charlotte: Spirit of the New South*. 1st ed. Tulsa, Okla.: Continental Heritage Press, 1980.

——. *Charlotte: Spirit of the New South*. 2nd ed. Winston-Salem, N.C.: John F. Blair, 1992.

——. *The Imaginative Spirit: Literary Heritage of Charlotte and Mecklenburg County*. Charlotte: Public Library of Charlotte and Mecklenburg County, 1988.

Kratt, Mary Norton, and Thomas W. Hanchett. *Legacy: The Myers Park Story*. Charlotte: Myers Park Foundation, 1986.

Krim, A. J. *Northwest Cambridge: Report Five, Survey of Architectural History in Cambridge*. Cambridge, Mass.: MIT Press for the Cambridge Historical Commission, 1977.

Krueckeberg, Donald A., ed. *The American Planner: Biographies and Recollections*. New York: Methuen, 1983.

Kulik, Gary, Roger Parks, and Theodore Z. Penn, eds. *The New England Mill Village, 1790–1860*. Cambridge, Mass.: MIT Press, 1982.

Kusmer, Kenneth. *A Ghetto Takes Shape: Black Cleveland, 1870–1930*. Urbana: University of Illinois Press, 1976.

Lafferty, Robert H. *The North Carolina Medical College, Davidson, and Charlotte, North Carolina*. Charlotte: Privately published, 1946.

Lancaster, Clay. "The American Bungalow." *Art Bulletin* 40, no. 3 (September 1958): 239–53.

———. *The American Bungalow, 1880–1930.* New York: Abbeville, 1985.

Langdon, Philip. *A Better Place to Live: Reshaping the American Suburb.* Amherst: University of Massachusetts Press, 1994.

Larsen, Lawrence. *The Rise of the Urban South.* Lexington: University Press of Kentucky, 1985.

Latham, Alexander & Co. *Cotton Movement and Fluctuations.* New York: Latham, Alexander & Co., 1880.

Laurie, Bruce. "Fire Companies and Gangs in Southwark in the 1840s." In *The Peoples of Philadelphia: A History of Ethnic Groups and Lower Class Life, 1790–1840,* edited by Allan F. Davis and Mark Haller, pp. 71–87. Philadelphia: Temple University Press, 1973.

Lawrence, Jeanne Catherine. "Geographical Space, Social Space, and the Realm of the Department Store." *Urban History* 19, no. 1 (April 1992): 64–83.

Lebsock, Suzanne. *The Free Women of Petersburg: Status and Culture in a Southern Town, 1784–1860.* New York: Norton, 1985.

Lefler, Hugh, and Albert Newsome. *North Carolina: The History of a Southern State.* Chapel Hill: University of North Carolina Press, 1973.

Leloudis, James. *Schooling the New South: Pedagogy, Self, and Society in North Carolina, 1880–1920.* Chapel Hill: University of North Carolina Press, 1996.

Levine, Lawrence. *Highbrow/Lowbrow: The Emergence of Cultural Hierarchy in America.* Cambridge, Mass.: Harvard University Press, 1988.

Levi-Strauss, Claude. *The Savage Mind.* Chicago: University of Chicago Press, 1966.

Lewis, Earl. *In Their Own Interests: Race, Class, and Power in Twentieth-Century Norfolk, Virginia.* Berkeley: University of California Press, 1991.

Lewis, F. Pierce. *New Orleans: The Making of a Southern Landscape.* Cambridge, Mass.: Ballinger, 1976.

Lewis, Robert. "The Segregated City: Class Residential Patterns and the Development of Industrial Districts in Montreal, 1861 and 1901." *Journal of Urban History* 17, no. 2 (February 1991): 123–52.

Liebs, Chester. *Main Street to Miracle Mile: American Roadside Architecture.* Boston: Little, Brown, 1985.

Link, William A. *A Hard Country and a Lonely Place: Schooling, Society, and Reform in Rural Virginia, 1870–1920.* Chapel Hill: University of North Carolina Press, 1986.

Lockwood, Charles. *Bricks and Brownstones: The New York Row House, 1783–1929.* New York: McGraw-Hill, 1972.

Logan, Frenise. *The Negro in North Carolina, 1876–1894.* Chapel Hill: University of North Carolina Press, 1964.

Longstreth, Richard. "The Neighborhood Shopping Center in Washington, D.C., 1930–1941." *Journal of the Society of Architectural Historians* 51, no. 1 (March 1992): 5–34.

Lord, J. Dennis. "Revitalization of Shopping Centers." In *Shopping Centre Development: Policies and Prospects,* edited by John A. Dawson and Dennis Lord. New York: Nichols, 1985.

Losch, August. *Economics of Location.* Translated from the 2nd rev. ed. by William Woglam and Wolfgang Stolper. New Haven: Yale University Press, 1954.

Lotchin, Roger W. *Fortress California, 1910–1961: From Warfare to Welfare*. New York: Oxford University Press, 1992.

———, ed. *The Martial Metropolis: United States Cities in War and Peace*. New York: Praeger, 1984.

Lubove, Roy. *Twentieth Century Pittsburgh: Government, Business, and Environmental Change*. New York: John Wiley and Sons, 1969.

Luebke, Paul. *Tar Heel Politics: Myths and Realities*. Chapel Hill: University of North Carolina Press, 1990.

Lynch, Kevin. *The Image of the City*. Cambridge, Mass.: MIT Press, 1960.

McCoy, Drew R. *The Elusive Republic: Political Economy in Jeffersonian America*. Chapel Hill: University of North Carolina Press, 1980.

McCullers, Carson. *The Heart Is a Lonely Hunter*. New York: Houghton Mifflin, 1940.

MacDonald, Lois. *Southern Mill Hills: A Study of Social and Economic Forces in Certain Textile Mill Villages*. New York: Alex Hillman, 1928.

MacDonald, Terence J. *The Parameters of Urban Fiscal Policy: Socioeconomic Change and Political Culture in San Francisco, 1860–1906*. Berkeley: University of California Press, 1986.

McEwen, Mildred Morse. *Queens College Yesterday and Today*. Charlotte: Queens College Alumnae Association, 1980.

McGuire, Peter. "The Seaboard Air Line." *North Carolina Historical Review* 11 (April 1934): 94–115.

Machor, James L. *Pastoral Cities: Urban Ideals and the Symbolic Landscape of America*. Madison: University of Wisconsin Press, 1987.

McLauren, Melton A. "The Knights of Labor in North Carolina Politics." *North Carolina Historical Review* 49 (July 1972): 298–315.

McMath, Robert C. *American Populism: A Social History, 1877–1898*. New York: Hill and Wang, 1993.

———. *Populist Vanguard: A History of the Southern Farmers' Alliance*. Chapel Hill: University of North Carolina Press, 1975.

MacPherson, James. "Antebellum Southern Exceptionalism: A New Look at an Old Question." *Civil War History* 29, no. 3 (September 1983): 230–44.

———. *Ordeal by Fire: The Civil War and Reconstruction*. New York: Knopf, 1982.

McShane, Clay. *Technology and Reform: Street Railways and the Growth of Milwaukee*. Madison: State Historical Society of Wisconsin, 1974.

McTigue, Geraldine. "Patterns of Residence: Housing Distribution by Color in Two Louisiana Towns, 1860–1880." *Louisiana Studies* 15, no. 4 (Winter 1976): 345–88.

Maisel, Sherman J. *Financing Real Estate: Principles and Practices*. New York: McGraw-Hill, 1965.

Marsh, Kenneth, and Blanche Marsh. *Charlotte: Carolinas' Queen City*. Columbia, S.C.: R. L. Bryan.

Marsh, Margaret. *Suburban Lives*. New Brunswick, N.J.: Rutgers University Press, 1990.

Massey, Douglas S. "Ethnic Residential Segregation: A Theoretical Synthesis and Empirical Review." *Sociology and Social Research* 69, no. 3 (April 1985): 316–50.

Massey, Douglas S., and Nancy Denton. *American Apartheid: Segregation and the Making of the Underclass*. Cambridge, Mass.: Harvard University Press, 1993.

Mathews, Donald G. *Religion in the Old South*. Chicago: University of Chicago Press, 1977.

Matthews, Louise Barber. *A History of Providence Presbyterian Church*. Matthews, N.C.: Providence Presbyterian Church, 1967.

Maynor, Joe. *Duke Power: The First Seventy-Five Years*. [Charlotte]: Duke Power, [1979].

Mead, Frank S. *Handbook of Denominations in the United States*. 5th ed. Nashville: Abingdon Press, 1970.

Meier, August, and Elliot Rudwick. "The Boycott Movement against Jim Crow Streetcars in the South, 1900–1906." *Journal of American History* 55, no. 4 (March 1969): 756–75.

Melvin, Patricia Mooney. *The Organic City: Urban Definition and Neighborhood Organization, 1880–1920*. Lexington: University Press of Kentucky, 1987.

Merrell, James H. *The Indians' New World: Catawbas and Their Neighbors from European Contact through the Era of Removal*. Chapel Hill: University of North Carolina Press, 1989.

Merrill, Gilbert. *American Cotton Handbook: Practical Text and Reference Book for the Entire Cotton Industry*. 2nd rev. ed. New York: Textile Book Publishers, 1949.

Miller, Marc S., ed. *Working Lives: The Southern Exposure History of Labor in the South*. New York: Pantheon, 1980.

Miller, William D. *Mr. Crump of Memphis*. Baton Rouge: Louisiana State University Press, 1964.

Miller, Zane L. *Boss Cox's Cincinnati: Urban Politics in the Progressive Era*. New York: Oxford University Press, 1968.

——. "The Role and the Concept of Neighborhood in American Cities." In *Community Organization for Social Change*, edited by Robert Fisher and Peter Romanofsky, pp. 3–32. Westport, Conn.: Greenwood Press, 1981.

——. *Suburb: Neighborhood and Community in Forest Park, Ohio, 1935–1976*. Knoxville: University of Tennessee Press, 1981.

Miller, Zane L., and Patricia Mooney Melvin. *The Urbanization of Modern America: A Brief History*. 2nd ed. San Diego: Harcourt Brace Jovanovich, 1987.

Mitchell, Broadus. *The Rise of Cotton Mills in the South*. Baltimore: Johns Hopkins University Press, 1921.

Mitchell, Broadus, and George Sinclair Mitchell. *The Industrial Revolution in the South*. Baltimore: Johns Hopkins University Press, 1930.

Mitchell, J. Paul. *Federal Housing Policy and Programs: Past and Present*. New Brunswick, N.J.: Center for Urban Policy Research, 1985.

Mobley, Joe. *James City: A Black Community in North Carolina, 1863–1900*. Raleigh: North Carolina Division of Archives and History, 1981.

Mohl, Raymond A. "Making the Second Ghetto in Metropolitan Miami, 1940–1960." *Journal of Urban History* 21, no. 3 (March 1995): 395–427.

——. "Trouble in Paradise: Race and Housing in Miami during the New Deal Era." In *The Making of Urban America*, edited by Raymond A. Mohl, pp. 214–27. Wilmington, Del.: SR Books, 1988.

——, ed. *The Making of Urban America*. Wilmington, Del.: SR Books, 1988.

Mollenkopf, John. *The Contested City*. Princeton: Princeton University Press, 1983.

Monchow, Helen. *The Use of Deed Restrictions in Suburban Development*. Chicago: Institute for Research in Land Economics and Public Utilities, 1928.

Monkkonen, Eric H. *America Becomes Urban: The Development of U.S. Cities and Towns, 1780–1980*. Berkeley: University of California Press, 1988.

Moody's Bank and Finance Manual. Vol. 1. New York: Moody's Investor's Service, 1955, 1960, 1965, 1970, 1990.

Moore, Winfred B., Jr., Joseph F. Tripp, and Lyon G. Tyler Jr., eds. *Developing Dixie: Modernization in a Traditional Society.* Westport, Conn.: Greenwood Press, 1988.

Moore-Parker, Inez. *The Biddle–Johnson C. Smith University Story.* Charlotte: Johnson C. Smith University, 1976.

Morland, John Kenneth. *Millways of Kent.* Chapel Hill: University of North Carolina Press, 1958.

Morrill, Dan L. "Edward Dilworth Latta and the Charlotte Consolidated Construction Company, 1890–1925: Builders of a New South City." *North Carolina Historical Review* 42 (July 1985): 293–316.

——. "The Road That Split Charlotte." *Parade Magazine,* May 2, 1982.

——. *Southern Campaigns of the American Revolution.* Baltimore: Nautical and Aviation Pub. Co. of America, 1993.

Morrison, Joseph L. *W. J. Cash: Southern Prophet.* New York: Knopf, 1967.

Moulton, Emma S. *Cotton Production and Distribution in the Gulf Southwest.* Domestic Commerce Series #49. Washington, D.C.: Department of Commerce, Government Printing Office, 1931.

Muller, Edward K., and Paul A. Groves. "The Emergence of Industrial Districts in Mid-Nineteenth Century Baltimore." *Geographical Review* 69 (April 1979): 159–78.

Murphy, Raymond E., J. E. Vance Jr., and Bart Epstein. "Internal Structure of the CBD." *Economic Geography* 31 (1955): 21–46.

Nash, Gary. *The Urban Crucible: Social Change, Political Consciousness, and the Origins of the American Revolution.* Cambridge, Mass.: Harvard University Press, 1979.

Nash, William W. *Residential Rehabilitation: Private Profits and Public Purposes.* New York: McGraw-Hill, 1959.

National Association of Real Estate Boards. *A Primer of Rehabilitation under Local Law Enforcement.* Washington, D.C.: National Association of Real Estate Boards, 1952.

Navin, Thomas R. *The Whitin Machine Works since 1831: A Textile Machinery Company in an Industrial Village.* Cambridge, Mass.: Harvard University Press, 1950.

Newby, Howard. "The Deferential Dialectic." *Comparative Studies in Society and History* 17 (1975): 139–64.

Newby, I. A. *Plain Folks in the New South: Social Change and Cultural Persistence, 1880–1915.* Baton Rouge: Louisiana State University Press, 1989.

Newton, Norman T. *Design on the Land: The Development of Landscape Architecture.* Cambridge, Mass.: Belknap Press of the Harvard University Press, 1971.

Nisbet, Robert, Susan Wagg, and Anne W. Tucker. *Money Matters: A Critical Look at Bank Architecture.* New York: McGraw-Hill, 1990.

Nolen, John. *Comprehensive City Plan: Roanoke, Virginia, 1928.* Roanoke: Stone Printing, 1928.

——. *New Ideals in the Planning of Cities, Towns, and Villages.* New York: American City Bureau, 1919.

———. *New Towns for Old: Achievements in Civic Improvement in Some American Small Towns and Neighborhoods.* Boston: Marshall Jones, 1927.

———. *Replanning Small Cities: Six Typical Studies.* New York: B. W. Huebsch, 1912.

———, ed. *City Planning: A Series of Papers Presenting the Essential Elements of a City Plan.* New York: Appleton, 1915.

North Carolina Authors: A Selective Handbook. Chapel Hill: University of North Carolina Press, 1952.

Nye, Bill. *Bill Nye: His Book, "A Universal Repository of Thought," Containing Two Hundred Sketches by America's Greatest Humorist.* Chicago: Hill, 1891.

Oakes, James. *The Ruling Race: A History of American Slaveholders.* New York: Vintage, 1983.

O'Brien, Gail Williams. *The Legal Fraternity and the Making of a New South Community, 1848–1882.* Athens: University of Georgia Press, 1986.

———. "Power and Influence in Mecklenburg County, 1850–1880." *North Carolina Historical Review* 56 (April 1977): 120–39.

Olmsted, Frederick Law, Jr., and John Nolen. "Public Open Space in American Towns and Cities." *South Atlantic Quarterly* 5, no. 3 (July 1906): 264–74.

Olson, Sherry H. *Baltimore: The Building of an American City.* Baltimore: Johns Hopkins University Press, 1980.

One Hundredth Anniversary: Young Men's Christian Association of Charlotte and Mecklenburg. Charlotte: Charlotte YMCA, 1974.

Orser, W. Edward. *Blockbusting in Baltimore: The Edmondson Village Story.* Lexington: University Press of Kentucky, 1994.

Park, Robert, Ernest W. Burgess, and Roderick McKenzie, eds. *The City.* Chicago: University of Chicago Press, 1925.

Parkinson, A. E. *The South: Its Economic-Geographic Development.* New York: John Wiley and Sons, 1938.

Pease, William H., and Jane H. Pease. *The Web of Progress: Private Values and Public Styles in Boston and Charleston, 1823–1843.* New York: Oxford University Press, 1985.

Perry, David C., and Alfred Watkins, eds. *The Rise of Sunbelt Cities.* Urban Affairs Annual Reviews, vol. 14. New York: Sage, 1977.

Pessen, Edward. *Riches, Class, and Power before the Civil War.* Lexington, Mass.: D. C. Heath, 1973.

Peterson, Jon A. "The City Beautiful Movement: Forgotten Origins and Lost Meanings." In *Introduction in Planning History in the United States,* edited by Donald A. Krueckeberg, pp. 40–57. New Brunswick, N.J.: Rutgers University Center for Urban Policy Research, 1983.

Philpott, Thomas Lee. *The Slum and the Ghetto: Neighborhood Deterioration and Middle-Class Reform, Chicago, 1880–1930.* New York: Oxford University Press, 1978.

Plank, David N. "Why Study the South?" In *Southern Cities, Southern Schools: Public Education in the Urban South,* edited by David N. Plank and Rick Ginsberg, pp. 3–4. Westport, Conn.: Greenwood Press, 1990.

Pocock, G. J. A. "The Classical Theory of Deference." *American Historical Review* 81 (June 1976): 516–23.

Poore, Patricia, and Clem Labine, eds. *The Old House Journal Compendium.* Garden City, N.J.: Doubleday, 1983.

Pope, Liston. *Millhands and Preachers: A Study of Gastonia*. New Haven: Yale University Press, 1942.

Potter, David M. *The South and Sectional Conflict*. Baton Rouge: Louisiana State University Press, 1968.

Potwin, Marjorie A. *Cotton Mill People of the Piedmont*. New York: Columbia University Press, 1927.

Powell, William S. *North Carolina through Four Centuries*. Chapel Hill: University of North Carolina Press, 1989.

——, ed. *Dictionary of North Carolina Biography*. Vol. 1, A–C. Chapel Hill: University of North Carolina Press, 1979.

Prather, H. Leon, Jr. *We Have Taken a City: Wilmington Racial Massacre and Coup of 1898*. Rutherford, N.J.: Fairleigh Dickinson University, 1984.

Pred, Allan. *Urban Growth and City Systems in the United States, 1840–1860*. Cambridge, Mass.: Harvard University Press, 1980.

Preston, Howard L. *Automobile Age Atlanta: The Making of a Southern Metropolis, 1900–1935*. Athens: University of Georgia Press, 1979.

Price, William S. "North Carolina in the First British Empire: Economy and Society in an Eighteenth Century Colony." In *The North Carolina Experience: An Interpretive and Documentary History*, edited by Lindley S. Butler and Alan D. Watson, pp. 79–87. Chapel Hill: University of North Carolina Press, 1984.

Pritchard, R. M. *Housing and the Spatial Structure of the City: Residential Mobility and the Housing Market in an English City since the Industrial Revolution*. Cambridge: Cambridge University Press, 1976.

Protestant Episcopal Church in the U.S., Domestic and Foreign Missionary Society. *The Church's Work among Negroes: The Good Samaritan Hospital, Charlotte, N.C.* 2nd ed. New York: Calumet Press, 1902.

Prude, Jonathan. *The Coming of the Industrial Order: Town and Factory Life in Rural Massachusetts, 1810–1860*. Cambridge: Cambridge University Press, 1983.

Pusateri, C. Joseph. *A History of American Business*. 2nd ed. Arlington Heights, Ill.: Harlan Davidson, 1988.

Rabin, Yale. "The Roots of Segregation in the Eighties: The Role of Local Government Actions." In *Divided Neighborhoods: Changing Patterns of Racial Segregation*, edited by Gary A. Tobin, pp. 208–26. Urban Affairs Annual Reviews, vol. 32. Beverly Hills, Calif.: Sage, 1987.

Rabinowitz, Howard. *The First New South, 1865–1920*. Arlington Heights, Ill.: Harlan Davidson, 1992.

——. *Race Relations in the Urban South, 1865–1890*. New York: Oxford University Press, 1978.

Rachleff, Peter J. *Black Labor in the South: Richmond, Virginia, 1865–1880*. Philadelphia: Temple University Press, 1984.

Radford, John P. "Race, Residence, and Ideology: Charleston, South Carolina, in the Mid-Nineteenth Century." *Journal of Historical Geography* 2, no. 4 (1976): 329–46.

——. "The Social Geography of the Nineteenth Century U.S. City." In *Geography and the Urban Environment: Progress in Research and Applications*, edited by D. T. Herbert and R. J. Johnston, 4:257–94. Chicester: John Wiley and Sons, 1981.

——. "Social Structure and Urban Form: Charleston, 1860–1880." In *From the Old South to the New: Essays on the Transitional South*, edited by Walter J. Fraser Jr. and Winfred B. Moore Jr., pp. 81–91. Westport, Conn.: Greenwood Press, 1981.

——. "Testing the Model of the Preindustrial City: The Case of Antebellum Charleston, South Carolina." *Transactions of the Institute of British Geographers*, n.s. 4 (1979): 393–410.

Rapoport, Amos. *House Form and Culture*. Englewood Cliffs, N.J.: Prentice-Hall, 1969.

Reps, John W. *The Making of Urban America: A History of City Planning in the United States*. Princeton: Princeton University Press, 1965.

——. *Town Planning in Frontier America*. Columbia: University of Missouri Press, 1980.

Reynolds, D. R., ed. *Charlotte Remembers*. Charlotte: Community Publishing, 1972.

Rice, Mitchell F., and Woodrow Jones Jr. *Public Policy and the Black Hospital: From Slavery to Segregation to Integration*. Westport, Conn.: Greenwood Press, 1994.

Rice, Roger L. "Residential Segregation by Law, 1910–1917." *Journal of Southern History* 34, no. 2 (May 1968): 179–99.

Ringer, Jim. *Bossmen: Bill Monroe and Muddy Waters*. New York: Dial, 1971.

Roberts, Claudia P., Diana E. Lea, and Robert M. Leary. *The Durham Architectural and Historic Inventory*. Durham, N.C.: Historic Preservation Society of Durham, 1982.

Roberts, Coleman W. *A Pattern for Charlotte*. Charlotte: Chamber of Commerce, 1944. The first edition of the report appeared in April. A revised and expanded edition came out later in the year.

Romine, Dannye. *Mecklenburg: A Bicentennial Story*. Charlotte: Independence Square Associates, 1975.

Roper, Laura Wood. *FLO: A Biography of Frederick Law Olmsted*. Baltimore: Johns Hopkins University Press, 1973.

Rose, Mark H. *Interstate: Express Highway Politics, 1939–1989*. Rev. ed. Knoxville: University of Tennessee Press, 1990.

Rouse, J. K. *The Noble Experiment of Warren C. Coleman*. Charlotte: Crabtree Press, 1972.

Rouse, Parke, Jr. *The Great Wagon Road from Philadelphia to the South*. New York: McGraw-Hill Book Co., 1973.

Rusk, David. *Cities without Suburbs*. Baltimore: Johns Hopkins University Press, 1993.

Russell, Horace. *Savings and Loan Associations*. 2nd ed. Albany, N.Y.: M. Bender, 1960.

Russell, James Michael. *Atlanta, 1847–1890: City Building in the Old South and New*. Baton Rouge: Louisiana State University Press, 1988.

Rust, Brian. *The Victor Master Book*. Vol. 2. Stanhope, N.J.: Walter C. Allen, 1970.

Ryan, Mary P. *Cradle of the Middle Class: Family in Oneida County, New York, 1790–1865*. Cambridge: Cambridge University Press, 1981.

Rybczynski, Witold. *Home: A Short History of an Idea*. New York: Viking, 1986.

Ryckman, Patricia. *Public Library of Charlotte and Mecklenburg County: A Century of Service*. Charlotte: Public Library of Charlotte and Mecklenburg County, 1989.

St. Martin's Chapel: A Brief History of Its Origin and Work, 1887–1937. Charlotte: Lassiter Press, 1937.

Sanders, Gail E. "Frederick Law Olmsted's Plan for Druid Hills." *Atlanta History* 31 (Spring–Summer 1987): 39–47.

Savage, Charles. *The Architecture of the Private Streets of St. Louis: The Architects and the Houses They Designed*. Columbia: University of Missouri Press, 1987.

Schalck, Harry G. "Planning Roland Park, 1891–1910." *Maryland Historical Magazine* 67, no. 4 (Winter 1972): 419–28.

Scharf, J. Thomas. *History of the Confederate States Navy from Its Organization to the Surrender of Its Last Vessel.* New York: Rogers and Sherwood, 1887.

Schiesl, Martin J. *The Politics of Efficiency: Municipal Administration and Reform in America, 1880–1920.* Berkeley: University of California Press, 1977.

Schmitt, Peter J. *Back to Nature: The Arcadian Myth in Urban America.* New York: Oxford University Press, 1969.

Schnore, Leo, ed. *The New Urban History: Quantitative Explorations by American Historians.* Princeton: Princeton University Press, 1975.

Schnore, Leo F., and Philip C. Evenson. "Segregation in Southern Cities." *American Journal of Sociology* 72, no. 1 (July 1966): 58–67.

Schulman, Bruce J. *From Cotton Belt to Sunbelt: Federal Policy, Economic Development, and the Transformation of the South, 1938–1980.* New York: Oxford University Press, 1991.

Schultz, Stanley. *Constructing Urban Culture: American Cities and City Planning, 1800–1920.* Philadelphia: Temple University Press, 1989.

Schuyler, David. *The New Urban Landscape: The Redefinition of City Form in Nineteenth-Century America.* Baltimore: Johns Hopkins University Press, 1986.

Scott, Anne Firor. *The Southern Lady: From Pedestal to Politics, 1830–1930.* Chicago: University of Chicago Press, 1970.

Scott, Mel. *American City Planning since 1860.* Berkeley: University of California Press, 1969.

Scranton, Philip. *Figured Tapestry: Production, Markets, and Power in Philadelphia Textiles, 1885–1941.* Cambridge: Cambridge University Press, 1989.

———. *Proprietary Capitalism: The Philadelphia Textile Manufacture, 1880–1885.* Cambridge: Cambridge University Press, 1983.

Sharpe, William, and Leonard Wallock. "Bold New City or Built-up 'Burb?: Redefining Contemporary Suburbia." *American Quarterly* 46 (1994): 1–30.

Silver, Christopher. "The Changing Face of Neighborhoods in Memphis and Richmond, 1940–1985." In *Shades of the Sunbelt: Essays in Ethnicity, Race, and Class in the Urban South,* edited by Randall Miller and George Pozetta, pp. 93–126. New York: Greenwood Press, 1988.

———. "The Racial Origins of Zoning: Southern Cities from 1910–1940." *Planning Perspectives* 6, no. 2 (May 1991): 189–205.

———. "Revitalizing the Urban South: Neighborhood Preservation and Planning since the 1920s." *Journal of the American Planning Association* 57, no. 1 (Winter 1991): 69–84.

———. *Twentieth Century Richmond: Planning, Politics, and Race.* Knoxville: University of Tennessee Press, 1984.

———. "Urban Planning in the New South." *Journal of Planning Literature* 2, no. 4 (Autumn 1987): 371–83.

Silver, Christopher, and John V. Moeser. *The Separate City: Black Communities in the Urban South, 1940–1968.* Lexington: University Press of Kentucky, 1995.

Sjoberg, Gideon. *The Preindustrial City, Past and Present.* New York: Free Press, 1960.

Skowronek, Stephen. *Building a New American State: The Expansion of National*

Administrative Capacities, 1877–1920. Cambridge: Cambridge University Press, 1982.

Smith, Beth Laney. *A Foundry*. Vol. 1, *Being the Story of the Charlotte Pipe & Foundry Company, Founded November 1901*. Charlotte: Laney-Smith, 1977.

Smith, Douglas L. *The New Deal in the Urban South*. Baton Rouge: Louisiana State University Press, 1973.

Sorensen, Annemette, Karl E. Taeuber, and Leslie J. Holingsworth Jr. *Indexes of Racial Segregation for 109 Cities in the United States, 1940 to 1970, with Methodological Appendix*. Madison: University of Wisconsin, Institute for Research on Poverty, 1974.

Southworth, Michael, and Eran Ben-Joseph. "Street Standards and the Shaping of Suburbia." *Journal of the American Planning Association* 61, no. 1 (Winter 1995): 65–81.

Spain, Daphne. "Race Relations and Residential Segregation in New Orleans: Two Centuries of Paradox." *Annals of the American Academy of Political and Social Science* 441 (January 1979): 82–96.

Spear, Allan H. *Black Chicago: The Making of a Negro Ghetto, 1890–1920*. Chicago: University of Chicago Press, 1967.

Springs, Katherine Wooten. *The Squires of Springfield*. Charlotte: William Loftin, 1965.

Squires, Gregory D. "Community Reinvestment: An Emerging Social Movement." In *From Redlining to Reinvestment: Community Responses to Urban Disinvestment*, edited by Gregory D. Squires, pp. 1–37. Philadelphia: Temple University Press, 1992.

Stach, Patricia Burgess. "Deed Restrictions and Subdivision Development in Columbus, Ohio, 1900–1970." *Journal of Urban History* 15, no. 1 (November 1988): 42–68.

Stancell, Christine. *City of Women: Sex and Class in New York, 1789–1860*. New York: Knopf, 1986.

Stave, Bruce, ed. *Urban Bosses, Machines, and Progressive Reformers*. Lexington, Mass.: D. C. Heath, 1972.

Stein, Clarence S. *Toward New Towns for America*. Rev. ed. Cambridge, Mass.: MIT Press, 1973.

Stephenson, Gilbert Thomas. *Race Distinctions in American Law*. New York: Appleton, 1910.

Stern, Robert A. M., ed. *The Anglo-American Suburb*. Architectural Design Profiles series. London: Architectural Design, 1981.

Stern, Stephen. "Ethnic Folklore and the Folklore of Ethnicity." *Western Folklore* 36, no. 1 (1977): 7–32.

Stilgoe, John R. *Borderland: Origins of the American Suburb, 1820–1939*. New Haven: Yale University Press, 1988.

———. *Metropolitan Corridor: Railroads and the American Scene*. New Haven: Yale University Press, 1983.

Stone, Harold A., Don K. Price, and Kathryn H. Stone. *City Manager Government in Charlotte, North Carolina*. Chicago: Public Administration Service, 1939.

Stott, Richard. *Workers in the Metropolis: Class, Ethnicity, and Youth in Antebellum New York City*. Ithaca, N.Y.: Cornell University Press, 1990.

Stover, John. *The Railroads of the South, 1865–1900: A Study in Finance and Control.* Chapel Hill: University of North Carolina Press, 1955.

Strong, Charles M. *History of Mecklenburg County Medicine.* Charlotte: News Printing House, 1929.

Sugrue, Thomas. "Crabgrass-Roots Politics: Race, Rights, and the Reaction against Liberalism in the Urban North, 1940–1964." *Journal of American History* 82, no. 2 (September 1995): 551–78.

———. "The Structures of Urban Poverty: The Reorganization of Space and Work in Three Periods of American History." In *The "Underclass" Debate: Views from History,* edited by Michael B. Katz, pp. 85–117. Princeton, N.J.: Princeton University Press, 1993.

Sumka, Howard J. "Racial Segregation in Small North Carolina Cities." *Southeastern Geographer* 17 (1977): 58–75.

Sydnor, Charles. *American Revolution in the Making: Political Practices in Washington's Virginia.* New York: Free Press, 1965.

Taeuber, Karl E., and Alma F. Taeuber. *Negroes in Cities: Residential Segregation and Neighborhood Change.* Chicago: Aldine, 1965.

Taylor, Graham Romeyn. *Satellite Cities: A Study of Industrial Suburbs.* New York: Arno Press, 1970.

Taylor, Henry Louis, Jr. "The Use of Maps in the Study of the Black Ghetto-Formation Process: Cincinnati, 1802–1910." *Historical Methods* 17, no. 2 (Spring 1984): 44–58.

Taylor, Henry Louis, Jr., and Vicki Dula. "The Black Residential Experience and Community Formation in Antebellum Cincinnati." In *Race and the City: Work Community and Protest in Cincinnati, 1820–1970,* edited by Henry Louis Taylor Jr., pp. 96–125. Urbana: University of Illinois Press, 1993.

Teaford, Jon C. *City and Suburb: The Political Fragmentation of Metropolitan America, 1850–1970.* Baltimore: Johns Hopkins University Press, 1979.

———. *The Rough Road to Renaissance: Urban Revitalization in America, 1940–1985.* Baltimore: Johns Hopkins University Press, 1990.

———. *The Twentieth Century American City: Problems, Promises, and Reality.* Baltimore: Johns Hopkins University Press, 1986.

———. *The Unheralded Triumph: City Government in America, 1870–1900.* Baltimore: Johns Hopkins University Press, 1984.

Tenth Anniversary: Grace African Methodist Episcopal Zion Church, Charlotte, North Carolina, 1900–1970. Charlotte: Grace AME Zion, 1970.

Thelen, David, Howard Rabinowitz, and C. Vann Woodward. "Perspectives: The Strange Career of Jim Crow." *Journal of American History* 75, no. 3 (December 1988): 841–68.

Thomas, Bernice L. "Five and Dime Design." *Historic Preservation* 41, no. 1 (January–February 1993): 62–70.

Thompson, E. P. *The Making of the English Working Class.* New York: Vintage, 1966.

Thompson, Edgar, ed. *Agricultural Mecklenburg and Industrial Charlotte.* Chapel Hill: University of North Carolina Press, 1926.

Thornton, J. Mills, III. *Politics and Power in a Slave Society: Alabama, 1800–1860.* Baton Rouge: Louisiana State University Press, 1977.

Tindall, George Brown. *America: A Narrative History*. 2nd ed. New York: Norton, 1988.

——. *The Emergence of the New South, 1913–1945*. Baton Rouge: Louisiana State University Press, 1967.

Tobey, Ronald, Charles Wetherell, and Jay Brigham. "Moving Out and Settling In: Residential Mobility, Home Owning, and the Public Enframing of Citizenship, 1921–1950." *American Historical Review* 95 (December 1990): 1395–1422.

Toll, Robert C. *Blacking Up: The Minstrel Show in Nineteenth-Century America*. London: Oxford University Press, 1974.

Tompkins, D. A. *Cotton Mill: Commercial Features*. Charlotte: Observer Job Print, 1899.

——. *History of Mecklenburg County and the City of Charlotte, from 1740 to 1903*. 2 vols. Charlotte: Observer Printing House, 1903.

Tonnies, Ferdinand. *Community and Society*. Translated and edited by Charles P. Loomis. New York: Harper and Row, 1963.

Towns, W. Stuart. "Honoring the Confederacy in Northwest Florida: The Confederate Monument Ritual." *Florida Historical Quarterly* 57 (October 1978): 205, 212.

Trelease, Allen W. *The North Carolina Railroad, 1849–1871, and the Modernization of North Carolina*. Chapel Hill: University of North Carolina Press, 1991.

Troen, Selwyn. *The Public and the Schools: Shaping the St. Louis School System, 1838–1920*. New York: Columbia University Press, 1975.

Trotter, Joe William, Jr. *Black Milwaukee: The Making of an Industrial Proletariate, 1915–1945*. Urbana: University of Illinois Press, 1985.

Tucker, Glenn. *Zeb Vance, Champion of Personal Freedom*. Indianapolis: Bobbs-Merrill, 1965.

Tullos, Allen. *Habits of Industry: White Culture and the Transformation of the Carolina Piedmont*. Chapel Hill: University of North Carolina Press, 1989.

Tunnard, Christopher, and Boris Pushkarev. *Man-Made America: Chaos or Control?* Rev. ed. New York: Harmony, 1981.

Ture, Norman B. *Accelerated Depreciation in the United States, 1954–1960*. New York: National Bureau of Economic Research, 1967.

Tyack, David B. *The One Best System: A History of American Urban Education*. Cambridge, Mass.: Harvard University Press, 1974.

Tyrell, Ian R. *Sobering Up: From Temperance to Prohibition in Antebellum America, 1800–1860*. Westport, Conn.: Greenwood Press, 1979.

Upton, Dell, and John Vlach, eds. *Common Places: Readings in American Vernacular Architecture*. Athens: University of Georgia Press, 1986.

Vance, James E., Jr. "Emerging Patterns of Commercial Structure in American Cities." In *Proceedings of the IGU Symposium in Urban Geography*, edited by K. Norburg, pp. 485–518. Lund Studies in Geography, series 3, 24 (1962).

——. "Housing the Worker: Determinative and Contingent Ties in Nineteenth Century Birmingham." *Economic Geography* 43 (1967): 95–127.

——. *The Merchant's World: The Geography of Wholesaling*. Englewood Cliffs, N.J.: Prentice-Hall, 1970.

——. *This Scene of Man: The Role and Structure of the City in the Geography of Western Civilization*. New York: Harper and Row, 1977. Revised as *The Continuing*

City: Urban Morphology in Western Civilization. Baltimore: Johns Hopkins University Press, 1990.

Vance, Rupert B., and Nicholas J. Demerath, eds. *The Urban South*. Chapel Hill: University of North Carolina Press, 1954.

Vose, Clement E. *Caucasians Only: The Supreme Court, the* NAACP, *and the Restrictive Covenants Cases*. Berkeley: University of California Press, 1959.

Wade, Richard C. *Slavery in the Cities: The South, 1820–1860*. New York: Oxford University Press, 1964.

——. *The Urban Frontier: The Rise of Cities in the West, 1790–1830*. Cambridge, Mass.: Harvard University Press, 1959.

——. "Urbanization." Section 4 of *The Comparative Approach to American History*, edited by C. Vann Woodward. New York: Basic Books, 1968.

Walker, Robert Averill. *The Planning Function in Urban Government*. 2nd ed. Chicago: University of Chicago Press, 1950.

Wallace, Anthony F. C. *Rockdale: The Growth of an American Village in the Early Industrial Revolution*. New York: Knopf, 1978.

Walls, William J. *The African Methodist Episcopal Zion Church*. Charlotte: AME Zion Publishing House, 1974.

Ward, David. *Cities and Immigrants: A Geography of Change in Nineteenth Century America*. New York: Oxford University Press, 1972.

——. "The Industrial Revolution and the Emergence of Boston's Central Business District." *Economic Geography* 42 (1966): 152–71.

——. "The Place of Victorian Cities in Developmental Approaches to Urbanization." In *The Expanding City: Essays in Honour of Professor Jean Gottman*, edited by John Patten, pp. 355–79. London: Academic Press, 1983.

Warner, Sam Bass, Jr. "If All the World Were Philadelphia: A Scaffolding for Urban History, 1774–1930." *American Historical Review* 74 (October 1968): 26–43.

——. *The Private City: Philadelphia in Three Periods of Its Growth*. Philadelphia: University of Pennsylvania Press, 1968.

——. *Streetcar Suburbs: The Process of Growth in Boston, 1870–1900*. Cambridge, Mass.: Harvard University and the MIT Press, 1962.

——. "Urban History: A Matter of Choice." *Public Historian* 8, no. 4 (Fall 1986): 75–80.

Warnes, A. M. "Early Separation of Homes from Workplaces and the Urban Structure of Chorley, 1780 to 1850." *Transactions of the Historical Society of Lancashire and Cheshire* 122 (1970): 105–36.

Watson, C. H., ed. *Colored Charlotte: Published in Connection with the Fiftieth Anniversary of the Freedom of the Negro in the County of Mecklenburg and the City of Charlotte, North Carolina*. Charlotte: AME Zion Printing House, 1914.

Weare, Walter B. *Black Business in the New South: A Social History of the North Carolina Mutual Life Insurance Company*. Urbana: University of Illinois Press, 1973.

Weaver, Robert C. *The Negro Ghetto*. New York: Harcourt, Brace, 1948.

Weiher, Kenneth. "The Cotton Industry and Southern Urbanization, 1880–1930." *Explorations in Economic History* 14 (1977): 120–40.

Weiner, Jonathan. *Social Origins of the New South: Alabama, 1860–1885*. Baton Rouge: Louisiana State University Press, 1978.

Weiss, Marc. *The Rise of the Community Builders: The American Real Estate Industry and Urban Land Planning*. New York: Columbia University Press, 1987.

Welter, Barbara. "The Cult of True Womanhood, 1820–1860." *American Quarterly* 16 (1966): 151–74.

Wheeler, Joanne. "Together in Egypt: A Pattern of Race Relations in Cairo, Illinois, 1865–1915." In *Toward a New South? Studies in Post–Civil War Communities,* edited by Orville Burton and Robert McMath Jr., pp. 103–34. Westport, Conn.: Greenwood Press, 1982.

Whiffen, Marcus. *American Architecture since 1780: A Guide to the Styles.* Cambridge, Mass.: MIT Press, 1981.

White, Dana F. "The Black Sides of Atlanta: A Geography of Expansion and Containment, 1970–1870." *Atlanta Historical Journal* 26, no. 2–3 (Summer–Fall 1982): 199–225.

White, Dana F., and Tim Crimmins. "Urban Structure, Atlanta." *Journal of Urban History* 2, no. 2 (February 1976): 231–52.

White, Dana F., and Victor A. Kramer, eds. *Olmsted South: Old South Critic/New South Planner.* Westport, Conn.: Greenwood Press, 1979.

White, Morton, and Lucia White. *The Intellectual Versus the City: From Thomas Jefferson to Frank Lloyd Wright.* New York: Mentor, 1962.

Whitt, Anne Hall. *The Suitcases.* New York: Signet, 1982.

Who's Who in America. Vol. 16. Chicago: A. N. Marquis, 1930.

Who's Who in America, 1908–1909. Chicago: A. N. Marquis, 1909.

Wiebe, Robert. *The Opening of American Society: From the Adoption of the Constitution to the Eve of Disunion.* New York: Knopf, 1984.

———. *The Search for Order, 1877–1920.* Westport, Conn.: Greenwood Press, 1980.

Wilentz, Sean. *Chants Democratic: New York City and the Rise of the American Working Class, 1788–1850.* New York: Oxford University Press, 1984.

Williams, Michael Ann. *Homeplace: The Social Use and Meaning of Folk Dwelling in Southwestern North Carolina.* Athens: University of Georgia Press, 1991.

Williamson, Joel. *The Crucible of Race: Black/White Relations in the American South since Emancipation.* New York: Oxford University Press, 1984.

———, ed. *Origins of Segregation.* Boston: D. C. Heath, 1968.

Wilson, Charles Reagan. *Baptized in Blood: The Religion of the Lost Cause, 1865–1920.* Athens: University of Georgia Press, 1980.

Wilson, William H. *The City Beautiful Movement.* Baltimore: Johns Hopkins University Press, 1989.

Winston, George Tayloe. *A Builder of the New South, Being the Story of the Life Work of Daniel Augustus Tompkins.* New York: Doubleday, Page, 1920.

Wintz, Cary D. "The Emergence of a Black Neighborhood: Houston's Fourth Ward, 1865–1915." In *Urban Texas: Politics and Development,* edited by Char Miller and Heywood T. Sanders, pp. 96–109. College Station: Texas A&M Press, 1990.

Withey, Henry F., and Elsie Rathburn Withey. *Biographical Dictionary of American Architects (Deceased).* Los Angeles: Hennessey and Ingall, 1970.

Wodehouse, Lawrence. "Frank Pierce Milburn, 1896–1926, a Major Southern Architect." *North Carolina Historical Review* 50 (July 1973): 289–303.

Wolfe, Margaret Ripley. *Kingsport, Tennessee: A Planned American City.* Lexington: University Press of Kentucky, 1987.

Woodman, Harold. "Sequel to Slavery: The New History Views the Postbellum South." *Journal of Southern History* 43, no. 4 (November 1977): 523–54.

Woods, Robert A., and Albert J. Kennedy, eds. *The Zone of Emergence: Observations* of the Lower Middle and Upper Working Class Communities of Boston, 1905–1914. 2nd abridged ed. Cambridge, Mass.: MIT Press, 1969.

Woodward, C. Vann. *Origins of the New South, 1877–1913*. Baton Rouge: Louisiana State University Press, 1951.

——. *The Strange Career of Jim Crow*. 2nd rev. ed. New York: Oxford University Press, 1966.

Woofter, T. J. *Negro Problem in Cities*. New York: Doubleday, Doran, 1928.

Works Progress Administration. *Charlotte: A Guide to the Queen City of North Carolina*. WPA American Guide series. Charlotte: WPA, 1939.

Worley, William S. *J. C. Nichols and the Shaping of Kansas City: Innovation in Planned Residential Communities*. Columbia: University of Missouri Press, 1990.

Wright, Gavin. *Old South, New South: Revolutions in the Southern Economy since the Civil War*. New York: Basic Books, 1986.

Wright, George C. *Life behind a Veil: Blacks in Louisville, Kentucky, 1865–1930*. Baton Rouge: Louisiana State University Press, 1985.

Wright, Gwendolyn. *Building the Dream: A Social History of Housing in America*. Cambridge, Mass.: MIT Press, 1981.

——. *Moralism and the Model Home: Domestic Architecture and Cultural Conflict in Chicago, 1873–1913*. Chicago: University of Chicago Press, 1980.

Wyatt-Brown, Bertram. *Southern Honor: Ethics and Behavior in the Old South*. New York: Oxford University Press, 1982.

Young, Marjorie, ed. *Textile Leaders of the South*. Columbia, S.C.: James R. Young, 1963.

Zaitzevsky, Cynthia. *Frederick Law Olmsted and the Boston Park System*. Cambridge, Mass.: Belknap Press of the Harvard University Press, 1982.

Zimiles, Martha, and Murray Zimiles. *Early American Mills*. New York: Bramhall House, 1973.

Zunz, Olivier. *The Changing Face of Inequality: Urbanization, Industrial Development, and Immigrants in Detroit, 1880–1920*. Chicago: University of Chicago Press, 1988.

THESES AND DISSERTATIONS

Akers, John McCorkle. "Finances of the City of Charlotte, North Carolina, 1917–1929." Master's thesis, University of North Carolina, 1933.

Ambrose, Andrew M. "Redrawing the Color Line: The History and Patterns of Black Housing in Atlanta, 1940–1973." Ph.D. dissertation, Emory University, 1992.

Anderson, Johnnie. "Heriot Clarkson: A Social Engineer of North Carolina." Master's thesis, Wake Forest University, 1972.

Barber, Rupert T., Jr. "A Historical Study of the Theatre in Charlotte, North Carolina, from 1873 to 1902." Ph.D. dissertation, Louisiana State University, 1970.

Buggs, Patricia A. "The Negro in Charlotte, North Carolina, as Reflected in the *Charlotte Observer* and Related Sources, 1900–1910." Master's thesis, Atlanta University, 1976.

Clay, Howard Bunyan. "Daniel Augustus Tompkins: An American Bourbon." Ph.D. dissertation, University of North Carolina, 1950.

Dillard, Geraldine. "The Negro in the Political, Economic, and Social Development of Charlotte, North Carolina, 1890–1900." Master's thesis, Atlanta University, 1972.

Douglas, Edna May. "An Analysis of the Retail Trading Area of Charlotte, North Carolina." Ph.D. dissertation, University of North Carolina, 1945.

Ferris, Abbott L. "North Carolina Trade Centers, 1910–1940: A Study in Ecology." Ph.D. dissertation, University of North Carolina, 1950.

Galenson, Carol Alice. "The Migration of the Cotton Textile Industry from New England to the South: 1880 to 1930." Ph.D. dissertation, Cornell University, 1975.

Glass, James Arthur. "John Nolen and the Planning of New Towns: Three Case Studies." Master's thesis, Cornell University, 1984.

Hanchett, Thomas W. "The Four Square House in America." Master's paper, University of Chicago, 1986.

———. "Sorting Out the New South City: Charlotte and Its Neighborhoods." Ph.D. dissertation, University of North Carolina, 1993.

Hancock, John L. "John Nolen and the American City Planning Movement: A History of Cultural Change and Community Response, 1900–1940." Ph.D. dissertation, University of Pennsylvania, 1964.

Hoffman, Carolyn F. "The Development of Town and Country: Charlotte and Mecklenburg County, North Carolina, 1850–1880." Ph.D. dissertation, University of Maryland, College Park, 1988.

Huggins, Koleen Alice Haire. "The Evolution of City and Regional Planning in North Carolina, 1900–1950." Ph.D. dissertation, Duke University, 1967.

Kipp, Samuel. "Urban Growth and Social Change in the South, 1870–1920: Greensboro, North Carolina, as a Case Study." Ph.D. dissertation, Princeton University, 1974.

Leach, Damaria Etta Brown. "Progress under Pressure: Changes in Charlotte Race Relations, 1955–1965." Master's thesis, University of North Carolina, 1976.

McKown, Harry Wilson, Jr. "Roads and Reform: The Good Roads Movement in North Carolina, 1885–1921." Master's thesis, University of North Carolina, 1972.

Michael, Michelle. "The Rise of the Regional Architect in North Carolina as Seen through the Manufacturers Record, 1890–1910." Master of Historic Preservation thesis, University of Georgia, 1994.

Moye, William T. "Charlotte-Mecklenburg Consolidation: Metrolina in Motion." Ph.D. dissertation, University of North Carolina, 1975.

Porter, Michael L. "Black Atlanta: An Interdisciplinary Study of Blacks on the East Side of Atlanta, 1890–1930." Ph.D. dissertation, Emory University, 1974.

Smith, Mary Philgar. "Municipal Development in North Carolina, 1665–1930: A History of Urbanization." Ph.D. dissertation, University of North Carolina, 1930.

Steelman, Joseph Flake. "The Progressive Era in North Carolina, 1884–1917." Ph.D. dissertation, University of North Carolina, 1955.

Tolbert, Lisa. "Constructing Townscapes: Architecture and Experience in Nineteenth Century County Seats of Middle Tennessee." Ph.D. dissertation, University of North Carolina, 1993.

Wheaton, William Cody. "The Evolution of Federal Housing Programs." Ph.D. dissertation, University of Chicago, 1953.

Wright, James Zebulon. "Thomas Dixon: The Mind of a Southern Apologist." Ph.D. dissertation, George Peabody College for Teachers, 1966.

PAMPHLETS AND UNPUBLISHED SOURCES

Ayers, Edward L. "Toward a Synthesis of the New South." Paper presented to the annual meeting of the Organization of American Historians, 1988.

Beers, F. W. *Map of Charlotte and Mecklenburg County, N.C., from Recent and Careful Surveys.* Richmond, Va.: Southern and Southwestern Surveying and Pub. Co., 1877. Copies are in the City of Charlotte Engineering Map Room and in the North Carolina Collection of the University of North Carolina, Chapel Hill.

Butler and Spratt. *Map of Charlotte Township, From Recent Surveys.* Charlotte: Butler and Spratt, 1892. Copies are in the collections of the City of Charlotte Historic Districts Commission and the History Department of the Mint Museum.

Bostic, Harry, Jr. "History of Presbyterian Hospital." Undated mimeographed essay in the files of the Public Information Office, Presbyterian Hospital, Charlotte, N.C.

Cheshire, Joseph Blount. "St. Peter's Church, Charlotte: Thirty Years in Its Life and Work." 1921. Pamphlet photocopy in the "Episcopal Church" vertical file, Robinson-Spangler Carolina Room, Public Library of Charlotte and Mecklenburg County.

Greenwood, Janette Thomas. "The Black Experience in Charlotte-Mecklenburg, 1850–1920: A Teaching Packet for Charlotte-Mecklenburg Teachers." Charlotte: Charlotte Mecklenburg Historic Properties Commission, 1984.

——. "The Early History of Mecklenburg County to 1825." 1984. Typescript in the collection of the History Department of the Mint Museum, Charlotte.

——. "Race and the Middle Class: New South Charlotte as a Model." Paper presented to the American Historical Association, 1989.

——. "Race, Class, and Prohibition: Charlotte, North Carolina, 1881–1904." Paper presented to Dr. Edward Ayers, University of Virginia, 1988.

E. C. Griffith Company files, Charlotte. "Eastover, a Residential District Developed for the Discriminating Homebuilder." 1927.

——. "Eastover Restriction Agreement." Undated.

——. "Subdivision Plat of Eastover." 1927.

Harding, Harry P. "Charlotte City Schools." 1966. Typescript, Robinson-Spangler Carolina Room, Public Library of Charlotte and Mecklenburg County.

Huggins, Kay Haire. "Town Planning in the New South: The Work of Earle Sumner Draper, 1915–1933." Paper presented to the Citadel Conference on the New South, Charleston, S.C., 1978.

Know Charlotte, Queen City of the South. Charlotte: Chamber of Commerce, 1929. Pamphlet in the collection of Lindsay Wiggins, Charlotte.

Myers Park Homeowners Association scrapbooks.

Ragan, Robert Allison. "Leading Textile Mills in Gaston County, N.C., 1904 to present, and Gaston County Textile Leaders." Looseleaf binder. Copies in the Robinson-Spangler Carolina Room, Public Library of Charlotte and Mecklenburg County, and the North Carolina Collection, Wilson Library, Chapel Hill.

Seventy-Fifth Anniversary, Mercy Hospital. Charlotte: Mercy Hospital Public Relations Department, 1981.

Wiese, Andrew. "Driving a Thin Wedge of Opportunity: Black Suburbanization in the Northern Metropolis, 1940–1960." Paper presented to the Urban History Association conference in Richmond, Va., 1991.

Sector pattern, 3–5, 8, 164, 223–24, 228, 234–35, 244–45, 252–53, 259–63, 326 (n. 1), 334 (n. 110)

Sedgefield, 243

Segregation, racial, 116–21, 143–44, 151, 164, 169, 221, 224–25, 229–33, 234–38, 249–55, 257–63, 334 (n. 110). *See also* African Americans

Seversville, 136, 334 (n. 110)

Sewer and water, 97, 107, 172, 206–7, 217

Shopping centers, 174, 225, 241–45, 263

Shotgun houses, 116, 122–26, 142, 158

Shue, George, 114

Sjoberg, Gideon, 9

Skyscrapers, 183–84, 196–200

Slavery, 16–18, 20–21, 41, 44

Sloan, J. H., 128

Slum clearance. *See* Public housing; Urban renewal

Smith, W. C., 139

Smith, W. W., 131–34, 303 (n. 48)

Smith, Wilbur, 220

Social pyramid, 16–19, 22, 27–28, 88, 152, 159, 258

South Atlantic Cotton Waste, 94, 110

Southern distinctiveness, 12, 260–61, 269 (n. 22)

Southern Power Company. *See* Duke Power

Southern Public Utilities Company, 171, 190, 292 (n. 61)

Southern Textile Bulletin, 110, 179, 296 (n. 86)

Spangler, C. D., Sr., 223, 236, 238

Spencer, Jesse, 106–7, 294 (n. 65), 296 (n. 87)

Spencer, N.C., 291 (n. 49)

Spratt, C. A., 149

Springs family, 31, 55, 180, 270 (n. 30). *See also* Myers, John Springs

Squires, 19

Staten, James, 157, 160, 191

Steele Creek Township, 71

Stephens, George, 148–49, 155–56, 171–73, 176–77, 179–80, 186, 217, 218, 220–21, 225

Stoddard, William, 186, 197

Stone, Harold and Kathryn, 222

Stowe family, 180

Streetcars, 9–10, 54–57, 62–63, 104, 111, 136, 140, 142, 163, 164–65, 167, 171–72, 174, 184, 207, 221, 259, 266 (n. 11), 279 (n. 35); and racial segregation, 119–21

Strikes, 73–74, 96, 103, 112

Suburbs, 139–42, 145–81, 206, 230–36, 241–45; annexation debates, 213–18; defined, 54

Sunnyside, 103

Swann, Herbert, 220

Swann v. Mecklenburg, 12, 251–53

Tanner family, 180

Tate, Thad, 125–26, 130–31, 139, 140, 143, 247, 330 (n. 46)

Tax shelters, 241–44

Taylor, C. S. L. A., 121, 139

Taylor, Z. V., 179

Tech High School, 202

Telegraph service, 271 (n. 42)

Telephone service, 136, 207

Textile mills, 48–53, 62–63, 80, 87, 89–114, 180, 186, 202, 225–26, 258; Ada Mill, 50, 52–53, 74; Alpha Mill, 50, 52–53, 97, 100, 289 (n. 13); Anchor Mill, 106; Atherton Mill, 62–63, 284 (n. 38), 286 (n. 70); Chadwick-Hoskins mills, 94, 112, 284 (n. 38), 289 (n. 13); Charlotte Cotton Mill, 48–49, 51, 99, 202; decline of, 226; Dover Mill, 289 (n. 13); Elizabeth Mill, 284 (n. 38); Highland Park mills (including Gingham Mill), 96, 98, 100, 106–14, 216–17, 226, 284 (n. 38), 293 (n. 64); Johnston Mill, 108, 217, 327 (n. 8); Larkwood Mill, 110; Louise Mill, 96, 101–3, 284 (n. 38), 289 (n. 13); Mecklenburg Mill, 108, 110, 217; millhands, 51–53, 70, 73–77, 80, 82–85, 88, 95–100, 103–14, 191, 202, 286 (n. 70); mill housing, 51–53, 62–64, 83–85, 95, 97–114, 158, 200, 216–17, 219, 226, 231, 251, 258, 315 (n. 107); related industries, 49–50, 55, 93–95, 107, 110, 186, 225, 289 (n. 11); Victor Mill, 50–53, 97, 98; Virgin Mill, 294 (n. 68)

Theaters, 185, 191, 243, 283 (n. 18)

Thies family, 171, 246, 328 (n. 21)

Thomas, Barzilla, 305 (n. 72)